Penguin Books

PEARLS OF WISDOM

A Book of Aphorisms

Vivien Foster was born in Yorkshire and studied at the College of Commerce and Hull Regional College of Art and, as a mature student, at the North Devon College. She has lived in Africa, the Middle East, the South of France and Canada and has travelled extensively to various other parts of the world.

Pearls of Wisdom is her first book, and she is currently working on a novel based on the fascinating experiences of her life.

She is divorced and lives in Devon with her three daughters.

Vivien Foster

PEARLS OF WISDOM

A Book of Aphorisms

Penguin Books

Penguin Books Ltd, 27 Wrights Lane, London w8 5tz (Publishing and Editorial)
and Harmondsworth, Middlesex, England (Distribution and Warehouse)
Viking Penguin Inc., 40 West 23rd Street, New York, New York 10010, USA
Penguin Books Australia Ltd, Ringwood, Victoria, Australia
Penguin Books Canada Ltd, 2801 John Street, Markham, Ontario, Canada l3r 1b4
Penguin Books (NZ) Ltd, 182–190 Wairau Road, Auckland 10, New Zealand

First published 1987

Made and printed in Great Britain by
Cox and Wyman Ltd, Reading, Berks
Typeset in 9/10½pt Linotron Palatino by
Rowland Phototypesetting Ltd, Bury St Edmunds, Suffolk

PREFACE

There is one attribute that is usually acquired through age and experience – wisdom. Since life seldom produces in any generation experiences that are wholly original, *Pearls of Wisdom* has been compiled to illuminate the wisdom of the past for the guidance of the present and the future. It contains many of those seeds of sagacity that philosophers and moralists have transformed into whole theoretical structures and ethical systems; for those, like me, who are not architects of human reasoning a truth encapsulated in a few words is easily recalled and useful for illustrating a train of thought – or for creating one. Some of the most important principles have been expressed succinctly. The Lord's Prayer contains fifty-six words; the Ten Commandments run to 297; the American Declaration of Independence extends to 300. On the other hand, an EEC directive on the import of caramel and caramel products requires, apparently, no fewer than 26,911 words.

A scholar would have marched in a disciplined fashion across the terrain of wisdom, tracking down sources, capturing variants and taking loose ends hostage. My approach has been different – more a series of skirmishes than a sustained campaign. I have gathered fragments wherever I could find them – in books and magazines, in conversation with friends and neighbours, from radio, films and television, on samplers and crockery. Sometimes I have known their sources; sometimes I have been able to discover them; sometimes I have had to rely on memory to reconstruct a phrase or saying and now have no idea where it came from. Always sheer delight in a deftly expressed thought has been my sole reason for its inclusion in this book. I hope that the meticulous reader will excuse the imperfections of my filing system over the years and will simply share my pleasure. I hope too that some readers will be generous enough to put me right if my enthusiasm has swept me past complete accuracy on occasion.

Vivien Foster
March 1987

ACKNOWLEDGEMENTS

I acknowledge all the help and interest and especially encouragement I received in compiling this book from many people, relatives, friends and strangers too numerous to mention but my biggest thank you goes to Miss Marilyn Tyrrell for being the perfect secretary.

ABILITY

Ability involves responsibility; power, to its last particle, is duty – *A. Maclaren*

Men, like bullets, go farthest when they are smoothest – *Jean Paul Richter*

As we advance in life, we learn the limit of our abilities – *James Anthony Froude*

What we do upon some great occasion will probably depend what we already are; and what we are will be the result of previous years of self-discipline – *Henry Parry Liddon*

The world is like a board with holes in it, and the square men get into the round holes – *Sydney Smith*

Ability is a poor man's wealth – *M. Wren*

They are able because they think they are able – *Virgil*

The dwarf sees farther than the giant, when he has the giant's shoulders to mount on – *Samuel Taylor Coleridge*

Natural ability without education has oftener raised men to glory and virtue, than education without natural ability – *Cicero*

No man's abilities are so remarkably shining as not to stand in need of a proper opportunity, a patron, and even the praises of a friend to recommend them to the notice of the world – *Pliny the Younger*

The winds and waves are always on the side of the ablest navigators – *Edward Gibbon*

Men are often capable of greater things than they perform. They are sent into the world with bills of credit, and seldom draw to their full extent.

He that would please all and himself too, undertakes what he cannot do.

Make the most of yourself for that is all there is of you.

Glory not in what you are, but in what you have the power to become.

The toughest form of mountain climbing is getting out of a rut.

ABSENCE

Short absence quickens love; long absence kills it – *Comte de Mirabeau*

Love reckons hours for months, and days for years; and every little absence is an age – *John Dryden*

Absence in love is like water upon fire; a little quickens, but much extinguishes it – *Hannah More*

The absent are like children, helpless to defend themselves – *Charles Reade*

Absence makes the heart grow fonder – *Thomas Haynes Bayly*

Absence lessens moderate passions and increases great ones; as the wind extinguishes the taper, but fans a fire – *François de La Rochefoucauld*

Absence, like death, sets a seal on the image of those we love: we cannot realize the intervening changes which time may have effected – *Oliver Goldsmith*

The absent are never without fault, nor the present without excuse – *Benjamin Franklin*

The joy of meeting pays the pangs of absence; else who could bear it?

ABSTINENCE

Always rise from the table with an appetite, and you will never sit down without one – *William Penn*

Against diseases the strongest fence is the defensive virtue, abstinence – *Robert Herrick*

Abstinence is whereby a man refraineth from anything which he may lawfully claim.

ABUSE

Abuse of anyone generally shows that he has marked traits of character. The stupid and indifferent are passed by in silence – *Tryon Edwards*

It is not he who gives abuse that affronts, but the view that we take of it as insulting; so that when one provokes you it is your own opinion which is provoking – *Epictetus*

Abuse me as much as you will; it is often a benefit rather than an injury – *E. Nott*

The difference between coarse and refined abuse is the difference between being bruised by a club and wounded by a poisoned arrow – *Samuel Johnson*

There are none more abusive to others than they that lie most open to it themselves; but the humour goes round, and he that laughs at me today will have somebody to laugh at him tomorrow – *Seneca*

ACCENT

Accent is the soul of language; it gives to it both feeling and truth – *Jean Jacques Rousseau*

ACCIDENT

Nothing is or can be accidental with God – *Henry Wadsworth Longfellow*

No accidents are so unlucky but that the wise may draw some advantage from them; nor are there any so lucky but that the foolish may turn them to their own prejudice – *François de La Rochefoucauld*

What men call accident is the doing of God's providence.

See also CHANCE.

ACCURACY

Accuracy is the twin brother of honesty; inaccuracy, of dishonesty –
  C. Simmons

ACQUAINTANCE

If a man does not make new acquaintances as he advances through life,
  he will soon find himself left alone; one should keep his friendships
  in constant repair – *Samuel Johnson*
Three days of uninterrupted company in a vehicle will make you better
  acquainted with another than one hour's conversation with him
  every day for three years – *Johann Kaspar Lavater*
Never say you know a man till you have divided an inheritance with him
  – *Lavater*
If a man is worth knowing at all, he is worth knowing well – *Alexander
  Smith*
See also ASSOCIATES, COMPANIONSHIP.

ACQUISITION

That which we acquire with most difficulty we retain the longest; as
  those who have earned a fortune are commonly more careful of it
  than those by whom it may have been inherited – *Charles Caleb Colton*
Every noble acquisition is attended with its risks; he who fears to
  encounter the one must not expect to obtain the other – *Metastasio*
A status symbol is anything you can't afford, but did.

ACTION

Action may not always bring happiness; but there is no happiness
  without action – *Benjamin Disraeli*
Our grand business is not to see what lies dimly at a distance, but to do
  what lies clearly at hand – *Thomas Carlyle*
Only actions give to life its strength as only moderation gives it its charm
  – *Jean Paul Richter*
Every noble activity makes room for itself – *Ralph Waldo Emerson*
Mark this well, ye proud men of action! Ye are, after all, nothing but
  unconscious instruments of the men of thought – *Heinrich Heine*
A right act strikes a chord that extends through the whole universe,
  touches all moral intelligence, visits every world, vibrates along its
  whole extent, and conveys its vibrations to the very bosom of God! –
  T. Binney
Doing is the great thing. For if, resolutely, people do what is right, in
  time they come to like doing it – *John Ruskin*

That action is not warrantable which either fears to ask the divine blessing on its performance, or having succeeded, does not come with thanksgiving to God for its success – *Francis Quarles*

The actions of men are the best interpreters of their thoughts – *John Locke*

Act well at the moment, and you have performed a good action for all eternity – *Johann Kaspar Lavater*

In activity we must find our joy as well as glory; and labour, like everything else that is good, is its own reward – *E. P. Whipple*

To do an evil act is base. To do a good one without incurring danger is common enough. But it is the part of a good man to do great and noble deeds though he risks everything in doing them – *Plutarch*

All our actions take their hue from the complexion of the heart, as landscapes do their variety from light – *W. T. Bacon*

A good action is never lost; it is a treasure laid up and guarded for the doer's need – *Pedro Calderón de la Barca*

Deliberate with caution, but act with decision; and yield with graciousness, or oppose with firmness – *Charles Caleb Colton*

Existence was given us for action. Our worth is determined by the good deeds we do, rather than by the fine emotions we feel – *E. L. Magoon*

The more we do, the more we can do; the more busy we are the more leisure we have – *William Hazlitt*

Activity may lead to evil; but inactivity cannot be led to good – *Hannah More*

Be not too tame neither, but let your own discretion be your tutor: suit the action to the word, the word to the action – *William Shakespeare*

In all exigencies or miseries, lamentation becomes fools, and action wise folk – *Sir Philip Sidney*

Nothing, says Goethe, is so terrible as activity without insight. Look before you leap is a maxim for the world – *E. P. Whipple*

Actions are ours; their consequences belong to heaven – *Sir Philip Francis*

The end of man is action, and not thought, though it be of the noblest – *Thomas Carlyle*

Thought and theory must precede all salutary action; yet action is nobler in itself than either thought or theory – *William Wordsworth*

Life, in all ranks and situations, is an outward occupation, an actual and active work – *W. Humboldt*

Every action of our lives touches on some chord that will vibrate in eternity – *E. H. Chapin*

Only the actions of the just / Smell sweet, and blossom in their dust – *James Shirley*

Action is eloquence, and the eyes of the ignorant / More learned than the ears – *Shakespeare*

An action is the perfection and publication of thought – *Emerson*

The actual is limited, the possible is immense – *Alphonse Marie Louis de Lamartine*

The firefly only shines when on the wing, so it is with the human mind – when it rests, it darkens – *L. E. Landon*

The acts of this life are the destiny of the next – *Eastern proverb*

Action is the proper fruit of knowledge.

The actions of men are like the index of a book; they point out what is most remarkable in them.

Unselfish and noble actions are the most radiant pages in the biography of souls.

Activity and sadness are incompatible.

See also DEEDS.

ACTORS

There is no strong performance without a little fanaticism in the performer.

The art of acting consists in keeping people from coughing.

ADMIRATION

Few men are admired by their servants – *Michel Eyquem de Montaigne*

We always like those who admire us, but we do not always like those whom we admire – *François de La Rochefoucauld*

There is a wide difference between admiration and love. The sublime, which is the cause of the former, always dwells on great objects and terrible; the latter on small ones and pleasing; we submit to what we admire, but we love what submits to us: in one case we are forced, in the other we are flattered, into compliance – *Edmund Burke*

ADVERSITY

Adversity is the trial of principle. Without it a man hardly knows whether he is honest or not – *Henry Fielding*

Adversity is the first path to truth – *Lord Byron*

Adversity has ever been considered the state in which a man most easily becomes acquainted with himself, then, especially, being free from flatterers – *Samuel Johnson*

Prosperity is no just scale; adversity is the only balance to weigh friends – *Plutarch*

Who hath not known ill fortune, never knew himself, or his own virtue – *David Mallet*

Stars may be seen from the bottom of a deep well when they cannot be discerned from the top of a mountain. So are many things learned in adversity which the prosperous man dreams not of – *Charles Haddon Spurgeon*

Adversity is the diamond dust Heaven polishes its jewels with – *Robert Leighton*

Adversity has the effect of eliciting talents which in prosperous circumstances would have lain dormant – *Horace*

Prosperity is a great teacher; adversity is a greater. Possession pampers the mind; privation trains and strengthens it – *William Hazlitt*

The flower that follows the sun does so even in cloudy days – *Leighton*

The good things of prosperity are to be wished; but the good things that belong to adversity are to be admired – *Seneca*

Adversity, sage useful guest, / Severe instructor, but the best; / It is from thee alone we know / Justly to value things below – *William Somerville*

Sweet are the uses of adversity, / Which like the toad, ugly and venomous, / Wears yet a precious jewel in his head – *William Shakespeare*

Genuine morality is preserved only in the school of adversity; a state of continuous prosperity may easily prove a quicksand to virtue – *Johann Christoph Friedrich von Schiller*

Those who have suffered much are like those who know many languages; they have learned to understand and be understood by all – *Mme Swetchine*

A noble heart, like the sun, showeth its greatest countenance in its lowest estate – *Sir Philip Sidney*

It is not the so-called blessings of life, its sunshine and calm and pleasant experiences that make men, but its rugged experiences, its storms and tempests and trials. Early adversity is often a blessing in disguise – *W. Mathews*

No man is more unhappy than the one who is never in adversity; the greatest affliction of life is never to be afflicted.

A smooth sea never made a skilful mariner.

Adversity, like winter weather, is of use to kill those vermin which the summer of prosperity is apt to produce and nourish.

Prosperity makes friends; adversity tests them.

See also AFFLICTION.

ADVERTISING

The advertising man is a liaison between the products of business and the mind of the nation. He must know both before he can serve either – *Glenn Frank*

There are more sales made today because buyers must have what they want than because of salesmen selling them something better.

ADVICE

Let no man presume to give advice to others who has not first given good
counsel to himself – *Seneca*

The greatest trust between man and man is the trust of giving counsel –
Francis Bacon

When a man seeks your advice he generally wants your praise – *Lord
Chesterfield*

When a man has been guilty of any vice or folly, the best atonement he
can make for it is to warn others not to fall into the like – *Joseph Addison*

It is easy when we are in prosperity to give advice to the afflicted –
Aeschylus

We ask advice: we mean approbation – *Charles Caleb Colton*

Advice is like snow; the softer it falls, the longer it dwells upon, and the
deeper it sinks into the mind – *Samuel Taylor Coleridge*

Let no man value at a little price a virtuous woman's counsel – *George
Chapman*

Men give away nothing so liberally as their advice – *François de La
Rochefoucauld*

Advice is seldom welcome. Those who need it most, like it least – *Samuel
Johnson*

Every man, however wise, needs the advice of some sagacious friend in
the affairs of life – *Plautus*

We give advice, by the bucket, but take it by the grain – *William
Rounseville Alger*

It takes nearly as much ability to know how to profit by good advice as to
know how to act for one's self – *La Rochefoucauld*

Harsh counsels have no effect: they are like hammers which are always
repulsed by the anvil – *Claude Adrien Helvétius*

Give every man thine ear, but few thy voice; / Take each man's censure,
but reserve thy judgment – *William Shakespeare*

Giving advice is sometimes only showing our wisdom at the expense of
another – *Lord Shaftesbury*

If you wish good advice, consult an old man – *Portuguese proverb*

Write down the advice of him that loves you, though you like it not at
present – *seventeenth-century proverb*

A man without a smiling face must not open a shop – *Chinese proverb*

To profit from good advice requires more wisdom than to give it.

A good scare does more for a man than good advice.

We often repent of saying too much but seldom of saying too little.

Better carry burden on the shoulder than worry in the heart.

Do not give to your friends the most agreeable counsels, but the most
advantageous.

Who we are and how we are are less important than what we are.

There's no better sign of a brave mind than a hard hand.

The smartest person we know is the one who asks our advice.

The worst men often give the best advice; our thoughts are better sometimes than our deeds.

AFFECTATION

All affectation is the vain and ridiculous attempt of poverty to appear rich
– *Johann Kaspar Lavater*

Affectation is a greater enemy to the face than the smallpox – *Seigneur de Saint-Evremond*

All affectation proceeds from the supposition of possessing something better than the rest of the world possesses – *Sydney Smith*

Affectation is a perpetual disguise of the real character by false appearances – *Samuel Johnson*

We are never so ridiculous by the qualities we have, as by those we affect to have – *François de La Rochefoucauld*

Be yourself. Ape no greatness. Be willing to pass for what you are. A good farthing is better than a bad sovereign – *S. Coley*

Affectation lights a candle to our defects, and though it may gratify ourselves, it disgusts all others – *Lavater*

Affectation is certain deformity. By forming themselves on fantastic models the young begin with being ridiculous, and often end in being vicious.

Hearts may be attracted by assumed qualities, but the affections can only be fixed and retained by those that are real.

All false practices and affectations of knowledge are more odious than any want or defect of knowledge can be.

AFFECTION

How often a new affection makes a new man. The sordid becomes liberal; the cowering, heroic; the frivolous girl, the steadfast martyr of patience and ministration, transfigured by deathless love – *E. H. Chapin*

Our affections are our life. We live by them; they supply our warmth – *William Ellery Channing*

The affections are like lightning: you cannot tell where they will strike till they have fallen – *Jean Baptiste Henri Lacordaire*

Of all earthly music that which reaches farthest into heaven is the beating of a truly loving heart – *Henry Ward Beecher*

If there is any thing that keeps the mind open to angel visits, and repels the ministry of evil, it is a pure human love – *Nathaniel Parker Willis*

Our sweetest experiences of affection are meant to point us to that realm
which is the real and endless home of the heart – *Beecher*

Affection, like melancholy, magnifies trifles; but the magnifying of the
one is like looking through a telescope at heavenly objects; that of the
other, like enlarging monsters with a microscope – *James Henry Leigh
Hunt*

The heart will commonly govern the head; and any strong passion, set
the wrong way, will soon infatuate even the wisest of men; therefore
the first part of wisdom is to watch the affections – *Daniel Waterland*

There is in life no blessing like affection; it soothes, it hallows, elevates,
subdues and bringeth down to earth its native heaven: life has
nought else that may supply its place – *Letitia Elizabeth London*

I'd rather than that crowds should sigh for me, that from some kindred
eye the trickling tear should steal – *Henry Kirke White*

Those who marry where they do not love, will be likely to love where
they do not marry.

AFFLICTION

The lord gets his best soldiers out of the highlands of affliction – *Charles
Haddon Spurgeon*

It has done me good to be somewhat parched by the heat and drenched
by the rain of life – *Henry Wadsworth Longfellow*

It is not from the tall, crowded workhouse of prosperity that men first or
clearest see the eternal stars of heaven – *Theodore Parker*

Ah! if you only knew the peace there is in an accepted sorrow – *Mme
Guion*

It is not until we have passed through the furnace that we are made to
know how much dross there is in our composition – *Charles Caleb
Colton*

It is a great thing, when the cup of bitterness is pressed to our lips, to feel
that it is not fate or necessity, but divine love working upon us for
good ends – *E. H. Chapin*

The soul that suffers is stronger than the soul that rejoices – *E. Shepard*

Tears are often the telescope by which men see far into heaven – *Henry
Ward Beecher*

Strength is born in the deep silence of long-suffering hearts; not amid joy
– *Felicia Dorothea Hemans*

With the wind of tribulation God separates, in the floor of the soul, the
wheat from the chaff – *Miguel de Molinos*

What seems to us but dim funeral tapers, may be heaven's distant lamps
– *Longfellow*

The gem cannot be polished without friction, nor men perfected without
trials – *Chinese proverb*

It is from the remembrance of joys we have lost that the arrows of affliction are pointed.

Heaven tries our virtue by afflictions; as oft the cloud that wraps the present hour, serves but to lighten all our future days.

Come then, affliction, if my Father wills, and be my frowning friend. A friend that frowns is better than a smiling enemy.

Heaven but tries our virtue by affliction, and oft the cloud that wraps the present hour serves but to brighten all our future days.

If you would not have affliction visit you twice, listen at once to what it teaches.

By afflictions God is spoiling us of what otherwise might have spoiled us.

We should always record our thoughts in affliction: set up way-marks, that we may recur to them in health; for then we are in other circumstances, and can never recover our sick-bed views.

See also ADVERSITY.

AGE

A graceful and honourable old age is the childhood of immortality – *Pindar*

How beautiful can time with goodness make an old man look – *Douglas William Jerrold*

Old age adds to the respect due to virtue, but it takes nothing from the contempt inspired by vice; it whitens only the hair – *J. P. Senn*

Age does not depend upon years but upon temperament and health. Some men are born old, and some never grow so – *Tryon Edwards*

A person is always startled when he hears himself seriously called old for the first time – *Oliver Wendell Holmes*

Let us respect grey hairs, especially our own – *Senn*

Our youth and manhood are due to our country, but our declining years are due to ourselves – *Pliny the Younger*

When we are young, we are slavishly employed in procuring something whereby we may live comfortably when we grow old; and when we are old, we perceive it is too late to live as we proposed – *Alexander Pope*

Old men's eyes are like old men's memories; they are strongest for things a long way off – *George Eliot*

No wise man ever wished to be younger – *Jonathan Swift*

Years do not make sages; they only make old men – *Mme Swetchine*

Every one desires to live long, but no one would be old – *Swift*

As we grow old we become both more foolish and more wise – *François de La Rochefoucauld*

Age that lessens the enjoyment of life, increases our desire of living – *Oliver Goldsmith*

Childhood itself is scarcely more lovely than a cheerful, kindly, sunshiny old age – *Lydia Maria Child*

Old age is a tyrant, which forbids the pleasures of youth on pain of death – *La Rochefoucauld*

The evening of a well-spent life brings its lamps with it – *Joseph Joubert*

Remember when he is old, that he has once been young – *Joseph Addison*

While one finds company in himself and his pursuits, he cannot feel old, no matter what his years may be – *Amos Bronson Alcott*

As we advance in life the circle of our pains enlarges, while that of our pleasures contracts – *Mme Swetchine*

When we are out of sympathy with the young, then I think our work in this world is over – *George Macdonald*

At twenty, the will reigns; at thirty, the wit; at forty, the judgment; afterward, proportion of character – *Henry Grattan*

When men grow virtuous in their old age, they are merely making a sacrifice to God of the devil's leavings – *Swift*

Probably the happiest period in life most frequently is in middle age, when the eager passions of youth are cooled, and the infirmities of age not yet begun – *Thomas Arnold*

It is not by the grey of the hair that one knows the age of the heart.

How many fancy they have experience simply because they have grown old.

A comfortable old age is the reward of a well-spent youth.

No snow falls lighter than the snow of age; but none lies heavier, for it never melts.

That man never grows old who keeps a child in his heart.

Old age is like everything else. To make a success of it you've got to start young.

One is never too old to feel young.

No one is old enough to know better.

If you are bored with life you are old.

Years know more than books.

Grow up as soon as you can. The only time you live fully is from thirty to sixty.

As we advance in life we learn the limits of our abilities.

Many a woman could add years to her life by telling her true age.

You are old if you are bored with life.

AGNOSTICISM

Agnosticism is the philosophical, ethical, and religious dry rot of the modern world – *F. E. Abbot*

An agnostic is a man who doesn't know whether there is a God or not, doesn't know whether he has a soul or not, doesn't know whether there is a future life or not, doesn't believe that anyone else knows any more about these matters than he does, and thinks it a waste of time to try to find out.

See also BELIEF.

AGRICULTURE

Agriculture not only gives riches to a nation, but the only riches she can call her own – *Samuel Johnson*

Let the farmer forevermore be honoured in his calling, for they who labour in the earth are the chosen people of God – *Thomas Jefferson*

Trade increases the wealth and glory of a country; but its real strength and stamina are to be looked for among the cultivators of the land – *Lord Chatham*

The farmers are the founders of civilization and prosperity – *Daniel Webster*

He that would look with contempt on the pursuits of the farmer, is not worthy the name of a man – *Henry Ward Beecher*

In the age of acorns, before the times of Ceres, a single barley-corn had been of more value to mankind than all the diamonds of the mines of India – *Henry Brooke*

Command large fields, but cultivate small ones – *Virgil*

Whoever makes two ears of corn, or two blades of grass to grow where only one grew before, deserves of mankind, and does more essential service to his country than the whole race of politicians put together – *Jonathan Swift*

The frost is God's plough which he drives through every inch of ground in the world, opening each clod, and pulverizing the whole.

We may talk as we please of lilies, and lions rampant, and spread eagles in fields of d'or or d'argent, but if heraldry were guided by reason, a plough in the field arable would be the most noble and ancient arms.

A cloudless sky could never produce a good harvest.

AIMS

High aims from high characters, and great objects bring out great minds – *Tryon Edwards*

Not failure, but low aim, is crime – *James Russell Lowell*

Aim at the sun, and you may not reach it; but your arrow will fly far higher than if aimed at an object on a level with yourself – *J. Hawes*

What are the aims which are at the same time duties? They are the perfecting of ourselves, and the happiness of others – *Immanuel Kant*

A purpose is the eternal condition of success – *T. T. Munger*

In great attempts it is glorious even to fail – *Longinus*

See also ASPIRATION.

AMBITION

Ambition is the germ from which all growth of nobleness proceeds – *Thomas Dunn English*

Ambition is the spur that makes man struggle with destiny – *Donald Grant Mitchell*

Ambition often puts men upon doing the meanest offices: so climbing is performed in the same posture as creeping – *Jonathan Swift*

The noblest spirit is most strongly attracted by the love of glory – *Cicero*

Ambition is the avarice of power – *Charles Caleb Colton*

Ambition is but the evil shadow of aspiration – *George Macdonald*

Ambition is not a vice of little people – *Michel Eyquem de Montaigne*

To have more ambition than ability is to be at once weak and unhappy – *G. S. Hillard*

It is by attempting to reach the top at a single leap, that so much misery is caused in the world – *William Cobbett*

Ambition has one heel nailed in well, though she stretch her fingers to touch the heavens – *William Lilly*

Ambition thinks no face so beautiful as that which looks from under a crown – *Sir Philip Sidney*

It is the constant fault and inseparable evil quality of ambition, that it never looks behind it – *Seneca*

The tallest trees are most in the power of the winds, and ambitious men of the blasts of fortune – *Penn*

Most people would succeed in small things if they were not troubled by great ambitions – *Henry Wadsworth Longfellow*

He who surpasses or subdues mankind, must look down on the hate of those below – *Lord Byron*

Ambition is so powerful a passion in the human breast, that however high we reach we are never satisfied – *Niccolò Machiavelli*

There is no sorrow I have thought more about than that – to love what is great, and try to reach it, and yet to fail – *George Eliot*

High seats are never but uneasy, and crown are always stuffed with thorns.

Ambition is like love, impatient both of delays and rivals.

Too low they build who build below the skies.

AMERICA

America is another name for opportunity. Our whole history appears like a last effort of divine Providence on behalf of the human race – *Ralph Waldo Emerson*

America is a fortunate country; she grows by the follies of our European nations – *Napoleon Bonaparte*

If all Europe were to become a prison, America would still present a
  loop-hole of escape; and, God be praised! that loop-hole is larger than
  the dungeon itself – *Heinrich Heine*

The home of freedom, and the hope of the downtrodden and oppressed
  among the nations of the earth – *Daniel Webster*

America has proved that it is practicable to elevate the mass of mankind –
  the labouring or lower class – to raise them to self-respect, to make
  them competent to act a part in the great right and the great duty of
  self-government; and she has proved that this may be done by
  education and the diffusion of knowledge. She holds out an example
  a thousand times more encouraging than ever was presented before
  to those nine-tenths of the human race who are born without
  hereditary fortune or hereditary rank – *Webster*

Americans are genuinely proud of all things enormous – *Luigi Pirandello*

America is a circus of grown-up children – *Eilbert Pastor*

In America you must live life with a smile, even before your toothbrush
  has had time to reach your mouth – *Prince William of Sweden*

The reason American cities are prosperous is that there is no place to sit
  down – *Alfred J. Talley*

America – half-brother of the world.

The home of the homeless all over the earth.

AMUSEMENTS

The mind ought sometimes to be diverted, that it may return the better to
  thinking – *Phaedrus*

It is a sober truth that people who live only to amuse themselves work
  harder at the task than most people do in earning their daily bread –
  Hannah More

I am a great friend to public amusements, for they keep people from vice
  – *Samuel Johnson*

Amusement to an observing mind is study – *Benjamin Disraeli*

It is doing some service to humanity to amuse innocently; and they know
  very little of society who think we can bear to be always employed,
  either in duties or meditations, without any relaxation – *Sir Philip
  Sidney*

All amusements to which virtuous women are not admitted are, rely
  upon it, deleterious in their nature – *William Makepeace Thackeray*

Dwell not too long upon sports; for as they refresh a man that is weary,
  so they weary a man that is refreshed.

ANCESTRY

Every man is his own ancestor, and every man is his own heir. He
  devises his own future and he inherits his own past – *H. F. Hedge*

They alone cry out against a noble ancestry who have none of their own
– *Ben Jonson*

We take rank by descent. Such of us as have the longest pedigree, and
are therefore the furthest removed from the first who made the
fortune and founded the family, we are the noblest – *James Anthony
Froude*

Breed is stronger than pasture – *George Eliot*

What can we see in the longest kingly line in Europe, save that it runs
back to a successful soldier? – *Sir Walter Scott*

It is of no consequence of what parents a man is born, so he be a man of
merit – *Horace*

Mere family never made a man great. Thought and deed, not pedigree,
are the passports to enduring fame – *Mikhail Dmitrievich Skobeleff*

Title and ancestry render a good man more illustrious, but an ill one
more contemptible – *Joseph Addison*

I am no herald to inquire after men's pedigrees: it sufficeth me if I know
of their virtues – *Sir Philip Sidney*

Some men by ancestry are only the shadow of a mighty name – *Lucan*

The inheritance of a distinguished and noble name is a proud inheritance
to him who lives worthily of it – *Charles Caleb Colton*

It would be more honourable to our distinguished ancestors to praise
them in words less, but in deeds to imitate them more – *Horace Mann*

The man who has nothing to boast of but his illustrious ancestry is like
the potato – the best part under ground – *Sir Thomas Overbury*

We inherit nothing truly, but what our actions make us worthy of –
George Chapman

Birth is nothing where virtue is not – *Molière*

They that on glorious ancestors enlarge, / Produce their debt, instead of
their discharge.

It is, indeed, a blessing, when the virtues of noble races are hereditary.

They who depend on the merits of ancestors search in the roots of the
tree for the fruits which the branches ought to produce.

See also ARISTOCRACY, BIRTH.

ANGER

Anger begins in folly, and ends in repentance – *Pythagoras*

To be angry is to revenge the faults of others on ourselves – *Alexander
Pope*

Temperate anger well becomes the wise – *Philemon*

Keep cool and you command everybody – *Louis Antoine Léon Florelle de
Saint-Just*

Beware of the fury of a patient man – *John Dryden*

A man that does not know how to be angry does not know how to be good. Now and then a man should be shaken to the core with indignation over things evil – *Henry Ward Beecher*

There is not in nature a thing that makes man so deformed, so beastly, as doth intemperate anger – *John Webster*

Men often make up in wrath what they want in reason – *William Rounseville Alger*

The greatest remedy for anger is delay – *Seneca*

When a man is wrong and won't admit it, he always gets angry – *Thomas Chandler Haliburton*

To rule one's anger is well; to prevent it is still better – *Tryon Edwards*

The intoxication of anger, like that of the grape, shows us to others, but hides us from ourselves. We injure our own cause in the opinion of the world when we too passionately defend it – *Charles Caleb Colton*

When angry, count ten before you speak; if very angry, count a hundred – *Thomas Jefferson*

When passion is on the throne reason is out of doors – *Matthew Henry*

An angry man is again angry with himself when he returns to reason – *Publius Syrus*

When anger rises, think of the consequences – *Confucius*

Rage is the most effective producer of courage in the world – *Helen Woodward*

The fire you kindle for your enemy often burns yourself more than him – *Chinese proverb*

Anger is as a stone cast into a wasp's nest – *Malabar proverb*

Anger is the most impotent of passions. It effects nothing it goes about, and hurts the one who is possessed by it more than the one against whom it is directed.

Anger is one of the sinews of the soul.

When anger rushes, unrestrained, to action, like a hot steed, it stumbles in its way.

Anger ventilated often hurries towards forgiveness; anger concealed often hardens into revenge.

He who can suppress a moment's anger may prevent a day of sorrow.

Violence in the voice is often only the death rattle of reason in the throat.

See also RAGE.

ANTICIPATION

He who foresees calamities suffers them twice over – *Beilby Porteous*

Suffering itself does less afflict the senses than the anticipation of suffering – *Quintilian*

Sorrow itself is not so hard to bear as the thought of sorrow coming – *Thomas Bailey Aldrich*

To tremble before anticipated evils is to bemoan what thou hast never lost – *Johann Wolfgang von Goethe*

Nothing is so good as it seems beforehand – *George Eliot*

Why need a man forestall his date of grief, and run to meet that he would most avoid? – *John Milton*

The joys we expect are not so bright, nor the troubles so dark as we fancy they will be – *Charles Reade*

Heaven were not heaven if we knew what it were – *Sir John Suckling*

It is worse to apprehend than to suffer – *Jean de La Bruyère*

All earthly delights are sweeter in expectation than in enjoyment.

We part more easily with what we possess than with our expectations of what we hope for.

The worst evils are those that never arrive.

ANXIETY

Anxiety is the rust of life, destroying its brightness and weakening its power – *Tryon Edwards*

Do not anticipate trouble, or worry about what may never happen. Keep in the sunlight – *Benjamin Franklin*

Better be despised for too anxious apprehensions, than ruined by too confident security – *Edmund Burke*

How much have cost us the evils that never happened! – *Thomas Jefferson*

It is not the cares of today, but the cares of tomorrow that weigh a man down – *George Macdonald*

It is not work that kills men; it is worry – *Henry Ward Beecher*

He is well along the road to perfect manhood who does not allow the thousand little worries of life to embitter his temper, or disturb his equanimity.

See also CARE.

APOLOGIES

Apologies only account for the evil which they cannot alter – *Benjamin Disraeli*

Apology is only egotism wrong side out – *Oliver Wendell Holmes*

No sensible person ever made an apology – *Ralph Waldo Emerson*

APOTHEGMS

Apothegms are the wisdom of the past condensed for the instruction and guidance of the present – *Tryon Edwards*

Apothegms are in history, the same as pearls in the sand, or gold in the mine – *Erasmus*

Aphorisms are portable wisdom, the quintessential extracts of thought and feeling – *William Rounseville Alger*

He is a benefactor of mankind who contracts the great rules of life into short sentences, that may be easily impressed on the memory, and so recur habitually to the mind – *Samuel Johnson*

The excellence of aphorisms consists not so much in the expression of some rare or abstruse sentiment, as in the comprehension of some useful truth in few words – *Johnson*

Under the veil of these curious sentences are hid those germs of morals which the masters of philosophy have afterwards developed into so many volumes – *Plutarch*

There are but few proverbial sayings that are not true, for they are all drawn from experience itself, which is the mother of all sciences – *Miguel de Cervantes Saavedra*

Sensible men show their sense by saying much in few words – *C. Simmons*

Apothegms to thinking minds are the seeds from which spring vast fields of new thought, that may be further cultivated, beautified, and enlarged.

See also MAXIMS, PROVERBS.

APPETITE

Reason should direct, and appetite obey – *Cicero*

Good cheer is no hindrance to a good life – *Aristippus*

Choose rather to punish your appetites than to be punished by them – *Tyrius Maximus*

There are so few that resist the allurements and luxuries of the table, that the usual civilities at a meal are very like being politely assisted to the grave – *Nathaniel Parker Willis*

Now good digestion wait on appetite, / And health on both! – *William Shakespeare*

Temperance and labour are the two best physicians of man; labour sharpens the appetite, and temperance prevents from indulging to excess – *Jean Jacques Rousseau*

A well-governed appetite is a great part of liberty – *Seneca*

See also EATING.

APPLAUSE

Applause is the spur of noble minds; the end and aim of weak ones – *Charles Caleb Colton*

Neither human applause nor human censure is to be taken as the test of truth; but either should set us upon testing ourselves – *Richard Whately*

When the million applaud you, seriously ask what harm you have done; when they censure you, what good! – *Colton*

A slowness to applaud betrays a cold temper or an envious spirit – *Hannah More*

Applause is the echo of a platitude – *Ambrose Bierce*

See also PRAISE.

APPRECIATION

Next to excellence is the appreciation of it – *William Makepeace Thackeray*

To love one that is great is almost to be great one's self – *Mme Neckar*

Contemporaries appreciate the man rather than the merit; but posterity will regard the merit rather than the man – *Charles Caleb Colton*

When a nation gives birth to a man who is able to produce a great thought, another is born who is able to understand and admire it – *Joseph Joubert*

You will find poetry nowhere unless you bring some with you – *Joubert*

In proportion as our own mind is enlarged we discover a greater number of men of originality – *Blaise Pascal*

Every man is valued in this world as he shows by his conduct that he wishes to be valued – *Jean de La Bruyère*

In the tumult of war both sides applaud a heroic deed – *Thomas Wentworth Higginson*

We are very much what others think of us – *William Hazlitt*

A work of real merit finds favour at last – *Amos Bronson Alcott*

To feel exquisitely is the lot of very many; but to appreciate belongs to the few – *A. Auchester*

We never miss the water till the well runs dry.

ARCHITECTURE

Architecture is the printing press of all ages, and gives a history of the state of society in which the structure was erected – *Lady Morgan*

Greek architecture is the flowering of geometry – *Ralph Waldo Emerson*

Architecture is a handmaid of devotion. A beautiful church is a sermon in stone, and its spire a finger pointing to heaven – *Philip Schaff*

Architecture is frozen music.

See also BUILDING.

ARGUMENT

Argument is the worst sort of conversation – *Jonathan Swift*

Wise men argue causes; fools decide them – *Anacharsis*

He who establishes his argument by noise and command shows that his
reason is weak – *Michel Eyquem de Montaigne*
Men's arguments often prove nothing but their wishes – *Charles Caleb
Colton*
Prejudices are rarely overcome by argument; not being founded in
reason they cannot be destroyed by logic – *Tryon Edwards*
Clear statement is argument – *W. G. T. Shedd*
The first duty of a wise advocate is to convince his opponents that he
understands their arguments, and sympathizes with their just
feelings – *Samuel Taylor Coleridge*
Debate is the death of conversation – *Emil Ludwig*
People generally quarrel because they cannot argue – *G. K. Chesterton*
There are two sides to every question – the wrong side and our side –
American proverb
In argument similes are like songs in love; they describe much, but prove
nothing.
When a man argues for victory and not the truth, he is sure of just one
ally, that is the devil.
Never argue at the dinner table, for the one who is not hungry always
gets the best of the argument.
There is no dispute managed without passion, and yet there is scarce a
dispute worth a passion.
The best way of answering a bad argument is to let it go on.
For the sake of harmony a woman will nurse a grievance.
See also CONTENTION, CONTROVERSY, DISCUSSION, QUARRELS.

ARISTOCRACY

And lords, whose parents were the Lord knows who – *Daniel Defoe*
Some will always be above others. Destroy the inequality today, and it
will appear again tomorrow – *Ralph Waldo Emerson*
Among the masses, even in revolutions, aristocracy must ever exist.
Destroy it in the nobility, and it becomes centred in the rich and
powerful Houses of Commons. Pull them down, and it still survives
in the master and foreman of the workshop – *François Pierre Guillaume
Guizot*
I never could believe that Providence had sent a few men into the world,
ready booted and spurred to ride, and millions ready saddled and
bridled to be ridden – *Richard Rumbold*
Aristocracy has three successive ages: the age of superiorities, that of
privileges, and that of vanities. Having passed out of the first, it
degenerates in the second, and dies away in the third – *François de
Chateaubriand*

A social life that worships money or makes social distinction its aim is, in spirit, an attempted aristocracy.

See also ANCESTRY, BIRTH, NOBILITY.

ARROGANCE

When men are most sure and arrogant they are commonly most mistaken, giving views to passion without that proper deliberation which alone can secure them from the grossest absurdities – *David Hume*

Nothing is more hateful to a poor man than the purse-proud arrogance of the rich. But let the poor man become rich and he runs at once into the vice against which he so feelingly declaimed. There are strange contradictions in human character.

See also PRIDE.

ART

All great art is the expression of man's delight in God's work, not his own – *John Ruskin*

The highest problem of any art is to cause by appearance the illusion of a higher reality – *Johann Wolfgang von Goethe*

The true work of art is but a shadow of the divine perfection – *Michelangelo Buonarroti*

All that is good in art is the expression of one soul to another, and is precious according to the greatness of the soul that utters it – *Ruskin*

The perfection of art is to conceal art – *Quintilian*

Never judge a work of art by its defects – *Washington Allston*

The highest triumph of art is the truest presentation of nature – *Nathaniel Parker Willis*

The mission of art is to represent nature; not to imitate her – *W. M. Hunt*

The learned understand the reason of art; the unlearned feel the pleasure – *Quintilian*

The mother of the useful art is necessity; that of the fine arts is luxury – *Arthur Schopenhauer*

Would that we could at once paint with the eyes! In the long way from the eye through the arm to the pencil, how much is lost – *Gotthold Ephraim Lessing*

Artists are nearest God. Into their souls he breathes his life, and from their hands it comes in fair, articulate forms to bless the world – *Josiah Gilbert Holland*

Art and life ought to be hurriedly remarried and brought to live together – *Hugh Walpole*

There is no such thing as modern art. There is art – and there is advertising – *Albert Sterner*

The object of art is to crystallize emotion into thought, and then fix it in
form.

ASPIRATION

Nothing will ever be attempted if all objections must first be overcome.
See also AIMS, EXCELSIOR.

ASSERTIONS

Weigh not so much what men assert, as what they prove – *Sir Philip
Sidney*

ASSOCIATES

Tell me with whom thou art found, and I will tell thee who thou art –
Johann Wolfgang von Goethe
If you wish to be held in esteem, you must associate only with those who
are estimable – *Jean de La Bruyère*
Evil communications corrupt good manners – *Menander*
You may depend upon it that he is a good man whose intimate friends
are all good, and whose enemies are decidedly bad – *Johann Kaspar
Lavater*
No company is preferable to bad, because we are more apt to catch the
vices of others than their virtues, as disease is far more contagious
than health – *Charles Caleb Colton*
Choose the company of your superiors whenever you can have it; that is
the right and true pride – *Lord Chesterfield*
A man should live with his superiors as he does with his fire: not too
near, lest he burn; nor too far off, lest he freeze – *Diogenes*
Those unacquainted with the world take pleasure in intimacy with great
men; those who are wiser fear the consequences – *Horace*
Tell me with whom you live and I will tell you who you are – *Spanish
proverb*
When one associates with vice, it is but one step from companionship to
slavery.
It is best to be with those in time, that we hope to be with in eternity.
See also ACQUAINTANCE, COMPANIONSHIP.

ATHEISM

The three great apostles of practical atheism that make converts without
persecuting, and retain them without preaching, are health, wealth
and power – *Charles Caleb Colton*

Atheism is rather in the life than in the heart of man – *Francis Bacon*

To be an atheist requires an infinitely greater measure of faith than to receive all the great truths which atheism would deny – *Joseph Addison*

The footprint of the savage in the sand is sufficient to prove the presence of man to the atheist who will not recognize God though his hand is impressed on the entire universe – *Hugh Miller*

Few men are so obstinate in their atheism that a pressing danger will not compel them to the acknowledgment of a divine power – *Plato*

Virtue in distress, and vice in triumph, make atheists of mankind – *John Dryden*

In agony or danger, no nature is atheist. The mind that knows not what to fly to flies to God – *Hannah More*

Atheism is a disease of the soul, before it becomes an error of the understanding – *Plato*

God never wrought miracles to convince atheism, because His ordinary works convince it – *Bacon*

Atheists put on a false courage in the midst of their darkness and misapprehensions, like children who, when they fear to go in the dark, will sing or whistle to keep up their courage – *Alexander Pope*

Whoever considers the study of anatomy can never be an atheist – *Lord Herbert*

Atheism is the death of hope, the suicide of the soul.

An irreligious man, a speculative or a practical atheist, is as a sovereign, who voluntarily takes off his crown and declares himself unworthy to reign.

See also RELIGION.

AUTHORITY

Nothing is more gratifying to the mind of man than power of dominion – *Joseph Addison*

Nothing sooner overthrows a weak head than opinion of authority; like too strong liquor for a frail glass – *Sir Philip Sidney*

They that govern make least noise, as they that row the barge do work and puff and sweat, while he that governs sits quietly at the stern, and scarce is seen to stir – *John Selden*

He who is firmly seated in authority soon learns to think security, and not progress, the highest lesson of statecraft – *J. R. Lovell*

Nothing more impairs authority than a too frequent or indiscreet use of it.

See also GOVERNMENT, POWER.

AUTHORSHIP

The two most engaging powers of an author, are, to make new things familiar, and familiar things new – *Samuel Johnson*

No fathers or mothers think their own children ugly; and this self-deceit is yet stronger with respect to the offspring of the mind – *Miguel de Cervantes Saavedra*

The most original authors are not so because they advance what is new, but because they put what they have to say as if it had never been said before – *Johann Wolfgang von Goethe*

Next to doing things that deserve to be written, nothing gets a man more credit, or gives him more pleasure than to write things that deserve to be read – *Lord Chesterfield*

There are three difficulties in authorship: to write anything worth publishing – to find honest men to publish it – and to get sensible men to read it – *Charles Caleb Colton*

Talent alone cannot make a writer; there must be a man behind the book – *Ralph Waldo Emerson*

Every author in some degree portrays himself in his works, even if it be against his will – *Goethe*

A great writer is the friend and benefactor of his readers – *Thomas Babington Macaulay*

Satire lies about men of letters during their lives, and eulogy after their death – *Voltaire*

No author is so poor that he cannot be of some service, if only as a witness of his time.

Writers are the main landmarks of the past.

See also BOOKS.

AUTUMN

The melancholy days are come, the saddest of the year – *William Cullen Bryant*

A moral character is attached to autumnal scenes. The flowers fading like our hopes, the leaves falling like our years, the clouds fleeting like our illusions, the light diminishing like our intelligence, the sun growing colder like our affections, the rivers becoming frozen like our lives – all bear secret relations to our destinies – *François de Chateaubriand*

Season of mists and mellow fruitfulness – *John Keats*

The leaves in autumn do not change colour from the blighting touch of frost, but from the process of natural decay. They fall when the fruit is ripened, and their work is done. And their splendid colouring is but their graceful and beautiful surrender of life when they have finished their summer offering of service to God and man. And one of the great lessons the fall of the leaf teaches, is this: Do your work well, and then be ready to depart when God shall call – *Tryon Edwards*

AVARICE

Avarice increases with the increasing pile of gold – *Juvenal*

The lust of gold, unfeeling and remorseless, the last corruption of degenerate man – *Samuel Johnson*

Study rather to fill your mind than your coffers; knowing that gold and silver were originally mingled with dirt, until avarice or ambition parted them – *Seneca*

The avaricious man is like the barren sandy ground of the desert which sucks in all the rain and dew with greediness, but yields no fruitful herbs or plants for the benefit of others – *Zeno*

Avarice, in old age, is foolish; for what can be more absurd than to increase our provisons for the road the nearer we approach to our journey's end? – *Cicero*

Avarice is the vice of declining years.

Poverty wants some things, luxury many, avarice all things.

BABBLERS

Fire and sword are but slow engines of destruction in comparison with the babbler – *Richard Steele*

Talkers are no good doers: be assur'd / We go to use our hands and not our tongues – *William Shakespeare*

See also LOQUACITY.

BABIES

A babe in the house is a well-spring of pleasure, a messenger of peace and love, a resting place for innocence on earth, a link between angels and men – *Martin Farquhar Tupper*

A sweet new blossom of humanity, fresh fallen from God's own home, to flower on earth – *Gerald Massey*

Some wonder that children should be given to young mothers. But what instruction does the babe bring to the mother! She learns patience, self-control, endurance; her very arm grows strong so that she holds the dear burden longer than the father can – *Thomas Wentworth Higginson*

A rose with all its sweetest leaves yet folded – *Lord Byron*

The coarsest father gains a new impulse to labour from the moment of his baby's birth. Every stroke he strikes is for his child. New social aims, and new moral motives come vaguely up to him – *Higginson*

Of all the joys that lighten suffering earth, what joy is welcomed like a
new-born child?
Living jewels, dropped unstained from heaven.
A baby is God's opinion that the world should go on.
See also CHILDREN.

BACHELORS

I have no wife or children, good or bad, to provide for; a mere spectator
of other men's fortunes and adventures, and how they play their
parts; which, methinks, are diversly presented unto me, as from a
common theatre or scene – *Robert Burton*
Because I will not do them the wrong to mistrust any, I will do myself the
right to trust none; and the fine is, – for the which I may go the finer, –
I will live a bachelor – *William Shakespeare*
A bachelor's life is a splendid breakfast; a tolerably flat dinner; and a
most miserable supper.

BARGAINS

Sometimes one pays most for the things one gets for nothing – *Alfred
Einstein*
A bargain is something you have to find a use for, once you've bought it.
Bargains made in speed are commonly repented at leisure.
The person who has a second-hand car knows how hard it is to drive a
bargain.

BASENESS

Every base occupation makes one sharp in its practice, and dull in every
other – *Sir Philip Sidney*
There is a law of forces which hinders bodies from sinking beyond a
certain depth in the sea; but in the ocean of baseness the deeper we
get the easier the sinking – *J. R. Lovell*
Baseness of character or conduct not only scars the conscience but
deranges the intellect. Right conduct is connected with right views of
truth – *Charles Caleb Colton*

BEAUTY

If virtue accompanies beauty it is the heart's paradise; if vice be associate
with it, it is the soul's purgatory. It is the wise man's bonfire, and the
fool's furnace – *Francis Quarles*

The best part of beauty is that which no picture can express – *Francis Bacon*

It is the divinity within that makes the divinity without – *George Washington*

Even virtue is more fair when it appears in a beautiful person – *Virgil*

That which is striking and beautiful is not always good; but that which is good is always beautiful – *Ninon de Lenclos*

Every trait of beauty may be referred to some virtue, as to innocence, candour, generosity, modesty, or heroism – *Jacques Henri Bernadin de Saint-Pierre*

To give pain is the tyranny; to make happy, the true empire of beauty – *Richard Steele*

If the nose of Cleopatra had been a little shorter, it would have changed the history of the world – *Blaise Pascal*

Beauty in a modest woman is like fire at a distance, or a sharp sword beyond reach. The one does not burn, or the other wound those that come not too near them – *Miguel de Cervantes Saavedra*

The most natural beauty in the world is honesty and moral truth. For all beauty is truth. True features make the beauty of the face; true proportions, the beauty of architecture; true measures, the beauty of harmony and music – *Lord Shaftesbury*

How goodness heightens beauty! – *Hannah More*

Beauty is the mark God sets on virtue – *Ralph Waldo Emerson*

Beauty is like an almanack: if it last a year it is well – *T. Adams*

The common foible of women who have been handsome is to forget that they are no longer so – *François de La Rochefoucauld*

Beauty is as summer fruits, which are easy to corrupt and cannot last; and for the most part it makes a dissolute youth, and an age a little out of countenance; but if it light well, it makes virtue shine and vice blush – *Francis Bacon*

Beauty is an outward gift which is seldom despised, except by those to whom it has been refused – *Edward Gibbon*

An appearance of delicacy, and even of fragility, is almost essential to beauty – *Edmund Burke*

I pray thee, O God, that I may be beautiful within – *Socrates*

All beauty does not inspire love; some beauties please the sight without captivating the affections – *Miguel de Cervantes Saavedra*

In all ranks of life the human heart yearns for the beautiful; and the beautiful things that God makes are his gift to all alike – *Harriet Beecher Stowe*

Beauty attracts us men; but if, like an armed magnet it is pointed, beside, with gold or silver, it attracts with tenfold power – *Jean Paul Richter*

There should be as little merit in loving a woman for her beauty, as a man for his prosperity, both being equally subject to change – *Alexander Pope*

O! how much more doth beauty beauteous seem / By that sweet ornament which truth doth give! – *William Shakespeare*

A thing of beauty is a joy for ever: / Its loveliness increases; it will never / Pass into nothingness – *John Keats*

Charms strike the sight but merit wins the soul – *Pope*

By cultivating the beautiful we scatter the seeds of heavenly flowers, as by doing good we cultivate those that belong to humanity.

Socrates called beauty a short-lived tyranny; Plato, a privilege of nature; Theophrastus, a silent cheat; Theocritus, a delightful prejudice; Carneades, a solitary kingdom; Aristotle said that it was better than all the letters of recommendation in the world; Homer, that it was a glorious gift of nature, and Ovid, that it was a favour bestowed by the gods.

Beauty is often worse than wine; intoxicating both the holder and beholder.

Beauty, unaccompanied by virtue, is as a flower without perfume.

The fountain of beauty is the heart, and every generous thought illustrates the walls of your chamber.

The beauty seen, is partly in him who sees it.

To cultivate the sense of the beautiful is one of the most effectual ways of cultivating an appreciation of the divine goodness.

The soul, by an instinct stronger than reason, ever associates beauty with truth.

No woman can be handsome by the force of features alone, any more than she can be witty by only the help of speech.

Beauty is the first present nature gives to women and the first it takes away.

If you tell a woman she is beautiful, whisper it softly; for if the devil hears it he will echo it many times.

Loveliness needs not the aid of foreign ornament, but is, when un-adorned, adorned the most.

BED

The bed is a bundle of paradoxes: we go to it with reluctance, yet we quit it with regret; we make up our minds every night to leave it early, but we make up our bodies every morning to keep it late – *Charles Caleb Colton*

What a delightful thing rest is! The bed has become a place of luxury to me. I would not exchange it for all the thrones in the world – *Napoleon Bonaparte*

In bed we laugh; in bed we cry; / In bed are born; in bed we die; / The near approach the bed doth show, / Of human bliss to human woe – *Isaac de Benserade*

Early to bed, and early to rise, makes a man healthy, wealthy, and wise – *Benjamin Franklin*

Night is the time for rest; how sweet when labours close, / To gather round an aching heart the curtain of repose; / Stretch the tired limbs, and lay the weary head / Down on our own delightful bed – *James Montgomery*

Early to bed and early to rise and you'll meet very few of our best people – *George Ade*

BEGINNINGS

Let us watch well our beginnings, and results will manage themselves – *Alex Clark*

When the ancients said a work well begun was half done, they meant to impress the importance of always endeavouring to make a good beginning – *Polybius*

BEHAVIOUR

Behaviour is a mirror in which every one displays his image – *Johann Wolfgang von Goethe*

What is becoming in behaviour is honourable, and what is honourable is becoming – *Cicero*

Levity of behaviour is the bane of all that is good and virtuous – *Seneca*

Oddities and singularities of behaviour may attend genius, but when they do, they are its misfortunes and blemishes – *William Temple*

A consciousness of inward knowledge gives confidence to the outward behaviour, which, of all things, is the best to grace a man in his carriage.

You and I are much more alike than we are different.

See also CONDUCT.

BELIEF

Nothing is so easy as to deceive one's self; for what we wish, that we readily believe – *Demosthenes*

There are many great truths which we do not deny, and which nevertheless we do not fully believe – *J. W. Alexander*

He that will believe only what he can fully comprehend must have a very long head or a very short creed – *Charles Caleb Colton*

Remember that what you believe will depend very much upon what you are – *Noah Porter*

We are slow to believe that which if believed would hurt our feelings – *Ovid*

The practical effect of a belief is the real test of its soundness – *James Anthony Froude*

You believe easily what you hope for earnestly – *Terence*

He who expects men to be always as good as their beliefs indulges a groundless hope; and he who expects men to be always as bad as their beliefs vexes himself with a needless fear – *J. S. Kieffer*

It is a singular fact that many men of action incline to the theory of fatalism, while the greater part of men of thought believe in a divine providence – *Honoré de Balzac*

Yes I shall see God as he is, face to face! – *Marquis de Vauvenargues*

Achieving starts with believing.

Some believe all that parents, tutors, and kindred believe. They take their principles by inheritance, and defend them as they would their estates, because they are born heirs to them.

In belief lies the secret of all valuable exertion.

A sceptical young man one day, conversing with the celebrated Dr Parr, observed, that he would believe nothing which he could not understand. 'Then, young man, your creed will be the shortest of any man's I know.'

See also AGNOSTICISM, FAITH.

BENEFICENCE

Christian beneficence takes a large sweep; that circumference cannot be small of which God is the centre – *Hannah More*

Doing good is the only certainly happy action of a man's life – *Sir Philip Sidney*

We enjoy thoroughly only the pleasure that we give – *Alexandre Dumas*

He that does good to another does good also to himself, not only in the consequences, but in the very act; for the consciousness of well doing is, in itself, ample reward – *Seneca*

Men resemble the gods in nothing so much as in doing good to their fellow creatures – *Cicero*

Rich people should consider that they are only trustees for what they possess, and should show their wealth to be more in doing good than merely in having it. They should not reserve their benevolence for purposes after they are dead, for those who give not of their property till they die show that they would not then if they could keep it any longer – *Bishop Hall*

It is another's fault if he be ungrateful; but it is mine if I do not give. To find one thankful man, I will oblige a great many that are not so. I had rather never receive a kindness than never bestow one. Not to return a benefit is a great sin; but not to confer one is a greater – *Seneca*

For his bounty, / There was no winter in't, an autumn 'twas / That grew
the more by reaping – *William Shakespeare*

I never knew a child of God being bankrupted by his benevolence. What
we keep we may lose, but what we give to Christ we are sure to keep –
T. L. Cuyler

Be charitable before wealth makes thee covetous – *Sir Thomas Browne*

Money spent on ourselves may be a millstone about the neck; spent on
others it may give us wings like eagles – *R. D. Hitchcock*

To pity distress is but human; to relieve it is Godlike.

The luxury of doing good surpasses every other personal enjoyment.

There is no use of money equal to that of beneficence; here the enjoyment grows on reflection; and our money is most truly ours when it
ceases to be in our possession.

See also CHARITY, GENEROSITY, GIFTS.

BENEVOLENCE

To feel much for others, and little for ourselves; to restrain our selfish,
and exercise our benevolent affections, constitutes the perfection of
human nature – *Adam Smith*

Benevolent feeling ennobles the most trifling actions – *William Makepeace
Thackeray*

In this world it is not what we take up, but what we give up, that makes
us rich – *Henry Ward Beecher*

Do not wait for extraordinary circumstances to do good actions: try to use
ordinary situations – *Jean Paul Richter*

This is the law of benefits between men; the one ought to forget at once
what he has given, and the other ought never to forget what he has
received – *Seneca*

The one who will be found in trial capable of great acts of love is ever the
one who is always doing considerate small ones – *Frederick William
Robertson*

He who wishes to secure the good of others has already secured his own
– *Confucius*

He only does not live in vain, who employs his wealth, his thoughts, his
speech to advance the good of others – *Hindu maxim*

Benevolence is allied to few vices; selfishness to fewer virtues.

They who scatter with one hand gather with two, not always in coin, but
in kind. Nothing multiplies so much as kindness.

The best way to do good to ourselves is to do it to others; the right way to
gather is to scatter.

The conqueror is regarded with awe; the wise man commands our
respect; but it is only the benevolent man that wins our affection.

See also CHARITY.

THE BIBLE

There is no book like the Bible for excellent wisdom and use – *Sir Matthew Hale*

There never was found in any age of the world, either religion or law that did so highly exalt the public good as the Bible – *Francis Bacon*

In this little book [the New Testament], is contained all the wisdom of the world – *Henrich Georg August von Ewald*

Do you know a book that you are willing to put under your head for a pillow when you lie dying? That is the book you want to study while you are living. There is but one such book in the world – *Joseph Cook*

A noble book! All men's book! It is our first oldest statement of the never-ending problem, – man's destiny – *Thomas Carlyle*

There is a Book worth all other books which were ever printed – *Patrick Henry*

The Bible furnishes the only fitting vehicle to express the thoughts that overwhelm us when contemplating the stellar universe – *O. M. Mitchell*

I can meet with anything in the Bible on my subjects, it always affords me a firm platform on which to stand – *Lieutenant Maury*

Holy Scripture is a stream of running water, where alike the elephant may swim, and the lamb walk without losing its feet – *Pope Gregory I, the Great*

The whole hope of human progress is suspended on the ever-growing influence of the Bible – *William Henry Seward*

The Bible stands alone in human literature in its elevated conception of manhood as to character and conduct. It is the invaluable training book of the world – *Henry Ward Beecher*

Nobody ever outgrows Scripture; the book widens and deepens with our years – *Charles Haddon Spurgeon*

I have read the Bible through many times, and now make it a practice to read it through once every year. It is a book of all others for lawyers, as well as divines; and I pity the man who cannot find in it a rich supply of thought and of rules for conduct – *Daniel Webster*

There is no book on which we can rest in a dying moment but the Bible – *John Selden*

A loving trust in the Author of the Bible is the best preparation for a wise and profitable study of the Bible itself – *H. C. Trumbull*

The Bible is the only source of all Christian truth; – the only rule for the Christian life; – the only book that unfolds to us the realities of eternity.

The Bible is a window in this prison of hope, through which we look into eternity.

All the distinctive features and superiority of our republican institutions
are derived from the teachings of Scripture.

The grand old Book of God still stands, and this old earth, the more its
leaves are turned over and pondered, the more it will sustain and
illustrate the sacred Word.

Wilmot, the infidel, when dying, laid his trembling, emaciated hand on
the Bible, and said solemnly and with unwonted energy, 'The only
objection against this book is a bad life!'

See also CHRISTIANITY.

BIGOTRY

The mind of the bigot is like the pupil of the eye; the more light you pour
upon it, the more it will contract – *Oliver Wendell Holmes*

There is no bigotry like that of 'free thought' run to seed – *Horace Greeley*

Bigotry murders religion to frighten fools with her ghost – *Charles Caleb
Colton*

A man must be both stupid and uncharitable who believes there is no
virtue or truth but on his own side – *Joseph Addison*

Bigotry has no head, and cannot think; no heart, and cannot feel.

The bigot for the most part clings to opinions adopted without investigation, and defended without argument, while he is intolerant of the
opinions of others.

BIOGRAPHY

One anecdote of a man is worth a volume of biography – *William Ellery
Channing*

Rich as we are in biography, a well-written life is almost as rare as a
well-spent one; and there are certainly many more men whose
history deserves to be recorded than persons able and willing to
furnish the record – *Thomas Carlyle*

To be ignorant of the lives of the most celebrated men of antiquity is to
continue in a state of childhood all our days – *Plutarch*

A life that is worth writing at all is worth writing minutely and truthfully
– *Henry Wadsworth Longfellow*

Biography is the most universally pleasant and profitable of all reading –
Carlyle

Those only who live with a man can write his life with any genuine
exactness and discrimination, and few people who have lived with a
man know what to remark about him – *Samuel Johnson*

History can be formed from permanent monuments and records; but
lives can only be written from personal knowledge, which is growing
every day less, and in a short time is lost forever – *Johnson*

My advice is, to consult the lives of other men as we would a looking-glass, and from thence fetch examples for our own imitation – *Terence*

Biography is the personal and home aspect of history.

The best teachers of humanity are the lives of great men.

Great men have often the shortest biographies. Their real life is in their books or deeds.

BIRTH

What is birth to a man if it be a stain to his dead ancestors to have left such an offspring? – *Sir Philip Sidney*

A noble birth and fortune, though they make not a bad man good, yet they are a real advantage to a worthy one, and place his virtues in the fairest light – *George Lillo*

High birth is a gift of fortune which should never challenge esteem toward those who receive it, since it costs them neither study nor labour – *Jean de La Bruyère*

Of all vanities and fopperies, the vanity of high birth is the greatest. True nobility is derived from virtue, not from birth. Titles, indeed, may be purchased; but virtue is the only coin that makes the bargain valid – *Sir Richard Burton*

Features alone do not run in the blood; vices and virtues, genius and folly, are transmitted through the same sure but unseen channel – *William Hazlitt*

Our birth is nothing but our death begun, as tapers waste the moment they take fire.

Custom forms us all; our thoughts, our morals, our most fixed belief, are consequences of the place of our birth.

I have learned to judge of men by their own deeds, and not to make the accident of birth the standard of their merit.

Birth is much, but breeding is more.

See also ANCESTRY, ARISTOCRACY.

BLESSEDNESS

True blessedness consisteth in a good life and a happy death – *Solon*

Reflect upon your present blessings, of which every man has many: not on your past misfortunes, of which all men have some – *Charles Dickens*

The beloved of the Almighty are the rich who have the humility of the poor, and the poor who have the magnanimity of the rich – *Sádi*

Nothing raises the price of a blessing like its removal; whereas, it was its continuance which should have taught us its value.

BLUSHING

A blush is the colour of virtue – *Diogenes*
Whoever blushes seems to be good – *Menander*
Whoever blushes, is already guilty; true innocence is ashamed of
    nothing – *Jean Jacques Rousseau*
A blush is beautiful, but often inconvenient – *Carlo Goldoni*
Better a blush on the face than a blot on the heart – *Miguel de Cervantes
    Saavedra*
Men blush less for their crimes, than for their weaknesses and vanity –
    Jean de La Bruyère
Blushing is the livery of virtue, though it may sometimes proceed from
    guilt – *Francis Bacon*
It is better for a young man to blush, than to turn pale – *Cicero*
The inconvenience, or the beauty of the blush, which is the greater? –
    Mme Neckar
The ambiguous livery worn alike by modesty and shame.
When a girl ceases to blush, she has lost the most powerful charm of her
    beauty.
A blush is a sign that nature hangs out, to show where chastity and
    honour dwell.
The man that blushes is not quite a brute.
The blush is nature's alarm at the approach of sin, and her testimony to
    the dignity of virtue.
Playful blushes, that seem but luminous escapes of thought.

BLUSTERING

A killing tongue and a quiet sword – *William Shakespeare*
It is with narrow souled people as with narrow necked bottles; the less
    they have in them, the more noise they make in pouring it out –
    Alexander Pope
They that are loudest in their threats are the weakest in the execution of
    them – *Charles Caleb Colton*
Commonly they whose tongue is their weapon, use their feet for defence
    – *Sir Philip Sidney*
A brave man is sometimes a desperado; but a bully is always a coward.

BOASTING

Where there is much pretension, much has been borrowed; nature never
    pretends – *Johann Kaspar Lavater*
Who knows himself a braggart, / Let him fear this; for it will come to pass /
    That every braggart shall be found an ass – *William Shakespeare*

Usually the greatest boasters are the smallest workers. The deep rivers pay a larger tribute to the sea than shallow brooks, and yet empty themselves with less noise – *W. Secker*

· With all his tumid boasts, he's like the sword-fish, who only wears his weapon in his mouth – *Sir Frederick Madden*

Conceit, more rich in matter than in words, / Brags of his substance, not of ornament: / They are but beggars that can count their worth – *Shakespeare*

A gentleman . . . that loves to hear himself talk, and will speak more in a minute than he will stand to in a month – *Shakespeare*

The empty vessel makes the greatest sound – *Shakespeare*

Where boasting ends, there dignity begins.

The less you speak of your greatness, the more shall I think of it.

BODY

Our body is a well-set clock, which keeps good time, but if it be too much or indiscreetly tampered with, the alarum runs out before the hour – *Bishop Hall*

God made the human body, and it is the most exquisite and wonderful organization which has come to us from the divine hand – *Henry Ward Beecher*

BOLDNESS

Boldness is ever blind, for it sees not dangers and inconveniences – *Francis Bacon*

Fools rush in where angels fear to tread – *Alexander Pope*

Who bravely dares must sometimes risk a fall – *Tobias Smollett*

Fortune befriends the bold – *John Dryden*

We make way for the man who boldly pushes past us.

It is wonderful what strength of purpose and boldness and energy of will are roused by the assurance that we are doing our duty.

See also BRAVERY, COURAGE, VALOUR.

BOOKS

A book is the only immortality – *Rufus Choate*

Books are lighthouses erected in the great sea of time – *E. P. Whipple*

If a book come from the heart it will contrive to reach other hearts – *Thomas Carlyle*

Some books are to be tasted; others swallowed; and some few to be chewed and digested – *Francis Bacon*

Books are those faithful mirrors that reflect to our mind the minds of sages and heroes – *Edward Gibbon*

Next to acquiring good friends, the best acquisition is that of good books – *Charles Caleb Colton*

A good book is the best of friends, the same today and forever – *Martin Farquhar Tupper*

Books are the legacies that genius leaves to mankind, to be delivered down from generation to generation, as presents to those that are yet unborn – *Joseph Addison*

There is no book so bad but something valuable may be derived from it – *Pliny the Younger*

Books are a guide in youth, and an entertainment for age – *Jeremy Collier*

Be as careful of the books you read, as of the company you keep; for your habits and character will be as much influenced by the former as by the latter – *Paxton Hood*

Books, like proverbs, receive their chief value from the stamp and esteem of the ages through which they have passed – *William Temple*

We are as liable to be corrupted by books, as by companions – *Henry Fielding*

Life's first danger has been said to be an empty mind which, like an unoccupied room, is open for base spirits to enter – *H. W. Grout*

The best books for a man are not always those which the wise recommend, but often those which meet the peculiar wants, the natural thirst of his mind, and therefore awaken interest and rivet thought – *William Ellery Channing*

A house without books is like a room without windows – *Horace Mann*

The books that help you most are those which make you think the most. The hardest way of learning is that of easy reading; but a great book that comes from a great thinker is a ship of thought, deep freighted with truth and beauty – *Theodore Parker*

There was a time when the world acted on books, now books act on the world – *Joseph Joubert*

To buy books only because they were published by an eminent printer is much as if a man should buy clothes that did not fit him, only because made by some famous tailor – *Alexander Pope*

The book to read is not the one which thinks for you, but the one which makes you think – *James McCosh*

The best of a book is not the thought which it contains, but the thought which it suggests – *Oliver Wendell Holmes*

Every man is a volume if you know how to read him – *Channing*

That is a good book which is opened with expectation, and closed with delight and profit – *Amos Bronson Alcott*

A book is a garden, an orchard, a storehouse, a party, a company by the way, a counsellor, a multitude of counsellors – *Henry Ward Beecher*

Deep versed in books, but shallow in himself – *John Milton*

The books that help you most are those that make you think the most –
Parker

No book can be so good as to be profitable when negligently read –
Seneca

Upon books the collective education of the race depends; they are the
sole instruments of registering, perpetuating, and transmitting
thought – *H. Rogers*

There is no worse robber than a bad book – *Italian proverb*

Books are embalmed minds.

Books, like friends, should be few and well chosen.

A book may be compared to your neighbour: if it be good, it cannot last
too long; if bad, you cannot get rid of it too early.

Books are but waste paper unless we spend in action the wisdom we get
from thought.

The books we read should be chosen with great care, that they may be, as
an Egyptian king wrote over his library, 'the medicines of the soul'.

Choose an author as you choose a friend.

Books are men of higher stature; the only men that speak aloud for future
times to hear.

Master books, but do not let them master you. Read to live, not live to
read.

Most books, like their authors, are born to die; of only a few books can it
be said that death hath no dominion over them; they live, and their
influence lives forever.

Books should to one of these four ends conduce, / For wisdom, piety,
delight, or use.

He that loves not books before he comes to thirty years of age, will hardly
love them enough afterward to understand them.

See also AUTHORSHIP, FICTION, LIBRARIES, LITERATURE, NOVELS,
READING.

BORES

The secret of making one's self tiresome is not to know when to stop –
Voltaire

There are some kinds of men who cannot pass their time alone; they are
the flails of occupied people – *Vicomte de Bonald*

There are few wild beasts more to be dreaded than a talking man having
nothing to say – *Jonathan Swift*

O! he's as tedious / As a tired horse, a railing wife; / Worse than a smoky
house – *William Shakespeare*

We are almost always wearied in the company of persons with whom we
are not permitted to be weary – *François de La Rochefoucauld*

BORROWING

Borrowing is not much better than begging – *Gotthold Ephraim Lessing*

If you would know the value of money, go and try to borrow some. He that goes a-borrowing goes a-sorrowing – *Benjamin Franklin*

Neither a borrower, nor a lender be; / For loan oft loses both itself and friend, / And borrowing dulls the edge of husbandry – *William Shakespeare*

Getting into debt is getting into a tanglesome net – *Franklin*

The borrower runs in his own debt – *Ralph Waldo Emerson*

He that would have a short Lent, let him borrow money to be repaid at Easter – *Franklin*

No remedy against this consumption of the purse; borrowing only lingers and lingers it out, but the disease is incurable – *Shakespeare*

The unpleasantness is not in living on the overdraft but in repaying it.

Many a man has a wolf at the door because his wife has a silver fox around her neck.

Brave actions never want a trumpet.

Before borrowing money from a friend decide which you need more.

See also CREDIT, DEBT, LENDING.

BRAVERY

The best hearts are ever the bravest – *Laurence Sterne*

A true knight is fuller of bravery in the midst, than in the beginning of danger – *Sir Philip Sidney*

There is a wide difference between true courage and a mere contempt of life – *Cato*

At the bottom of not a little of the bravery that appears in the world, there lurks a miserable cowardice. Men will face powder and steel because they have not the courage to face public opinion – *E. H. Chapin*

True bravery is shown by performing without witnesses what one might be capable of doing before all the world – *François de La Rochefoucauld*

Nature often enshrines gallant and noble hearts in weak bosoms; oftenest, God bless her, in woman's breast – *Charles Dickens*

All brave men love; for he only is brave who has affections to fight for, whether in the daily battle of life, or in physical contests – *Nathaniel Hawthorne*

See also BOLDNESS, COURAGE, VALOUR.

BREVITY

Brevity is the soul of wit – *William Shakespeare*

Have something to say; say it, and stop when you've done – *Tryon Edwards*

When one has no design but to speak plain truth, he may say a great deal in a very narrow compass – *Richard Steele*

The one prudence of life is concentration – *Ralph Waldo Emerson*

One rare, strange virtue in speeches, and the secret of their mastery, is that they are short – *Fitz-Greene Halleck*

Brevity is the best recommendation of speech, whether in a senator or an orator – *Cicero*

Talk to the point, and stop when you have reached it – *John Neal*

Words are like leaves, and where they most abound, / Much fruit of sense beneath is rarely found – *Alexander Pope*

If you would be pungent, be brief; for it is with words as with sunbeams – the more they are condensed, the deeper they burn – *Robert Southey*

When you introduce a moral lesson let it be brief – *Horace*

Never be so brief as to become obscure – *Edwards*

BRIBERY

Judges and senators have been bought with gold – *Alexander Pope*

Though authority be a stubborn bear, yet he is oft led by the nose with gold – *William Shakespeare*

Petitions not sweetened with gold, are but unsavory, and often refused; or if received, are pocketed, not read – *Philip Massinger*

Who thinketh to buy villainy with gold, / Shall find such faith so bought, so sold – *John Marston*

A man who is furnished with arguments from the mint will convince his antagonist much sooner than one who draws them from reason and philosophy – *Joseph Addison*

The universe is not rich enough to buy the vote of an honest man.

BROTHERHOOD

To live is not to live for one's self alone; let us help one another – *Menander*

Whoever in prayer can say 'Our Father', acknowledges and should feel the brotherhood of the whole race of mankind – *Tryon Edwards*

There is no brotherhood of man without the fatherhood of God – *H. M. Field*

If God is the father, man is thy brother – *Alphonse Marie Louis de Lamartine*

However degraded or wretched a fellow mortal may be, he is still a member of our common species – *Seneca*

Jesus throws down the dividing prejudices of nationality, and teaches universal love, without distinction of race, merit, or rank. A man's neighbour is everyone that needs help. All men, from the slave to the highest, are sons of the one father in heaven – *J. C. Geikie*

Give bread to the stranger, in the name of the universal brotherhood
which binds together all men under the common fatherhood of
nature – *Quintilian*

BUILDING

He that is fond of building will soon ruin himself without the help of
enemies – *Plutarch*

Houses are built to live in, more than to look at; therefore let use be
preferred before uniformity, except where both may be had – *Francis
Bacon*

Never build after you are five-and-forty; have five years' income in hand
before you lay a brick; and always calculate the expense at double the
estimate.

See also ARCHITECTURE, HOUSE.

BUSINESS

Not because of any extraordinary talents did he succeed, but because he
had a capacity on a level for business and not above it – *Tacitus*

Avoid multiplicity of business; the man of one thing is the man of
success – *Tryon Edwards*

It is a wise man who knows his own business; and it is a wiser man who
thoroughly attends to it – *H. L. Wayland*

To business that we love we rise betime, / And go to't with delight –
William Shakespeare

All the money in the world is not worth so much to you as one good
staunch friend – *Henry Ward Beecher*

Call on a business man only at business times, and on business; transact
your business, and go about your business, in order to give him time
to finish his business – *Duke of Wellington*

Nobody has ever established a successful business without dreaming
about it at the beginning – *James Ramsay MacDonald*

American business is in a state of realization; it is cashing in on the
foresight of the pioneers – *Merryle Stanley Rukeyser*

The 'tired business man' is one whose business is usually not a successful one – *Joseph R. Grundy*

In business, three things are necessary, knowledge, temper and time.

Never shrink from doing anything your business calls you to do. The
man who is above his business may one day find his business above
him.

Formerly when great fortunes were only made in war, war was a
business; but now when great fortunes are only made by business,
business is war.

It was a beautiful truth which our forefathers symbolized when in the old market towns they erected a market cross, as if to teach both buyers and sellers to rule their actions and sanctify their gains by the remembrance of the cross.

Business? It's quite simple; it's other people's money.

See also COMMERCE.

BUSYBODIES

Always occupied with the duties of others, never, alas! with our own – *Joseph Joubert*

I never knew anyone interfere with other people's disputes, but that he heartily repented of it – *Lord Carlisle*

One who is too wise an observer of the business of others, like one who is too curious in observing the labour of bees, will often be stung for his curiosity – *Alexander Pope*

CALAMITY

Calamity is man's true touchstone – *Francis Beaumont and John Fletcher*

Calamity is the perfect glass wherein we truly see and know ourselves – *Sir William Davenant*

When any calamity has been suffered, the first thing to be remembered is how much has been escaped – *Samuel Johnson*

He who foresees calamities, suffers them twice over – *Beilby Porteus*

It is only from the belief of the goodness and wisdom of a supreme being that our calamities can be borne in the manner which becomes a man.

CANDOUR

I can promise to be candid, though I may not be impartial – *Johann Wolfgang von Goethe*

Candour is the brightest gem of criticism – *Benjamin Disraeli*

I make it my rule, to lay hold of light and embrace it, wherever I see it, though held forth by a child or an enemy – *Jonathan Edwards*

Examine what is said, not him who speaks – *Arabian proverb*

Candour is the seal of a noble mind, the ornament and pride of man, the sweetest charm of women, the scorn of rascals, and the rarest virtue of sociability.

It is great and manly to disdain disguise; it shows our spirit, and proves our strength.

In reasoning upon moral subjects, we have great occasion for candour, in order to compare circumstances, and weigh arguments with impartiality.

CARE

Care is no cure, but rather corrosive, / For things that are not to be remedied – *William Shakespeare*

Cares are often more difficult to throw off than sorrows; the latter die with time; the former grow upon it – *Jean Paul Richter*

You have too much respect upon the world: / They lose it that do buy it with much care – *Shakespeare*

Providence has given us hope and sleep as a compensation for the many cares of life – *Voltaire*

Only man clogs his happiness with care destroying what is, with thoughts of what may be – *John Dryden*

Care keeps his watch in every old man's eye, / And where care lodges, sleep will never lie – *Shakespeare*

Measure thrice before you cut once – *Italian proverb*

Care admitted as a guest quickly turns to be master.

This world has cares enough to plague us but he who meditates on others' woe shall, in that meditation, lose his care.

Better the foot slip than the tongue.

See also ANXIETY, CAUTION.

CASTLES IN THE AIR

Charming Alnaschar vision! It is the happy privilege of youth to construct you! – *William Makepeace Thackeray*

If you have built castles in the air, your work need not be lost; that is where they should be. Now put foundations under them – *Henry David Thoreau*

CAUTION

It is well to learn caution by the misfortunes of others – *Publius Syrus*

All is to be feared where all is to be lost – *Lord Byron*

Look before you leap; see before you go – *Thomas Tusser*

When clouds are seen, wise men put on their cloaks – *William Shakespeare*

None pities him that's in the snare, / Who, warned before, would not beware – *Robert Herrick*

Trust not him that hath once broken faith – *Shakespeare*

Things done well, / And with a care, exempt themselves from fear – *Shakespeare*

I don't like these cold, precise, perfect people, who, in order not to speak wrong, never speak at all, and in order not to do wrong, never do anything – *Henry Ward Beecher*

Open your mouth and purse cautiously, and your stock of wealth and reputation shall, at least in repute, be great.

More firm and sure the hand of courage strikes, when it obeys the watchful eye of caution.

If you think you have someone eating out of your hand it's a good idea to count your fingers.

See also CARE.

CENSURE

Censure is the tax a man pays to the public for being eminent – *Jonathan Swift*

The censure of those who are opposed to us is the highest commendation that can be given us – *Seigneur de Saint-Evremond*

Forbear to judge, for we are sinners all – *William Shakespeare*

The readiest and surest way to get rid of censure is to correct ourselves – *Demosthenes*

Censure pardons the ravens, but rebukes the doves – *Juvenal*

Few persons have sufficient wisdom to prefer censure, which is useful, to praise, which deceives them – *François de La Rochefoucauld*

The villain's censure is extorted praise – *Alexander Pope*

It is harder to avoid censure than to gain applause, for this may be done by one great or wise action in an age; but to escape censure a man must pass his whole life without saying or doing one ill or foolish thing – *David Hume*

He is always the severest censor on the merits of others who has the least worth of his own – *E. L. Magoon*

We hand folks over to God's mercy, and show none ourselves – *George Eliot*

They must first judge themselves, that presume to censure others.

See also CRITICISM.

CHANCE

There is no such thing as chance; and what seems to us the merest accident springs from the deepest source of destiny – *Johann Christoph Friedrich von Schiller*

Be not too presumptuously sure in any business; for things of this world depend on such a train of unseen chances that if it were in man's hands to set the tables, still he would not be certain to win the game – *George Herbert*

Chance is always powerful. Let your hook be always cast; in the pool where you least expect it, there will be a fish – *Ovid*

Chance is a word void of sense; nothing can exist without a cause – *Voltaire*

Chance generally favours the prudent – *Joseph Joubert*

The doctrine of chances is the bible of the fool.

There is no doubt such a thing as chance; but I see no reason why Providence should not make use of it.

Many shining actions owe their success to chance, though the general or statesman runs away with the applause.

See also ACCIDENT, LUCK.

CHANGE

The circumstances of the world are so variable that an irrevocable purpose or opinion is almost synonymous with a foolish one – *William Henry Seward*

What I possess I would gladly retain. Change amuses the mind, yet scarcely profits – *Johann Wolfgang von Goethe*

He that will not apply new remedies must expect new evils – *Francis Bacon*

Change, indeed, is painful, yet ever needful; and if memory have its force and worth, so also has hope – *Thomas Carlyle*

Remember the wheel of Providence is always in motion; and the spoke that is uppermost will be under; and therefore mix trembling always with your joy – *Philip Henry*

This world is not for aye, nor 'tis not strange, / That even our love should with our fortunes change – *William Shakespeare*

In this world of change naught which comes stays, and naught which goes is lost – *Mme Swetchine*

The world is a scene of changes; to be constant in nature were inconstancy.

Change is not made without inconvenience even from worse to better.

CHARACTER

Character is perfectly educated will – *Novalis*

The noblest contribution which any man can make for the benefit of posterity is that of a good character. The richest bequest which any man can leave to the youth of his native land is that of a shining, spotless example – *Robert Charles Winthrop*

Let us not say, Every man is the architect of his own fortune; but let us say, Every man is the architect of his own character – *G. D. Boardman*

Talents are best nurtured in solitude; character is best formed in the stormy billows of the world – *Johann Wolfgang von Goethe*

He who acts wickedly in private life can never be expected to show himself noble in public conduct – *Aeschines*

Character and personal force are the only investments that are worth anything – *Walt Whitman*

A man's character is the reality of himself. His reputation is the opinion others have formed of him. Character is in him; reputation is from other people – that is the substance, this is the shadow – *Henry Ward Beecher*

Characters do not change. Opinions alter, but characters are only developed – *Benjamin Disraeli*

Character is built out of circumstances. From exactly the same materials one man builds palaces, while another builds hovels – *G. H. Lewes*

The character that needs law to mend it is hardly worth the tinkering – *Douglas William Jerrold*

As there is nothing in the world great but man, there is nothing truly great in man but character – *William Maxwell Evarts*

If you would create something, you must be something – *Goethe*

If I take care of my character, my reputation will take care of itself – *Dwight Lyman Moody*

Character must stand behind and back up everything – the sermon, the poem, the picture, the play. None of them is worth a straw without it – *Josiah Gilbert Holland*

Make but few explanations. The character that cannot defend itself is not worth vindicating – *Frederick William Robertson*

The great thing in this world is not so much where we are, but in what direction we are moving – *Oliver Wendell Holmes*

Do what you know and perception is converted into character – *Ralph Waldo Emerson*

Good character is human nature in its best form – *Samuel Smiles*

Never does a man portray his own character more vividly than in his manner of portraying another – *Jean Paul Richter*

Should one tell you that a mountain had changed its place, you are at liberty to doubt it; but if anyone tells you that a man has changed his character, do not believe it – *Muhammad*

A good heart, benevolent feelings, and a balanced mind lie at the foundation of character – *John Todd*

You cannot dream yourself into a character; you must hammer and forge one for yourself – *James Anthony Froude*

Win without boasting. Lose without excuse – *Albert Payson Terhune*

When the fight begins within himself, / A man's worth something – *Robert Browning*

The measure of a man's character is what he would do if he knew he would not be found out – *Thomas Babington Macaulay*

Charms strike the sight but merit wins the soul – *Alexander Pope*

Character is before money or property or anything else. Money cannot buy it – *John Pierpont Morgan*

Only what we have wrought into our character during life can we take away with us.

Character is a diamond that scratches every other stone.

A good character is, in all cases, the fruit of personal exertion. It is not inherited from parents; it is not created by external advantages; it is not a necessary appendage of birth, wealth, talents, or station; but it is the result of one's own endeavours – the fruit and reward of good principles manifested in a course of virtuous and honourable action.

As the sun is best seen at his rising and setting, so men's native dispositions are clearest seen when they are children, and when they are dying.

The character is like paper; if once blotted it can hardly ever be made to appear white as before.

Our character is but the stamp on our souls of the free choices of good and evil we have made through life.

Truthfulness is a cornerstone in character, and if it be not firmly laid in youth, there will ever after be a weak spot in the foundation.

Character is like stock in trade; the more of it a man possesses, the greater his facilities for making additions to it. Character is power – is influence; it makes friends; creates funds; draws patronage and support; and opens a sure and easy way to wealth, honour, and happiness.

Not education, but character, is man's greatest need and man's greatest safeguard.

Some men are self-made and others are the revised work of a wife and daughters.

No man was ever great by imitation.

You can mould a mannerism, but you must chisel a character.

A person's character is like a fence – it cannot be strengthened by whitewash.

See also DISPOSITION.

CHARITY

Posthumous charities are the very essence of selfishness when bequeathed by those who, even alive, would part with nothing – *Charles Caleb Colton*

To pity is but human; to relieve it is Godlike – *Horace Mann*

Proportion thy charity to the strength of thine estate, lest God in anger proportion thine estate to the weakness of thy charity – *Francis Quarles*

Let him who neglects to raise the fallen fear lest, when he falls, no one will stretch out his hand to lift him up – *Sádi*

Loving kindness is greater than laws; and the charities of life are more than all ceremonies – *Talmud*

Charity gives itself rich; covetousness hoards itself poor – *German proverb*

Give a man a fish and you give him a meal, give a man a net and he will never be hungry again.

First daughter to the love of God, is charity to man.

Charity is never lost; it may meet with ingratitude, or be of no service to those on whom it was bestowed, yet it ever does a work of beauty and grace upon the heart of the giver.

The deeds of charity we have done shall stay with us forever. Only the wealth we have so bestowed do we keep; the other is not ours.

The charity that hastens to proclaim its good deeds ceases to be charity, and is only pride and ostentation.

When faith and hope fail, as they do sometimes, we must try charity, which is love in action.

Give work rather than alms to the poor. The former drives out indolence, the latter industry.

The place of charity, like that of God, is everywhere.

Our true acquisitions lie only in our charities, we gain only as we give.

The truly generous is truly wise, and he who loves not others lives unblest.

See also BENEFICENCE, BENEVOLENCE, GENEROSITY, GIFTS, LIBERALITY.

CHASTITY

A pure mind in a chaste body is the mother of wisdom and deliberation – *Jeremy Taylor*

Chastity enables the soul to breathe a pure air in the foulest places – *Joseph Joubert*

A man defines his standing at the court of chastity by his views of women. He cannot be any man's friend, nor his own, if not hers – *Amos Bronson Alcott*

There needs not strength to be added to inviolate chastity; the excellency of the mind makes the body impregnable – *Sir Philip Sidney*

That chastity of honour, which feels a stain like a wound – *Edmund Burke*

See also PURITY.

CHEERFULNESS

I had rather have a fool to make me merry than experience to make me sad – *William Shakespeare*

Oh, give us the man who sings at his work – *Thomas Carlyle*

The highest wisdom is continual cheerfulness; such a state, like the region above the moon, is always clear and serene – *Michel Eyquem de Montaigne*

Wondrous is the strength of cheerfulness, and its power of endurance –

the cheerful man will do more in the same time, will do it better, will persevere in it longer than the sad or sullen – *Carlyle*

Honest good humour is the oil and wine of a merry meeting, and there is no jovial companionship equal to that where the jokes are rather small and the laughter abundant – *Washington Irving*

Cheerfulness is as natural to the heart of a man in strong health as colour to his cheeks; and wherever there is habitual gloom, there must be either bad air, unwholesome food, improperly severe labour, or erring habits of life – *John Ruskin*

A light heart lives long – *Shakespeare*

The true source of cheerfulness is benevolence – *Parke Godwin*

If I can put one touch of a rosy sunset into the life of any man or woman, I shall feel that I have worked with God – *George Macdonald*

Burdens become light when cheerfully borne – *Ovid*

The cheerful live longest in years, and afterwards in our regards. Cheerfulness is the offshoot of goodness.

Cheerful looks make every dish a feast; and it is that which crowns a welcome – *Philip Massinger*

Everyone must have felt that a cheerful friend is like a sunny day, which sheds its brightness on all around; and most of us can, as we choose, make of this world either a palace or a prison – *Sir J. Luddock*

Every time a man smiles, and much more when he laughs, it adds something to his fragment of life – *Laurence Sterne*

Cheerfulness is the principal ingredient in the composition of health.

How great the virtue and the art to live on little with a cheerful heart.

He started to sing as he tackled the thing that couldn't be done, and he did it.

What sunshine is to flowers, smiles are to humanity.

Get into the habit of looking for the silver lining of the cloud, and, when you have found it, continue to look at it, rather than at the leaden grey in the middle. It will help you over many hard places.

Cheerfulness is health; its opposite, melancholy, is disease.

Climate has much to do with cheerfulness, but nourishing food, a good digestion, and good health much more.

An ounce of cheerfulness is worth a pound of sadness.

The sourest temper must sweeten in the atmosphere of continuous good humour.

See also GOOD HUMOUR, HAPPINESS.

CHILDREN

Childhood shows the man, as morning shows the day – *John Milton*

The child is father of the man – *William Wordsworth*

Children have more need of models than of critics – *Joseph Joubert*

In bringing up a child, think of its old age – *Joubert*

Call not that man wretched who, whatever ills he suffers, has a child to love – *Robert Southey*

I have often thought what a melancholy world this would be without children; and what an inhuman world without the aged – *Samuel Taylor Coleridge*

God sends children for another purpose than merely to keep up the race – to enlarge our hearts; and to make us unselfish and full of kindly sympathies and affections; to give our souls higher aims; to call out all our facilities to extended enterprise and exertion; and to bring round our firesides bright faces, happy smiles, and loving, tender hearts. My soul blesses the great Father, every day, that he has gladdened the earth with little children – *Mary Howitt*

Children are God's apostles, sent forth, day by day, to preach of love, and hope and peace – *J. R. Lovell*

A torn jacket is soon mended, but hard words bruise the heart of a child – *Henry Wadsworth Longfellow*

Blessed be the hand that prepares a pleasure for a child, for there is no saying when and where it may bloom forth – *Douglas William Jerrold*

You cannot teach a child to take care of himself unless you will let him try to take care of himself. He will make mistakes; and out of these mistakes will come his wisdom – *Henry Ward Beecher*

The child's grief throbs against its little heart as heavily as the man's sorrow; and the one finds as much delight in his kite or drum, as the other in striking the springs of enterprise, or soaring on the wings of fame – *E. H. Chapin*

The sensible child will dread the frown of a judicious mother more than all the rods, dark rooms, and scolding school-mistresses in the universe – *Henry Kirke White*

We step not over the threshold of childhood till we are led by love – *L. E. Landon*

Children are not so much to be taught as to be trained. To teach a child is to give him ideas; to train him is to enable him to reduce those ideas to practice – *Beecher*

Where there is a houseful of children, one or two of the eldest may be restricted, and the youngest ruined by indulgence; but in the midst, some are, as it were, forgotten, who many times, nevertheless, prove the best – *Francis Bacon*

In praising or loving a child, we love and praise not that which is, but that which we hope for – *Johann Wolfgang von Goethe*

Better be driven out from among men, than to be disliked by children.

Just as the twig is bent, the tree is inclined – *Alexander Pope*

The plays of natural lively children are the infancy of art – *Adam Gottlob Oehlenschläger*

Childhood has no forebodings; but then it is soothed by no memories of outlived sorrow – *George Eliot*

Where children are, there is the golden age – *Novalis*

Childhood sometimes does pay a second visit to a man; youth never – *Anna Jameson*

Children have neither past nor future; they enjoy the present, which very few of us do – *Jean de La Bruyère*

A baby is something you carry inside you for nine months, in your arms for three years and in your heart till the day you die – *M. Mason*

Many children, many cares; no children, no felicity.

The interest of childhood and youth are the interests of mankind.

Never fear spoiling children by making them too happy.

Someone says, 'Boys will be boys'; he forgets to add, 'Boys will be men.'

When parents spoil their children, it is less to please them than to please themselves.

An infallible way to make your child miserable is to satisfy all his demands.

Childhood and genius have the same master-organ in common – inquisitiveness. Let childhood have its way, and as it began where genius begins, it may find what genius finds.

Children and fools speak the truth.

Every newborn child brings the message that God still has hope for mankind.

A perfect example of minority rule is a baby in the house.

See also BABIES.

CHOICE

The measure of choosing well is whether a man likes and finds good in what he has chosen – *Charles Lamb*

Life often presents us with a choice of evils than of good – *Charles Caleb Colton*

Between two evils, choose neither; between two goods, choose both – *Tryon Edwards*

CHRISTIANITY

Heathenism was the seeking religion; Judaism the hoping religion; Christianity is the reality of what heathenism sought and Judaism hoped for – *Christoph Ernst Luthardt*

Christianity is not a theory or speculation, but a life; not a philosophy of life, but a life and a living process – *Samuel Taylor Coleridge*

The distinction between Christianity and all other systems of religion consists largely in this, that in these others men are found seeking after God, while Christianity is God seeking after men – *Thomas Arnold*

Where science speaks of improvement Christianity speaks of renovation – *J. P. Thompson*

Christianity is the companion of liberty in all its conflicts – the cradle of its infancy, and the divine source of its claims – *Alexis de Tocqueville*

Christianity will gain by every step that is taken in the knowledge of man – *Johann Caspar Spurzheim*

Christianity proves itself – *Coleridge*

The moral and religious system which Jesus Christ transmitted to us is the best the world has ever seen, or can see – *Benjamin Franklin*

There's not much practical Christianity in the man who lives on better terms with angels and seraphs than with his children, servants, and neighbours – *Henry Ward Beecher*

Christianity always suits us well enough so long as we suit it. With most of us it is not reason that makes faith hard, but life – *Jean Ingelow*

Christianity ruined emperors, but saved peoples – *Alfred de Musset*

'Learn of me', says the philosopher, 'and ye shall find restlessness.' 'Learn of me', says Christ, 'and ye shall find rest.'

Christianity is the only system of faith which combines religious beliefs with corresponding principles of morality. It builds ethics on religion.

Christ built no church, wrote no book, left no money, and erected no monuments; yet show me ten square miles in the whole earth without Christianity, where the life and man and the purity of women are respected, and I will give up Christianity.

Christianity is intensely practical. She has no trait more striking than her common sense.

See also THE BIBLE, THE CROSS, RELIGION.

CHRISTIANS

The Christian has greatly the advantage of the unbeliever, having everything to gain and nothing to lose – *Lord Byron*

A Christian is nothing but a sinful man who has put himself to school to Christ for the honest purpose of becoming better – *Henry Ward Beecher*

The best advertisement of a workshop is first-class work. The strongest attraction to Christianity is a well-made Christian character – *T. L. Cuyler*

The modern Christian differs from his grandparents, even from his parents, perhaps, in being a Christian from choice – *Hamford Henderson*

He is no good Christian who thinks he can be safe without God, or not
    safe with him.
It does not require great learning to be a Christian and be convinced of
    the truth of the Bible. It requires only an honest heart and a willing-
    ness to obey God.
Faith makes, life proves, trials confirm, and death crowns the Christian.

THE CHURCH

The way to preserve the peace of the church is to preserve its purity –
    Matthew Henry
Surely the church is a place where one day's truce ought to be allowed to
    the dissensions and animosities of mankind – *Edmund Burke*
It is the province of the church not only to offer salvation in the future,
    but to teach men how they ought to live in the present life – *F. C.
    Monfort*
The church is not a gallery for the exhibition of eminent Christians, but a
    school for the education of imperfect ones, a nursery for the care of
    weak ones, a hospital for the healing of those who need assiduous
    care – *Henry Ward Beecher*
Men say the principles of the churches point to heaven; so does every
    tree that buds, and every bird that rises and sings. They say their
    aisles are good for worship; so is every rough seashore and mountain
    glen. But this they have of distinct and indisputable glory, that their
    mighty walls were never raised, and never shall be, but by men who
    love and aid each other in their weakness, and on the way to heaven –
    John Ruskin
That is the only true church organization when heads and hearts unite in
    working for the welfare of the human race – *Lydia Maria Child*
See also RELIGION.

CIRCUMSTANCES

He is happy whose circumstances suit his temper; but he is more
    excellent who can suit his temper to any circumstances – *David Hume*
Men are the sport of circumstances, when the circumstances seem the
    sport of men – *Lord Byron*
Circumstances are the rulers of the weak; they are but the instruments of
    the wise – *Samuel Lover*
Circumstances form the character; but like petrifying waters they harden
    while they form – *L. E. Landon*
Circumstances do not make a man either strong or weak, but they show
    what he is – *Thomas à Kempis*
It is our relation to circumstances that determines their influence over us.

The same wind that carries one vessel into port may blow another off shore.

Shape circumstances; don't allow them to shape you.

CITIES

Cities force growth, and make men talkative and entertaining, but they make them artificial – *Ralph Waldo Emerson*

Cities have always been the fireplaces of civilization, whence light and heat radiated out into the dark, cold world – *Theodore Parker*

If you suppress the exorbitant love of pleasure and money, idle curiosity, iniquitous purpose, and wanton mirth, what a stillness would there be in the greatest cities – *Jean de La Bruyère*

As goes the city so goes the world – *S. J. McPherson*

If you would know and not be known, live in a city – *Charles Caleb Colton*

Men, by associating in large masses, as in camps and cities, improve their talents, but impair their virtues; and strengthen their minds, but weaken their morals – *Colton*

In the country, a man's mind is free and easy, and at his own disposal; but in the city, the persons of friends and acquaintance, one's own and other people's business, foolish quarrels, ceremonies, visits, impertinent discourses, and a thousand other fopperies and diversions steal away the greatest part of our time, and leave no leisure for better and more necessary employment. Great towns are but a larger sort of prison to the soul, like cages to birds, or pounds to beasts – *Pierre Charron*

God the first garden made, and Cain the first city.

There is no solitude more dreadful for a stranger, an isolated man, than a great city. So many thousands of men, and not one friend.

CIVILITY

Civility is a charm that attracts the love of all men; and too much is better than to show too little – *Bishop Horne*

While thou livest, keep a good tongue in thy head – *William Shakespeare*

Nothing costs less, nor is cheaper, than the compliments of civility – *Miguel de Cervantes Saavedra*

See also COURTESY, GOOD BREEDING, MANNERS, POLITENESS.

CIVILIZATION

All that is best in the civilization of today is the fruit of Christ's appearance among men – *Daniel Webster*

If you would civilize a man, begin with his grandmother – *Victor Hugo*

The most civilized people are as near to barbarism as the most polished steel is to rust. Nations, like metals, have only a superficial brilliancy – *Antoine Rivarol*

The true test of civilization is, not the census, nor the size of cities, nor the crops, but the kind of man that the country turns out – *Ralph Waldo Emerson*

A sufficient and sure method of civilization is the influence of good women – *Emerson*

The ultimate tendency of civilization is toward barbarism.

Civilization is the upward struggle of mankind, in which millions are trampled to death that thousands may mount on their bodies.

CLEANLINESS

Certainly, this is a duty – not a sin. Cleanliness is, indeed, next to Godliness – *John Wesley*

Let thy mind's sweetness have its operation upon thy body, thy clothes, and thy habitation – *George Herbert*

The consciousness of clean linen is, in, and of itself, a source of moral strength, second only to that of a clean conscience – *E. S. Phelps*

Beauty commonly produces love, but cleanliness preserves it – *Joseph Addison*

Even from the body's purity the mind receives a secret sympathetic aid.

So great is the effect of cleanliness upon man, that it extends even to his moral character. Virtues never dwelt long with filth.

CLEMENCY

Lenity will operate with greater force, in some instances, than rigour – *George Washington*

In general, indulgence for those we know is rarer than pity for those we know not – *Antoine Rivarol*

It is the brightest jewel in a monarch's crown.

As meekness moderates anger, so clemency moderates punishment.

Clemency is profitable for all; mischiefs condemned lose their force.

See also LENITY, MERCY, PARDON.

COMFORT

It is a little thing to speak a phrase of common comfort, which by daily use has almost lost its sense; and yet, on the ear of him who thought to die unmourned, it will fall like the choicest music – *Sir Thomas Noon Talfourd*

Of all created comforts, God is the leader; you are the borrower, not the owner.

Most of our comforts grow up between our crosses.
See also CONSOLATION.

COMMANDERS

It is better to have a lion at the head of an army of sheep than a sheep at the head of an army of lions – *Daniel Defoe*

The right of commanding is no longer an advantage transmitted by nature; like an inheritance, it is the fruit of labours, the price of courage – *Voltaire*

A brave captain is as a root, out of which, as branches, the courage of his soldiers doth spring – *Sir Philip Sidney*

COMMERCE

Perfect freedom is as necessary to the health and vigour of commerce, as it is to the health and vigour of citizenship – *Patrick Henry*

Commerce has made all winds her messengers; all climes her tributaries; all people her servants – *Tryon Edwards*

Commerce may well be termed the younger sister, for in all emergencies she looks to agriculture both for defence and for supply – *Charles Caleb Colton*

A well regulated commerce is not like law, physic or divinity, to be overstocked with hands; but, on the contrary, flourishes by multitudes, and gives employment to all its professors – *Joseph Addison*

Every dollar spent for missions has added hundreds to the commerce of the world.

It may almost be held that the hope of commercial gain has done nearly as much for the cause of truth as even the love of truth itself.

A statesman may do much for commerce – most, by leaving it alone. A river never flows so smoothly as when it follows its own course, without either aid or check. Let it make its own bed; it will do so better than you can.

See also BUSINESS.

COMMON SENSE

Common sense is, of all kinds, the most uncommon. It implies judgement, sound discretion, and true and practical wisdom applied to common life – *Tryon Edwards*

Common sense is the knack of seeing things as they are, and doing things as they ought to be done – *C. E. Stowe*

If a man can have only one kind of sense, let him have common sense – *Henry Ward Beecher*

He was one of those men who possess almost every gift, except the gift of
the power to use them – *Charles Kingsley*

If you haven't grace, the Lord can give it to you. If you haven't learning,
I'll help you to get it. But if you haven't common sense, neither I, nor
the Lord can give it to you – *John Brown*

One pound of learning requires ten pounds of common sense to apply
it – *Persian proverb*

The crown of all faculties is common sense. It is not enough to do the
right thing, it must be done at the right time and place. Talent knows
what to do; tact knows when and how to do it.

Common sense is only a modification of talent. Genius is an exaltation of
it. The difference is, therefore, in degree, not nature.

Good sense; spending less for things you don't need, to impress people
you don't like.

A handful of common sense is worth a bushel of learning.

There are forty kinds of lunacy, but only one kind of common sense.

Common sense is in spite of, not the result of, education.

COMMUNISM

What is a communist? One who has a yearning for equal division of
unequal earnings – *Ebenezer Elliott*

Communism possesses a language which every people can understand.
Its elements are hunger, envy, and death – *Heinrich Heine*

See also LEVELLERS.

COMPANIONSHIP

No company is preferable to bad, because we are more apt to catch the
vices of others than their virtues, as disease is far more contagious
than health – *Charles Caleb Colton*

No man can possibly improve in any company for which he has
not respect enough to be under some degree of restraint – *Lord
Chesterfield*

No man can be provident of his time, who is not prudent in the choice of
his company – *Jeremy Taylor*

Take rather than give the tone of the company you are in – *Chesterfield*

The most agreeable of all companions is a simple, frank man, without
any high pretensions to an oppressive greatness; one who loves life,
and understands the use of it; obliging, alike, at all hours; above all,
of a golden temper, and steadfast as an anchor. For such a one we
gladly exchange the greatest genius, the most brilliant wit, the
profoundest thinker – *Gotthold Ephraim Lessing*

See also ACQUAINTANCE, ASSOCIATES.

COMPARISON

If we rightly estimate what we call good and evil, we shall find it lies much in comparison – *John Locke*

The superiority of some men is merely local. They are great because their associates are little – *Samuel Johnson*

COMPASSION

There never was any heart truly great and generous, that was not also tender and compassionate – *Robert South*

It is the crown of justice and the glory, where it may kill with right, to save with pity – *Francis Beaumont and John Fletcher*

The dew of compassion is a tear – *Lord Byron*

Compassion to an offender who has grossly violated the laws is, in effect, a cruelty to the peaceable subject who has observed them – *Junius*

Blessed are they who have nothing to say and know what to do instead.

See also PITY.

COMPENSATION

No evil is without its compensation. The less money, the less trouble. The less favour, the less envy. Even in those cases which put us out of wits, it is not the loss itself, but the estimate of the loss that troubles us – *Seneca*

If poverty makes man groan, he yawns in opulence. When fortune exempts us from labour, nature overwhelms us with time – *Antoine Rivarol*

When you are disposed to be vain of your mental acquirements, look up to those who are more accomplished than yourself, that you may be fired with emulation; but when you feel dissatisfied with your circumstances, look down on those beneath you, that you may learn contentment – *Hannah More*

When fate has allowed to any man more than one great gift, accident or necessity seems usually to contrive that one shall encumber and impede the other – *Algernon Charles Swinburne*

As there is no worldly gain without some loss, so there is no worldly loss without some gain. If thou hast lost thy wealth, thou hast lost some trouble with it. If thou art degraded from thy honour, thou art likewise freed from the stroke of envy. If sickness hath blurred thy beauty, it hath delivered thee from pride. Set the allowance against the loss and thou shalt find no loss great. He loses little or nothing who reserves himself – *Francis Quarles*

Whatever difference may appear in the fortunes of mankind, there is

nevertheless a certain compensation of good and evil which makes
them equal.
If the poor man cannot always get meat, the rich man cannot always
digest it.

COMPLACENCY

Self-complacency is the thickest form of armour plating.
See also CONCEIT, SELF-CONCEIT.

COMPLIMENTS

Compliments are only lies in court clothes – *John Sterling*
Compliments or congratulations are always kindly taken, and cost
nothing but pen, ink, and paper. I consider them as draughts upon
good breeding where the exchange is always greatly in favour of the
drawer – *Lord Chesterfield*
Compliments which we think are deserved, we accept only as debts,
with indifference; but those which conscience informs us we do not
merit, we receive with the same gratitude that we do favours given
away – *Oliver Goldsmith*
A compliment is usually accompanied with a bow, as if to beg pardon for
paying it.
Proud looks lose hearts, but courteous words win them.
See also GALLANTRY.

COMPROMISE

Compromise is but the sacrifice of one right or good in the hope of
retaining another, too often ending in the loss of both – *Tryon Edwards*

CONCEALMENT

I can never close my lips where I have opened my heart – *Charles Dickens*
He who can conceal his joys is greater than he who can hide his griefs –
Johann Kaspar Lavater
It is great cleverness to know how to conceal our cleverness – *François de
La Rochefoucauld*
'Thou shalt not get found out' is not one of God's commandments; and
no man can be saved by trying to keep it – *Leonard Bacon*

CONCEIT

It is vanity driven from all other shifts, and forced to appeal to itself for
admiration – *William Hazlitt*

It is wonderful how near conceit is to insanity – *Douglas William Jerrold*

He who gives himself airs of importance exhibits the credentials of impotence – *Johann Kaspar Lavater*

The overweening self-respect of conceited men relieves others from the duty of respecting them at all – *Henry Ward Beecher*

Conceit is to nature, what paint is to beauty; it is not only needless, but it impairs what it would improve – *Alexander Pope*

The more one speaks of himself, the less he likes to hear another talked of – *Lavater*

A man – poet, prophet, or whatever he may be – readily persuades himself of his right to all the worship that is voluntarily tendered – *Nathaniel Hawthorne*

It is the admirer of himself, and not the admirer of virtue, that thinks himself superior to others – *Plutarch*

The best of lessons, for a good many people, would be to listen at a key-hole – *Mme Swetchine*

If he could only see how small a vacancy his death would leave, the proud man would think less of the place he occupies in his lifetime – *Ernest Legouvé*

I've never any pity for conceited people, because I think they carry their comfort about with them – *George Eliot*

Conceit may puff a man up, but can never prop him up – *John Ruskin*

Every man has a right to be conceited until he is successful – *Benjamin Disraeli*

Conceit and confidence are both of them cheats. The first always imposes on itself; the second frequently deceives others.

No man was ever so much deceived by another as by himself.

The weakest spot in every man is where he thinks himself to be the wisest.

Life is so humbling, that a great man's idea of himself gets washed out of him by the time he is forty.

Self-conceit is specially the mark of a small and narrow mind.

A man wrapped up in himself makes a very small parcel.

See also COMPLACENCY.

CONDUCT

What a man does tells us what he is – *F. D. Huntington*

The integrity of men is to be measured by their conduct, not by their professions – *Junius*

What does it signify to make anything a secret to my neighbour, when to God, who is the searcher of our hearts, all our privacies are open – *Seneca*

Every one of us, whatever our speculative opinions, knows better than he practises, and recognizes a better law than he obeys – *James Anthony Froude*

In all the affairs of life let it be your great care, not to hurt your mind, or offend your judgement – *Epictetus*

All the while that thou livest ill, thou hast the trouble, distraction, and inconveniences of life, but not the sweet and true use of it.

Climbing and crawling are performed in much the same attitude.

See also BEHAVIOUR, DECENCY.

CONFESSION

A man should never be ashamed to own he has been in the wrong, therefore being wiser today than he was yesterday – *Alexander Pope*

The confession of evil works is the first beginning of good works – *Augustine*

It is not our wrong actions which it requires courage to confess, so much as those which are ridiculous and foolish – *Jean Jacques Rousseau*

Live as if you were to die tomorrow.

Confessions may be good for the soul but they are bad for the reputation.

CONFIDENCE

Trust men and they will be true to you; treat them greatly and they will show themselves great – *Ralph Waldo Emerson*

Confidence is a plant of slow growth; especially in an aged bosom – *Samuel Johnson*

Trust him with little, who, without proofs, trusts you with everything, or when he has proved you, with nothing – *Johann Kaspar Lavater*

When young, we trust ourselves too much; and we trust others too little when old – *Charles Caleb Colton*

Society is built upon trust, and trust upon confidence in one another's integrity – *Robert South*

Let us have a care not to disclose our hearts to those who shut up theirs against us – *Francis Beaumont*

Fields are won by those who believe in winning – *Thomas Wentworth Higginson*

They can conquer who believe they can – *John Dryden*

Confidence imparts a wondrous inspiration to its possessor – *John Milton*

The human heart, at whatever age, opens only to the heart that opens in return – *Maria Edgeworth*

Self-trust is the essence of heroism – *Ralph Waldo Emerson*

Confidence, in conversation, has a greater share than wit – *François de La Rochefoucauld*

Confidence in another man's virtue is no slight evidence of one's own – *Michel Eyquem de Montaigne*

Trust him little who praises all; him less who censures all; and him least who is indifferent to all – *Lavater*

He that does not respect a confidence will never find happiness in his path.

If we are truly prudent we shall cherish those noblest and happiest of our tendencies – to love and to confide.

To confide, even though to be betrayed, is much better than to learn only to conceal.

Never put much confidence in such as put no confidence in others.

See also CREDIT, TRUST.

CONSCIENCE

Conscience! conscience! man's most faithful friend! – *George Crabbe*

Man's conscience is the oracle of God – *Lord Byron*

The truth is not so much that man has conscience, as that conscience has man – *Isaak August Dorner*

It is far more important to me to preserve an unblemished conscience than to compass any object however great – *William Ellery Channing*

He will easily be content and at peace, whose conscience is pure – *Thomas à Kempis*

What other dungeon is so dark as one's own heart! What gaoler so inexorable as one's self – *Nathaniel Hawthorne*

A good conscience is a continual Christmas – *Benjamin Franklin*

We cannot live better than in seeking to become better, nor more agreeably than in having a clear conscience – *Socrates*

The voice of conscience is so delicate that it is easy to stifle it; but it is also so clear that it is impossible to mistake it – *Mme de Staël*

Conscience is the voice of the soul, as the passions are the voice of the body – *Jean Jacques Rousseau*

Conscience is the true vicar of Christ in the soul – *John Henry Newman*

There is no witness so terrible – no accuser so powerful as conscience which dwells within us – *Sophocles*

Conscience tells us that we ought to do right, but it does not tell us what right is – that we are taught by God's word – *H. C. Trumbull*

Labour to keep alive in your heart that little spark of celestial fire called conscience – *George Washington*

There is no class of men so difficult to be managed in a state as those whose intentions are honest, but whose consciences are bewitched – *Napoleon Bonaparte*

The men who succeed best in public life are those who take the risk of standing by their own convictions – *James Abram Garfield*

The torture of a bad conscience is the hell of a living soul – *John Calvin*

Many a lash in the dark doth conscience give the wicked – *Thomas Boston*

Trust that man in nothing who has not a conscience in everything – *Laurence Sterne*

Conscience does make cowards of us all – *William Shakespeare*

The foundation of true joy is in the conscience – *Seneca*

A quiet conscience makes one so serene – *Byron*

A clean and sensitive conscience is the most valuable of all possessions, to a nation as to an individual – *H. J. Van Dyke*

Conscience whose still, small voice the loudest revelry cannot drown – *William Henry Harrison*

A good conscience fears no witness, but a guilty conscience is solicitous even in solitude – *Seneca*

Conscience, though ever so small a worm while we live, grows suddenly into a serpent on our deathbed – *Douglas William Jerrold*

If conscience smite thee once, it is an admonition; if twice, it is a condemnation.

Conscience, in most men, is but the anticipation of the opinions of others.

Conscience warns us as a friend before it punishes as a judge.

A disciplined conscience is a man's best friend. It may not be his most amiable, but it is his most faithful monitor.

Cowardice asks, Is it safe? Expediency asks, Is it politic? Vanity asks, Is it popular? but Conscience asks, Is it right?

A man of integrity will never listen to any reason against conscience.

What we call conscience is, in many instances, only a wholesome fear of the constable.

Conscience is the inner voice which warns us someone may be looking.

A twinge of conscience is a glimpse of God.

The dictates of conscience make a reliable guide.

CONSERVATISM

The highest function of conservatism is to keep what progressiveness has accomplished – *R. H. Fulton*

A conservative young man has wound up his life before it was unreeled. We expect old men to be conservative, but when a nation's young men are so, its funeral bell is already tolled – *Henry Ward Beecher*

The conservative may clamour against reform and sighs for 'the good old times'. He might as well wish the oak back into the acorn – *E. H. Chapin*

A conservative is a man who will not look at the new moon, out of respect for that 'ancient institution' the old one – *Douglas William Jerrold*

CONSIDERATION

Consideration is the soil in which wisdom may be expected to grow, and strength be given to every upspringing plant of duty – *Ralph Waldo Emerson*

CONSISTENCY

With consistency a great soul has simply nothing to do. He may as well concern himself with his shadow on the wall – *Ralph Waldo Emerson*

Inconsistency with past views or conduct may be but a mark of increasing knowledge and wisdom – *Tryon Edwards*

Those who honestly mean to be true contradict themselves more rarely than those who try to be consistent – *Oliver Wendell Holmes*

Without consistency there is no moral strength.

CONSOLATION

Before an affliction is digested, consolation comes too soon; and after it is digested, it comes too late; but there is a mark between these two, as fine almost as a hair, for a comforter to take aim at – *Laurence Sterne*

God has commanded time to console the unhappy – *Joseph Joubert*

For every bad there might be a worse; and when one breaks his leg let him be thankful it was not his neck – *Bishop Hall*

Consolation, indiscreetly pressed upon us when we are suffering under affliction, only serves to increase our pain and to render our grief more poignant – *Jean Jacques Rousseau*

Quiet and sincere sympathy is often the most welcome and efficient consolation to the afflicted – *Tryon Edwards*

The powers of Time as a comforter can hardly be overstated; but the agency by which he works is exhaustion – *L. E. Landon*

The defects of great men are the consolation of the dunces.

See also COMFORT.

CONSPIRACY

Conspiracies, like thunder clouds, should in a moment form and strike like lightning, ere the sound is heard.

A game invented for the amusement of unoccupied men of rank.

CONSTANCY

Constancy is the complement of all other human virtues – *Giuseppe Mazzini*

The secret of success is constancy of purpose – *Benjamin Disraeli*

Without constancy there is neither love, friendship, nor virtue in the
   world – *Joseph Addison*
See also FIDELITY.

CONTEMPLATION

In order to improve the mind, we ought less to learn than to contemplate
   – *René Descartes*
Contemplation is to knowledge what digestion is to food – the way to get
   life out of it – *Tryon Edwards*

CONTEMPT

Wrongs are often forgiven; contempt never – *Lord Chesterfield*
None but the contemptible are apprehensive of contempt – *François de La
   Rochefoucauld*
Speak with contempt of no man. Everyone hath a tender sense of
   reputation. And every man hath a sting, which he may, if provoked
   too far, dart out at one time or another – *Robert Burton*
Despise not any man, and do not spurn anything; for there is no man
   that hath not his honour, nor is there anything that hath not its
   place – *Rabbi Ben Azai*
The basest and meanest of all human beings are generally the most
   forward to despise others. So that the most contemptible are
   generally the most contemptuous – *Henry Fielding*
Contempt is commonly taken by the young for an evidence of understanding. To discover the imperfections of others is penetration; to
   hate them for their faults is contempt – *Sydney Smith*
Christ saw much in this world to weep over, and much to pray over; but
 · he saw nothing in it to look upon with contempt – *E. H. Chapin*

CONTENTION

Weakness on both sides is, as we know, the trait of all quarrels – *Voltaire*
Religious contention is the devil's harvest – *Jean de La Fontaine*
Where two discourse, if the anger of one rises, he is the wise man who
   lets the contest fall – *Plutarch*
Contention is like fire, for both burn so long as there is any exhaustible
   matter to contend within.
See also ARGUMENT, CONTROVERSY, DISCUSSION, QUARRELS.

CONTENTMENT

A contented mind is the greatest blessing a man can enjoy in this world –
   Joseph Addison

If you are but content you have enough to live upon with comfort –
  Plautus

Contentment is natural wealth, luxury is artificial poverty – *Socrates*

Contentment gives a crown, where fortune hath denied it – *John Ford*

They that deserve nothing should be content with anything – *Erskine
  Mason*

You traverse the world in search of happiness, which is within the reach
  of every man; a contented mind confers it all – *Horace*

The noblest mind the best contentment has – *Edmund Spenser*

If everyone were satisfied no one would buy the new thing – *Charles F.
  Kettering*

Since we cannot get what we like, let us like what we can get – *Spanish
  proverb*

It is right to be contented with what we have, never with what we are.

If we fasten our attention on what we have, rather than on what we lack,
  a very little wealth is sufficient.

I never complained of my condition but once, said an old man – when my
  feet were bare, and I had no money to buy shoes; but I met a man
  without feet, and became contented.

The contented man is never poor; the discontented never rich.

An ounce of contentment is worth a pound of sadness, to serve God
  with.

He who is not contented with what he has, would not be contented with
  what he would like to have.

One who is contented with what he has done will never become famous
  for what he will do.

Contentment is a pearl of great price, and whoever procures it at the
  expense of ten thousand desires makes a wise and a happy purchase.

It is a great blessing to possess what one wishes, said one to an ancient
  philosopher. It is a greater still, was the reply, not to desire what one
  does not possess.

He who wants little always has enough.

CONTRADICTION

A downright contradiction is equally mysterious to wise men as to fools.

CONTRAST

The rose and the thorn, and sorrow and gladness are linked together –
  Sádi

Where there is much light, the shadow is deep – *Johann Wolfgang von
  Goethe*

If there be light, then there is darkness; if cold, then heat; if height, depth also; if solid, then fluid; hardness and softness; roughness and smoothness; calm and tempest; prosperity and adversity; life and death – *Pythagoras*

Joy and grief are never far apart. A wedding party returns from the church; and a funeral winds to its door.

CONTROVERSY

Most controversies would soon be ended, if those engaged in them would first accurately define their terms, and then adhere to their definitions – *Tryon Edwards*

Controversy is wretched when it is only an attempt to prove another wrong – *Frederick William Robertson*

The evils of controversy are transitory, while its benefits are permanent – *Robert Hill*

Controversy should always be so managed as to remember that the only true end of it is peace – *Alexander Pope*

See also ARGUMENT, CONTENTION.

CONVERSATION

It is good to rub and polish our brain against that of others – *Michel Eyquem de Montaigne*

The first ingredient in conversation is truth; the next, good sense; the third, good humour; and the fourth, wit – *William Temple*

One of the best rules in conversation is, never to say a thing which any of the company can reasonably wish had been left unsaid – *Jonathan Swift*

Know how to listen, and you will profit even from those who talk badly – *Plutarch*

The reason why so few people are agreeable in conversation is that each is thinking more of what he is intending to say than of what others are saying – *François de La Rochefoucauld*

He who sedulously attends, pointedly asks, calmly speaks, coolly answers, and ceases when he has no more to say, is in possession of some of the best requisites of conversation – *Johann Kaspar Lavater*

Never hold anyone by the button, or the hand, in order to be heard out; for if people are unwilling to hear you, you had better hold your tongue than them – *Lord Chesterfield*

Silence is one great art of conversation – *William Hazlitt*

Conversation is an art in which a man has all mankind for competitors – *Ralph Waldo Emerson*

In conversation, humour is more than wit, and easiness more than knowledge – *Temple*

As it is the characteristic of great wits to say much in few words, so it is of small wits to talk much, and say nothing – *François de La Rochefoucauld*

Not only to say the right thing in the right place, but far more difficult, to leave unsaid the wrong thing at the tempting moment – *George Sala*

The less men think, the more they talk – *Charles de Montesquieu*

In table talk, I prefer the pleasant and witty before the learned and grave – *Montaigne*

It is when you come close to a man in conversation that you discover what his real abilities are. To make a speech in a public assembly is a knack – *Samuel Johnson*

That is the happiest conversation where there is no competition, no vanity, but only a calm, quiet interchange of sentiment – *Johnson*

I would establish but one general rule to be observed in all conversation, which is this, that men should not talk to please themselves, but those that hear them – *Richard Steele*

Take as many half-minutes as you can get, but never talk more than half a minute without pausing and giving others an opportunity to strike in – *Swift*

Repose is as necessary in conversation as in a picture – *Hazlitt*

In private conversation between intimate friends the wisest men very often talk like the weakest; for, indeed, the talking with a friend is nothing else but thinking aloud – *Joseph Addison*

Conversation is never so much straitened and confined as in large assemblies – *Addison*

To listen well is as powerful a means of influence as to talk well, and is as essential to all true conversation.

A single conversation across the table with a wise man is worth a month's study of books – *Chinese proverb*

When in the company of sensible men we ought to be doubly cautious of talking too much, lest we lose two good things – their good opinion and our own improvement.

'Tis a task indeed to learn to hear; in that the skill of conversation lies; that shows or makes you both polite and wise.

Conversation derives its greatest charm not from the multitude of ideas but from their application.

CONVERSION

Conversion is not implanting eyes, for they exist already; but giving them a right direction, which they have not – *Plato*

The time when I was converted was when religion became no longer a mere duty, but a pleasure.

COQUETTES

A coquette is a young lady of more beauty than sense, more accomplishments than learning, more charms of person than graces of mind,
more admirers than friends, more fools than wise men for attendants
– *Henry Wadsworth Longfellow*

An accomplished coquette excites the passions of others, in proportion
as she feels none herself – *William Hazlitt*

A coquette is like a recruiting sergeant, always on the lookout for fresh
victims – *Douglas William Jerrold*

There is one antidote only for coquetry, and that is true love – *Mme
Deluzy*

The adoration of his heart had been to her only as the perfume of a wild
flower, which she had carelessly crushed with her foot in passing –
Longfellow

The most effective coquetry is innocence – *Alphonse Marie Louis de
Lamartine*

She who only finds her self-esteem in admiration depends on others for
her daily food and is the very servant of her slaves – *Joanna Baillie*

God created the coquette as soon as he had made the fool – *Victor Hugo*

A coquette is a woman without any heart, who makes a fool of a man that
hasn't got any head.

COUNTENANCE

Thy cheek / Is apter than thy tongue to tell thy errand – *William
Shakespeare*

A cheerful, easy, open countenance will make fools think you a good-
natured man, and make designing men think you an undesigning
one – *Lord Chesterfield*

It is hard for the face to conceal the thoughts of the heart – the true
character of the soul. The look without is an index of what is within.

See also FACE, LOOKS.

COUNTRY

If you would be known and not know, vegetate in a village. If you would
know and not be known, live in a city – *Charles Caleb Colton*

The country is both the philosopher's garden and his library, in which he
reads and contemplates the power, wisdom, and goodness – *William
Penn*

There is virtue in country houses, in gardens and orchards, in fields,
streams, and groves, in rustic recreations and plain manners, that
neither cities nor universities enjoy – *Amos Bronson Alcott*

Men are taught virtue and a love of independence, by living in the country – *Menander*

If country life be healthful to the body, it is no less so to the mind – *Giovanni Domenico Ruffini*

I consider it the best part of an education to have been born and brought up in the country – *Alcott*

God made the country, and man made the town – *William Cowper*

I fancy the proper means for increasing the love we bear to our native country is to reside some time in a foreign one – *William Shenstone*

COURAGE

Courage consists not in blindly overlooking danger, but in seeing and conquering it – *Jean Paul Richter*

The truest courage is always mixed with circumspection – *Jones of Nayland*

Courage from hearts and not from numbers grows – *John Dryden*

Courage is, on all hands, considered as an essential of high character – *James Anthony Froude*

Conscience is the root of all true courage; if a man would be brave let him obey his conscience – *J. F. Clarke*

Courage in danger is half the battle – *Plautus*

No man can answer for his courage who has never been in danger – *François de La Rochefoucauld*

Moral courage is a virtue of higher cast and nobler origin than physical courage – *Samuel Griswold Goodrich*

To see what is right and not to do it is want of courage – *Confucius*

A great deal of talent is lost in this world for the want of a little courage – *Sydney Smith*

Women and men of retiring timidity are cowardly only in dangers which affect themselves, but are the first to rescue when others are endangered – *Richter*

Courage ought to be guided by skill, and skill armed by courage – *Sir Philip Sidney*

True courage is not the brutal force of vulgar heroes, but the firm resolve of virtue and reason.

If we survive danger it steels our courage more than anything else.

Probably the most courageous thing a man can do is to be himself.

Courage is not freedom from fear; it is being afraid and going on.

See also BOLDNESS, BRAVERY, VALOUR.

COURTESY

Life is not so short but that there is always time for courtesy – *Ralph Waldo Emerson*

There is no outward sign of true courtesy that does not rest on a deep moral foundation – *Johann Wolfgang von Goethe*

A churlish courtesy rarely comes but either for gain or falsehood – *Sir Philip Sidney*

We should be as courteous to a man as we are to a picture, which we are willing to give the advantage of the best light – *Emerson*

The courtesies of a small and trivial character are the ones which strike deepest to the grateful and appreciating heart – *Henry Clay*

Approved valour is made precious by natural courtesy – *Sidney*

The small courtesies sweeten life; the greater ennoble it.

As the sword of the best tempered metal is most flexible, so the truly generous are most pliant and courteous in their behaviour to their inferiors.

See also CIVILITY, GALLANTRY, GOOD BREEDING, MANNERS, POLITENESS.

COURTS AND COURTIERS

A court is an assemblage of noble and distinguished beggars – *Charles Maurice de Talleyrand-Périgord*

The court is a golden, but fatal circle, upon whose magic skirts a thousand devils sit tempting innocence, and beckon early virtue from its centre – *Nathaniel Lee*

The court is like a palace built of marble – made up of very hard, and very polished materials – *Jean de La Bruyère*

The chief requisites for a courtier are a flexible conscience and an inflexible politeness – *Lady Blessington*

Poor wretches, that depend / On greatness' favour dream as I have done; / Wake, and find nothing – *William Shakespeare*

COURTSHIP

Courtship consists in a number of quiet attentions, not so pointed as to alarm, nor so vague as not to be understood – *Laurence Sterne*

She half consents, who silently denies – *Ovid*

She is a woman, therefore may be woo'd; / She is a woman, therefore may be won – *William Shakespeare*

If you cannot inspire a woman with love of yourself, fill her above the brim with love of herself; all that runs over will be yours – *Charles Caleb Colton*

Men are April when they woo, December when they wed – *Shakespeare*

That man that hath a tongue, I say, is no man, / If with his tongue he cannot win a woman – *Shakespeare*

With women worth being won, the softest lover ever best succeeds.

See also LOVE.

COVETOUSNESS

Desire of having is the sin of covetousness – *William Shakespeare*

If money be not thy servant, it will be thy master – *Francis Bacon*

The only gratification a covetous man gives his neighbours is to let them see that he himself is as little better for what he has, as they are – *William Penn*

The air fills not the body, neither does money the covetous heart of man – *Edmund Spenser*

Covetousness is both the beginning and end of the devil's alphabet – the first vice in corrupt nature that moves, and the last which dies – *Robert South*

Why are we so blind? That which we improve, we have; that which we hoard, is not for ourselves – *Mme Deluzy*

Refrain from covetousness, and thy estate shall prosper – *Plato*

It serves the devil without receiving his wages, and for the empty foolery of dying rich, pays down its health, happiness, and integrity – *Charles Caleb Colton*

The covetous man pines in plenty, like Tantalus up to the chin in water, and yet thirsty.

See also ENVY.

COWARDICE

The craven's fear is but selfishness, like his merriment – *John Greenleaf Whittier*

It is the coward who fawns upon those above him. It is the coward who is insolent whenever he dares be so – *Junius*

Cowards falter, but danger is often overcome by those who nobly dare – *Elizabeth I*

Plenty and peace breeds cowards – *William Shakespeare*

Cowards die many times before their deaths; / The valiant never taste of death but once – *Shakespeare*.

CREDIT

Credit is like a looking-glass, which, when once sullied by a breath, may be wiped clear again; but if once cracked can never be repaired – *Walter Scott*

The most trifling actions that affect a man's credit are to be regarded. The sound of your hammer at five in the morning, or nine at night, heard by a creditor, makes him easier six months longer; but if he sees you at a billiard table, or hears your voice at a tavern when you should be at work, he sends for his money the next day – *Benjamin Franklin*

Too large a credit has made many a bankrupt; taking even less than a
    man can answer with ease is a sure fund for extending it whenever
    his occasions require – *Guardian*
Nothing so cements and holds together all the parts of a society as faith
    or credit, which can never be kept up unless men are under some
    force or necessity of honestly paying what they owe to one another –
    Cicero
A nation's economic credit is like a woman's reputation – the more it is
    debated, the more it is endangered – *Sir Josiah Stamp*
See also BORROWING, CONFIDENCE, DEBT, REPUTATION.

CREDITORS

Creditors have better memories than debtors; they are a superstitious
    sect, great of set days and times – *Benjamin Franklin*
The creditor whose appearance gladdens the heart of a debtor may hold
    his head in sunbeams, and his foot on storms – *Johann Kaspar Lavater*
See also DEBT.

CREDULITY

Credulity is belief on slight evidence, with no evidence, or against
    evidence – *Tryon Edwards*
The only disadvantage of an honest heart is credulity – *Sir Philip Sidney*
Credulity is a more peaceful possession of the mind than curiosity –
    Jonathan Swift
I cannot spare the luxury of believing that all things beautiful are what
    they seem – *Fitz-Greene Halleck*
It is a curious paradox that precisely in proportion to our own intellectual
    weakness will be our credulity as to the mysterious powers assumed
    by others – *Charles Caleb Colton*
You believe easily that which you hope for earnestly – *Terence*
The most positive men are the most credulous, since they most believe
    themselves – *Alexander Pope*
Generous souls are still most subject to credulity – *William Davenant*
To take for granted as truth all that is alleged against the fame of others is
    a species of credulity that men would blush at on any other subject –
    Jane Porter
Credulity is perhaps a weakness, almost inseparable from eminently
    truthful characters.
Your noblest natures are most credulous.
Beyond all credulity is the credulousness of atheists, who believe that
    chance could make the world, when it cannot build a house.

CRIME

Of all the adult male criminals in London, not two in a hundred have entered upon a course of crime who have lived an honest life up to the age of twenty. Almost all who enter on a course of crime do so between the ages of eight and sixteen – *Lord Shaftesbury*

Small crimes always precede great ones. Never have we seen timid innocence pass suddenly to extreme licentiousness – *Jean Racine*

Fear follows crime, and is its punishment – *Voltaire*

Criminals together corrupt each other. They are worse than ever when, at the termination of their punishment, they return to society – *Napoleon Bonaparte*

Those who are themselves incapable of great crimes are ever backward to suspect others – *François de La Rochefoucauld*

If poverty is the mother of crimes, want of sense is the father of them – *Jean de La Bruyère*

We easily forget crimes that are known only to ourselves – *La Rochefoucauld*

Crimes lead into one another. They who are capable of being forgers are capable of being incendiaries – *Edmund Burke*

Society prepares the crime; the criminal commits it.

Whenever man commits a crime heaven finds a witness.

Crimes sometimes shock us too much; vices almost always too little.

Man's crimes are his worst enemies, following him like shadows, till they drive his steps into the pit he dug.

CRITICISM

Criticism, as it was first instituted by Aristotle, was meant as a standard of judging well – *Samuel Johnson*

It is ridiculous for any man to criticize the works of another if he has not distinguished himself by his own performances – *Joseph Addison*

Criticism often takes from the tree caterpillars and blossoms together – *Jean Paul Richter*

It is easy to criticize an author, but difficult to appreciate him – *Marquis de Vauvenargues*

Silence is sometimes the severest criticism – *Charles Buxton*

The most noble criticism is that in which the critic is not the antagonist so much as the rival of the author – *Benjamin Disraeli*

Get your enemies to read your works in order to mend them; for your friend is so much your second self that he will judge too much like you – *Alexander Pope*

Is it in destroying and pulling down that skill is displayed? The shallowest understanding, the rudest hand, is more than equal to that task – *Edmund Burke*

The pleasure of criticism takes from us that of being deeply moved by very beautiful things – *Jean de La Bruyère*

It is a barren kind of criticism which tells you what a thing is not – *Rufus Wilmot Griswold*

The strength of criticism lies only in the weakness of the thing criticized – *Henry Wadsworth Longfellow*

People ask you for criticism, but they only want praise – *William Somerset Maugham*

Neither praise nor blame is the object of true criticism. Justly to discriminate, firmly to establish, wisely to prescribe, and honestly to aware – these are the true aims and duties of criticism.

It is a maxim with me, that no man was ever written out of a reputation but him himself.

It is quite cruel that a poet cannot wander through his regions of enchantment without having a critic, forever, like the old man of the sea, upon his back.

Criticism is something you can avoid, by saying nothing, doing nothing and being nothing.

The only criticism which hurts is that which we deserve.

It is much easier to be critical than to be correct.

See also CENSURE.

CRITICS

Critics are sentinels in the grand army of letters, stationed at the corners of newspapers and reviews, to challenge every new author – *Henry Wadsworth Longfellow*

Critics must excuse me if I compare them to certain animals called asses, who, by gnawing vines, originally taught the great advantage of pruning them – *William Shenstone*

The eyes of critics, whether in commending or carping, are both on one side, like those of a turbot – *Walter Savage Landor*

Some critics are like chimney-sweepers; they put out the fire below, and frighten the swallows from their nests above; they scrape a long time in the chimney, cover themselves with soot, and bring nothing away but a bag of cinders, and then sing out from the top of the house, as if they had built it – *Longfellow*

Only God can form and paint a flower, but any foolish child can pull it to pieces – *J. M. Gibson*

To be a mere verbal critic is what no man of genius would be if the could; but to be a critic of true taste and feeling is what no man without genius could be if he would – *Charles Caleb Colton*

Critics are like deer, goats, and diverse other graminivorous animals, who gain subsistence by gorging upon buds and leaves of the young shrubs of the forest, thereby robbing them of their verdure and retarding their progress to maturity – *Washington Irving*

The severest critics are always those who have either never attempted or who have failed in original composition – *William Hazlitt*

He whose first emotion, on the view of an excellent production, is to undervalue it will never have one of his own to show.

THE CROSS

The cross is the only ladder high enough to touch Heaven's threshold – *G. D. Boardman*

Carry the cross patiently, and with perfect submission; and in the end it shall carry you – *Thomas à Kempis*

While to the reluctant the cross is too heavy to be borne, it grows light to the heart of willing trust.

The cross of Christ, on which he was extended, points, in the length of it, to heaven and earth, reconciling them together; and in the breadth of it, to former and following ages, as being equally salvation to both.

The cross of Christ is the sweetest burden that I ever bore; it is such a burden as wings are to a bird, or sails to a ship, to carry me forward to my harbour.

See also CHRISTIANITY.

CRUELTY

All cruelty springs from hard-heartedness and weakness – *Seneca*

Cruelty and fear shake hands together – *Honoré de Balzac*

Man's inhumanity to man / Makes countless thousands mourn! – *Robert Burns*

Cruelty, like every other vice, requires no motive outside of itself; it only requires opportunity – *George Eliot*

Detested sport, / That owes its pleasures to another's pain – *William Cowper*

One of the ill effects of cruelty is that it makes the bystanders cruel.

CULTIVATION

The highest purpose of intellectual cultivation is to give a man a perfect knowledge and mastery of his own inner self – *Novalis*

It matters little whether a man be mathematically, or philologically, or artistically cultivated, so he be but cultivated – *Johann Wolfgang von Goethe*

It is very rare to find ground which produces nothing. If it is not covered with flowers, fruit trees, and grains, it produces briars and pines. It is the same with man; if he is not virtuous, he becomes vicious – *Jean de La Bruyère*

Cultivation to the mind is as necessary as food to the body – *Cicero*

As the soil, however rich it may be, cannot be productive without culture, so the mind, without cultivation, can never produce good fruit – *Seneca*

Partial culture runs to the ornate; extreme culture to simplicity.

CUNNING

Cunning is the ape of wisdom – *John Locke*

Cleverness and cunning are incompatible – *Lord Byron*

Cunning is none of the best nor worst qualities; it floats between virtue and vice – *Jean de La Bruyère*

Cunning pays no regard to virtue, and is but the low mimic of wisdom – *Henry St John Bolingbroke*

The certain way to be cheated is to fancy one's self more cunning than others – *Pierre Charron*

We take cunning for a sinister or crooked wisdom, and certainly there is a great difference between a cunning man and a wise man, not only in point of honesty, but in point of ability – *Francis Bacon*

In a great business there is nothing so fatal as cunning management – *Junius*

A cunning man overreaches no one half as much as himself – *Henry Ward Beecher*

The most sure way of subjecting yourself to be deceived is to consider yourself more cunning than others – *François de La Rochefoucauld*

We should do by our cunning as we do by our courage – always have it ready to defend ourselves, never to offend others.

The very cunning conceal their cunning; the indifferently shrewd boast of it.

CURIOSITY

The first and simplest emotion which we discover in the human mind is curiosity – *Edmund Burke*

Curiosity in children is but an appetite for knowledge – *John Locke*

Men are more inclined to ask curious questions than to obtain necessary instruction – *Pasquier Quesnel*

The over curious are not over wise – *Philip Massinger*

Inquisitive people are the funnels of conversation; they do not take anything for their own use, but merely to pass it on to others – *Richard Steele*

The gratification of curiosity rather frees us from uneasiness, than confers pleasure – *Samuel Johnson*

Curiosity is looking over other people's affairs, and overlooking our own – *H. L. Wayland*

Seize the moment of excited curiosity on any subject, to solve your doubts; for if you let it pass, the desire may never return, and you may remain in ignorance.

How, many a noble art, now widely known, / Owes its young impulse to this power alone.

Eve, with all the fruits of Eden blest, save only one, rather than leave that one unknown, lost all the rest.

See also INQUISITIVENESS.

CUSTOM

The way of the world is to make laws, but follow customs – *Michel Eyquem de Montaigne*

Custom may lead a man into many errors, but it justifies none – *Henry Fielding*

Custom is the law of fools – *Sir John Vanbrugh*

As the world leads, we follow – *Seneca*

Men commonly think according to their inclinations, speak according to their learning and imbibed opinions, but generally act according to custom – *Francis Bacon*

In this great society wide lying around us, a critical analysis would find very few spontaneous actions. It is almost all custom and gross sense – *Ralph Waldo Emerson*

New customs, / Though they be never so ridiculous, / Nay, let 'em be unmanly, yet are follow'd – *William Shakespeare*

There are not unfrequently substantial reasons underneath for customs that appear to us absurd – *Charlotte Brontë*

The custom and fashion of today will be the awkwardness and outrage of tomorrow – so arbitrary are these transient laws – *Alexandre Dumas*

To follow foolish precedents, and wink with both our eyes, is easier than to think – *William Cowper*

Man yields to custom, as he bows to fate – / In all things ruled, mind, body, and estate – *George Crabbe*

There is no tyrant like custom, and no freedom where its edicts are not resisted.

The influence of custom is incalculable; dress a boy as a man, and he will at once change his conception of himself.

Be not so bigoted to any custom as to worship it at the expense of truth.

CYNICS

It will generally be found that those who sneer habitually at human nature, and affect to despise it, are among its worst and least pleasant samples – *Charles Dickens*

The cynic is one who never sees a good quality in a man, and never fails to see a bad one. He is the human owl, vigilant in darkness and blind to light, mousing for vermin, and never seeing noble game – *Henry Ward Beecher*

DANGER

Danger levels man and brute, and all are fellows in their need – *Lord Byron*

We should never so entirely avoid danger as to appear irresolute and cowardly; but, at the same time, we should avoid unnecessarily exposing ourselves to danger, than which nothing can be more foolish – *Cicero*

A timid person is frightened before a danger; a coward during the time; and a courageous person afterward – *Jean Paul Richter*

Let the fear of a danger be a spur to prevent it; he that fears not, gives advantage to the danger – *Francis Quarles*

It is better to meet danger than to wait for it. He that is on a lee shore, and foresees a hurricane, stands out to sea and encounters a storm to avoid a shipwreck – *Charles Caleb Colton*

To ignore the danger is to deserve the disaster.

DAY

Every day is a little life, and our whole life is but a day repeated. Therefore live every day as if it would be the last – *Bishop Hall*

Enjoy the blessings of the day if God sends them: and the evils bear patiently and sweetly; for this day only is ours: we are dead to yesterday, and not born to tomorrow – *Jeremy Taylor*

Count that day lost, whose low descending sun / Views from thy hand no worthy action done.

Greet every new day as the start of the rest of your life.

DEATH

This world is the land of the dying; the next is the land of the living – *Tryon Edwards*

We understand death for the first time when he puts his hand upon one whom we love – *Mme de Staël*

The gods conceal from men the happiness of death, that they may endure life – *Lucan*

One may live as a conqueror, a king, or a magistrate; but he must die a man – *Daniel Webster*

Death is the golden key that opens the palace of eternity – *John Milton*

Death expecteth thee everywhere; be wise, therefore, and expect death everywhere – *Francis Quarles*

The ancients feared death; we, thanks to Christianity, fear only dying – *Guesses at Truth*

Death shuts the gate of envy after it – *Laurence Sterne*

Be absolute for death; either death or life / Shall thereby be the sweeter – *William Shakespeare*

He who should teach men to die, would, at the same time, teach them to live – *Michel Eyquem de Montaigne*

Is death the last sleep? No, it is the last and final awakening – *Walter Scott*

The darkness of death is like the evening twilight; it makes all objects appear more lovely to the dying – *Jean Paul Richter*

Death is the liberator of him whom freedom cannot release; the physician of him whom medicine cannot cure; the comforter of him whom time cannot console – *Charles Caleb Colton*

Let death be daily before your eyes, and you will never entertain any abject thought, nor too eagerly covet anything – *Epictetus*

On death and judgment, heaven and hell, / Who oft doth think, must needs die well – *Walter Raleigh*

Death and love are the two wings that bear the good man to heaven – *Michelangelo Buonarroti*

Each departed friend is a magnet that attracts us to the next world – *Richter*

It is as natural to man to die, as to be born – *Francis Bacon*

Ah! what a sign it is of evil life / Where death's approach is seen so terrible – *William Shakespeare*

When the sun goes below the horizon, he is not set; the heavens glow for a full hour after his departure. And when a great and good man sets, the sky of this word is luminous long after he is out of sight – *Henry Ward Beecher*

Death is but the dropping of the flower that the fruit may swell – *Beecher*

The sense of death is most in apprehension, / And the poor beetle, that we tread upon, / In corporal sufferance finds a pang as great / As when a giant dies – *Shakespeare*

As long as we are living, God will give us living grace, and he won't give us dying grace till it's time to die. What's the use of trying to feel like dying when you ain't dying, nor anywhere near it? – *Beecher*

Be of good cheer about death, and know this of a truth, that no evil can happen to a good man, either in life or after death – *Socrates*

Some people are so afraid to die that they never begin to live – *Henry van Dyke*

Men fear death, as if unquestionably the greatest evil, and yet no man knows that it may not be the greatest good.

Death is paying the debt of nature.

One of the fathers says, 'There is but this difference between the death of old men and young; that old men go to death, and death comes to the young.'

Men may live fools, but fools they cannot die.

How shocking must thy summons be, O death, to him that is at ease in his possessions! who, counting on long years of pleasure here, is quite unfurnished for the world to come.

Alexander the Great, seeing Diogenes looking attentively at a parcel of human bones, asked the philosopher what he was looking for. 'That which I cannot find,' was the reply; 'the difference between your father's bones and those of his slaves.'

A good man being asked during his last illness, whether he thought himself dying, 'Really, friend, I care not whether I am or not; for if I die I shall be with God; if I live, He will be with me.'

See also GRAVES, GRIEF, LIFE, MORTALITY.

DEBT

Debt is the secret foe of thrift, as vice and idleness are its open foes. The debt habit is the twin brother of poverty – *T. T. Munger*

Do not accustom yourself to consider debt only as an inconvenience; you will find it a calamity – *Samuel Johnson*

Poverty is hard, but debt is horrible – *Charles Haddon Spurgeon*

Think what you do when you run in debt; you give to another power over your liberty – *Benjamin Franklin*

Debt follows debt, as lie follows lie – *Samuel Smiles*

A man who owes a little can clear it off in a little time – *Lord Chesterfield*

A small debt produces a debtor; a large one, an enemy – *Publius Syrus*

Youth is in danger until it learns to look upon debts as furies.

Time flies, especially between instalments.

See also BORROWING, CREDIT, CREDITORS.

DECEIT

Of all the evil spirits abroad in the word, insincerity is the most dangerous – *James Anthony Froude*

Deceivers are the most dangerous members of society. They trifle with the best affections of our nature, and violate the most sacred obligations – *George Crabbe*

It is as easy to deceive one's self without perceiving it, as it is difficult to deceive others without their finding it out – *François de La Rochefoucauld*

We never deceive for a good purpose – *Jean de La Bruyère*

Who dares think one thing and another tell, / My heart detests him as the gates of hell – *Alexander Pope*

He that has no real esteem for any of the virtues can best assume the appearance of them all – *Charles Caleb Colton*

O what a tangled web we weave, / When first we practise to deceive! – *Walter Scott*

All deception in the course of life is indeed nothing else but a lie reduced to practice – *Robert South*

No man was ever so much deceived by another as by himself.

Deceit is the false road to happiness.

The first and worst of all frauds is to cheat one's self. All sin is easy after that.

There are three persons you should never deceive: your physician, your confessor, and your lawyer.

See also FALSEHOOD, HYPOCRISY, LIARS, LYING.

DECENCY

Virtue and decency are so nearly related that it is difficult to separate them from each other but in our imagination – *Cicero*

Decency is the least of all laws, but yet it is the law which is most strictly observed – *François de La Rochefoucauld*

Want of decency is want of sense.

See also CONDUCT, HONESTY.

DECISIVENESS

When desperate ills demand a speedy cure, distrust is cowardice, and prudence folly – *Samuel Johnson*

The block of granite which was an obstacle in the pathway of the weak becomes a stepping-stone in the pathway of the strong – *Thomas Carlyle*

A determinate purpose in life and a steady adhesion to it through all disadvantages are indispensable conditions of success – *W. M. Punshon*

The man who has not learned to say no will be a weak if not a wretched man as long as he lives.

I hate to see things done by halves. If it be right, do it boldly, if it be wrong leave it undone.

Decision of character will often give to an inferior mind command over a
superior.
The souls of men of undecided and feeble purpose are the graveyards of
good intentions.

DEEDS

Our deeds determine us, as much as we determine our deeds – *George
Eliot*
Our deeds are seeds of fate, sown here on earth, but bringing forth their
harvest in eternity – *G. D. Boardman*
Our deeds follow us, and what we have been makes us what we are.
A word that has been said may be unsaid – it is but air. But when a deed is
done, it cannot be undone – *Henry Wadsworth Longfellow*
Good actions ennoble us, and we are the sons of our own deeds – *Miguel
de Cervantes Saavedra*
No matter what a man's aims, or resolutions, or professions may be, it is
by one's deeds that he is to be judged, both by God and man – *Henry
Ward Beecher*
Blessings ever wait on virtuous deeds, and though a late, a sure reward
succeeds – *William Congreve*
Good deeds ring clear through heaven like a bell – *Jean Paul Richter*
A noble deed is a step toward God – *Josiah Gilbert Holland*
A life spent worthily should be measured by deeds, not years – *Richard
Brinsley Sheridan*
We should believe only in deeds; words go for nothing everywhere.
Blessed are they who have nothing to say and know what to do instead.
See also ACTION.

DEFEAT

What is defeat? Nothing but education; nothing but the first step to
something better – *Wendell Phillips*
Defeat is a school in which truth always grows strong – *Henry Ward Beecher*
You are never so near to victory as when defeated in a good cause –
Beecher

DELAY

Delay has always been injurious to those whose are prepared – *Lucan*
Defer no time, delays have dangerous ends – *William Shakespeare*
He that takes time to resolve gives leisure to deny, and warning to
prepare – *Francis Quarles*
In delay / We waste our lights in vain, like lamps by day – *Shakespeare*

Tomorrow I will live, the fool does say: / Today itself's too late; the wise
lived yesterday – *Martial*

Every delay is hateful, but it gives wisdom – *Publius Syrus*

Someone speaks admirably of the well-ripened fruit of sage delay –
Honoré de Balzac

Where duty is plain delay is both foolish and hazardous; where it is not,
delay may be both wisdom and safety – *Tryon Edwards*

When the fool has made up his mind the market has gone by – *Spanish proverb*

Procrastination is the thief of time; year after year it steals till all are fled.

See also PROCRASTINATION.

DELICACY

The finest qualities of our nature, like the bloom on fruits, can be
preserved only by the most delicate handling – *Henry David Thoreau*

An appearance of delicacy, and even of fragility, is almost essential to
beauty – *Edmund Burke*

Delicacy is to the affections what gravity is to beauty.

If you destroy delicacy and a sense of shame in a young girl you deprave
her very fast.

Delicacy is to the mind what fragrance is to the fruit.

DELIGHT

What more felicity can fall to man than to enjoy delight with liberty –
Edmund Spenser

As high as we have mounted in delight, / In our abjection do we sing as
low – *William Wordsworth*

I am convinced that we have a degree of delight, and that no small one, in
the real misfortunes and pains of others – *Edmund Burke*

Sensual delights soon end in loathing, quickly bring a glutting surfeit,
and degenerate into torments when they are continued and unintermitted – *John Howe*

See also JOY.

DELUSION

Were we perfectly acquainted with the object, we should never
passionately desire it – *François de La Rochefoucauld*

It many times falls out that we deem ourselves much deceived in others,
because we are first deceived in ourselves – *Sir Philip Sidney*

When our vices quit us, we flatter ourselves with the belief that it is we
who quit them – *La Rochefoucauld*

O, thoughts of men accurst! / Past and to come seem best; things present worst – *William Shakespeare*

The disappointment of manhood succeeds the delusion of youth – *Benjamin Disraeli*

Delusions are as necessary to our happiness as realities.

The worst deluded are the self-deluded.

Mankind in the gross is a gaping monster, that loves to be deceived, and has seldom been disappointed.

Hope tells a flattering tale, delusive, vain, and hollow.

DEMOCRACY

The love of democracy is that of equality – *Charles de Montesquieu*

In every village there will arise some miscreant, to establish the most grinding tyranny by calling himself the people – *Sir Robert Peel*

If there were a people consisting of gods, they would be governed democratically; so perfect a government is not suitable to men – *Jean Jacques Rousseau*

To be the favourite of an ignorant multitude, a man must descend to their level; he must desire what they desire, and detest all they do not approve: he must yield to their prejudices, and substitute them for principles. Instead of enlightening their errors, he must adopt them, and must furnish the sophistry that will propagate and defend them – *Fisher Ames*

Democracy will itself accomplish the salutary universal change from the delusive to the real, and make a new blessed world of us by and by – *Thomas Carlyle*

The devil was the first democrat – *Lord Byron*

The real democratic American idea is, not that every man shall be on a level with every other, but that everyone shall have liberty, without hindrance, to be what God made him – *Henry Ward Beecher*

The democracy must depend upon organization much more than the aristocracy – *David Lloyd George*

Democracy is based upon the conviction that there are extraordinary possibilities in ordinary people – *Harry Emerson Fosdick*

You little child is your only true democrat.

DEPENDENCE

There is none so great but he may both need the help and service of the meanest of mortals – *Seneca*

Heaven's eternal wisdom has decreed, that man should ever stand in need of man – *Theocritus*

God has ordered, that men, being in need of each other, should learn to love each other, and to bear each other's burdens – *George Sala*

Depend on no man, on no friend but him who can depend on himself.
He only who acts conscientiously towards himself will act so towards
others – *Johann Kaspar Lavater*

God has made no one absolute. The rich depend on the poor, as well as
the poor on the rich. The world is but a magnificent building; all the
stones are gradually cemented together. No one subsists by himself
alone.

The greatest man living may stand in need of the meanest, as much as
the meanest does of him.

The gentle needs the strong to sustain it.

DEPRAVITY

We are all sinful; and whatever one of us blames in another each one will
find in his own heart – *Seneca*

Controlled depravity is not innocence – *Edmund Burke*

Every man has his devilish moments – *Johann Kaspar Lavater*

DESIRE

The thirst of desire is never filled, nor fully satisfied – *Cicero*

It is much easier to suppress a first desire than to satisfy those that follow
– *François de La Rochefoucauld*

Some desire is necessary to keep life in motion; he whose real wants are
supplied must admit those of fancy – *Samuel Johnson*

Every man without passions has within him no principle of action, nor
motive to act – *Claude Adrien Helvétius*

Every desire bears its death in its very gratification – *Washington Irving*

Unlawful desires are punished after the effect of enjoying; but impossible desires are punished in the desire itself – *Sir Philip Sidney*

Before we passionately desire anything which another enjoys, we
should examine as to the happiness of its possessor – *La Rochefoucauld*

In moderating, not in satisfying desires, lies peace – *Reginald Heber*

The soul of man is infinite in what it covets – *Ben Jonson*

A wise man will desire no more than he may get justly, use soberly,
distribute cheerfully, and leave contentedly.

When a man's desires are boundless, his labours are endless.

See also WANTS.

DESOLATION

No one is so utterly desolate, but some heart, though unknown, re-
sponds unto his own – *Henry Wadsworth Longfellow*

No soul is desolate as long as there is a human being for whom it can feel
trust and reverence – *George Eliot*

My desolation begins to make / A better life – *William Shakespeare*

What is the worst of woes that wait on age? What stamps the wrinkle deeper on the brow? To view each loved one blotted from life's page, and be alone on earth – *Lord Byron*

DESPAIR

What we call despair is often only the painful eagerness of unfed hope – *George Eliot*

He who despairs wants love and faith, for faith, hope, and love are three torches which blend their light together, nor does the one shine without the other – *Metastasio*

Despair is the damp of hell, as joy is the serenity of heaven – *John Donne*

Despair gives the shocking ease to the mind that mortification gives to the body.

DESPONDENCY

To believe a business impossible is the way to make it so – *Jeremy Collier*

In the lottery of life there are more prizes drawn than blanks. Despondency is the most unprofitable feeling a man can indulge in – *De Witt Talmage*

Despondency is ingratitude; hope is God's worship – *Henry Ward Beecher*

As to feel that we can do a thing is often success, so to doubt and despond is a sure step to failure.

DESTINY

Man proposes, but God disposes – *Thomas à Kempis*

We are but the instruments of heaven; our work is not design, but destiny – *Owen Meredith*

No man of woman born, coward or brave, can shun his destiny – *Homer*

That which God writes on thy forehead, thou wilt come to it – *Koran*

The clue of our destiny, wander where we will, lies at the cradle foot – *Jean Paul Richter*

Our fate is decreed, and every man's portion of joy or sorrow is predetermined – *Seneca*

That which is not allotted the hand cannot reach; and what is allotted you will find wherever you may be – *Sádi*

Man supposes that he directs his life and governs his actions, when his existence is irretrievably under the control of destiny – *Johann Wolfgang von Goethe*

Death and life have their determined appointments; riches and honours depend upon heaven – *Confucius*

The wheels of nature are not made to roll backward – *Robert Hall*

Thoughts lead on to purposes; purposes go forth in action; actions form
  habits; habits decide character; and character fixes our destiny –
  Tryon Edwards
The acts of this life are the destiny of the next – *Eastern proverb*
See also FATE, FORTUNE, PROVIDENCE.

DETRACTION

Traduc'd by ignorant tongues. . . / 'Tis but the fate of place, and the
  rough brake / That virtue must go through – *William Shakespeare*
To make beads of the faults of others, and tell them over every day, is
  infernal. If you want to know how devils feel, you do know if you are
  such an one – *Henry Ward Beecher*
Happy are they that hear their detractions, and can put them to mending
  – *Shakespeare*
Base natures joy to see hard hap happen to them they deem happy – *Sir
  Philip Sidney*
There is no readier way for a man to bring his own worth into question
  than by endeavouring to detract from the worth of other men – *John
  Tillotson*
Unjustifiable detraction always proves the weakness as well as mean-
  ness of the one who employs it – *E. L. Magoon*
Much depends upon a man's courage when he is slandered and tra-
  duced. Weak men are crushed by detraction; but the brave hold on
  and succeed.
Whoever feels pain in hearing a good character of his neighbour, will feel
  pleasure in the reverse; and those who despair to rise to distinction
  by their virtues are happy if others can be depressed to a level with
  themselves.
The man that makes a character makes foes.

DEVIATION

When people once begin to deviate, they do not know where to stop –
  George III
Ah! to what gulfs a single deviation from the track of human duties lead!
  – *Lord Byron*
Deviation from either truth or duty is a downward path, and none can
  say where the descent will end – *Tryon Edwards*

DEVIL

As no good is done, or spoken or thought by any man without the
  assistance of God, all the works of our evil nature are the work of the
  devil – *John Wesley*

What, man! defy the devil: consider, he's an enemy to mankind – *William Shakespeare*

He who would fight the devil with his own weapons must not wonder if he finds him an overmatch – *Robert South*

The devil knoweth his own, and is a particularly bad paymaster – *Francis Marion Crawford*

The devil has at least one good quality, that he will flee if we resist him. Though cowardly in him, it is safety for us – *Tryon Edwards*

The devil tempts all, but the idle man tempts the devil – *Turkish proverb*

The devil is no idle spirit, but a vagrant, runagate walker, that never rests in one place. The motive, cause, and main intention of his walking is to ruin man.

No sooner is a temple built to God, but the devil builds a chapel hard by.

DEVOTION

All is holy where devotion kneels – *Oliver Wendell Holmes*

The private devotions and secret offices of religion are like the refreshing of a garden with the distilling and petty drops of a waterpot; but addressed from the temple, they are like rain from heaven – *Jeremy Taylor*

Satan rocks the cradle when we sleep at our devotions – *Bishop Hall*

The secret heart is devotion's temple; there the saint lights the flame of purest sacrifice, which burns unseen but not unaccepted – *Hannah More*

The inward sighs of humble penitence rise to the ear of heaven, when pealed hymns are scattered to the common air – *Joanna Baillie*

The best and sweetest flowers in paradise, God gives to his people when they are on their knees in the closet.

Once I sought a time and place for solitude and prayer; / But now where'er I find thy face I find a closet there.

See also PRAYER.

DEW

The dews of evening – those tears of the sky for the loss of the sun – *Lord Chesterfield*

Stars of the morning dew-drops which the sun impearls on every leaf and flower – *John Milton*

Dew-drops are the gems of morning, but the tears of mournful eve – *Samuel Taylor Coleridge*

Dew-drops nature's tears, which she sheds on her own breast for the fair which die. The sun insists on gladness; but at night, when he is gone, poor nature loves to weep.

Earth's liquid jewellery, wrought of the air.

DICE

I never hear the rattling of dice that it does not sound to me like the funeral bell of the whole family – *Douglas William Jerrold*

I look upon every man as a suicide from the moment he takes the dice-box desperately in his hand; all that follows in his career from that fatal time is only sharpening the dagger before he strikes it to his heart.

The best throw with the dice is to throw them away.

See also GAMBLING.

DIET

Regimen is better than physic. Everyone should be his own physician. We should assist, not force, nature. Eat with moderation what you know by experience agrees with your constitution. Nothing is good for the body but what we can digest. What can procure digestion? Exercise. What will recruit strength? Sleep. What will alleviate incurable evils? Patience – *Voltaire*

In general, mankind, since the improvement of cookery, eats twice as much as nature requires – *Benjamin Franklin*

All courageous animals are carnivorous, and greater courage is to be expected in a people whose food is strong and hearty, than in the half-starved of other countries – *William Temple*

Simple diet is best; for many dishes bring many diseases; and rich sauces are worse than even heaping several meats upon each other – *Pliny the Younger*

The chief pleasure in eating does not consist in costly seasoning, or exquisite flavour, but in yourself – *Horace*

If thou wouldst preserve a sound body, use fasting and walking; if a healthful soul, fasting and praying. Walking exercises the body; praying exercises the soul; fasting cleanses both – *Francis Quarles*

A fig for your bill of fare; show me your bill of company – *Jonathan Swift*

One meal a day is enough for a lion, and it ought to be for a man.

DIFFICULTY

The greatest difficulties lie where we are not looking for them – *Johann Wolfgang von Goethe*

The weak sinews become strong by their conflict with difficulties – *E. H. Chapin*

Difficulties strengthen the mind, as labour does the body – *Seneca*

The greater the obstacle, the more glory we have in overcoming it; the difficulties with which we are met are the maids of honour which set off virtue – *Molière*

Difficulties show men what they are – *Epictetus*

We attempt nothing great but from a sense of the difficulties we have to encounter; we persevere in nothing great but from a pride in overcoming them – *William Hazlitt*

There are difficulties in your path. Be thankful for them. They will test your capabilities of resistance; you will be impelled to persevere from the very energy of the opposition. But what of him that fails? What does he gain? Strength for life. The real merit is not in the success, but in the endeavour; and win or lose, he will be honoured and crowned – *W. Punshon*

Difficulty is the soil in which all manly and womanly qualities best flourish; and the true worker, in any sphere, is continually coping with difficulties. His very failures, throwing him upon his own resources, cultivate energy and resolution; his hardships teach him fortitude; his successes inspire self-reliance.

There is no merit where there is no trial; and till experience stamps the mark of strength, cowards may pass for heroes, and faith for falsehood.

To overcome difficulties is to experience the full delight of existence.

The best way out of a difficulty is through it.

DIFFIDENCE

We are as often duped by diffidence as by confidence – *Lord Chesterfield*

Nothing sinks a person into low company so surely as timidity and diffidence of himself. If he thinks he shall not please, he may depend upon it that he will not. But with proper endeavours to please, and a degree of persuasion that he shall, it is almost certain that he will – *Chesterfield*

One with more of soul in his face than words on his tongue – *William Wordsworth*

Persons extremely reserved and diffident are like old enamelled watches, which had painted covers that hindered your seeing what o'clock it was.

DIGNITY

True dignity is never gained by place, and never lost when honours are withdrawn – *Philip Massinger*

Dignity consists not in possessing honours, but in the consciousness that we deserve them – *Aristotle*

Dignity and love do not blend well, nor do they continue long together – *Ovid*

Dignity is like a top-hat. It is hardly worth having if you are always standing on it – *Christopher Hollis*

Dignity of position adds to dignity of character, as well as to dignity of carriage.

Dignity consists not in preserving honours but in deserving them.

You add nothing to your height by standing on your dignity.

DILIGENCE

What we hope ever to do with ease, we must learn first to do with diligence – *Samuel Johnson*

The expectations of life depend upon diligence; the mechanic that would perfect his work must first sharpen his tools – *Confucius*

Diligence is the mother of good luck, and God gives all things to industry. Work while it is called today, for you know not how much you may be hindered tomorrow. One today is worth two tomorrows; never put off till tomorrow that which you can do today – *Benjamin Franklin*

Who makes quick use of the moment is a genius of prudence – *Johann Kaspar Lavater*

He who labours diligently need never despair; for all things are accomplished by diligence and labour – *Menander*

In all departments of activity, to have one thing to do, and then to do it, is the secret of success.

Diligence is the next best thing to having Saturday afternoon off.

It is better to wear out than rust out.

DINNER

A good dinner sharpens wit, while it softens the heart – *John Doran*

A dinner lubricates business.

DIRT

'Ignorance', says Ajax, 'is a painless evil.' So, I should think, is dirt, considering the merry faces that go along with it – *George Eliot*

Dirt is not dirt, but only something in the wrong place – *Lord Palmerston*

DISAPPOINTMENT

The disappointment of manhood succeeds to the delusion of youth – *Benjamin Disraeli*

Oft expectation fails, and most oft there / Where most it promises; and oft it hits / Where hope is coldest and despair most fits – *William Shakespeare*

How disappointment tracks the steps of hope – *L. E. Landon*

He who expects much will be often disappointed; yet disappointment seldom cures us of expectation – *Samuel Johnson*

Mean spirits under disappointment, like small beer in a thunderstorm, always turn sour – *John Randolph*

An old man once said, 'When I was young, I was poor; when old, I became rich; but in each condition I found disappointment. When I had the faculties for enjoyment, I had not the means; when the means came, the faculties were gone' – *Mme Gasparin*

We mount to heaven mostly on the ruins of our cherished schemes finding our failures were successes – *Amos Bronson Alcott*

No man, with a man's heart in him, gets far on his way without some bitter, soul-searching disappointment.

The best enjoyment is half disappointment to what we intend or would have in this world.

Man must be disappointed with the lesser things of life before he can comprehend the full value of the greater.

A frequent disappointment is meeting someone we have heard so much about.

DISCERNMENT

After a spirit of discernment, the next rarest things in the world are diamonds and pearls – *Jean de La Bruyère*

To succeed in the world, it is much more necessary to possess the penetration to discern who is a fool, than to discover who is a clever man – *Charles Maurice de Talleyrand-Périgord*

The idiot, the Indian, the child, and the unschooled farmer's boy stand nearer to the light by which nature is to be read, than the dissector or the antiquary – *Ralph Waldo Emerson*

DISCIPLINE

A stern discipline pervades all nature, which is a little cruel that it may be very kind – *Edmund Spenser*

No pain, no palm; no thorns, no throne; no gall, no glory; no cross, no crown – *William Penn*

A man in old age is like a sword in a shop window. Men that look upon the perfect blade do not imagine the process by which it was completed. Man is a sword; daily life is the workshop; and God is the artificer; and those cares which beat upon the anvil, and file the edge, and eat in, acid-like, the inscription on the hilt – those are the very things that fashion the man – *Henry Ward Beecher*

Let the evening's enjoyment bear the morning's reflection.

DISCONTENT

Discontent is the want of self-reliance; it is infirmity of will – *Ralph Waldo Emerson*

Our condition never satisfies us; the present is always the worst – *Jean de La Fontaine*

Noble discontent is the path to heaven – *Thomas Wentworth Higginson*

The best remedy for our discontent is to count our mercies. By the time we have reckoned up a part of these, we shall be on our knees praising the Lord for His great mercy and love – *The Quiver*

We love in others what we lack ourselves, and would be everything but what we are – *C. A. Stoddard*

A good man and a wise man may, at times, be angry with the world, and at times grieved for it; but no man was ever discontented with the world if he did his duty in it – *Robert Southey*

Discontent is like ink poured into water, which fills the whole fountain full of blackness. It casts a cloud over the mind, and renders it more occupied about the evil which disquiets than about the means of removing it.

The root of all discontent is self-love.

The more self is indulged the more it demands, and, therefore, of all men the selfish are the most discontented.

That which makes people dissatisfied with their condition is the chimerical idea they form of the happiness of others.

DISCOVERY

A new principle is an inexhaustible source of new views – *Marquis de Vauvenargues*

It is a mortifying truth, and ought to teach the wisest of us humility, that many of the most valuable discoveries have been the result of chance rather than of contemplation, and of accident rather than of design – *Charles Caleb Colton*

If I have ever made any valuable discoveries, it has been owing more to patient attention, than to any other talent – *Sir Isaac Newton*

It is a profound mistake to think that everything has been discovered; as well think the horizon the boundary of the world.

He who sins against me may fear discovery; but he who sins against God is sure of it.

DISCRETION

Be discreet in all things, and so render it unnecessary to be mysterious about any – *Duke of Wellington*

There are many shining qualities in the mind of man; but none so useful
   as discretion – *Joseph Addison*

Discretion in speech is more than eloquence – *Francis Bacon*

The better part of valour is discretion; in the which better part, I have
   saved my life – *William Shakespeare*

Discretion is the perfection of reason, and a guide to us in all the duties of
   life. It is only found in men of sound sense and good understanding –
   Jean de La Bruyère

Discretion is the salt, and fancy the sugar of life; the one preserves, the
   other sweetens it.

Open your mouth and purse cautiously, and your stock of wealth and
   reputation shall, at least in repute, be great.

A sound discretion is not so much indicated by never making a mistake,
   as by never repeating it.

If thou art a master, be sometimes blind, if a servant, sometimes deaf.

An ounce of discretion is worth a pound of learning.

See also TACT.

DISCUSSION

He who knows only his own side of the case knows little of that – *John
   Stuart Mill*

He that is not open to conviction is not qualified for discussion – *Richard
   Whately*

Gratuitous violence in argument betrays a conscious weakness of the
   cause, and is usually a signal of despair – *Junius*

Men are never so likely to settle a question rightly, as when they discuss
   it freely – *Thomas Babington Macaulay*

In debate, rather pull to pieces the argument of thine antagonist, than
   offer him any of thine own; for thus thou wilt fight him in his own
   country – *Henry Fielding*

If you take delight in idle argumentation, you may be qualified to
   combat with the sophists, but will never know how to live with men –
   Socrates

Reply with wit to gravity, and with gravity to wit – *Charles Caleb Colton*

It is in disputes, as in armies, where the weaker side sets up false lights,
   and makes a great noise to make the enemy believe them more
   numerous and strong than they really are – *Jonathan Swift*

There is no dispute managed without passion, and yet there is scarce a
   dispute worth a passion.

Free and fair discussion will ever be found the firmest friend to truth.

It is an excellent rule to be observed in all discussions, that men should
   give soft words and hard arguments.

Whosoever is afraid of submitting any question, civil or religious, to the test of free discussion, is more in love with his own opinion than with truth.

Understand your antagonist before you answer him.

See also ARGUMENT, CONTENTION.

DISEASE

The disease and its medicine are like two factions in a besieged town; they tear one another to pieces, but both unite against their common enemy – Nature – *Francis Jeffrey*

It is with diseases of the mind, as with those of the body; we are half dead before we understand our disorder, and half cured when we do – *Charles Caleb Colton*

Diseases are the penalties we pay for over-indulgence, or for our neglect of the means of health.

In these days half our diseases come from the neglect of the body, and the over-work of the brain. We live longer than our forefathers; but we suffer more, from a thousand artificial anxieties and cares. They fatigued only the muscles; we exhaust the finer strength of the nerves.

Taking medicine is often only making a new disease to cure or hide the old one.

DISGRACE

Disgrace is not in the punishment, but in the crime – *Vittorio Alfieri*

Whatever disgrace we may have deserved or incurred, it is almost always in our power to re-establish our character – *François de La Rochefoucauld*

Do not talk about disgrace from a thing being known, when the disgrace is that the thing should exist.

DISGUISE

Men would not live long in society, were they not the mutual dupes of each other – *François de La Rochefoucauld*

Were we to take as much pains to be what we ought to be, as we do to disguise what we really are, we might appear like ourselves without being at the trouble of any disguise whatever – *La Rochefoucauld*

Disguise yourself as you may to your fellow men, if you are honest with yourself conscience will make known your real character, and the heart-searching one always knows it.

DISHONESTY

Dishonesty will stare honesty out of countenance any day of the week, if there is anything to be got by it – *Charles Dickens*

He who purposely cheats his friend would cheat his God – *Johann Kaspar Lavater*

Every man takes care that his neighbour shall not cheat him. But a day comes when he begins to care that he do not cheat his neighbour. Then all goes well. He has changed his market-cart into a chariot of the sun – *Ralph Waldo Emerson*

That which is won ill will never wear well, for there is a curse attends it which will waste it – *Henry Ward Beecher*

I could never draw the line between meanness and dishonesty. What is mean, so far as I can see, slides by indistinguishable gradations into what is dishonest – *George Macdonald*

Dishonesty is a forsaking of permanent for temporary advantages.

DISOBEDIENCE

Rogues differ little. Each began first as a disobedient son – *Chinese proverb*

Wherever there is authority, there is a natural inclination to disobedience.

Disobedient children, if preserved from the gallows, are reserved for the rack, to be tortured by their own posterity.

DISPOSITION

A good disposition is more valuable than gold; for the latter is the gift of fortune, but the former is the dower of nature – *Joseph Addison*

The most phlegmatic dispositions often contain the most inflammable spirits, as fire is struck from the hardest flints – *William Hazlitt*

The man who has so little knowledge of human nature as to seek happiness by changing anything but his own dispositions will waste his life in fruitless efforts, and multiply the griefs which he proposes to remove – *Charles Caleb Colton*

A tender-hearted, compassionate disposition, which inclines men to pity and to feel the misfortunes of others, and which is incapable of involving any man in ruin and misery, is, of all tempers of mind, the most amiable; and though it seldom receives much honour, is worthy of the highest – *Henry Fielding*

See also CHARACTER.

DISTANCE

Sweetest melodies are those that are by distance made more sweet – *William Wordsworth*

Glories, like glow-worms afar off, shine bright, / But looked at near have neither heat nor light – *John Webster*

Distance lends enchantment to the view.

Distance sometimes endears friendship, and absence sweeteneth it.

DISTINCTION

You may fail to shine in the opinion of others, both in your conversation and actions, from being superior, as well as inferior to them.

How men long for celebrity! Some would willingly sacrifice their lives for fame, and not a few would rather be known by their crimes than not known at all.

DISTRUST

A certain amount of distrust is wholesome, but not so much of others as of ourselves – *Mme Neckar*

The feeling of distrust is always the last which a great mind acquires – *Jean Racine*

Nothing is more certain of destroying any good feelings that may be cherished toward us than to show distrust – *Mme de Sévigné*

What loneliness is more lonely than distrust? – *George Eliot*

Self-distrust is the cause of most of our failures. In the assurance of strength, there is strength, and they are the weakest, however strong, who have no faith in themselves or their own powers.

To think and feel we are able, is often to be so.

DOCTRINE

Doctrine is the framework of life, the skeleton of truth, to be clothed and rounded out by the living grace of a holy life – *A. J. Gordon*

Pure doctrine always bears fruit in pure benefits – *Ralph Waldo Emerson*

Doctrine is the necessary foundation of duty; if the theory is not correct, the practice cannot be right.

The question is not whether a doctrine is beautiful but whether it is true.

DOGMATISM

Those who differ most from the opinions of their fellow men are the most confident of the truth of their own.

Those who refuse the long drudgery of thought, and think with the heart rather than the head, are ever most fiercely dogmatic.

DOING WELL

Whatever is worth doing at all is worth doing well – *Lord Chesterfield*

We do not choose our own parts in life, and have nothing to do with those parts. Our duty is confined to playing them well – *Epictetus*

Rest satisfied with doing well, and leave others to talk of you as they please – *Pythagoras*

Thinking well is wise; planning well, wiser; doing well wisest and best of all – *Persian proverb*

DOMESTICITY

Domestic happiness, thou only bliss / Of Paradise that has surviv'd the fall! – *William Cowper*

Domestic happiness is the end of almost all our pursuits, and the common reward of all our pains – *Henry Fielding*

A prince wants only the pleasure of private life to complete his happiness – *Jean de La Bruyère*

Our notion of the perfect society embraces the family as its centre and ornament. Nor is there a paradise planted till the children appear in the foreground to animate and complete the picture – *Amos Bronson Alcott*

No money is better spent than what is laid out for domestic satisfaction. A man is pleased that his wife is dressed as well as other people, and the wife is pleased that she is so dressed – *Samuel Johnson*

See also HOME, HOUSE, MARRIAGE.

DOUBT

Modest doubt is call'd / The beacon of the wise, the tent that searches / To the bottom of the worst – *William Shakespeare*

In contemplation, if a man begins with certainties he shall end in doubts; but if he be content to begin with doubts, he shall end in certainties – *Francis Bacon*

Doubt, indulged and cherished, is in danger of becoming denial; but if honest, and bent on thorough investigation, it may soon lead to full establishment in the truth – *Tryon Edwards*

When you doubt, abstain – *Zoroaster*

We know accurately only when we know little; with knowledge doubt increases – *Johann Wolfgang von Goethe*

Our doubts are traitors, / And make us lose the good we oft might win, / By fearing to attempt – *Shakespeare*

Misgive, that you may not mistake – *Richard Whately*

Doubt comes in at the window when inquiry is denied at the door – *Benjamin Jowett*

It is never worth while to suggest doubts in order to show how cleverly we can answer them – *Whately*

Give me the benefit of your convictions, if you have any, but keep your doubts to yourself, for I have enough of my own – *Goethe*

The end of doubt is the beginning of repose – *Petrarch*

Doubt is hell in the human soul – *Mme Gasparin*

Human knowledge is the parent of doubt.

The doubter's dissatisfaction with his doubt is as great and widespread as the doubt itself.

Doubt is the disease of this inquisitive, restless age. It is the price we pay for our advanced intelligence and civilization.

The vain man is generally a doubter.

Doubt is an incentive to search for truth, and patient inquiry leads the way to it.

Who never doubted never half believed. Where doubt is, there truth is – it is her shadow.

Uncertain ways unsafest are, and doubt a greater mischief than despair.

The man who speaks his positive convictions is worth a regiment of men who are always proclaiming their doubts and suspicions.

See also SCEPTICISM, UNCERTAINTY.

DREAMS

Dreams full oft are found of real events the forms and shadows – *Joanna Baillie*

Let not our babbling dreams affright our souls – *William Shakespeare*

Children of the night, of indigestion bred.

We are somewhat more than ourselves in our sleeps, and the slumber of the body seems to be but the waking of the soul.

As dreams are the fancies of those that sleep, so fancies are but the dreams of those awake.

Dreaming is an act of pure imagination, attesting in all men a creative power, which, if it were available in waking, would make every man a Dante or a Shakespeare.

Nothing so much convinces me of the boundlessness of the human mind as its operations in dreaming.

Many a man wastes his present by dreaming of his future.

Castles in the air cost a vast deal to keep up.

DRESS

Dress has a moral effect upon the conduct of mankind – *Sir John Barrington*

As you treat your body, so your house, your domestics, your enemies, your friends. Dress is the table of your contents – *Johann Kaspar Lavater*

Out of clothes, out of countenance; out of countenance, out of wit – *Ben Jonson*

Eat to please thyself, but dress to please others – *Benjamin Franklin*

An emperor in his night-cap would not meet with half the respect of an emperor with a crown – *Oliver Goldsmith*

As the index tells the contents of the book, and directs to the particular chapter, even so do garments, in man or woman, give us a taste of the spirit, and point to the internal quality of the soul; and there cannot be a more evident and gross manifestation of poor, degenerate, dung-hilly blood and breeding, than a rude, unpolished, disordered, and slovenly outside – *Philip Massinger*

As to matters of dress, I would recommend one never to be first in the fashion nor the last out of it – *John Wesley*

Costly thy habit as thy purse can buy, / But not express'd in fancy; rich, not gaudy; / For the apparel oft proclaims the man – *William Shakespeare*

No man is esteemed for gay garments, but by fools and women – *Walter Raleigh*

The vanity of loving fine clothes and new fashions, and valuing ourselves by them, is one of the most childish pieces of folly – *Sir Matthew Hale*

Where the eye is the jury, thine apparel is the evidence – *Francis Quarles*

Dress adds but little to the beauty of a person; it may possibly create a deference, but that is rather an enemy to love – *William Shenstone*

Worldly wisdom dictates the propriety of dressing somewhat beyond one's means, but of living within them, for everyone sees how we dress, but none see how we live unless we choose to let them – *Charles Caleb Colton*

We sacrifice to dress till household joys and comforts cease. Dress drains our cellar dry, and keeps our larder clean; puts out our fires, and introduces hunger, frost, and woe, where peace and hospitality might reign – *William Cowper*

In clothes clean and fresh there is a kind of youth with which age should surround itself – *Joseph Joubert*

Too great carelessness, equally with excess in dress, multiplies the wrinkles of old age, and makes its decay more conspicuous – *Jean de La Bruyère*

In the indications of female poverty there can be no disguise. No woman dresses below herself from caprice – *Charles Lamb*

In civilized society external advantages make us more respected. A man with a good coat on his back meets with a better reception than he who has a bad one – *Samuel Johnson*

The only medicine which does women more good than harm is dress –
Jean Paul Richter

Those who think that in order to dress well it is necessary to dress
extravagantly or gaudily make a great mistake. Nothing so well
becomes true feminine beauty as simplicity.

The body is the shell of the soul, and dress the husk of that shell; but the
husk often tells what the kernel is.

If honour be your clothing, the suit will last a lifetime; but if clothing be
your honour, it will soon be worn threadbare.

The perfection of dress is in the union of three requisites – in its being
comfortable, cheap, and tasteful.

The plainer the dress with greater lustre does beauty appear. Virtue is
the greatest ornament, and good sense the best equipage.

Beauty gains little, and homeliness and deformity lose much by gaudy
attire.

Persons are often misled in regard to their choice of dress by attending to
the beauty of colours, rather than selecting such colours as may
increase their own beauty.

DRINKING

The first draught serveth for health, the second for pleasure, the third for
shame, and the fourth for madness – *Anacharsis*

The Japanese say, 'A man takes a drink, then the drink takes a drink, and
the next drink takes the man.'

The bar-room is a bank: you deposit your money – and lose it; your time
– and lose it; your character – and lose it; your manly independence –
and lose it; your home comfort – and lose it; your self-control – and
lose it; your children's happiness – and lose it; your own soul – and
lose it.

Whisky is a good thing in its place. There is nothing like it for preserving
a man when he is dead. If you want to keep a dead man, put him in
whisky; if you want to kill a live man put whisky in him.

In the bottle, discontent seeks for comfort; cowardice, for courage;
bashfulness, for confidence; sadness, for joy; and all find ruin!

DRUNKENNESS

Drunkenness is nothing else but a voluntary madness – *Seneca*

Some of the domestic evils of drunkenness are houses without windows,
gardens without fences, fields without tillage, barns without roofs,
children without clothing, principles, morals, or manners – *Benjamin
Franklin*

All the armies on earth do not destroy so many of the human race, nor
alienate so much property, as drunkenness – *Francis Bacon*

Habitual intoxication is the epitome of every crime – *Douglas William Jerrold*

Let there be an entire abstinence from intoxicating drinks throughout this country during the period of a single generation, and a mob would be as impossible as combustion without oxygen – *Horace Mann*

There is scarcely a crime before me that is not, directly or indirectly, caused by strong drink – *John Taylor Coleridge*

A drunkard is the annoyance of modesty; the trouble of civility; the spoil of wealth; the distraction of reason. He is the brewer's agent; the tavern and ale-house benefactor; the beggar's companion; the constable's trouble; his wife's woe; his children's sorrow; his neighbour's scoff; his own shame. In short he is a tub of swill, a spirit of unrest, a thing below a beast, and a monster of a man.

Drunkenness places man as much below the level of the brutes, as reason elevates him above them.

The sight of a drunkard is a better sermon against that vice than the best that was ever preached on that subject.

See also INTEMPERANCE.

DUTY

Every duty which we omit obscures some truth which we should have known – *John Ruskin*

We do not choose our own parts in life, and have nothing to do with selecting those parts. Our simple duty is confined to playing them well – *Epictetus*

The reward of one duty done is the power to fulfil another – *George Eliot*

God always has an angel of help for those who are willing to do their duty – *T. L. Cuyler*

Who escapes a duty avoids a gain – *Theodore Parker*

Men do less than they ought, unless they do all that they can – *Thomas Carlyle*

It is one of the worst of errors to suppose that there is any path of safety except that of duty – *William Vevins*

Every duty that is bidden to wait comes back with seven fresh duties at its back – *Charles Kingsley*

Duty performed is a moral tonic – *Tryon Edwards*

Do thy duty; that is best; / Leave unto the Lord the rest – *Henry Wadsworth Longfellow*

By doing our duty, we learn to do it – *Edward Bouverie Pusey*

If I am faithful to the duties of the present, God will provide for the future – *William Bedell*

Do the truth you know, and you shall learn the truth you need to know – *George Macdonald*

Duty by habit is to pleasure turned – *Sir Samuel Egerton Brydges*

Our grand business is not to see what lies dimly in the distance, but to do what lies clearly at hand – *Thomas Carlyle*

The brave man wants no charms to encourage him to duty, and the good man scorns all warnings that would deter him from doing it.

Let us never forget that every station in life is necessary; that each deserves our respect; that not the station itself, but the worthy fulfilment of its duties does honour to man.

Duties in general, like that class of them called debts, give more trouble the longer they remain undischarged.

Exactness in little duties is a wonderful source of cheerfulness.

Duty, too often, is the thing that one expects from others.

EARLY RISING

When one turns over in bed, it is time to turn out – *Duke of Wellington*

It is well to be up before daybreak, for such habits contribute to health, wealth, and wisdom – *Aristotle*

Early rising not only gives us more life in the same number of years, but adds, likewise, to their number – *Charles Caleb Colton*

The early morning hath gold in its mouth – *Benjamin Franklin*

He who rises late may trot all day, and not overtake his business at night – *Franklin*

I never knew a man come to greatness or eminence who lay abed late in the morning – *Jonathan Swift*

Few ever lived to old age, and fewer still ever became distinguished, who were not in the habit of early rising.

Better to get up late and be wide awake then, than to get up early and be asleep all day.

EARNESTNESS

Earnestness is enthusiasm tempered by reason – *Blaise Pascal*

A man in earnest finds means, or if he cannot find, creates them – *William Ellery Channing*

The difference between half a heart and a whole heart makes the difference between signal defeat and a splendid victory – *A. H. K. Boyd*

The superior man is slow in his words and earnest in his conduct – *Confucius*

Without earnestness no man is ever great or does really great things.

To impress others we must be earnest; to amuse them, it is only necessary to be kindly and fanciful.

EATING

For the sake of health, medicines are taken by weight and measure; so ought food to be, or by some similar rule – *John Skelton*

The difference between a rich man and a poor man, is this – the former eats when he pleases, and the latter when he can get it – *Walter Raleigh*

One should eat to live, not live to eat – *Benjamin Franklin*

See also APPETITE, FEASTING

ECONOMY

If you know how to spend less than you get, you have the philosopher's stone – *Benjamin Franklin*

Economy is in itself a source of great revenue – *Seneca*

To make three guineas do the work of five – *Robert Burns*

Without economy none can be rich and with it few will be poor – *Samuel Johnson*

He who is taught to live upon little owes more to his father's wisdom than he that has a great deal left him does to his father's care – *William Penn*

The habit of saving is itself an education – *T. T. Munger*

The man who will live above his present circumstances is in great danger of soon living much beneath them – *Joseph Addison*

Economy is half the battle of life; it is not so hard to earn money as to spend it well – *Charles Haddon Spurgeon*

Ere you consult fancy, consult your purse – *Franklin*

Take care of the pence, and the pounds will take care of themselves – *Franklin*

Economy is the parent of integrity and liberty.

Men talk in raptures of youth and beauty, wit and sprightliness; but after seven years of union, not one of them is to be compared to good family management, which is seen at every meal, and felt every hour in the husband's purse.

No man is rich whose expenditure exceed his means; and no one is poor whose incomings exceed his outgoings.

Economy is frequently a way of spending money without getting any fun out of it.

Take care to be an economist in prosperity; there is no fear of your not being one in adversity.

See also FRUGALITY.

EDUCATION

A human being is not, in any proper sense, a human being till he is educated – *Horace Mann*

The great end of education is to discipline rather than to furnish the mind; to train it to the use of its own powers, rather than fill it with the accumulations of others – *Tryon Edwards*

An investment in knowledge always pays the best interest – *Benjamin Franklin*

Observation more than books, experience rather than persons, are the prime educators – *Amos Bronson Alcott*

Education is a companion which no misfortune can depress – *Varle*

Educate men without religion, and you make them but clever devils – *Duke of Wellington*

Capacity without education is deplorable, and education without capacity is thrown away – *Sádi*

The parent who sends his son out into the world uneducated defrauds the community of a useful citizen, and bequeaths a nuisance – *James Kent*

The true object of education should be to train one to think clearly and act rightly – *H. J. Van Dyke*

An industrious and virtuous education of children is a better inheritance for them than a great estate – *Joseph Addison*

The secret of education lies in respecting the pupil – *Ralph Waldo Emerson*

Education is the cheap defence of nations – *Edmund Burke*

Instruction ends in the schoolroom but education ends only with life – *Frederick William Robertson*

The best education in the world is that got by struggling to get a living – *Wendell Phillips*

Education is a debt due from the present to future generations – *George Peabody*

The aim of education should be to convert the mind into a living fountain, and not a reservoir – *John M. Mason*

Education commences at the mother's knee – *Hosea Ballou*

The wisest man may always learn something from the humblest peasant – *J. P. Senn*

Public instruction should be the first object of government – *Napoleon Bonaparte*

All who have meditated on the art of governing mankind have been convinced that the fate of empires depends on the education of youth – *Aristotle*

It is by education I learn to do by choice what other men do by the constraint of fear – *Aristotle*

Never educate a child to be a gentleman or lady only, but to be a man, a woman – *Herbert Spencer*

It is on the sound education of the people that the security and destiny of every nation chiefly rest – *Lajos Kossuth*

'Tis education forms the common mind; / Just as the twig is bent, the tree's inclined – *Alexander Pope*

The first thing education teaches you is to walk alone – *Trader Horn*

There are obviously two educations. One should teach us how to make a living and the other how to live – *James Truslow Adams*

Finding out – not knowledge – is the spring which makes life fascinating.

Education is the apprenticeship of life.

The aim of education should be to teach us rather how to think, than what to think.

We speak of educating our children. Do we know that our children also educate us?

Planting colleges and filling them with studious young men and women is planting seed corn for the world.

The public mind is educated quickly by events – slowly by arguments.

Education is a better safeguard of liberty than a standing army.

The poorest education that teaches self-control is better than the best that neglects it.

The education of the human mind commences in the cradle.

Every day's experience shows how much more actively education goes on out of the schoolroom than in it.

The true order of learning should be, first, what is necessary; second what is useful; and third, what is ornamental.

No woman is educated who is not equal to the successful management of a family.

See also INSTRUCTION, LEARNING.

EFFORT

Things don't turn up in this world until somebody turns them up – *James Abram Garfield*

The fact is, nothing comes; at least, nothing good. All has to be fetched – *Charles Buxton*

If you would relish food, labour for it before you take it; if enjoy clothing, pay for it before you wear it; if you would sleep soundly, take a clear conscience to bed with you – *Benjamin Franklin*

Labour is the real measure of the exchangeable value of all commodities.

The tree falls not at the first stroke.

EGOTISM

The more anyone speaks of himself, the less he likes to hear another talked of – *Johann Kaspar Lavater*

Do you wish men to speak well of you? Then never speak well of yourself – *Blaise Pascal*

There's not one wise man among twenty that will praise himself – *William Shakespeare*

The personal pronoun 'I', might well be the coat of arms of some individuals – *Antoine Rivarol*

The reason why lovers are never weary of one another is this – they are ever talking of themselves – *François de La Rochefoucauld*

The more you speak of yourself, the more you are likely to lie.

An egotist is a person of low taste more interested in himself than in me.

ELOQUENCE

True eloquence consists in saying all that is proper, and nothing more – *François de La Rochefoucauld*

Brevity is a great charm of eloquence – *Cicero*

Action is eloquence, and the eyes of the ignorant / More learned than the ears – *William Shakespeare*

It is but a poor eloquence which only shows that the orator can talk – *Joshua Reynolds*

Eloquence is in the assembly not merely in the speaker – *William Pitt*

Eloquence is logic on fire – *Lyman Beecher*

There is no eloquence without a man behind it – *Ralph Waldo Emerson*

Eloquence is the transference of thought and emotion from one heart to another – *John B. Gough*

There is not less eloquence in the voice, the eye, the gesture, than in words – *La Rochefoucauld*

Talking and eloquence are not the same – *Ben Jonson*

The prime purpose of eloquence is to keep other people from speaking.

The truest eloquence is that which holds us too mute for applause.

Those who would make us feel must feel themselves.

Eloquence is vehement simplicity.

Speech is the body; thought, the soul, and suitable action the life of eloquence.

See also ORATORY.

EMPIRE

As a general truth, nothing is more opposed to the well-being and freedom of men, than vast empires – *Alexis de Tocqueville*

Extended empire, like expanded gold, exchanges solid strength for feeble splendour – *Samuel Johnson*

It is not their long reigns, nor their frequent changes which occasion the fall of empires, but their abuse of power – *George Crabbe*

EMPLOYMENT

Employment is nature's physician, and is essential to human happiness
– *Galen*

Employment gives health, sobriety and morals – *Daniel Webster*

The devil never tempted a man whom he found judiciously employed –
Charles Haddon Spurgeon

The safe and general antidote against sorrow is employment – *Samuel Johnson*

The wise prove, and the foolish confess, by their conduct, that a life of
employment is the only life worth leading – *William Paley*

Occupation is one great source of enjoyment. No man, properly
occupied, was ever miserable – *L. E. Landon*

The employer generally gets the employees he deserves – *Walter Gilbey*

Be always employed about some rational thing, that the devil find thee
not idle.

He that does not bring up his son to some honest calling and employment, brings him up to be a thief – *Jewish maxim*

Not to enjoy life, but to employ life, ought to be our aim and inspiration.

EMPTINESS

Four things are grievously empty; a head without brains, a wit without
judgement, a heart without honesty, and a purse without money.

EMULATION

Emulation admires and strives to imitate great actions; envy is only
moved to malice – *Honoré de Balzac*

Emulation is the devil-shadow of aspiration – *George Macdonald*

Where there is emulation, there will be vanity; where there is vanity,
there will be folly – *Samuel Johnson*

There is a long and wearisome step between admiration and imitation –
Jean Paul Richter

Without emulation we sink into mediocrity, for nothing great or excellent can be done without it.

ENCOURAGEMENT

Correction does much, but encouragement does more – *Johann Wolfgang
von Goethe*

It is more pleasing to see smoke brightening into flame, than flame
sinking into smoke – *Samuel Johnson*

END

Let the end try the man – *William Shakespeare*

If well thou hast begun, go on; it is the end that crowns us, not the fight – *Robert Herrick*

The end crowns all, / And that old common arbitrator, Time, / Will one day end it – *Shakespeare*

ENDURANCE

The greater the difficulty, the more glory in surmounting – *Epicurus*

The palm-tree grows best beneath a ponderous weight, and even so the character of man – *Lajos Kossuth*

There is nothing in the world so much admired as a man who knows how to bear unhappiness with courage – *Seneca*

Our strength often increases in proportion to the obstacles imposed upon it – *Paul de Rapin*

He conquers who endures – *Persius*

ENEMIES

If we could read the secret history of our enemies we should find in each man's life sorrow and suffering enough to disarm all hostility – *Henry Wadsworth Longfellow*

There is no little enemy – *Benjamin Franklin*

Observe your enemies, for they first find out your faults – *Antisthenes*

Men of sense often learn from their enemies. It is from their foes, not their friends, that cities learn the lesson of building high walls and ships of war; and this lesson saves their children, their homes, and their properties – *Aristophanes*

They are our outward consciences / And preachers to us all – *William Shakespeare*

In order to have an enemy, one must be somebody – *Mme Swetchine*

Heat not a furnace for your foe so hot / That it do singe yourself – *Shakespeare*

If you want enemies, excel others; if friends, let others excel you – *Charles Caleb Colton*

Our enemies come nearer the truth in the opinions they form of us than we do in our opinion of ourselves – *François de La Rochefoucauld*

O wise man, wash your hands of that friend who associates with your enemies – *Sádi*

The fine and noble way to destroy a foe is not to kill him; with kindness you may so change him that he shall cease to be so; then he's slain.

Have you fifty friends? It is not enough. Have you one enemy? It is too much – *Italian proverb*

It is much safer to reconcile an enemy than to conquer him; victory may deprive him of his poison, but reconciliation of his will.

We should never make enemies, if for no other reason, because it is so hard to behave toward them as we ought.

It is the enemy whom we do not suspect who is the most dangerous.

I am persuaded that he who is capable of being a bitter enemy can never possess the necessary virtues that constitute a true friend.

Did a person but know the value of an enemy, he would purchase him with pure gold.

ENERGY

This world belongs to the energetic – *Ralph Waldo Emerson*

Energy will do anything that can be done in the world – *Johann Wolfgang von Goethe*

To think we are able is almost to be so – *Samuel Smiles*

He alone has energy who cannot be deprived of it – *Johann Kaspar Lavater*

The reward of a thing well done is to have done it – *Emerson*

The wise and active conquer difficulties by daring to attempt them.

ENJOYMENT

Gratitude is the memory of the heart – *Lydia Maria Child*

Sleep, riches, health, and so every blessing, are not truly and fully enjoyed till after they have been interrupted – *Jean Paul Richter*

Those who would enjoyment gain must find it in the purpose they pursue.

He scatters enjoyment, who enjoys much; and he will enjoy much who scatters enjoyments to others.

Whatever can lead an intelligent being to the exercise of enjoyment, contributes more to his happiness than the highest sensual or mere bodily pleasures. The one feeds the soul, while the other only exhausts the frame, and too often injures the immortal part.

All solitary enjoyments quickly pall, or become painful.

See also PLEASURE.

ENTERPRISE

Kites rise against, not with the wind. No man ever worked his passage anywhere in a dead calm – *John Neal*

Attempt the end, and never stand to doubt; / Nothing's so hard, but search will find it out – *Robert Herrick*

ENTHUSIASM

Nothing great was ever achieved without it – *Ralph Waldo Emerson*

The sense of this word among the Greeks affords the noblest definition of it; enthusiasm signifies 'God in us' – *Mme de Staël*

Opposition always inflames the enthusiast, never converts him – *Johann Christoph Friedrich von Schiller*

All noble enthusiasms pass through a feverish stage, and grow wiser and more serene – *William Ellery Channing*

Every production of genius must be the production of enthusiasm – *Benjamin Disraeli*

No wild enthusiast ever yet could rest, / Till half mankind were, like himself, possessed – *William Cowper*

Enthusiasm flourishes in adversity, kindles in the hour of danger, and awakens to deeds of renown.

Nothing is so contagious as enthusiasm.

Great designs are not accomplished without enthusiasm.

Enthusiasm is the strongest motive force for production.

ENVY

Envy has no other quality but that of detracting from virtue – *Livy*

Envy is a passion so full of cowardice and shame, that nobody ever had the confidence to own it – *Earl of Rochester*

Whoever feels pain in hearing a good character of his neighbour will feel a pleasure in the reverse – *Benjamin Franklin*

Fools may our scorn, not envy raise, / For envy is a kind of praise – *John Gay*

All envy is proportionate to desire – *Samuel Johnson*

The truest mark of being born with great qualities is being born without envy – *François de La Rochefoucauld*

Envy feels not its own happiness but when it may be compared with the misery of others – *Johnson*

There is power in ambition, pleasure in luxury, and pelf in covetousness; but envy can gain nothing but vexation – *Michel Eyquem de Montaigne*

Base rivals maliciously aspire to gain renown, / By standing up, and pulling others down – *John Dryden*

Envy always implies conscious inferiority wherever it resides – *Pliny the Younger*

Envy is so shameful a passion that we never dare to acknowledge it – *La Rochefoucauld*

Envy, like the scorpion confined within a circle of fire, will sting itself to death – *Charles Caleb Colton*

As a moth gnaws a garment, so doth envy consume a man – *St John Chrysostom*

The envious man grows lean at the success of his neighbour – *Horace*

If we did but know how little some enjoy of the great things that they possess, there would not be much envy in the world.

Envy is like a fly that passes all a body's sounder parts, and dwells upon the sores.

There is no surer mark of the absence of the highest moral and intellectual qualities than a cold reception of excellence.

Base envy withers at another's joy, and hates the excellence it cannot reach.

Envy, like the worm, never runs but to the fairest fruit.

Envy is but the smoke of low estate, / Ascending still against the fortunate.

No crime is so great to envy as daring to excel.

See also COVETOUSNESS, JEALOUSY.

EPITAPHS

Do ye not laugh, O, listening friends, when men praise those dead whose virtues they discovered not when living?

If all would speak as kindly of the living as in epitaphs they do of the dead, slander and censorious gossip would soon be strangers in the world.

EQUALITY

All men are by nature equal, made all of the same earth by the same Creator and however we deceive ourselves, as dear to God is the poor peasant as the mighty prince – *Giuseppe Mazzini*

By the law of God, given by him to humanity, all men are free, are brothers and are equals – *Mazzini*

In the gates of eternity the black hand and the white hold each other with an equal clasp – *Lucy Stone*

Liberty, equality – bad principles! The only true principle for humanity is justice; and justice to the feeble is protection and kindness – *Henri Frédéric Amiel*

It is not true that equality is a law of nature. Nature has no equality. Its sovereign law is subordination and dependence – *Marquis de Vauvenargues*

If by saying that all men are born free and equal you mean that they are all equally born, it is true, but true in no other sense; birth, talent, labour, virtue and providence, are forever making differences – *Eugene Edwards*

Let them case their hearts with prate of equal rights, which man never knew – *Lord Byron*

So far is it from being true that men are naturally equal, that no two
people can be half an hour together but one shall acquire an evident
superiority over the other – *Samuel Johnson*

Some must follow, and some command though all are made of clay –
Henry Wadsworth Longfellow

Whatever difference there may appear to be in men's fortunes, there is
still a certain compensation of good and ill in all that makes them
equal – *Pierre Charron*

The less enterprising and less hard working cannot be made equal by
simply cutting down the achievement of the enterprising and the
striving – *Lee Kuan Yew*

Woman was made from the rib of man, not from his head to top him, nor
from his feet to be trampled upon, but from out of his side, under his
arm to be protected, and close to his heart to be loved.

Equality is the share of everyone at their advent upon earth; and equality
is also theirs when placed beneath it.

See also LEVELLERS.

ERROR

Men are apt to prefer a prosperous error to an afflicted truth – *Jeremy
Taylor*

A man should never be ashamed to own he has been in the wrong, which
is but saying, in other words, that he is wiser today than he was
yesterday – *Alexander Pope*

Our greatest glory is not in never falling, but in rising every time we fall –
Confucius

Error of opinion may be tolerated where reason is left free to combat it –
Thomas Jefferson

Error is not a fault of our knowledge, but a mistake of our judgement
giving assent to that which is not true – *John Locke*

Sometimes we may learn more from a man's errors than from his virtues
– *Henry Wadsworth Longfellow*

From the errors of others a wise man corrects his own – *Publius Syrus*

To make no mistakes is not in the power of man; but from their errors and
mistakes the wise and good learn wisdom for the future – *Plutarch*

Honest error is to be pitied, not ridiculed – *Lord Chesterfield*

There will be mistakes in divinity while men preach, and errors in
governments while men govern – *Dudley Carleton*

Find earth where grows no weed, and you may find a heart wherein no
error grows.

No tempting form of error is without some latent charm derived from
truth.

In all science error precedes the truth and it is better it should go first than
   last.
The least error should humble, but we should never permit even the
   greatest to discourage us.

ESTEEM

The chief ingredients in the composition of those qualities that gain
   esteem and praise are good nature, truth, good sense and good
   breeding – *Joseph Addison*
The esteem of wise and good men is the greatest of all temporal
   encouragements to virtue – *Edmund Burke*
Esteem has more engaging charms than friendship – *François de La
   Rochefoucauld*
It is difficult to esteem a man as highly as he would wish – *Marquis de
   Vauvenargues*
Esteem cannot be where there is no confidence; and there can be no
   confidence where there is no respect.
All true love is founded on esteem.

ESTIMATION

A life spent worthily should be measured by deeds, not years – *Richard
   Brinsley Sheridan*
It is seldom that a man labours well in his minor department unless he
   overrates it. It is lucky for us that the bee does not look upon the
   honeycomb in the same light we do – *Richard Whately*
Men judge us by the success of our efforts. God looks at the efforts
   themselves – *Charlotte Elizabeth*
To judge of the real importance of an individual, we should think of the
   effect his death would produce.

ETERNITY

Eternity is a negative idea clothed with a positive name – *William Paley*
Eternity looks grander and kinder if time grows meaner and more hostile
   – *Thomas Carlyle*
The thought of eternity consoles for the shortness of life – *Chrétien
   Guillaume de Malesherbes*
Let me dream that love goes with us to the shore unknown – *Felicia
   Dorothea Hemans*
No man can pass into eternity, for he is already in it.
This is the world of seeds, of causes, and of tendencies; the other is
   the world of harvests and results and of perfected and eternal
   consequences.

ETIQUETTE

Good taste rejects excessive nicety; it treats little things as little things, and is not hurt by them – *François de Fénelon*

We must conform, to a certain extent, to the conventionalities of society, for they are the ripened results of a varied and long experience.

EVASION

Evasions are the common shelter of the hard-hearted, the false, and the impotent when called upon to assist; the real great alone plan instantaneous help, even when their looks or words presage difficulties – *Johann Kaspar Lavater*

Evasion is unworthy of us, and is always the intimate of equivocation – *Honoré de Balzac*

Evasion, like equivocation, comes generally from a cowardly or a deceiving spirit or from both; afraid to speak out its sentiments, or from guile concealing them.

EVENING

There is an evening twilight of the heart, when its wild passion waves are lulled to rest – *Fitz-Greene Halleck*

Evening is the delight of virtuous age; it seems an emblem of the tranquil close of a busy life – serene, placid, and mild.

EVENTS

In today already walks tomorrow – *Samuel Taylor Coleridge*

Coming events cast their shadows before.

EVIDENCE

Upon any given point, contradictory evidence seldom puzzles the man who has mastered the laws of evidence, but he knows little of the laws of evidence who has not studied the unwritten law of the human heart.

Hear one side and you will be in the dark; hear both sides, and all will be clear.

EVILS

Evil is in antagonism with the entire creation – *Johann Heinrich Daniel Zschokke*

If we rightly estimate what we call good and evil, we shall find it lies much in comparison – *John Locke*

Physical evils destroy themselves, or they destroy us – *Jean Jacques Rousseau*

This is the course of every evil deed that, propagating still it brings forth evil – *Samuel Taylor Coleridge*

To be free from evil thoughts is God's best gift – *Aeschylus*

The first lesson of history is that evil is good – *Ralph Waldo Emerson*

Good has but one enemy, the evil; but the evil has two enemies, the good and itself – *Johannes von Müller*

There is nothing truly evil, but what is within us; the rest is either natural or accidental – *Sir Philip Sidney*

We sometimes learn more from the sight of evil than from an example of good; and it is well to accustom ourselves to profit by the evil which is so common, while that which is good is so rare – *Blaise Pascal*

The lives of the best of us are spent in choosing between evils – *Junius*

If you do what you should not, you must bear what you would not – *Benjamin Franklin*

He who is in evil is also in the punishment of evil – *Emanuel Swedenborg*

Much that we call evil is really good in disguise; and we should not quarrel rashly with adversities not yet understood, nor overlook the mercies often bound up in them – *Sir Thomas Browne*

The evil that men do lives after them; / The good is oft interred with their bones – *William Shakespeare*

Evils in the journey of life are like the hills which alarm travellers on their road. Both appear great at a distance, but when we approach them we find they are far less insurmountable than we had conceived – *Charles Caleb Colton*

There is some soul of goodness in things evil, / Would men observingly distil it out – *Shakespeare*

Every evil to which we do not succumb is a benefactor. As the Sandwich Islander believes that the strength and valour of the enemy he kills passes into himself, so we gain the strength of the temptation we resist – *Emerson*

There are thousands hacking at the branches of evil to one who is striking at the root – *Henry David Thoreau*

There are three modes of bearing the ills of life: by indifference, which is the most common; by philosophy, which is the most ostentatious; and by religion, which is the most effectual – *Colton*

In the history of man it has been very generally the case, that when evils have grown insufferable they have touched the point of cure – *E. H. Chapin*

Evil is wrought by want of thought, as well as by want of heart – *Thomas Hood*

As surely as God is good, so surely there is no such thing as necessary evil – *Robert Southey*

Evil spreads as necessarily as disease – *George Eliot*

By the very constitution of our nature, moral evil is its own curse.

It is some compensation for great evils, that they enforce great lessons.

All physical evils are so many beacon lights to warn us from vice.

He who does evil that good may come, pays a toll to the devil to let him into heaven.

If we could annihilate evil we should annihilate hope, and hope is the avenue of faith.

It is a great evil not to be able to bear an evil.

We cannot do evil to others without doing it to ourselves.

It is a proof of our natural bias to evil, that in all things good, gain is harder and slower than loss; but in all things bad or evil, getting is quicker and easier than getting rid of them.

For every evil there is a remedy, or there is not; if there is one I try to find it; and if there is not, I never mind it.

The evil is half cured whose cause we know.

Man creates the evil he endures.

EVIL SPEAKING

A good word is an easy obligation; but not to speak ill requires only our silence, which costs us nothing – *John Tillotson*

Ill deeds are doubled with an evil word – *William Shakespeare*

How much better it is that he should speak ill of me to all the world, than all the world speak ill of me to him – *Torquato Tasso*

Where the speech is corrupted, the mind is also – *Seneca*

To speak ill upon knowledge shows a want of charity; to speak ill upon suspicion shows a want of honesty. To know evil of others and not speak it is sometimes discretion; to speak evil of others and not know it is always dishonesty.

When will talkers refrain from evil speaking? When listeners refrain from evil hearing.

EXAGGERATION

There is a sort of harmless liars, frequently to be met with in company, who deal much in the marvellous. Their usual intention is to please and entertain: but as men are most delighted with what they conceive to be truth, these people mistake the means of pleasing, and incur universal blame – *David Hume*

Exaggerated language employed on trivial occasions spoils that simplicity and singleness of mind so necessary to a right judgement of ourselves and others.

Those who exaggerate in their statements belittle themselves.

Some men can never state an ordinary fact in ordinary terms. All their geese are swans, till you see the birds.

There is no strength in exaggeration; even the truth is weakened by being expressed too strongly.

Exaggeration, as to rhetoric, is using a vast force to lift a feather; as to morals and character, it is using falsehood to lift oneself out of the confidence of one's fellow men.

There are some persons who would not for their lives tell a direct and wilful lie, but who so exaggerate that it seems as if for their lives they could not tell the exact truth.

EXAMPLE

There is a transcendent power in example. We reform others unconsciously, when we walk uprightly – *Mme Swetchine*

People seldom improve when they have no model but themselves to copy after – *Oliver Goldsmith*

Nothing is so infectious as example – *Charles Kingsley*

We can do more good by being good, than in any other way – *Rowland Hill*

Example is the school of mankind; they will learn at no other – *Edmund Burke*

Noble examples stir us up to noble actions, and the very history of large and public souls inspires a man with generous thoughts – *Seneca*

I am satisfied that we are less convinced by what we hear than by what we see – *Herodotus*

It is certain that either wise bearing or ignorant carriage is caught, as men take diseases, one of another: therefore let men take heed of their company – *William Shakespeare*

No man is so insignificant as to be sure his example can do no hurt – *Lord Clarendon*

A wise and good man will turn examples of all sorts to his own advantage. The good he will make his patterns, and strive to equal or excel them. The bad he will by all means avoid – *Thomas à Kempis*

Thou canst not rebuke in children what they see practised in thee. Till reason be ripe, examples direct more than precepts. Such as is thy behaviour before thy children's faces, such is theirs behind thy back – *Francis Quarles*

The conscience of children is formed by the influences that surround them; their notions of good and evil are the result of the moral atmosphere they breathe – *Jean Paul Richter*

Of all commentaries upon the Scriptures, good examples are the best and the liveliest – *John Donne*

Precept is instruction written in the sand. The tide flows over it, and the record is gone. Example is graven on the rock, and the lesson is not soon lost – *William Ellery Channing*

There are bad examples that are worse than crimes; and more states have perished from the violation of morality than from the violation of law – *Charles de Montesquieu*

Examples of vicious courses, practised in a domestic circle, corrupt more readily and more deeply, when we behold them in persons of authority – *Juvenal*

Live with wolves, and you will learn to howl – *Spanish proverb*

Not the cry but the flight of the wild duck leads the flock to fly and follow – *Chinese proverb*

Example is more forcible than precept. People look at my six days in the week to see what I mean on the seventh.

A father that whipped his son for swearing, and swore himself whilst he whipped him, did more harm by his example than good by his correction.

The first great gift we can bestow on others is a good example.

One watch set right will do to set many by; one that goes wrong may be the means of misleading a whole neighbourhood; and the same may be said of example.

You can preach a better sermon with your life than with your lips.

Whatever parent gives his children good instruction, and sets them at the same time a bad example, may be considered as bringing them food in one hand, and poison in the other.

EXCELLENCE

Whose virtue and whose general graces speak / That which none else can utter – *William Shakespeare*

Those who attain to any excellence commonly spend life in some one single pursuit, for excellence is not often gained upon easier terms – *Samuel Johnson*

Nothing is such an obstacle to the production of excellence as the power of producing what is good with ease and rapidity.

Excellence is never granted to man but as the reward of labour.

EXCELSIOR

People never improve unless they look to some standard or example higher and better than themselves – *Tryon Edwards*

While we converse with what is above us, we do not grow old, but grow young – *Ralph Waldo Emerson*

Who shoots at the midday sun, though sure he shall never hit the mark, yet sure he is that he shall shoot higher than he who aims but at a bush – *Sir Philip Sidney*

Fearless minds climb soonest unto crowns – *William Shakespeare*

O sacred hunger of ambitious minds! – *Edmund Spenser*

Too low they build who build beneath the stars.

See also ASPIRATION.

EXCESS

Let's teach ourselves that honourable stop, / Not to outsport discretion – *William Shakespeare*

The excesses of our youth are drafts upon our old age, payable with interest, about thirty years after date – *Charles Caleb Colton*

They are as sick that surfeit with too much as they that starve with nothing – *Shakespeare*

Pliability and liberality, when not restrained within due bounds, must ever turn to the ruin of their possessor – *Tacitus*

The desire of power in excess caused angels to fall; the desire of knowledge in excess caused man to fall; but in charity is no excess, neither can man or angels come into danger by it – *Francis Bacon*

There can be no excess to love, to knowledge, to beauty, when these attributes are considered in the purest sense – *Ralph Waldo Emerson*

Too much noise deafens us; too much light blinds us; too great a distance, or too much of promixity equally prevents us from being able to see; too long or too short a discourse obscures our knowledge of a subject; too much of truth stuns us – *Blaise Pascal*

Excess generally causes reaction and produces a change in the opposite direction, whether it be in the seasons, or in individuals, or in government – *Plato*

EXCITEMENT

Violent excitement exhausts the mind, and leaves it withered and sterile – *François de Fénelon*

Never be afraid because the community teems with excitement. Silence and death are dreadful. The rush of life, the vigour of earnest men, and the conflict of realities, invigorate, cleanse, and establish the truth – *Henry Ward Beecher*

Excitement is so engraven on our nature that it may be regarded as an appetite; and like all other appetites it is not sinful unless indulged unlawfully, or to excess.

Religious excitement is to the steady influence of Christian principle as is the flush of fever to the uniform glow of health.

Excitement is of impulse, while earnestness is of principle; the one a glow, the other a fire; the one common, the other rare; the one theorizes, the other acts; the one needs company, the other can live alone. The two are oftener found in separation than in union, though neither is incompatible with the other.

EXCUSES

He that is good for making excuses is seldom good for anything else – *Benjamin Franklin*

Oftentimes excusing of a fault / Doth make the fault the worse by the excuse – *William Shakespeare*

'Tis not the eating, nor 'tis not the drinking that is to be blamed, but the excess – *John Selden*

Uncalled for excuses are practical confessions.

One of the most labour-saving inventions of today is tomorrow.

EXERCISE

I take the true definition of exercise to be labour without weariness – *Samuel Johnson*

The only way for a rich man to be healthy is by exercise and abstinence, to live as if he was poor; which are esteemed the worst parts of poverty – *William Temple*

The wise, for cure, on exercise depend. / Better to hunt in fields for health unbought / Than fee the doctor for a nauseous draught – *John Dryden*

Such is the constitution of man, that labour may be styled its own reward. Nor will any external incitements be requisite if it be considered how much happiness is gained, and how much misery escaped, by frequent and violent agitation of the body – *Johnson*

Health is the vital principle of bliss; and exercise, of health.

There are many troubles which you cannot cure by the Bible and the hymnbook, but which you can cure by a good perspiration and a breath of fresh air.

It is exercise alone that supports the spirits and keeps the mind in vigour.

EXERTION

Every man's task is his life preserver – *Ralph Waldo Emerson*

Experience shows that success is due less to ability than to zeal. The winner is he who gives himself to his work, body and soul – *Charles Buxton*

Never live in hope or expectation while your arms are folded. God helps those that help themselves. Providence smiles on those who put their shoulders to the wheel that propels to wealth and happiness.

EXPECTATION

Nothing is so good as it seems beforehand – *George Eliot*

'Tis expectation makes a blessing dear; heaven were not heaven if we knew what it were – *Sir John Suckling*

We love to expect, and when expectation is either disappointed or gratified, we want to be again expecting – *Samuel Johnson*

With what a heavy and retarding weight does expectation load the wing of time.

We part more easily with what we possess than with the expectation of what we wish for: and the reason of it is that what we expect is always greater than what we enjoy.

EXPERIENCE

Experience is the extract of suffering – *Arthur Helps*

Experience is the name men give to their follies or their sorrows – *Alfred de Musset*

No man was ever so completely skilled in the conduct of life as not to receive new information from age and experience – *Terence*

Experience joined with common sense, / To mortals is a providence – *Matthew Green*

He cannot be a perfect man, / Not being tried and tutor'd in the world: / Experience is by industry achiev'd / And perfected by the swift course of time – *William Shakespeare*

When I was young I was sure of everything; in a few years, having been mistaken a thousand times, I was not half so sure of most things as I was before; at present, I am hardly sure of anything but what God has revealed to me – *John Wesley*

To wilful men, / The injuries that they themselves procure / Must be their schoolmasters – *Shakespeare*

It may serve as a comfort to us in all our calamities and afflictions that he who loses anything and gets wisdom by it is a gainer by the loss – *Sir Roger L'Estrange*

That man is wise to some purpose who gains his wisdom at the expense and from the experience of another – *Plautus*

A jewel that I have purchased at an infinite rate – *Shakespeare*

Each succeeding day is the scholar of that which went before it – *Publius Syrus*

Experience takes dreadfully high school-wages, but he teaches like no other – *Thomas Carlyle*

We are often prophets to others, only because we are our own historians – *Mme Swetchine*

Experience, that chill touchstone whose sad proof reduces all things from their false hue – *Lord Byron*

Experience teaches slowly, and at the cost of mistakes – *James Anthony Froude*

Experience, if wisdom's friend, her best; if not, her foe.

Life consists in the alternate process of learning and unlearning, but it is often wiser to unlearn than to learn.

Experience – making all futures, fruits of all the pasts.

Experience is the shroud of illusions.

This is one of the sad conditions of life, that experience is not transmissible. No man will learn from the suffering of another; he must suffer himself.

However learned or eloquent, man knows nothing truly that he has not learned from experience.

No man was ever endowed with a judgement so correct and judicious, but that circumstances, time, and experience, would teach him something new.

Experience is simply the name we give to our mistakes.

The most instructive experiences are those in everyday life.

Error is the discipline through which we advance.

Experience shows that success is due less to ability.

Maturity consists in no longer being deceived by oneself.

Experience is a comb, which nature gives to men when they are bald.

EXTRAVAGANCE

Riches are for spending, and spending for honour and good actions; therefore extraordinary expense must be limited by the worth of the occasion – *Francis Bacon*

Buy what thou hast no need of, and ere long thou shalt sell thy necessaries – *Benjamin Franklin*

Gain may be temporary and uncertain; but ever while you live, expense is constant and certain: and it is easier to build two chimneys than to keep one in fuel – *Franklin*

He that is extravagant will soon become poor, and poverty will enforce dependence, and invite corruption – *Samuel Johnson*

The passion of acquiring riches in order to support a vain expense corrupts the purest souls – *François de Fénelon*

Waste of time is the most extravagant and costly of all expenses – *Theophrastus*

The covetous man never has money; the prodigal will have none shortly – *Ben Jonson*

Laws cannot prevent extravagance; and this perhaps is not always an evil to the public. A shilling spent idly by a fool may be picked up by a wiser person, who knows better what to do with it; it is, therefore, not lost – *Franklin*

A small leak will sink a great ship.

He that buys what he does not want, will soon want what he cannot buy.

The man who builds, and lacks wherewith to pay, / Provides a home from which to run away.

EXTREMES

The blast that blows loudest is soonest overblown – *Tobias Smollett*

Mistrust the man who finds everything good; the man who finds everything evil; and still more the man who is indifferent to everything – *Johann Kaspar Lavater*

The greatest flood has soonest ebb; the sorest tempest, the most sudden calm; the hottest love, the coldest end; and from the deepest desire often ensues the deadliest hate – *Socrates*

It is a hard but good law of fate, that as every evil, so every excessive power wears itself out – *Johann Gottfried Herder*

Neither great poverty nor great riches will hear reason – *Henry Fielding*

Too austere a philosophy makes few wise men; too rigorous politics, few good subjects; too hard a religion, few persons whose devotion is of long continuance – *Seigneur de Saint-Evremond*

No violent extremes endure; a sober moderation stands secure.

All extremes are error. The reverse of error is not truth, but error still. Truth lies between these extremes.

Extremes meet in almost everything: it is hard to tell whether the statesman at the top of the world, or the ploughman at the bottom, labours hardest.

Extreme views are never just; something always turns up which disturbs the calculations founded on their data.

Extremes, though contrary, have the like effects. Extreme heat kills, and so extreme cold; extreme love breeds satiety, and so extreme hatred; and too violent rigour tempts chastity, as does too much licence.

EYE

One of the most wonderful things in nature is a glance of the eye; it transcends speech; it is the bodily symbol of identity – *Ralph Waldo Emerson*

It is the eyes of other people that ruin us. If all but myself were blind I should neither want a fine house nor fine furniture – *Benjamin Franklin*

The balls of sight are so formed, that one man's eyes are spectacles to another, to read his heart with – *Samuel Johnson*

Men are born with two eyes, but only one tongue, in order that they should see twice as much as they say – *Charles Caleb Colton*

The eyes are the pioneers that first announce the soft tale of love – *Sextus Propertius*

Who has a daring eye tells downright truths and downright lies – *Johann Kaspar Lavater*

Where is any author in the world / Teaches such beauty as a woman's eye! – *William Shakespeare*

Lovers are angry, reconciled, entreat, thank, appoint, and finally speak all things by their eyes – *Michel Eyquem de Montaigne*

A wanton eye is the messenger of an unchaste heart – *Augustine*

Eyes are bold as lions, roving, running, leaping, here and there, far and near. They speak all languages; wait for no introduction; ask no leave of age or rank; respect neither poverty nor riches, neither learning nor power, nor virtue, nor sex, but intrude, and come again, and go through and through you in a moment of time. What inundation of life and thought is discharged from one soul into another through them! – *Emerson*

Men of cold passions have quick eyes – *Nathaniel Hawthorne*

Eyes will not see when the heart wishes them to be blind. Desire conceals truth, as darkness does the earth – *Seneca*

The heart's hushed secret in the soft dark eye – *L. E. Landon*

The intelligence of affection is carried on by the eye only. Good breeding has made the tongue falsify the heart and act a part of continued restraint, while Nature has preserved the eyes to herself, that she may not be disguised or misrepresented – *Joseph Addison*

Eyes raised toward heaven are always beautiful, whatever they may be – *Joseph Joubert*

Sweet silent rhetoric of persuading eyes – *William Davenant*

Her eyes are homes of silent prayer – *Alfred, Lord Tennyson*

A lover's eyes will gaze an eagle blind – *Shakespeare*

The eyes have one language everywhere – *Seventeenth-century proverb*

The eye speaks with an eloquence and truthfulness surpassing speech. It is the window out of which the winged thoughts often fly unwittingly. It is the tiny magic mirror on whose crystal surface the moods of feeling fitfully play, like the sunlight and shadow on a quiet stream.

The eye is the pulse of the soul; as physicians judge the heart by the pulse, so we by the eye.

The eye is the window of the soul.

Whatever of goodness emanates from the soul gathers its soft halo in the eyes; and if the heart be a lurking place of crime, the eyes are sure to betray the secret.

FACE

A good face is the best letter of recommendation – *Elizabeth I*

Look in the face of the person to whom you are speaking if you wish to know his real sentiments, for he can command his words more easily than his countenance – *Lord Chesterfield*

A cheerful face is nearly as good for an invalid as healthy weather – *Benjamin Franklin*

All men's faces are true, whatsoe'er their hands are – *William Shakespeare*

Truth makes the face of that person shine who speaks and owns it – *Robert South*

The faces which have charmed us the most escape us the soonest – *Walter Scott*

Features are the visible expression of the soul – the outward manifestation of the feeling and character within – *Tryon Edwards*

In thy face I see / The map of honour, truth and loyalty – *Shakespeare*

A beautiful face is a silent commendation – *Francis Bacon*

If we could but read it, every human being carries his life in his face, and is good-looking, or the reverse, as that life has been good or evil. On our features the fine chisels of thought and emotion are eternally at work – *Alexander Smith*

The countenance is the title-page which heralds the contents of the human volume, but like other title-pages it sometimes puzzles, often misleads, and often says nothing to the purpose.

The loveliest faces are to be seen by moonlight, when one sees half with the eye, and half with the fancy.

See also COUNTENANCE, LOOKS.

FACTION

A feeble government produces more factions than an oppressive one – *Fisher Ames*

Faction is the demon of discord armed with power to do endless mischief, and intent only on destroying whatever opposes its progress. Woe to that state in which it has found an entrance.

Faction is the excess and abuse of party. It begins when the first idea of private interest, preferred to public good, gets footing in the heart. It is always dangerous, yet always contemptible.

Seldom is faction's ire in haughty minds extinguished but by death; it oft, like flame suppressed, breaks forth again, and blazes higher.

FACTS

Facts are to the mind what food is to the body – *Edmund Burke*

There should always be some foundation of fact for the most airy fabric; pure invention is but the talent of a deceiver – *Lord Byron*

Facts are God's arguments; we should be careful never to misunderstand or pervert them – *Tryon Edwards*

Comment is free but facts are sacred – *C. P. Scott*

Any fact is better established by two or three good testimonies, than by a thousand arguments.

From principles is derived probability, but truth or certainty is obtained only from facts.

FAILINGS

Everyone has a wallet behind for his own failings, and one before for the failings of others – *Jean de La Fontaine*

If we had no failings ourselves we should not take so much pleasure in finding out those of others – *François de La Rochefoucauld*

Such is the force of envy and ill-nature that the failings of good men are more published to the world than their good deeds; and one fault of a well deserving man shall meet with more reproaches than all his virtues will with praise – *Nathaniel Parker Willis*

The finest composition of human nature, as well as the finest china, may have flaws in it, though the pattern may be of the highest value.

FAILURE

We mount to heaven mostly on the ruins of our cherished schemes, finding our failures were successes – *Amos Bronson Alcott*

Every failure is a step to success; every detection of what is false directs us toward what is true; every trial exhausts some tempting form of error – *William Whewell*

Failure is often God's own tool for carving some of the finest outlines in the character of his children; and, even in this life, bitter and crushing failures have often in them the germs of new and quite unimagined happiness – *Thomas Hodgkin*

He only is exempt from failures who makes no efforts – *Richard Whately*

They never fail who die in a great cause – *Lord Byron*

That word Fate is the refuge of every self-confessed failure – *Andrew Soutar*

Sometimes a noble failure serves the world as faithfully as a distinguished success.

In the lexicon of youth, which fate reserves for a bright manhood, there is no such word as fail.

A failure establishes only this, that our determination to succeed was not strong enough.

FAITH

All the scholastic scaffolding falls, as a ruined edifice, before one single word – faith – *Napoleon Bonaparte*

There is a limit where the intellect fails and breaks down, and this limit is where the questions concerning God, and freewill, and immortality arise – *Immanuel Kant*

Faith marches at the head of the army of progress. It is found beside the most refined life, the freest government, the profoundest philosophy, the noblest poetry, the purest humanity – *T. T. Munger*

We cannot live on probabilities. The faith in which we can live bravely and die in peace must be a certainty, so far as it professes to be a faith at all, or it is nothing – *James Anthony Froude*

Epochs of faith are epochs of fruitfulness; but epochs of unbelief, however glittering, are barren of all permanent good – *Johann Wolfgang von Goethe*

The saddest thing that can befall a soul is when it loses faith in God and woman – *Alexander Smith*

There never was found in any age of the world, either philosopher or sect, or law, or discipline which did so highly exalt the public good as the Christian faith – *Francis Bacon*

Despotism may govern without faith, but Liberty cannot – *Alexis de Tocqueville*

Faith evermore looks upward and describes objects remote; but reason can discover things only near – sees nothing that's above her – *Francis Quarles*

Science has sometimes been said to be opposed to faith, and inconsistent with it. But all science, in fact, rests on a basis of faith, for it assumes the permanence and uniformity of natural laws – a thing which can never be demonstrated – *Tryon Edwards*

The steps of faith fall on the seeming void, but find the rock beneath – *John Greenleaf Whittier*

When men cease to be faithful to their God, he who expects to find them so to each other will be much disappointed – *Bishop Horne*

To believe is to be strong. Doubt cramps energy. Belief is power – *Frederick William Robertson*

Faith is the root of all good works; a root that produces nothing is dead – *Bishop Wilson*

As the flower is before the fruit, so is faith before good works – *Richard Whately*

All I have seen teaches me to trust the Creator for all I have not seen – *Ralph Waldo Emerson*

Understanding is the wages of a lively faith; and faith is the reward of an humble ignorance – *Quarles*

Much knowledge of divine things is lost to us through want of faith – *Heraclitus*

Faith is like love: it cannot be forced. As trying to force love begets hatred, so trying to compel religious belief leads to unbelief – *Arthur Schopenhauer*

I, too, have loved and lost; but without faith there would be no light in all the world – *Helen Keller*

You may be deceived if you trust too much – but you will live in torment if you do not trust enough – *Frank Crane*

Faith must have adequate evidence else it is mere superstition.

Some wish they did, but no man disbelieves.

In actual life every great enterprise begins with and takes its first forward step in faith.

Man is not made to question, but adore.

Naturally, men are prone to spin themselves a web of opinions out of their own brain, and to have a religion that may be called their own. They are far readier to make themselves a faith, than to receive that which God hath formed to their hands; are far readier to receive a doctrine that tends to their carnal commodity, or honour, or delight, than one that tends to self-denial.

Faith is not reason's labour, but repose.

Faith makes the discords of the present the harmonies of the future.

Faith and works are like the light and heat of a candle; they cannot be separated.

What I admire in Columbus is not his having discovered a world, but his having gone to search for it on the faith of an opinion.

Faith is the pencil of the soul that pictures heavenly things.

While reason is puzzling herself about the mystery, faith is turning it into her daily bread and feeding on it thankfully in her heart of hearts.

Strike from mankind the principle of faith, and men would have no more history than a flock of sheep.

See also BELIEF.

FALSEHOOD

Falsehoods not only disagree with truths, but usually quarrel among themselves – *Daniel Webster*

The gain of lying is nothing else but not to be trusted of any, nor to be believed when we say the truth – *Walter Raleigh*

A liar begins with making falsehood appear like truth, and ends with making truth itself appear like falsehood – *William Shenstone*

He who tells a lie is not sensible how great a task he undertakes; for he must invent twenty more to maintain that one – *Alexander Pope*

It is more from carelessness about the truth, than from intention of lying, that there is so much falsehood in the world – *Samuel Johnson*

The telling of a falsehood is like the cut of a sabre; for though the wound may heal, the scar of it will remain – *Sádi*

Falsehood, like poison, will generally be rejected, when administered alone; but when blended with wholesome ingredients, may be swallowed unperceived – *Richard Whately*

A goodly apple rotten at the heart. / O, what a goodly outside falsehood hath! – *William Shakespeare*

Every lie, great or small, is the brink of a precipice, the depth of which nothing but Omniscience can fathom – *Charles Reade*

This above all: to thine own self be true; / And it must follow, as the night the day, / Thou canst not then be false to any man – *Shakespeare*

Dare to be true; nothing can need a lie.

A lie has always a certain amount of weight with those who wish to believe it.

None but cowards lie.

When Aristotle was asked what a man could gain by telling a falsehood, he replied, 'Never to be credited when he speaks the truth.'

Falsehood often lurks upon the tongue of him, who, by self-praise, seeks to enhance his value in the eyes of others.

See also DECEIT, LIARS, LYING

FAME

The way to fame is like the way to heaven, through much tribulation – *Laurence Sterne*

Fame is no sure test of merit, but only a probability of such; it is an accident, not a property of man – *Thomas Carlyle*

Fame is the perfume of heroic deeds – *Socrates*

I courted fame but as a spur to brave and honest deeds; who despises fame will soon renounce the virtues that deserve it – *David Mallet*

There is not in the world so toilsome a trade as the pursuit of fame: life concludes before you have so much as sketched your work – *Jean de La Bruyère*

Fame, like the river, is narrowest where it is bred, and broadest afar off – *William Davenant*

Few people make much noise after their deaths who did not do so while living – *William Hazlitt*

Our admiration of a famous man lessens upon our nearer acquaintance with him; and we seldom hear of a celebrated person without a catalogue of some of his weaknesses and infirmities – *Joseph Addison*

Even the best things are not equal to their fame – *Henry David Thoreau*

What a heavy burden is a name that has too soon become famous – *Voltaire*

I am not covetous for gold, / . . . / But if it be a sin to covet honour, / I am the most offending soul alive – *William Shakespeare*

Fame is a flower upon a dead man's heart – *William Motherwell*

If fame is only to come after death, I am in no hurry for it – *Martial*

To leave something so written, to after ages, that they should not willingly let it die – *Charles Caleb Colton*

Good fame is like fire; when you have kindled you may easily preserve it; but if you extinguish it, you will not easily kindle it again – *Francis Bacon*

Of all the possessions of this life fame is the noblest: when the body has sunk into the dust the great name still lives – *Johann Christoph Friedrich von Schiller*

To get a name can happen but to a few: it is one of the few things that cannot be bought. It is the free gift of mankind, which must be deserved before it will be granted, and is at last unwillingly bestowed – *Samuel Johnson*

Time has a doomsday book, on whose pages he is continually recording illustrious names. But as often as a new name is written there, an old one disappears. Only a few stand in illuminated characters never to be effaced – *Henry Wadsworth Longfellow*

Men's evil manners live in brass; their virtues / We write in water – *Shakespeare*

What is fame? The advantage of being known by people of whom you yourself know nothing, and for whom you care as little.

Fame, to the ambitious, is like salt water to the thirsty – the more one gets, the more he wants.

It often happens that those of whom we speak least on earth are best known in heaven.

Men think highly of those who rise rapidly in the world, whereas nothing rises quicker than dust, straw, and feathers.

A man who cannot win fame in his own age will have a very small chance of winning it from posterity.

In fame's temple there is always to be found a niche for rich dunces, importunate scoundrels, or successful butchers of the human race.

He who would acquire fame must not show himself afraid of censure. The dread of censure is the death of genius.

Men's fame is like their hair, which grows after they are dead, and with just as little use to them.

The man who wakes up and finds himself famous hasn't been asleep.

He who leaves the fame of good works after him does not die.

Always begin somewhere. You can't build a reputation on what you intend to do.

FAMILIARITY

All objects lose by too familiar a view – *John Dryden*

Though familiarity may not breed contempt, it takes off the edge of admiration – *William Hazlitt*

The confidant of my vices is my master, though he were my valet – *Johann Wolfgang von Goethe*

Familiarities are the aphides that imperceptibly suck out the juices intended for the germ of love – *Walter Savage Landor*

When a man becomes familiar with his goddess, she quickly sinks into a woman – *Joseph Addison*

Make not thy friend too cheap to thee, nor thyself to thy friend.

Be not too familiar with thy servants. At first it may beget love, but in the end it will breed contempt.

FAMILY

If I might control the literature of the household, I would guarantee the well-being of the church and state – *Francis Bacon*

'The last word' is the most dangerous of infernal machines, and the husband and wife should no more fight to get it than they would struggle for the possession of a lighted bombshell – *Douglas William Jerrold*

Woman is the salvation or the destruction of the family. She carries its destiny in the folds of her mantle – *Henri Frédéric Amiel*

All happy families resemble one another; every unhappy family is unhappy in its own way – *Leo Tolstoy*

Happy are the families where the government of parents is the reign of affection, and obedience of the children the submission of love.

As are families, so is society. If well ordered, well instructed, and well governed, they are the springs from which go forth the streams of national greatness and prosperity – of civil order and public happiness.

A happy family is but an earlier heaven.

FANATICISM

Of all things wisdom is the most terrified with epidemical fanaticism because, of all enemies, it is that against which she is the least able to furnish any kind of resource – *Edmund Burke*

We often excuse our own want of philanthropy by giving the name of fanaticism to the more ardent zeal of others – *Henry Wadsworth Longfellow*

The blind fanaticism of one foolish honest man may cause more evil than
* the united efforts of twenty rogues.

FASHION

It is the rule of rules, and the general law of all laws, that every person should observe the fashions of the place where he is – *Michel Eyquem de Montaigne*

Fashion is the science of appearances, and it inspires one with the desire to seem rather than to be – *E. H. Chapin*

Every generation laughs at the old fashions, but follows religiously the new – *Henry David Thoreau*

Fashion is, for the most part, nothing but the ostentation of riches – *John Locke*

A fop of fashion is the mercer's friend, the tailor's fool, and his own foe – *Johann Kaspar Lavater*

Change of fashions is the tax which industry imposes on the vanity of the rich – *Nicolas Sébastian Roch Camfort*

Avoid singularity. There may often be less vanity in following the new modes than in adhering to the old ones. It is true that the foolish invent them, but the wise may conform to, instead of contradicting them – *Joseph Joubert*

Those who seem to lead the public taste, are, in general, merely outrunning it in the direction it is spontaneously pursuing – *Thomas Babington Macaulay*

Fashion is only the attempt to realize art in living forms and social intercourse – *Oliver Wendell Holmes*

Fashion is the great governor of the world. It presides not only in matters of dress and amusement, but in law, physic, politics, religion, and all other things of the gravest kind. Indeed, the wisest man would be puzzled to give any better reason why particular forms in all these have been at certain times universally received, and at other times universally rejected, than that they were in, or out of fashion – *Henry Fielding*

To be happy is of far less consequence to the worshippers of fashion than to appear so; even pleasure itself they sacrifice to parade, and enjoyment to ostentation – *Charles Caleb Colton*

Fashion must be forever new, or she becomes insipid – *J. R. Lovell*

Be not too early in the fashion, nor too long out of it; not at any time in the extremes of it – *Lavater*

Fashion seldom interferes with nature without diminishing her grace and efficiency.

It is as absurd to suppose that everything fashionable is bad, as it would be to suppose that everything unfashionable is good.

FATE

What must be shall be; and that which is a necessity to him that struggles is little more than choice to him that is willing – *Seneca*

If fate means you to lose, give him a good fight anyhow – *William McFee*

If you believe in fate, believe in it, at least, for your good – *Ralph Waldo Emerson*

Fate is the friend of the good, the guide of the wise, the tyrant of the
    foolish, the enemy of the bad – *William Rounseville Alger*
All is created and goes according to order, yet o'er our lifetime rules an
    uncertain fate – *Johann Wolfgang von Goethe*
Fate is not the ruler, but the servant of Providence.
The things we don't want come more quickly than those we crave.
When things are at the worst they will mend.
Whosoever quarrels with his fate does not understand.
See also DESTINY, FORTUNE, PROVIDENCE.

FAULTS

We confess small faults, in order to insinuate that we have no great ones
    – *François de La Rochefoucauld*
You will find it less easy to uproot faults than to choke them by gaining
    virtues – *John Ruskin*
If thou wouldst bear thy neighbours' faults, cast thine eyes upon thine
    own – *Miguel de Molinos*
He who exhibits no faults is a fool or a hypocrite whom we should
    distrust – *Joseph Joubert*
We easily forget our faults when they are known only to ourselves – *La
    Rochefoucauld*
If we were faultless we should not be so much annoyed by the defects of
    those with whom we associate – *François de Fénelon*
Everyone is eagle-eyed to see another's faults and deformity – *John
    Dryden*
The greatest of faults is to be conscious of none – *Thomas Carlyle*
If you are pleased at finding faults, you are displeased at finding
    perfections – *Johann Kaspar Lavater*
Bad men excuse their faults; good men will leave them – *Ben Jonson*
Ten thousand of the greatest faults in our neighbours are of less conse-
    quence to us than one of the smallest in ourselves – *Richard Whately*
To find fault is easy; to do better may be difficult – *Plutarch*
He will be immortal who liveth till he be stoned by one without fault.
If the best man's faults were written on his forehead, he would draw his
    hat over his eyes.
We should correct our own faults by seeing how uncomely they appear
    in others.
No one sees the wallet on his own back, though every one carries two
    packs, one before, stuffed with the faults of his neighbours; the other
    behind, filled with his own.
To reprove small faults with undue vehemence is as absurd as if a man
    should take a great hammer to kill a fly on his friend's forehead.
People are commonly so employed in pointing out faults in those before

them, as to forget that some behind may at the same time be descanting on their own.

The wise man has his foibles as well as the fool. Those of the one are known to himself, and concealed from the world; while those of the other are known to the world, and concealed from himself.

To defend yourself for your fault is to commit another fault.

See also IMPERFECTION.

FEAR

Present fears / Are less than horrible imaginings – *William Shakespeare*

We often pretend to fear what we really despise, and more often to despise what we really fear – *Charles Caleb Colton*

In time we hate that which we often fear – *Shakespeare*

Fear is more painful to cowardice than death to true courage – *Sir Philip Sidney*

He who fears being conquered is sure of defeat – *Napoleon Bonaparte*

Early and provident fear is the mother of safety – *Edmund Burke*

Fear manifested invites danger; concealed cowards insult known ones – *Lord Chesterfield*

In morals, what begins in fear usually ends in wickedness; in religion, what begins in fear usually ends in fanaticism – *Anna Jameson*

No one loves the man whom he fears – *Aristotle*

Fear is the tax that conscience pays to guilt.

Fear is the mother of foresight.

There is great beauty in going through life without anxiety or fear.

Fear never robs tomorrow of its sorrow – it only robs today of its strength.

FEASTING

The road to people's hearts, I find, lies through their mouths – *Peter Pindar*

'Tis not the eating, nor 'tis not the drinking that is to be blamed, but the excess – *John Selden*

It is not the quality of the meat, but the cheerfulness of the guests, which makes the feast.

He who feasts every day, feasts no day.

He that feasts his body with banquets and delicate fare, and starves his soul for want of spiritual food, is like him that feasts his slave and starves his wife.

See also DINNER, EATING.

FEELINGS

There are moments and feelings which it is impossible to express in any
language – *Anatoly Scharansky*
Feeling in the young precedes philosophy, and often acts with a better
and more certain aim.
Strong feelings do not necessarily make a strong character.
Cultivate consideration for the feelings of other people if you would not
have your own injured.
Some people carry their hearts in their heads; very many carry their
heads in their hearts. The difficulty is to keep them apart, and yet
both actively working together.
Feelings come and go but principles stand fast.
The heart that is soonest awake to the flowers is always the first to be
touched by the thorns.
Thought is deeper than all speech; / Feeling deeper than all thought; /
Soul to souls can never teach / What unto themselves was taught.

FICKLENESS

They are the weakest-minded and the hardest-hearted men that most
love change – *John Ruskin*
Everything by starts, and nothing long – *John Dryden*
He wears his faith but as the fashion of his hat; it ever changes with the
next block – *William Shakespeare*
A fickle memory is bad; a fickle course of conduct is worse; but a fickle
heart and purposes, worst of all.

FICTION

I have often maintained that fiction may be much more instructive than
real history – *John Foster*
The most influential books of fiction repeat, rearrange, and clarify the
lessons of life – *Robert Louis Stevenson*
Every fiction that has ever laid strong hold on human belief is the
mistaken image of some great truth.
See also BOOKS, NOVELS, ROMANCE.

FIDELITY

Fidelity is the sister of justice – *Horace*
It goes far toward making a man faithful to let him understand that you
think him so; and he that does but suspect I will deceive him gives me
a sort of right to do it – *Seneca*
Trust reposed in noble natures obliges them the more – *John Dryden*

Fidelity is seven-tenths of business success – *James Parton*

O heaven! were man / But constant, he were perfect; that one error / Fills him with faults – *William Shakespeare*

To God, thy country, and thy friend be true, then thou'lt ne'er be false to anyone.

See also CONSTANCY.

FIRMNESS

When firmness is sufficient, rashness is unnecessary – *Napoleon Bonaparte*

The firm, without pliancy, and the pliant, without firmness, resemble vessels without water, and water without vessels – *Johann Kaspar Lavater*

The greatest firmness is the greatest mercy – *Henry Wadsworth Longfellow*

It is only persons of firmness that can have real gentleness – *François de La Rochefoucauld*

The purpose firm is equal to the deed.

FLATTERY

Men find it more easy to flatter than to praise – *Jean Paul Richter*

Of all wild beasts preserve me from a tyrant; and of all tame, from a flatterer – *Ben Jonson*

If we would not flatter ourselves, the flattery of others could not harm us – *François de La Rochefoucauld*

Flatterers are the worst kind of traitors for they will strengthen thy imperfections, encourage thee in all evils, correct thee in nothing – *Walter Raleigh*

He that is much flattered soon learns to flatter himself – *Samuel Johnson*

Flattery, though a base coin, is the necessary pocket-money at court – *Lord Chesterfield*

Know thyself, thine evil as well as thy good, and flattery shall not harm thee – *Martin Farquhar Tupper*

Flattery is a base coin which gains currency only from our vanity – *La Rochefoucauld*

Imitation is the sincerest flattery – *Charles Caleb Cotton*

It is better to fall among crows than flatterers; for those devour only the dead – these the living – *Antisthenes*

The rich man despises those who flatter him too much, and hates those who do not flatter him at all – *Charles Maurice de Talleyrand-Périgord*

The lie that flatters I abhor the most – *William Cowper*

Flatterers are the worst kind of enemies – *Tacitus*

The most skilful flattery is to let a person talk on, and be a listener – *Joseph Addison*

The most subtle flattery a woman can receive is that conveyed by actions, not by words – *Mme Neckar*

It is a dangerous crisis when a proud heart meets with flattering lips – *John Flavel*

When flatterers meet the devil goes to dinner – *Daniel Defoe*

We love flattery, even when we see through it, and are not deceived by it, for it shows that we are of importance enough to be courted – *Ralph Waldo Emerson*

The only benefit of flattery is that by hearing what we are not we may be instructed what we ought to be – *Jonathan Swift*

Flattery, like perfume, should be used with discretion.

No man flatters the woman he truly loves.

A fool flatters himself; the wise man flatters the fool.

There is no remedy against the bite of a flatterer.

FLOWERS

Flowers are the sweetest things that God ever made and forgot to put a soul into – *Henry Ward Beecher*

The flowers are nature's jewels, with whose wealth she decks her summer beauty – *George Croly*

How the universal heart of man blesses flowers! They are wreathed round the cradle, the marriage altar, and the tomb – *Lydia Maria Child*

Your voiceless lips, O, flowers, are living preachers – each cup a pulpit, and each leaf a book – *Horace Smith*

Every rose is an autograph from the hand of God on his world about us – *Theodore Parker*

A world without flowers is like a face without smiles.

Lovely flowers are the smiles of God's goodness.

Flowers are love's truest language.

To analyse the charms of flowers is like dissecting music; it is one of those things which it is far better to enjoy than to attempt fully to understand.

In eastern lands they talk in flowers, and tell in a garland their loves and cares.

To cultivate a garden is to walk with God.

Flowers are God's thoughts of beauty taking form to gladden mortal gaze.

FOLLY

There is a foolish corner even in the brain of a sage – *Aristotle*

The follies of the fool are known to the world, but are hidden from himself; the follies of the wise man are known to himself, but hidden from the world – *Charles Caleb Colton*

Want and sorrow are the wages that folly earns for itself, and they are
generally paid – *Christian Friedrich Daniel Schubart*

He who lives without folly is not so wise as he imagines – *François de La
Rochefoucauld*

FOOLS

The world is full of fools; and he who would not wish to see one, must
not only shut himself up alone, but must also break his looking-glass
– *Nicolas Boileau*

A fool always finds some greater fool to admire him – *Boileau*

A fool may have his coat embroidered with gold, but it is a fool's coat still
– *Antoine Rivarol*

A fool can no more see his own folly than he can see his ears – *William
Makepeace Thackeray*

Young men think old men fools, and old men know young men to be
so.

What the fool does in the end the wise man does in the beginning –
Spanish maxim

A fool may be known by six things: anger, without cause; speech,
without profit; change, without progress; inquiry, without object;
putting trust in a stranger, and mistaking foes for friends – *Arabian
proverb*

A fool in a high station is like a man on the top of a high mountain –
everything appears small to him and he appears small to everybody.

A fool at forty is a fool indeed.

None but a fool is always right.

Wise men learn by other men's mistakes; fools, by their own.

Even a fool, when he holdeth his peace, is counted wise.

It takes much more penetration to discover a fool than a clever man.

Fools do more harm in the world than rascals.

When you are taken in you feel put out.

A fellow who's always declaring he's no fool usually has his surprises.

FORBEARANCE

It is a noble and great thing to cover the blemishes and excuse the failings
of a friend and to proclaim his virtues on the house-top – *Robert
South*

There is a limit at which forbearance ceases to be a virtue – *Edmund Burke*

If thou would'st be borne with, then bear with others.

See also TOLERATION.

FORCE

Who overcomes by force, hath overcome but half his foe – *John Milton*

Force rules the world – not opinion; but it is opinion that makes use of force – *Blaise Pascal*

FOREBODING

A heavy summons lies like lead upon me – *William Shakespeare*

Half our forebodings of our neighbours are but our wishes, which we are ashamed to utter in any other form – *L. E. Landon*

FORETHOUGHT

To fear the worst, oft cures the worst – *William Shakespeare*

To have too much forethought is the part of a wretch; to have too little is the part of a fool.

He that foretells his own calamity, and makes events before they come, doth twice endure the pains of evil destiny – *William Davenant*

Human foresight often leaves its proudest possessor only a choice of evils – *Charles Caleb Colton*

If life, as in chess, forethought wins.

Whatever is foretold by God will be done by man; but nothing will be done by man because it is foretold by God – *William Wordsworth*

Few things are brought to a successful issue by impetuous desire, but most by calm and prudent forethought – *Thucydides*

FORGETFULNESS

Though the past haunt me as a spirit, I do not ask to forget – *Felicia Dorothea Hemans*

When out of sight, quickly also out of mind – *Thomas à Kempis*

There is a noble forgetfulness – that which does not remember injuries.

FORGIVENESS

To err is human; to forgive, divine – *Alexander Pope*

His heart was as great as the world, but there was no room in it to hold the memory of a wrong – *Ralph Waldo Emerson*

We hand folks over to God's mercy, and show none ourselves – *George Eliot*

A brave man thinks no one his superior who does him an injury; for he has it then in his power to make himself superior to the other by forgiving it – *Pope*

The heart has always the pardoning power – *Mme Swetchine*

Never does the human soul appear so strong and noble as when it forgoes revenge, and dares to forgive an injury – *E. H. Chapin*

They never pardon who commit the wrong – *John Dryden*

The sun should not set on our anger; neither should it rise on our confidence – *Charles Caleb Colton*

To be able to bear provocation is an argument of great reason, and to forgive it of a great mind – *John Tillotson*

Only the brave know how to forgive; it is the most refined and generous pitch of virtue human nature can arrive at – *Laurence Sterne*

We forgive too little; forget too much – *Mme Swetchine*

As you from crimes would pardon'd be, / Let your indulgence set me free – *William Shakespeare*

The more we know, the better we forgive. Whoe'er feels deeply, feels for all that live – *Mme de Staël*

Forgive many things in others; nothing in yourself – *Ausonius*

He that cannot forgive others, breaks the bridge over which he himself must pass if he would ever reach heaven.

Said General Oglethorpe to John Wesley, 'I never forgive.' 'Then I hope, sir,' said Wesley, 'you never sin.'

Life that ever needs forgiveness has for its first duty to forgive.

A wise man will make haste to forgive, because he knows the full value of time and will not suffer it to pass away in unnecessary pain.

It is easier for the generous to forgive than for the offender to ask forgiveness.

The narrow soul knows not the godlike glory of forgiving.

FORTITUDE

In itself an essential virtue, it is a guard to every other virtue – *John Locke*

True fortitude is seen in great exploits that justice warrants and that wisdom guides – *Joseph Addison*

Who fights with passions and overcomes, that man is armed with the best virtue – passive fortitude.

FORTUNE

Human life is more governed by fortune than by reason – *David Hume*

'Fortune knocks at every man's door once in a life' but in a good many cases the man is in a neighbouring saloon and does not hear her – *Mark Twain*

We do not know what is really good or bad fortune – *Jean Jacques Rousseau*

The bad fortune of the good turns their faces up to heaven; the good fortune of the bad bows their heads down to the earth – *Sádi*

Fortune is the rod of the weak, and the staff of the brave – *James Russell Lowell*

The fortunate circumstances of our lives are generally found, at last, to be of our own producing – *Oliver Goldsmith*

Poverty treads upon the heels of great and unexpected riches – *Jean de La Bruyère*

Fortune gives too much to many, but to none enough – *Martial*

Fortune is ever seen accompanying industry – *Goldsmith*

We make our fortunes, and we call them fate.

Fortune does not change men; it only unmasks them.

Every man is the maker of his own fortune.

Many have been ruined by their fortunes, and many have escaped ruin by the want of fortune.

See also DESTINY, FATE, PROVIDENCE

FREEDOM

It is a strange desire men have, to seek power and lose liberty – *Francis Bacon*

He is the free man whom the truth makes free, / And all are slaves beside – *William Cowper*

Countries are well cultivated, not as they are fertile, but as they are free – *Charles de Montesquieu*

The only freedom worth possessing is that which gives enlargement to a people's energy, intellect and virtues – *William Ellery Channing*

Void of freedom, what would virtue be? – *Alphonse Marie Louis de Lamartine*

There is no legitimacy on earth but in a government which is the choice of the nation – *Joseph Bonaparte*

None are more hopelessly enslaved than those who falsely believe they are free – *Johann Wolfgang von Goethe*

There are two freedoms: the false, where a man is free to do what he likes; the true, where a man is free to do what he ought – *Charles Kingsley*

A man that loves his own fireside, and can govern his house without falling by the ears with his neighbours, or engaging in suits at law, is free – *Michel Eyquem de Montaigne*

To be truly free, nations must believe, and so must the individuals that compose them – *Alexis de Tocqueville*

Many politicians lay it down as a self-evident proposition, that no people ought to be free till they are fit to use their freedom. The maxim is worthy of the fool in the old story, who resolved not to go into the water till he had learned to swim – *Thomas Babington Macaulay*

No man is free who is not master of himself – *Epictetus*
The free world is not just a fortress, it is also a promised land.
Where the Bible forms public opinion, a nation must be free.
There is only one way of being free – being a slave of the law.
The greatest glory of a free-born people is to transmit that freedom to their children.
See also INDEPENDENCE, LIBERTY.

FRIENDSHIP

Be slow to fall into friendship; but when thou art in, continue firm and constant – *Socrates*
The loss of a friend is like that of a limb, time may heal the anguish of the wound, but the loss cannot be repaired – *Robert Southey*
Two persons cannot long be friends if they cannot forgive each other's little failings – *Jean de La Bruyère*
Friendship improves happiness and abates misery, by doubling our joy, and dividing our grief – *Joseph Addison*
In poverty and other misfortunes of life, true friends are a sure refuge. The young they keep out of mischief; to the old they are a comfort and aid in their weakness, and those in the prime of life they incite to noble deeds – *Aristotle*
Life has no blessing like a prudent friend – *Euripides*
Friendship is the shadow of the evening which strengthens with the setting sun of life – *Jean de La Fontaine*
Nothing is more dangerous than a friend without discretion; even a prudent enemy is preferable – *La Fontaine*
Life is to be fortified by many friendships. To love and to be loved is the greatest happiness of existence – *Sydney Smith*
That friendship will continue to the end which is begun for an end – *Francis Quarles*
He is our friend who loves far more than admires us, and would aid us in our great work – *William Ellery Channing*
If you have friends, you can endure anything – *Helen Keller*
Friendship is a plant of slow growth, and must undergo and withstand the shocks of adversity before it can grow.
Friendship hath the skill and observation of the best physician, the diligence and vigilance of the best nurse, and the tenderness and patience of the best mother.
We learn our virtues from the friends who love us: our faults from the enemy who hates us.
The difficulty is not so great to die for a friend, as to find a friend worth dying for.
That is a choice friend who conceals our faults from the view of others and discovers them to our own.

Friends are lost by calling often and calling seldom.

The only way to have a friend is to be one.

Friends are the flowers in the garden of life.

May it please God not to make our friends so happy as to forget us.

Friendships last when each friend thinks he has a superiority over the other.

The rich knows not who is his friend.

The happiest miser on earth is the man who saves up every friend he has.

Old friends are best, like old shoes they are the easiest.

Money may not buy friends but it does attract the better class of enemy.

Be not the fourth friend of him who had three before and lost them.

Be more prompt to go to a friend in adversity than in prosperity.

All men have their frailties; and whoever looks for a friend without imperfections will never find what he seeks.

We love ourselves notwithstanding our faults and we ought to love our friends in like manner.

False friendship, like the ivy, decays and ruins the walls it embraces; but true friendship gives new life and animation to the object it supports.

Purchase not friends by gifts; when thou ceasest to give, such will cease to love.

You'll find the friendship of the world mere outward show! 'Tis like the harlot's tears, the statesman's promise, or the false patriot's zeal, full of fair seeming, but delusion all.

Make not thy friends too cheap to thee, nor thyself to thy friend.

The light of friendship is like the light of phosphorus, seen plainest when all around is dark.

False friends are like our shadow, keeping close to us while we walk in the sunshine, but leaving us the instant we cross into the shade.

Kindred weaknesses induce friendships as often as kindred virtues.

Heaven gives us friends to bless the present scene, removes them to prepare us for the next.

It is chance that makes brothers, hearts that make friends.

A friend that isn't in need is a friend indeed.

No man can be happy without a friend, nor be sure of him till he's unhappy.

See also ACQUAINTANCE.

FRUGALITY

Frugality is founded on the principle that all riches have limits – *Edmund Burke*

He seldom lives frugally who lives by chance – *Samuel Johnson*

Frugality is a fair fortune; and habits of industry a good estate – *Benjamin Franklin*

Without industry and frugality will do; with them, everything – *Franklin*
By sowing frugality we reap liberty, a golden harvest – *Agesilaus*
Frugality is good if liberality be joined with it – *William Penn*
With parsimony a little is sufficient; without it nothing is sufficient; but frugality makes a poor man rich – *Seneca*
Nature is avariciously frugal. It gathers up the fragments that nothing be lost.
See also ECONOMY.

FUTURE

The future is always a fairy land to the young – *George Sala*
The golden age is not in the past, but in the future – *E. H. Chapin*
The best preparation for the future is the present well seen to – *George Macdonald*
We always live prospectively, never retrospectively – *Friedrich Heinrich Jacobi*
If there were no future life, our souls would not thirst for it – *Jean Paul Richter*
Belief in a future life is the appetite of reason – *Walter Savage Landor*
Another life, if it were not better than this, would be less a promise than a threat – *J. P. Senn*
Our ideal, whatever it may be, lies further on.
The veil which covers the face of the future is woven by the hand of mercy.
Future will grow out of what has already passed, or is now passing.
Age and sorrow have the gift of reading the future by the past.
Every tomorrow has two handles. We can take hold of it with the handle of anxiety or the handle of faith.
The future is only the past again, entered through another gate.
If you want a better world get busy in your own little corner.
Don't try to plan the future from the past.
The best of all prophets of the future is the past.
No one can walk backwards into the future.

GAIN

He is not rich that possesses much, but he that covets no more.
Sometimes the best gain is to lose.

GALLANTRY

Gallantry consists in saying the most empty things in an agreeable manner – *François de La Rochefoucauld*

Gallantry to women – the sure road to their favour – *William Hazlitt*
Gallantry thrives most in the atmosphere of the court – *Mme Neckar*
Conscience has no more to do with gallantry than it has with politics –
    Richard Brinsley Sheridan
See also COMPLIMENTS, COURTESY.

GAMBLING

Gambling is the child of avarice, but the parent of prodigality – *Charles
    Caleb Colton*
Gambling is getting money without giving an equivalent for it – *Henry
    Ward Beecher*
Keep flax from fire, and youth from gaming – *Benjamin Franklin*
Gambling is the child of avarice, the brother of iniquity, and the father of
    mischief – *George Washington*
By gambling we lose both our time and treasure, two things most
    precious to the life of man.
Play not for gain, but sport; who plays for more than he can lose with
    pleasure stakes his heart.
He that dares not venture must not complain of ill-luck.
See also DICE.

GENEROSITY

There is wisdom in generosity, as in everything else. A friend to
    everybody is often a friend to nobody – *Charles Haddon Spurgeon*
He that gives all, though but little, gives much; because God looks not
    to the quantity of the gift, but to the quality of the givers – *Francis
    Quarles*
Generosity during life is a very different thing from generosity in the
    hour of death; one proceeds from genuine liberality and benev-
    olence, the other from pride or fear – *Horace Mann*
Generosity is the accompaniment of high birth; pity and gratitude are its
    attendants – *Pierre Corneille*
Some are unwisely liberal, and more delight to give presents than to pay
    debts – *Sir Philip Sidney*
A man there was, and they called him mad; / The more he gave, the more
    he had – *John Bunyan*
What seems to be generosity is often no more than disguised ambition,
    which overlooks a small interest in order to secure a great one –
    François de La Rochefoucauld
If there be any truer measure of a man than by what he does, it must be
    by what he gives – *Robert South*
He who gives what he would as readily throw away, gives without

generosity; for the essence of generosity is in self-sacrifice – *Henry Taylor*

What I gave, I have; what I spent, I had; what I kept, I lost – *Epitaph*

When you give, take to yourself no credit for generosity, unless you deny yourself something in order that you may give.

Give all you can and a little more. Take that which is offered and be grateful.

He gives by halves who hesitates to give.

Men of the noblest dispositions think themselves happiest when others share their happiness with them.

Generosity, wrong placed, becometh a vice.

See also BENEFICENCE, CHARITY, GIFTS, GRATITUDE, LIBERALITY.

GENIUS

Genius is nothing but continued attention – *Claude Adrien Helvétius*

I know no such thing as genius; it is nothing but labour and diligence – *William Hogarth*

Genius is but a mind of large general powers accidentally determined in a particular direction – *Samuel Johnson*

Genius is only a superior power of seeing – *John Ruskin*

Talent, lying in the understanding, is often inherited; genius, being the action of reason and imagination, rarely or never – *Samuel Taylor Coleridge*

Men of genius are often dull and inert in society; as the blazing meteor, when it descends to earth, is only a stone – *Henry Wadsworth Longfellow*

Genius is the gold in the mine; talent is the miner who works and brings it out – *Lady Blessington*

Great geniuses have the shortest biographies – *Ralph Waldo Emerson*

Genius must be born; it never can be taught – *John Dryden*

Genius does what it must, and talent what it can – *Owen Meredith*

One of the strongest characteristics of genius is the power of lighting its own fire – *John Foster*

Genius is an infinite capacity for picking brains.

Genius is 1 per cent inspiration and 99 per cent perspiration.

Genius is a superior aptitude to patience.

The popular notion of genius is – of one who can do almost everything – except make a living.

Genius finds its own road, and carries its own lamp.

Genius may be described as the spirit of discovery – the pioneer for the generation which it precedes.

Genius is entitled to respect, only when it promotes the peace and improves the happiness of mankind.

GENTILITY

There cannot be a surer proof of low origin than to be always talking and
thinking about being genteel – *William Hazlitt*

Gentility is neither in birth, wealth, manner, nor fashion – but in the
mind.

GENTLEMEN

The flowering of civilization is the finished man – the man of sense, of
grace, of accomplishment, of social power – the gentleman – *Ralph
Waldo Emerson*

Education begins the gentleman, but reading, good company, and
reflection must finish him – *John Locke*

The taste of beauty, and the relish of what is decent, just, and amiable,
perfect the character of the gentleman – *Lord Shaftesbury*

No gentleman can be so termed unless a truly gentle man – *Elbert Hubbard*

Elegance is necessary to the fine gentleman; dignity is proper to noble-
men; and majesty to kings – *William Hazlitt*

We sometimes meet an original gentleman, who, if manners had not
existed, would have invented them – *Emerson*

Thoughtfulness for others, generosity, modesty, and self-respect are the
qualities which make a real gentleman or lady, as distinguished from
the veneered article which commonly goes by that name.

A gentleman is one who expects much from himself but little from
others.

Gentleman is a term that does not apply to any station, but to the mind
and feelings in every station.

See also GOOD BREEDING.

GENTLENESS

Nothing is so strong as gentleness; nothing so gentle as real strength –
Francis of Sales

What thou wilt, / Thou rather shalt enforce it with thy smile / Than hew
to't with thy sword – *William Shakespeare*

The great mind knows the power of gentleness – *Robert Browning*

We are indebted to Christianity for gentleness.

True gentleness is love in society.

True gentleness is founded on a sense of what we owe to him who made
us, and to the common nature which we all share.

GIFTS

It is the will, and not the gift that makes the giver – *Gotthold Ephraim
Lessing*

The manner of giving shows the character of the giver, more than the gift itself – *Johann Kaspar Lavater*

Give what you have. To someone it may be better than you dare to think – *Henry Wadsworth Longfellow*

We should give as we would receive, cheerfully, quickly, and without hesitation; for there is no grace in a benefit that sticks to the fingers – *Seneca*

Give according to your means, or God will make your means according to your giving – *John Hall*

He who loves with purity considers not the gift of the lover, but the love of the giver – *Thomas à Kempis*

One must be poor to know the luxury of giving – *George Eliot*

It is a proof of boorishness to confer a favour with a bad grace. How little does a smile cost! – *Jean de La Bruyère*

Every gift, though it be small, is in reality great if given with affection – *Pindar*

Rich gifts wax poor when givers prove unkind – *William Shakespeare*

The heart of the giver makes the gift dear and precious – *Martin Luther*

Who gives a trifle meanly is meaner than the trifle – *Lavater*

That which is given with pride and ostentation is rather an ambition than a bounty – *Seneca*

God's gifts put man's best gifts to shame – *Elizabeth Barrett Browning*

Examples are few of men ruined by giving.

When a friend asks, there is no tomorrow.

The best thing to give to your enemy is forgiveness; to an opponent, tolerance; to a friend, your heart; to your child, a good example; to a father, deference; to your mother, conduct that will make her proud of you; to yourself, respect; to all men, charity.

He gives not best who gives most; but he gives most who gives best.

See also BENEFICENCE, CHARITY, GENEROSITY, GRATITUDE.

GLORY

Our greatest glory consists not in never falling, but in rising every time we fall – *Oliver Goldsmith*

Glory, built on selfish principles, is shame and guilt – *William Cowper*

Like madness is the glory of this life – *William Shakespeare*

Glory, like the shadow, goes sometimes before the body, and sometimes in length infinitely exceeds it – *Michel Eyquem de Montaigne*

Real glory springs from the silent conquest of ourselves.

The glory of a people, and of an age, is always the work of a small number of great men, and disappears with them.

GOD

We know God easily, if we do not constrain ourselves to define him –
Joseph Joubert

God is a circle whose centre is everywhere, and its circumference
nowhere – *Empedocles*

The ancient hieroglyphic for God was the figure of an eye upon a sceptre,
to denote that he sees and rules all things.

It were better to have no opinion of God at all than such an one as is
unworthy of him; for the one is only unbelief – the other is contempt –
Plutarch

If God did not exist it would be necessary to invent him – *Voltaire*

Nature is too thin a screen; the glory of the omnipresent God bursts
through everywhere – *Ralph Waldo Emerson*

How often we look upon God as our last and feeblest resource! We go to
him because we have nowhere else to go. And then we learn that the
storms of life have driven us, not upon the rocks, but into the desired
haven – *George Macdonald*

If God were not a necessary being of himself, he might almost seem to be
made for the use and benefit of men – *John Tillotson*

We cannot too often think, that there is a never sleeping eye that reads
the heart, and registers our thoughts – *Francis Bacon*

I fear God, and next to God I chiefly fear him who fears him not –
Sádi

Amid all the war and contention and variety of human opinion, you will
find one consenting conviction in every land, that there is one God,
the king and father of all – *Maximus Tyrius*

Live near to God, and so all things will appear to you little in comparison
with eternal realities – *R. M. McCheyne*

As a countenance is made beautiful by the soul's shining through it, so
the world is beautified by the shining through it of God – *Friedrich
Heinrich Jacobi*

God comes to see us without a bell – *Spanish proverb*

God is great, and therefore he will be sought: he is good, and therefore
he will be found.

The Muhammadans have ninety-nine names for God, but among them
all they have not 'our Father'.

We should give God the same place in our hearts that he holds in the
universe.

I have read up many religions; and have found none that will work
without a God.

God is an unutterable sigh in the innermost depths of the soul.

A foe to God was never a true friend to man.

See also RELIGION.

GOLD

The lust of gold, unfeeling and remorseless; the last corruption of degenerate man – *Samuel Johnson*

Gold, like the sun, which melts wax, but hardens clay, expands great souls and contracts bad hearts – *Antoine Rivarol*

It is observed of gold, in an old epigram, that to have it is to be in fear, and to want it is to be in sorrow – *Johnson*

Give him gold enough and marry him to a puppet or an aglet-baby; or an old trot with ne'er a tooth in her head, though she have as many diseases as two-and-fifty horses; why, nothing comes amiss, so money comes withal – *William Shakespeare*

A mask of gold hides all deformities – *Thomas Dekker*

How quickly nature falls into revolt / When gold becomes her object! – *Shakespeare*

Gold is the fool's curtain, which hides all his defects from the world.

It is much better to have your gold in the hand than in the heart.

There is no place so high that an ass laden with gold cannot reach it.

O cursed lust of gold! when for thy sake, the fool throws up his interest in both worlds, first starved in this, then damned in that to come!

A vain man's motto is: 'Win gold and wear it'; a generous, 'Win gold and share it'; a miser's, 'Win gold and hoard it'; a profligate's, 'Win gold and spend it'; a broker's, 'Win gold and lend it'; a gambler's, 'Win gold and lose it'; a wise man's, 'Win gold and use it.'

As the touchstone tries gold, so gold tries men.

See also PROSPERITY, RICHES, WEALTH.

GOOD BREEDING

Good breeding is surface Christianity – *Oliver Wendell Holmes*

Good breeding is the art of showing men, by external signs, the internal regard we have for them – *Cato*

One principal point of good breeding is to suit our behaviour to the three several degrees of men – our superiors, our equals, and those below us – *Jonathan Swift*

Good breeding is the result of much good sense, some good nature, and a little self-denial for the sake of others, and with a view to obtain the same indulgence from them – *Lord Chesterfield*

A man's own good breeding is the best security against other people's ill manners – *Chesterfield*

Nothing can constitute good breeding which has not good nature for its foundation.

Virtue itself often offends, when coupled with bad manners.

There are few defects in our nature so glaring as not to be veiled from observation by politeness and good breeding.
See also CIVILITY, COURTESY, GENTLEMEN.

GOOD HUMOUR

Honest good humour is the oil and wine of a merry meeting, and there is no jovial companionship equal to that where the jokes are rather small, and the laughter abundant – *Washington Irving*
Good humour is the health of the soul: sadness is its poison.
Good humour will sometimes conquer ill humour, but ill humour will conquer it oftener; and for this plain reason, good humour must operate on generosity; ill humour on meanness.
See also CHEERFULNESS.

GOOD NATURE

An inexhaustible good nature is one of the most precious gifts of heaven
– *Washington Irving*
Good nature is one of the richest fruits of true Christianity – *Henry Ward Beecher*
Good nature is stronger than tomahawks – *Ralph Waldo Emerson*
Good sense and good nature are never separated; and good nature is the product of right reason – *John Dryden*
Good nature is the very air of a good mind; the sign of a large and generous soul, and the peculiar soil in which virtue prospers.
Good nature, like a bee, collects honey from every herb. Ill nature, like the spider, sucks poison from the sweetest flower.
Good nature is the beauty of the mind, and like personal beauty, wins almost without anything else – sometimes, indeed, in spite of positive deficiencies.

GOODNESS

Be not merely good; be good for something – *Henry David Thoreau*
In nothing do men approach so nearly to the gods as in doing good to men – *Cicero*
There may be a certain pleasure in vice, but there is a higher in purity and virtue – *Independent*
He that is a good man is three quarters of his way toward being a good Christian – *Robert South*
To be doing good is man's most glorious task – *Sophocles*
To be good, we must do good – *Tryon Edwards*
The good are heaven's peculiar care – *Ovid*

He who loves goodness harbours angels, reveres reverence, and lives with God – *Ralph Waldo Emerson*

A good man is kinder to his enemy than bad men to their friends – *Bishop Hall*

The best portion of a good man's life is his little, nameless, unremembered acts of kindness and of love – *William Wordsworth*

It is only great souls that know how much glory there is in being good – *Sophocles*

How far that little candle throws his beams! / So shines a good deed in a naughty world – *William Shakespeare*

Goodness consists not in the outward things we do, but in the inward thing we are – *E. H. Chapin*

A good man doubles the length of his existence; to have lived so as to look back with pleasure on our past life is to live twice – *Martial*

You are not very good if you are not better than your best friends imagine you to be – *Johann Kaspar Lavater*

It seems to me 'tis only noble to be good. / Kind hearts are more than coronets – *Alfred, Lord Tennyson*

Do all the good you can, in all the ways you can, to all the souls you can, in every place you can, at all the times you can, with all the zeal you can, as long as ever you can – *John Wesley*

Nothing is rarer than real goodness – *François de La Rochefoucauld*

Goodness thinks no ill where no ill seems – *John Milton*

There are two perfectly good men: one dead, and the other unborn – *Chinese proverb*

Goodness is the only investment that never fails.

If there be a divine providence, no good man need be afraid to do right; he will only fear to do wrong.

The heart that gives, gathers!

A good deed is never lost. He who sows courtesy, reaps friendship; he who plants kindness, gathers love.

Goodness is love in action.

Your actions, in passing, pass not away, for every good work is a grain of seed for eternal life.

That is good which doth good.

See also RECTITUDE.

GOSSIP

I hold it to be a fact, that if all persons knew what each said of the other, there would not be four friends in the world – *Blaise Pascal*

There is a set of malicious, prating, prudent gossips, both male and female, who murder characters to kill time; and will rob a young fellow of his good name before he has years to know the value of it – *Richard Brinsley Sheridan*

Fire and sword are but slow engines of destruction in comparison with the babbler – *Richard Steele*

Gossip is the henchman of rumour and scandal – *Octave Feuillet*

Tale bearers are just as bad as tale makers – *Sheridan*

What people say behind your back is your standing in the community – *Edgar Watson-Howe*

Love and scandal are the best sweeteners of tea.

Scandal is like an egg; when it is hatched it has wings.

Thorns and thistles sting very sore, but old maids' tongues sting more.

Don't talk about yourself – it will be done when you leave.

Gossip has been well defined as putting two and two together, and making it five.

News-hunters have great leisure, with little thought; much petty ambition to be thought intelligent, without any other pretension than being able to communicate what they have just learned.

When of a gossiping circle it was asked, 'What are they doing?' the answer was, 'Swapping lies.'

Truth is not exciting enough to those who depend on the character and lives of their neighbours for all their amusement.

An empty brain and a tattling tongue are very apt to go together.

Gossip, pretending to have the eyes of an Argus, has all the blindness of a bat.

A small town is one where the postmaster knows more than the schoolmaster.

No matter what you do, someone always knew you would.

See also RUMOUR, SCANDAL, SLANDER.

GOVERNMENT

The antidote to abuse of formal government is the influence of private character, the growth of the individual – *Ralph Waldo Emerson*

Men well governed should seek after no other liberty, for there can be no greater liberty than a good government – *Walter Raleigh*

The best of all governments is that which teaches us to govern ourselves – *Johann Wolfgang von Goethe*

No government ought to exist for the purpose of checking the prosperity of its people or to allow such a principle in its policy – *Edmund Burke*

The less of government the better, if society be kept in peace and prosperity – *William Ellery Channing*

That is the most perfect government under which a wrong to the humblest is an affront to all – *Solon*

Government is not mere advice; it is authority, with power to enforce its law – *George Washington*

The principal foundation of all states is in good laws and good arms – *Niccolò Machiavelli*

The punishment suffered by the wise who refuse to take part in the government is to live under the government of bad men – *Plato*

Government is only a necessary evil, like other go-carts and crutches. Our need of it shows exactly how far we are still children. All overmuch governing kills the self-help and energy of the governed – *Wendell Phillips*

The proper function of a government is to make it easy for the people to do good, and difficult for them to do evil – *William Gladstone*

This nation, under God, shall have a new birth of freedom, that government of the people, by the people, for the people, shall not perish from the earth – *Abraham Lincoln*

Government is a contrivance of human wisdom to provide for human wants – *Burke*

The culminating point of administration is to know well how much power, great or small, we ought to use in all circumstances – *Charles de Montesquieu*

Society is well governed when the people obey the magistrates, and the magistrates obey the laws – *Solon*

He that would govern others, first should be the master of himself, richly endued with depth of understanding and height of knowledge – *Philip Massinger*

All government and exercise of power, no matter in what form, which is not based on love, and directed by knowledge, is tyranny – *Anna Jameson*

Power exercised with violence has seldom been of long duration – *Seneca*

The aggregate happiness of society, which is best promoted by the practice of a virtuous policy, is, or ought to be, the end of all government – *George Washington*

No government is respectable which is not just – *Daniel Webster*

It is better for a city to be governed by a good man than even by good laws – *Aristotle*

For forms of government let fools contest. / That which is best administered is best – *Alexander Pope*

It may pass for a maxim in state, that the administration cannot be placed in too few hands, nor the legislation in too many – *Jonathan Swift*

All free governments, whatever their name, are in reality governments by public opinion; and it is on the quality of this public opinion that their prosperity depends – *James Russell Lowell*

All good government must begin in the home.

The worst of governments are always the most changeable, and cost the people dearest.

See also AUTHORITY.

GRACE

The king-becoming graces, / As justice, verity, temperance, stableness, / Bounty, perseverance, mercy, lowliness, / Devotion, patience, courage, fortitude – *William Shakespeare*

Let grace and goodness be the principal lodestone of thy affections – *John Dryden*

Whatever is graceful is virtuous, and whatever is virtuous is graceful – *Cicero*

Grace is but glory begun and glory is but grace perfected – *Jonathan Edwards*

God appoints our graces to be nurses to other men's weaknesses – *Henry Ward Beecher*

Virtue, wisdom, goodness, and real worth, like the lodestone, never lose their power.

There is no such way to attain to greater measure of grace as for a man to live up to the little grace he has.

As heat is opposed to cold, and light to darkness, so grace is opposed to sin. Fire and water may as well agree in the same vessel, as grace and sin in the same heart.

GRACEFULNESS

Grace is to the body what good sense is to the mind – *François de La Rochefoucauld*

Gracefulness has been defined to be the outward expression of the inward harmony of the soul – *William Hazlitt*

All the actions and attitudes of children are graceful because they are the offspring of the moment, without affectation, and free from all pretence – *Henry Fuseli*

How inimitably graceful children are before they learn to dance – *Samuel Taylor Coleridge*

GRATITUDE

Gratitude is not only the memory but the homage of the heart – *Nathaniel Parker Willis*

A grateful thought toward heaven is of itself a prayer – *Gotthold Ephraim Lessing*

Revenge is a much more punctual paymaster than gratitude – *Charles Caleb Colton*

He who receives a benefit should never forget it; he who bestows should never remember it – *Pierre Charron*

To the generous mind the heaviest debt is that of gratitude, when it is not in our power to repay it – *Benjamin Franklin*

When I find a great deal of gratitude in a poor man, I take it for granted there would be as much generosity if he were rich – *Alexander Pope*

There is as much greatness of mind in acknowledging a good turn as in doing it – *Seneca*

We can be thankful to a friend for a few acres or a little money; and yet for the freedom and command of the whole earth, and for the great benefits of our being, our life, health, and reason, we look upon ourselves as under no obligation – *Seneca*

O Lord! that lends me life, / Lend me a heart replete with thankfulness! – *William Shakespeare*

If gratitude is due from children to their earthly parent, how much more is the gratitude of the great family of men due to our father in heaven – *Hosea Ballou*

To receive honestly is the best thanks for a good thing – *George Macdonald*

Gratitude is the mother of virtues.

Gratitude to God makes even a temporal blessing a taste of heaven.

He enjoys much who is thankful for little.

See also GENEROSITY, GIFTS, THANKFULNESS.

GRAVES

A grave, wherever found, preaches a short and pithy sermon to the soul – *Nathaniel Hawthorne*

The grave buries every error, covers every defect, extinguishes every resentment – *Washington Irving*

A Christian graveyard is a cradle, where in the quiet motions of the globe, Jesus rocks his sleeping children. By and by he will wake them from their slumber, and in the arms of angels they shall be translated to the skies – *G. B. Cheever*

The disciples found angels at the grave of him they loved, and we should always find them, too, but that our eyes are too full of tears for seeing – *Henry Ward Beecher*

We go to the grave of a friend saying, 'A man is dead' but angels throng about him saying, 'A man is born.' – *Beecher*

We weep over the graves of infants and the little ones taken from us by death; but an early grave may be the shortest way to heaven – *Tryon Edwards*

The ancients feared death; we, thanks to Christianity, fear only dying.

It is sadness to sense to look to the grave, but gladness to faith to look beyond it.

See also DEATH.

GRAVITY

Gravity is only the bark of wisdom; but it preserves it – *Confucius*

Too much gravity argues a shallow mind – *Johann Kaspar Lavater*

Those wanting wit affect gravity, and go by the name of solid men – *John Dryden*

Gravity is a mysterious carriage of the body, invented to cover the defects of the mind – *François de La Rochefoucauld*

Gravity is but the rind of wisdom; but it is a preservative rind – *Joseph Joubert*

Gravity is the ballast of the soul, which keeps the mind steady.

Gravity – the body's wisdom to conceal the mind.

GREATNESS

A really great man is known by three signs – generosity in the design, humanity in the execution, moderation in success – *Otto von Bismarck*

He only is great who has the habits of greatness; who, after performing what none in ten thousand could accomplish, passes on like Samson, and 'tells neither father nor mother of it' – *Johann Kaspar Lavater*

If any man seeks for greatness, let him forget greatness and ask for truth, and he will find both – *Horace Mann*

The superiority of some men is merely local. They are great because their associates are little – *Samuel Johnson*

No man has come to true greatness who has not felt in some degree that his life belongs to his race, and that what God gives him he gives for mankind – *Phillips Brooks*

In life we shall find many men that are great, and some that are good, but very few men that are both great and good – *Charles Caleb Colton*

Subtract from the great man all that he owes to opportunity, all that he owes to chance, and all that he has gained by the wisdom of his friends and the folly of his enemies, and the giant will often be seen to be a pygmy – *Colton*

Distinction is the consequence, never the object, of a great mind – *Washington Allston*

He is great enough that is his own master – *Bishop Hall*

The most substantial glory of a country is in its virtuous great men. Its prosperity will depend on its docility to learn from their example – *Fisher Ames*

Some are born great, some achieve greatness, and some have greatness thrust upon them – *William Shakespeare*

There never was yet a truly great man that was not at the same time truly virtuous – *Benjamin Franklin*

It is to be lamented that great characters are seldom without a blot – *George Washington*

Great men lose somewhat of their greatness by being near us; ordinary men gain much – *Walter Savage Landor*

Great minds must be ready not only to take opportunities, but to make them – *Colton*

Great men undertake great things because they are great; fools, because they think them easy – *Marquis de Vauvenargues*

He who comes up to his own idea of greatness must always have had a very low standard of it in his mind – *John Ruskin*

Greatness lies not in being strong, but in the right using of strength – *Henry Ward Beecher*

The true test of a great man is his having been in advance of his age.

The greatest men in all ages have been lovers of their kind. All true leaders of men have it. Faith in men and love to men are unfailing marks of true greatness.

He is great who can do what he wishes; he is wise who wishes to do what he can.

Great minds, like heaven, are pleased in doing good, though the ungrateful subjects of their favours are barren in return.

What millions died that Caesar might be great.

High stations tumult not bliss create. / None think the great unhappy, but the great.

GRIEF

Never does a man know the force that is in him till some mighty affection or grief has humanized the soul – *Frederick William Robertson*

There is no greater grief than to remember days of joy when misery is at hand – *Dante Alighieri*

Sorrow's crown of sorrow is remembering happier things – *Alfred, Lord Tennyson*

Great grief makes sacred those upon whom its hand is laid. Joy may elevate, ambition glorify, but only sorrow can consecrate – *Horace Greeley*

Light griefs are plaintive, but great ones are dumb – *Seneca*

Everyone can master a grief but he that has it – *William Shakespeare*

No grief is so acute but that time ameliorates it – *Cicero*

Moderate lamentation is the right of the dead, excessive grief the enemy to the living – *Shakespeare*

Well has it been said that there is no grief like the grief which does not speak – *Henry Wadsworth Longfellow*

Grief knits two hearts in closer bonds than happiness ever can – *Alphonse Marie Louis de Lamartine*

Give sorrow words; the grief that does not speak / Whispers the o'er-fraught heart and bids it break – *Shakespeare*

Grief hallows hearts even while it ages heads.

Sorrow's best antidote is employment.

See also SADNESS, SORROW.

GRUMBLING

Just as you are pleased at finding faults, you are displeased at finding
perfections – *Johann Kaspar Lavater*

Those who complain most are most to be complained of – *Matthew Henry*

There is a very large and very knowing class of misanthropes who rejoice
in the name of grumblers whose chief pleasure is being displeased –
E. P. Whipple

Had we not faults of our own, we should take less pleasure in complaining of others – *François de Fénelon*

Everyone may see daily instances of people who complain from the
mere habit of complaining.

There is an unfortunate disposition in man to attend much more to the
faults of his companions that offend him, than to their perfections
which please him.

Grumblers are commonly an idle set. Having no disposition to work
themselves, they spend their time in whining and complaining both
about their own affairs and those of their neighbours.

GUESTS

True friendship's laws are by this rule expressed: / Welcome the coming,
speed the parting guest – *Alexander Pope*

The first day, a guest; the second, a burden; the third, a pest – *Edouard
René de Laboulaye*

Unbidden guests / Are often welcomest when they are gone – *William
Shakespeare*

Let the one you would welcome to your hospitality be one you can
welcome to your respect and esteem, if not to your personal
friendship.

See also HOSPITALITY.

GUIDANCE

That man may safely venture on his way, / Who is so guided that he
cannot stray – *Walter Scott*

A sound head, an honest heart, and an humble spirit are the three best
guides through time and to eternity.

Reason and authority, the two brightest lights in the world.

GUILT

Guilt is the very nerve of sorrow – *Horace Bushnell*

O! full of scorpions is my mind – *William Shakespeare*

From the body of one guilty deed / A thousand ghostly fears and haunting thoughts proceed – *William Wordsworth*

Better 'twere / That all the miseries which nature owes / Were mine at once – *Shakespeare*

To what deep gulfs a single deviation from the track of human duties leads – *Lord Byron*

They whose guilt within their bosoms lies, / Imagine every eye beholds their blame – *Shakespeare*

Guilt upon the conscience, like rust upon iron, both defiles and consumes it, gnawing and creeping into it, as that does which at last eats out the very heart and substance of the metal – *Robert South*

Guilt, once harboured in the conscious breast, intimidates the brave, degrades the great – *Samuel Johnson*

The guilt being great, the fear doth still exceed – *Shakespeare*

The greatest incitement to guilt is the hope of sinning with impunity – *Cicero*

Guiltiness will speak, / Though tongues were out of use – *Shakespeare*

Oh, that pang, where more than madness lies, / The worm that will not sleep, and never dies – *Lord Byron*

The consequences of our crimes long survive their commission, and, like the ghosts of the murdered, forever haunt the steps of the malefactor – *Walter Scott*

Suspicion always haunts the guilty mind; / The thief doth fear each bush an officer – *Shakespeare*

Let wickedness escape, as it may at the bar, it never fails of doing justice upon itself; for every guilty person is his own hangman – *Seneca*

The sin lessens in the guilty one's estimation, only as the guilt increases – *Johann Christoph Friedrich von Schiller*

Adversity, how blunt are all the arrows of thy quiver in comparison with those of guilt.

The guilty mind debases the great image that it wears, and levels us with brutes.

The guilt that feels not its own shame is wholly incurable.

Beside one deed of guilt, how blest is guileless woe!

HABIT

How use doth breed a habit in a man! – *William Shakespeare*

All habits gather, by unseen degrees, / As brooks make rivers, rivers run to seas – *John Dryden*

Habit is a cable. We weave a thread of it every day, and at last we cannot break it – *Horace Mann*

If an idiot were to tell you the same story every day for a year, you would end by believing him – *Edmund Burke*

Habit is the deepest law of human nature – *Thomas Carlyle*

The chains of habit are generally too small to be felt until they are too strong to be broken – *Samuel Johnson*

Habits are to the soul what the veins and arteries are to the blood, the courses in which it moves – *Horace Bushnell*

The phrases that men hear or repeat continually end by becoming convictions and ossify the organs of intelligence – *Johann Wolfgang von Goethe*

Bad habits are as infectious by example as the plague itself is by contact – *Henry Fielding*

Refrain tonight; / And that shall lend a kind of easiness / To the next abstinence; the next more easy; / For use almost can change the stamp of nature, / And master ev'n the devil or throw him out / With wondrous potency – *Shakespeare*

Habits are soon assumed; but when we endeavour to strip them off, it is being flayed alive – *William Cowper*

Habit is the beneficent harness of routine which enables silly men to live respectably, and unhappy men to live calmly – *George Eliot*

Long customs are not easily broken; he that attempts to change the course of his own life very often labours in vain – *Johnson*

Young persons are creatures of impulse; old persons are creatures of habit – *G. B. Cheever*

Early to bed and early to rise and you'll meet very few of our best people – *George Ade*

We first make our habits, and then our habits make us.

Habit is either the best of servants, or the worst of masters.

The habit of virtue cannot be formed in the closet; good habits are formed by acts of reason in a persevering struggle with temptation.

Habit, if not resisted, soon becomes necessity.

In early childhood you may lay the foundations of poverty or riches, industry or idleness, good or evil, by the habits to which you train your children. Teach them right habits then, and their future life is safe.

Sow an act, and you reap a habit; sow a habit, and you reap a character; sow a character, and you reap a destiny.

Good habits are the best magistrates.

HAIR

The hair is the richest ornament of women. Of old, virgins used to wear it loose, except when they were in mourning – *Martin Luther*

Her head was bare, but for her native ornament of hair, which in a simple knot was tied; sweet negligence – unheeded bait of love – *John Dryden*

Fair tresses man's imperial race ensnare, / And beauty draws us with a single hair – *Alexander Pope*

How ill white hairs become a fool and jester! – *William Shakespeare*

Those curious locks, so aptly twined, / Whose every hair a soul doth bind – *Thomas Carew*

Beware of her fair locks, for when she winds them round a young man's neck she will not set him free again – *Johann Wolfgang von Goethe*

Her sunny locks / Hang on her temples like a golden fleece – *Shakespeare*

By common consent grey hairs are a crown of glory; the only object of respect that can never excite envy.

HAND

I love a hand that meets my own with a grasp that causes some sensation – *F. S. Osgood*

Other parts of the body assist the speaker but the hands speak themselves – *Quintilian*

HAPPINESS

Happiness can be built only on virtue, and must of necessity have truth for its foundation – *Samuel Taylor Coleridge*

No man is happy who does not think himself so – *Aurelius*

Happiness is neither within us only, or without us; it is the union of ourselves with God – *Blaise Pascal*

It is not how much we have, but how much we enjoy, that makes happiness – *Charles Haddon Spurgeon*

Men of the noblest dispositions think themselves happiest when others share their happiness with them – *Jeremy Taylor*

All who would win joy must share it; happiness was born a twin – *Lord Byron*

Happiness in this world, when it comes, comes incidentally – *Nathaniel Hawthorne*

If one only wished to be happy, this could be easily accomplished; but we wish to be happier than other people, and this is always difficult, for we believe others to be happier than they are – *Charles de Montesquieu*

Few things are needful to make the wise man happy, but nothing satisfies the fool – *François de La Rochefoucauld*

Call no man happy till you know the end of his life. Till then, at most, he can only be counted fortunate – *Herodotus*

The rays of happiness, like those of light, are colourless when unbroken – *Henry Wadsworth Longfellow*

Happiness is dependent on the taste, and not on things. It is by having what we like that we are made happy, not by having what others think desirable – *La Rochefoucauld*

Happiness is not the end of life; character is – *Henry Ward Beecher*

There is this difference between happiness and wisdom, that he that thinks himself the happiest man, really is so; but he that thinks himself the wisest, is generally the greatest fool – *Charles Caleb Colton*

No person is either so happy or so unhappy as he imagines – *La Rochefoucauld*

We take greater pains to persuade others that we are happy than in endeavouring to be so ourselves – *Oliver Goldsmith*

You traverse the world in search of happiness, which is within the reach of every man; a contented mind confers it on all – *Horace*

True happiness renders men kind and sensible; and that happiness is always shared with others – *Montesquieu*

The most happy man is he who knows how to bring into relation the end and the beginning of his life – *Johann Wolfgang von Goethe*

The haunts of happiness are varied, but I have more often found her among little children, home firesides, and country houses than anywhere else – *Sydney Smith*

He only is happy as well as great who needs neither to obey nor command in order to be something – *Goethe*

That state of life is most happy where superfluities are not required, and necessaries are not wanting – *Plutarch*

It is not the place, nor the condition, but the mind alone that can make anyone happy or miserable – *Sir Roger L'Estrange*

The happiest life is that which constantly exercises and educates what is best in us – *Philip Gilbert Hamerton*

Do not speak of your happiness to one less fortunate than yourself – *Plutarch*

Objects we ardently pursue bring little happiness when gained; most of our pleasures come from unexpected sources – *Herbert Spencer*

To be happy is not the purpose of our being, but to deserve happiness – *Johann Gottlieb Fichte*

All mankind are happier for having been happy, so that if you make them happy now, you make them happy twenty years hence by the memory of it – *Smith*

The happiest women, like the happiest nations, have no history – *George Eliot*

Human happiness has no perfect security but freedom – *Josiah Quincy*

The best advice on the art of being happy is about as easy to follow as advice to be well when one is sick – *Mme Swetchine*

Reason's whole pleasure, all the joys of sense, / Lie in three words, health, peace, and competence – *Alexander Pope*

To forget oneself is to be happy – *Robert Louis Stevenson*

Happiness is like a sunbeam, which the least shadow intercepts, while adversity is often as the rain of spring – *Chinese proverb*

Happiness consists in being perfectly satisfied with what we have got and with what we haven't got.

I am more and more convinced that our happiness or unhappiness depends far more on the way we meet the events of life than on the nature of those events themselves.

Happiness is a butterfly, which, when pursued, is always just beyond your grasp, but which, if you will sit down quietly, may alight upon you.

The grand essentials to happiness in this life are something to do, something to love, and something to hope for.

Happiness and virtue rest upon each other; the best are not only the happiest, but the happiest are usually the best.

Happiness consists in activity. Such is the constitution of our nature. It is a running stream, and not a stagnant pool.

A little house well filled, a little land well tilled, and a little wife well willed, are great riches.

Happiness is nearly always a rebound from hard work.

The happiest people are those who don't want things they can't get.

The secret of happiness is to admire without desiring.

The happiest person is the person who thinks the most interesting thoughts.

None think the great unhappy but the great.

My idea of happiness is four feet on a fireplace fender.

See also CHEERFULNESS.

HARDSHIP

Kites rise against, not with the wind. No man ever worked his passage anywhere in a dead calm – *John Neal*

Peril is the element in which power is developed.

Not facilities but difficulties makes men.

HASTE

Though I am always in haste, I am never in a hurry – *John Wesley*

No two things differ more than hurry and dispatch. Hurry is the mark of a weak mind; dispatch of a strong one – *Charles Caleb Colton*

Haste is of the devil – *Koran*

Wisely and slow; they stumble that run fast – *William Shakespeare*

Unreasonable haste is the direct road to error – *Molière*

Fraud and deceit are ever in a hurry. Take time for all things. Great haste makes great waste – *Benjamin Franklin*

Manners require time, and nothing is more vulgar than haste – *Ralph Waldo Emerson*

Modest wisdom plucks me / From overcredulous haste – *Shakespeare*

Hurry and cunning are the two apprentices of dispatch and skill, but neither of them ever learns the master's trade – *Colton*

He who hesitates is last – *Mae West*

The longest way round is the shortest way home.

Haste usually turns upon being late, and may be avoided by a habit like that of Lord Nelson, to which he ascribed his success in life, of always being ten minutes too early.

HATRED

If I wanted to punish an enemy it should be by fastening on him the trouble of constantly hating somebody – *Hannah More*

When our hatred is violent, it sinks us even beneath those we hate – *François de La Rochefoucauld*

Hate no one; hate their vices, not themselves – *J. G. C. Brainard*

Hatred is the madness of the heart – *Lord Byron*

Thousands are hated, while none are loved, without a real cause – *Johann Kaspar Lavater*

Hatred is active and envy passive dislike; there is but one step from envy to hate – *Johann Wolfgang von Goethe*

It is human nature to hate him whom you have injured – *Tacitus*

Hatred does not cease by hatred, but only by love; this is the eternal rule – *Buddha*

We hate some persons because we do not know them; and we will not know them because we hate them – *Charles Caleb Colton*

The hatred of those who are most nearly connected is the most inveterate – *Tacitus*

Heaven has no rage like love to hatred turned – *William Congreve*

There are glances of hatred that stab, and raise no cry of murder – *George Eliot*

Hating people is like burning down your own house to get rid of a rat – *Harry Emerson Fosdick*

Malice can always find a mark to shoot at, and a pretence to fire.

If there is any person whom you dislike, that is the one of whom you should never speak.

Hatred is like fire, it makes even light rubbish deadly.

Hate, like love, mellows with the years.

HEALTH

A sound mind in a sound body; if the former be the glory of the latter, the latter is indispensable to the former – *Tryon Edwards*

The building of a perfect body crowned by a perfect brain is at once the greatest earthly problem and grandest hope of the race – *Dio Lewis*

Without health life is not life; it is only a state of languor and suffering – an image of death – *François Rabelais*

Health is the soul that animates all the enjoyments of life, which fade and are tasteless without it – *William Temple*

Wet feet are some of the most effective agents death has in the field. It has peopled more graves than all the gory engines of war – *John Abernethy*

Life is not to live, but to be well – *Martial*

There is this difference between the two temporal blessings – health and money; money is the most envied, but the least enjoyed; health is the most enjoyed, but the least envied – *Charles Caleb Colton*

The first wealth is health – *Ralph Waldo Emerson*

The ingredients of health and long life are great temperance, open air, easy labour, and little care – *Sir Philip Sidney*

Youth will never live to age unless they keep themselves in health with exercise, and in heart with joyfulness – *Sidney*

The only way for a rich man to be healthy is by exercise and abstinence, to live as if he were poor – *Temple*

Seldom shall we see in cities, courts, and rich families, where men live plentifully, and eat and drink freely, that perfect health and athletic soundness and vigour of constitution which are commonly seen in the country, where nature is the cook, and necessity the caterer, and where they have no other doctor but the sun and fresh air – *Robert South*

Joy, temperance, and repose, / Slam the door on the doctor's nose – *Henry Wadsworth Longfellow*

Be sober and temperate, and you will be healthy – *Benjamin Franklin*

Health is not valued until sickness comes – *Thomas Fuller*

He who has health, has hope; and he who has hope, has everything – *Arabian proverb*

Dyspepsia is the remorse of a guilty stomach.

The first sure symptoms of a mind in health are rest of heart and pleasure found at home.

Gold that buys health can never be ill spent; / Nor hours laid out in harmless merriment.

HEART

The heart is the best logician – *Wendell Phillips*
There is no instinct like that of the heart – *Lord Byron*
A good heart's worth gold – *William Shakespeare*
A loving heart is the truest wisdom – *Charles Dickens*

The heart has reasons that reason does not understand – *Jacques Bénigne Bossuet*

All who know their own minds do not know their own hearts – *François de La Rochefoucauld*

The wrinkles of the heart are more indelible than those of the brow – *Mme Deluzy*

When the heart goes before, like a lamp, and illumines the pathway, many things are made clear that else lie hidden in darkness – *Henry Wadsworth Longfellow*

When the heart speaks, glory itself is an illusion – *Napoleon Bonaparte*

Memory, wit, fancy, acuteness, cannot grow young again in old age; but the heart can – *Jean Paul Richter*

All our actions take their hue from the complexion of the heart, as landscapes their variety from light – *Francis Bacon*

The heart grows better by age; I fear rather worse; always harder – *Lord Chesterfield*

Mind is the partial side of man; the heart is everything – *Antoine Rivarol*

The heart of a wise man should resemble a mirror, which reflects every object without being sullied by any – *Confucius*

Each heart is a world. You find all within yourself that you find without – *Johann Kaspar Lavater*

What the heart has once owned and had, it shall never lose – *Henry Ward Beecher*

Nothing is less in our power than the heart, and far from commanding we are forced to obey it – *Jean Jacques Rousseau*

Many flowers open to the sun, but only one follows him constantly. Heart, be thou the sunflower, not only open to receive God's blessing, but constant in looking to him – *Richter*

Want and wealth equally harden the human heart, as frost and fire are both alien to the human flesh. Famine and gluttony alike drive away nature from the heart of man – *Theodore Parker*

A noble heart, like the sun, showeth its greatest countenance in its lowest estate – *Sir Philip Sidney*

The heart is an astrologer that always divines the truth – *Pedro Calderón de la Barca*

Men, as well as women, are oftener led by their hearts than their understandings. The way to the heart is through the senses; please the eyes and ears, and the work is half done – *Chesterfield*

If wrong our hearts, our heads are right in vain.

The heart gets weary, but never gets old.

The ways of the heart, like the ways of providence, are mysterious.

If a good face is a letter of recommendation, a good heart is a letter of credit.

To judge human character rightly, a man may sometimes have very small experience, provided he has a very large heart.

The hardest trial of the heart is whether it can bear a rival's failure without triumph.

When the heart is won, the understanding is easily convinced.

HEAVEN

If I ever reach heaven I expect to find three wonders there: first, to meet some I had not thought to see there; second, to miss some I had expected to see there; and third, the greatest wonder of all, to find myself there – *John Newton*

It is heaven upon earth to have a man's mind move in charity, rest in providence, and turn upon the poles of truth – *Francis Bacon*

The generous who is always just, and the just who is always generous, may, unannounced, approach the throne of heaven – *Johann Kaspar Lavater*

Heaven will be the endless portion of every man who has heaven in his soul – *Henry Ward Beecher*

The treasury of everlasting joy – *Shakespeare*

Perfect purity, fullness of joy, everlasting freedom, perfect rest, health, and fruition, complete security, substantial and eternal good – *Hannah More*

He who seldoms thinks of heaven is not likely to get there; the only way to hit the mark is to keep the eye fixed upon it – *Bishop Horne*

Every man is received in heaven who receives heaven in himself – *Emanuel Swedenborg*

It is not talking but walking that will bring us to heaven – *Matthew Henry*

Heaven must be in me before I can be in heaven.

Earth has no sorrow that heaven cannot heal.

Nothing is farther than the earth from heaven; nothing is nearer than heaven to earth.

If the way to heaven be narrow, it is not long; and if the gate be strait, it opens into endless life.

The hope of heaven under troubles is like wind and sails to the soul.

HELL

Hell is truth seen too late – duty neglected in its season – *Tryon Edwards*

Hell is as ubiquitous as condemning conscience – *Frederick William Robertson*

When the world dissolves, all places will be hell that are not heaven – *Christopher Marlowe*

The mind is its own place, and in itself can make a heaven of hell, a hell of heaven – *John Milton*

Men might go to heaven with half the labour they put forth to go to hell,
   if they would but venture their industry in the right way – *Ben Jonson*
Hell is full of good meanings and wishings.
If there be a paradise for virtues, there must be a hell for crimes.
A guilty conscience is a hell on earth, and points to one beyond.

HELP

Light is the task where many share the toil – *Homer*
'Tis not enough to help the feeble up, / But to support him after – *William
   Shakespeare*
God be prais'd, that to believing souls / Gives light in darkness, comfort
   in despair! – *Shakespeare*
Wise men know that the only way to help themselves is to help others –
   Elbert Hubbard
Help thyself, and God will help thee.
When a person is down in the world, an ounce of help is better than a
   pound of preaching.
God helps them that help themselves.
It is one of the most beautiful compensations of this life, that no man can
   sincerely try to help another without helping himself.

HEROISM

Worship your heroes from afar; contact withers them – *Mme Neckar*
There are heroes in evil as well as in good – *François de La Rochefoucauld*
The prudent see only the difficulties, the bold only the advantages, of a
   great enterprise; the hero sees both; diminishes the former and
   makes the latter preponderate, and so conquers – *Johann Kaspar
   Lavater*
A light supper, a good night's sleep, and a fine morning have often made
   a hero of the same man who, by indigestion, a restless night, and a
   rainy morning, would have proved a coward – *Lord Chesterfield*
Mankind is not disposed to look narrowly into the conduct of great
   victors when their victory is on the right side – *George Eliot*
Heroes are not known by the loftiness of their carriage; the greatest
   braggarts are generally the merest cowards – *Jean Jacques Rousseau*
The heroes of literary history have been no less remarkable for what they
   have suffered than for what they have achieved – *Samuel Johnson*
However great the advantages which nature bestows on us, it is not she
   alone, but fortune in conjunction with her, which makes heroes – *La
   Rochefoucauld*
Self-trust is the essence of heroism – *Ralph Waldo Emerson*
The grandest of heroic deeds are those which are performed within four
   walls and in domestic privacy – *Jean Paul Richter*

Every man is a hero and an oracle to somebody, and to that person, whatever he says, has an enhanced value – *Emerson*

Dream not that helm and harness are signs of valour true. / Peace hath higher tests of manhood than battle ever knew – *John Greenleaf Whittier*

Take away ambition and vanity, and where will be your heroes and patriots? – *Seneca*

The greatest obstacle to being heroic is the doubt whether one may not be going to prove oneself a fool. The truest heroism is to resist the doubt – *Nathaniel Hawthorne*

Unbounded courage and compassion joined proclaim him good and great, and make the hero and the man complete – *Joseph Addison*

One murder makes a villain; millions a hero – *Bielby Porteus*

Of two heroes, he is the greatest who esteems his rivals most.

Fear nothing so much as sin, and your moral heroism is complete.

HISTORY

History is but the unrolled scroll of prophecy – *James Abram Garfield*

All history is a lie – *Sir Robert Walpole*

History is little more than the register of the crimes, follies, and misfortunes of mankind – *Edward Gibbon*

History is but a kind of Newgate calendar, a register of the crimes and miseries that man has inflicted on his fellow man – *Washington Irving*

History is but the development and revelation of providence – *Lajos Kossuth*

We read history through our prejudices – *Wendell Phillips*

What is history but a fable agreed upon? *Napoleon Bonaparte*

Truth is very liable to be left-handed in history – *Alexandre Dumas*

History is neither more nor less than biography on a large scale – *Alphonse Marie Louis de Lamartine*

The best thing which we derive from history is the enthusiasm that it raises in us – *Johann Wolfgang von Goethe*

Grecian history is a poem; Latin history, a picture; modern history, a chronicle – *François de Chateaubriand*

The men who make history have not time to write it – *Prince Clemens Lothar Wenzel Metternich*

All history is but a romance, unless it is studied as an example – *George Croly*

What is public history but a register of the successes and disappointments, the vices, the follies and the quarrels of those who engage in contention for power – *William Paley*

Providence conceals itself in the details of human affairs, but becomes unveiled in the generalities of history – *Lamartine*

Many historians take pleasure in putting into the mouths of princes what they have neither said nor ought to have said – *Voltaire*

The present state of things is the consequence of the past – *Samuel Johnson*

Historians give us the extraordinary events, and omit just what we want, the everyday life of each particular time and country – *Richard Whately*

History needs distance, perspective. Facts and events which are too well attested cease, in some sort, to be malleable – *Joseph Joubert*

Biography is the only true history – *Thomas Carlyle*

History makes us some amends for the shortness of life – *John Skelton*

History is the first distinct product of man's spiritual nature, his earliest expression of what can be called thought – *Carlyle*

We may gather out of history a policy no less wise than eternal, by the comparison and application of other men's forepast miseries with our own like errors and ill deservings – *Walter Raleigh*

Anybody can make history but only a great man can write it – *Oscar Wilde*

History is philosophy teaching by example, and also by warning.

History maketh a young man to be old, without wrinkles or grey hairs, privileging him with the experience of age, without either the infirmities or inconveniences thereof.

Historians may lie but history cannot.

HOLIDAYS

Who first invented work, and bound the free and holiday rejoicing spirit down? *Charles Lamb*

If all the year were playing holidays, / To sport would be as tedious as to work; / But when they seldom come, they wish'd for come – *William Shakespeare*

The holiest of all holidays are those / Kept by ourselves in silence and apart, / The secret anniversaries of the heart, / When the full tide of feeling overflows – *Henry Wadsworth Longfellow*

Let your holidays be associated with great public events, and they may be the life of patriotism as well as a source of relaxation and personal employment – *Tryon Edwards*

Under the leaves, amid the grass, lazily the day shall pass, yet not be wasted. From my drowsy ease I borrow health and strength to bear my boat through the great life ocean.

See also LEISURE.

HOLINESS

Holiness is the symmetry of the soul – *Philip Henry*

A holy life is living above the world while we are still in it – *Tryon Edwards*

Blessed is the memory of those who have kept themselves unspotted from the world. Yet more blessed and more dear the memory of those who have kept themselves unspotted in the world – *Anna Jameson*

Holiness is the architectural plan on which God buildeth up his living temple – *Charles Haddon Spurgeon*

Our holy lives must win a new world's crown – *Shakespeare*

Not all the pomp and pageantry of worlds reflect such glory on the eye supreme, as the meek virtues of the holy man – *Robert Montgomery*

Man does not properly rise to the highest, but first sinks down from it, and then afterward rises again – *Jean Paul Richter*

A holy life is a voice; it speaks when the tongue is silent, and is either a constant attraction or a perpetual reproof – *Robert Leighton*

The serene, silent beauty of a holy life is the most powerful influence in the world – *Blaise Pascal*

Real holiness has love for its essence, humility for its clothing, the good of others as its employment, and the honour of God as its end.

Holiness is not the way to Christ, but Christ is the way to holiness.

Holiness is religious principle put into action.

The essence of true holiness consists in conformity to the nature and will of God.

See also RELIGION.

HOME

Without hearts there is no home – *Lord Byron*

Our home joys are the most delightful earth affords – *Johann Heinrich Pestalozzi*

The first indication of domestic happiness is the love of one's home.

He is the happiest, be he king or peasant, who finds peace in his home – *Johann Wolfgang von Goethe*

Any feeling that takes a man away from his home is a traitor to the household – *Henry Ward Beecher*

It is very dangerous for any man to find any spot on this broad globe that is sweeter to him than his home – *Beecher*

The sweetest type of heaven is home – *Josiah Gilbert Holland*

At evening, home is the best place for man – *Goethe*

The paternal hearth, that rallying place of the affections – *Washington Irving*

There is a magic in that little word, home; it is a mystic circle that surrounds comforts and virtues never known beyond its hallowed limits – *Robert Southey*

Be it ever so humble, there's no place like home – *John Howard Payne*

Home is the seminary of all other institutions – *E. H. Chapin*

A man is always nearest to his good when at home, and farthest from it when away – *Holland*

To be happy at home is the ultimate aim of all ambition – *Samuel Johnson*

We need not power or splendour; / Wide hall or lordly dome; / The good, the true, the tender, / These form the wealth of home – *Sarah Josepha Hale*

Only the home can found a state – *Joseph Cook*

A hundred men may make an encampment, but it takes a woman to make a home – *Chinese proverb*

To Adam paradise was home. To the good among his descendants, home is paradise.

The first sure symptom of a mind in health is rest of heart, and pleasure felt at home.

What a man is at home, that he is indeed, if not to the world, yet to his own conscience and to God.

The virtuous home is at the basis of all national prosperity.

Home is the resort of love, of joy, of peace, and plenty.

Educating the homes we evangelize the world.

To make men out of boys, and women out of girls, there is no place like home.

A cottage, if God be there, will hold as much happiness as might stock a palace.

Home, the spot of earth supremely blest, / A dearer, sweeter spot than all the rest.

A good home implies good living.

See also DOMESTICITY.

HONESTY

An honest man's the noblest work of God – *Alexander Pope*

Honesty is the best policy – *Benjamin Franklin*

Make yourself an honest man, and then you may be sure there is one rascal less in the world – *Thomas Carlyle*

To be honest, as this world goes, is to be one man picked out of ten thousand – *William Shakespeare*

All other knowledge is hurtful to him who has not honesty and good nature – *Michel Eyquem de Montaigne*

The only disadvantage of an honest heart is credulity – *Sir Philip Sidney*

A straight line is shortest in morals as well as in geometry – *Maria Edgeworth*

He who says there is no such thing as an honest man is himself a knave – *George Berkeley*

It would be an unspeakable advantage, both to the public and private, if men would consider that great truth, that no man is wise or safe, but he that is honest – *Walter Raleigh*

Money dishonestly acquired is never worth its cost, while a good conscience never costs as much as it is worth – *J. P. Senn*

If he does really think that there is no distinction between virtue and vice, when he leaves our houses let us count our spoons – *Samuel Johnson*

If honesty did not exist, we ought to invent it as the best means of getting rich – *Comte de Mirabeau*

No legacy is so rich as honesty – *Shakespeare*

There is no terror . . . in your threats; / For I am arm'd so strong in honesty / That they pass by me as the idle wind, / Which I respect not – *Shakespeare*

Lands mortgaged may return, but honesty once pawned is ne'er redeemed – *Thomas Middleton*

Hope of ill gain is the beginning of loss – *Democritus*

Put it out of the power of truth to give you an ill character. If anybody reports you not to be an honest man let your practice give him the lie – *Aurelius*

It was a grand trait of the old Roman that with him one and the same word meant both honour and honesty.

God looks only to the pure, not to the full, hands.

To one who said, 'I do not believe that there is an honest man in the world', another replied, 'It is impossible that any one man should know all the world, but quite possible that one may know himself.'

Socrates being asked the way to honest fame said, 'Study to be what you wish to seem.'

Prefer loss before unjust gain: for that brings grief but once; this forever.

You can cheat an honest man but you cannot fool him.

See also DECENCY, INTEGRITY.

HONOUR

Honour and shame from no condition rise; / Act well your part, there all the honour lies – *Alexander Pope*

That nation is worthless that will not, with pleasure, venture all for its honour – *Johann Christopher Friedrich von Schiller*

Mine honour is my life; both grow in one; / Take honour from me, and my life is done – *William Shakespeare*

Woman's honour is nice as ermine; it will not bear a soil – *John Dryden*

If it be a sin to covet honour, / I am the most offending soul alive – *Shakespeare*

Let honour be to us as strong an obligation as necessity is to others – *Pliny the Younger*

Our own heart, and not other men's opinion, forms our true honour – *Samuel Taylor Coleridge*

Hereditary honours are a noble and splendid treasure to descendants – *Plato*

Honour is like the eye, which cannot suffer the least impurity without damage. It is a precious stone, the price of which is lessened by a single flaw – *Jacques Bénigne Bossuet*

The giving of riches and honours to a wicked man is like giving strong wine to him that hath a fever – *Plutarch*

Better to die ten thousand deaths than wound my honour – *Joseph Addison*

Life every man holds dear; but the dear man / Holds honour far more precious-dear than life – *Shakespeare*

Honour is not a matter of any man's calling merely, but rather of his own actions in it.

Purity is the feminine truth, the masculine of honour.

HOPE

Hope springs eternal in the human breast; / Man never is, but always to be blest – *Alexander Pope*

Hope is a prodigal young heir, and experience is his banker, but his drafts are seldom honoured since there is often a heavy balance against him, because he draws largely on a small capital and is not yet in possession – *Charles Caleb Colton*

The hours we pass with happy prospects in view are more pleasing than those crowded with fruition – *Oliver Goldsmith*

We speak of hope; but is not hope only a more gentle name for fear – *L. E. Landon*

Hope is a flatterer, but the most upright of all parasites; for she frequents the poor man's hut, as well as the palace of his superior – *William Shenstone*

Hope is the last thing that dies in man – *François de La Rochefoucauld*

The miserable have no other medicine / But only hope – *William Shakespeare*

True hope is swift, and flies with swallow's wings; / Kings it makes gods, and meaner creatures kings – *Shakespeare*

A propensity to hope and joy is real riches; one to fear and sorrow, real poverty – *David Hume*

It is worth a thousand pounds a year to have the habit of looking on the bright side of things – *Samuel Johnson*

Hope is like the sun, which, as we journey toward it, casts the shadow of our burden behind us – *Samuel Smiles*

Hope is always liberal, and they that trust her promises make little scruple of revelling today on the profits of tomorrow – *Johnson*

Hope is a delusion; no hand can grasp a wave or a shadow – *Victor Hugo*

Hope is the only good that is common to all men; those who have nothing else possess hope still – *Thales*

Hope is a lover's staff; walk hence with that / And manage it against despairing thoughts – *Shakespeare*

Hope is brightest when it dawns from fears – *Walter Scott*

Where there is no hope, there can be no endeavour – *Johnson*

He that lives on hopes will die fasting – *Benjamin Franklin*

Hope is love's happiness, but not its life – *Landon*

The flights of the human mind are not from enjoyment to enjoyment, but from hope to hope – *Johnson*

Hope is a vigorous principle; it sets the head and heart to work, and animates a man to do his utmost – *Jeremy Collier*

Hope writes the poetry of the boy, but memory that of the man – *Ralph Waldo Emerson*

He [who] loses hope may part with anything – *William Congreve*

In all the wedding cake, hope is the sweetest plum – *Douglas William Jerrold*

The man who lives only by hope will die with despair – *Italian proverb*

You cannot put a great hope into a small soul.

Auspicious hope, in thy sweet garden grow wreaths for each toil, a charm for every woe.

Hope is but the dream of those that wake.

Hope – of all ills that men endure, / The only cheap and universal cure; / The captive's freedom, and the sick man's health, / The lover's victory, and the beggar's wealth.

Hope warps judgement in council, but quickens energy in action.

Hope – fortune's cheating lottery, where for one prize, a hundred blanks there be.

For present grief there is always a remedy; however much thou sufferest, hope; hope is the greatest happiness of man.

Hope is a pleasant acquaintance, but an unsafe friend.

Hope without action is a barren undoer.

When the heart is light with hope, all pleases; nothing comes amiss.

Hope is a good breakfast but it is a bad supper.

HOSPITALITY

As you receive the stranger, so you receive your God – *Johann Kaspar Lavater*

There is an emanation from the heart in genuine hospitality which cannot be described but is immediately felt, and puts the stranger at once at his ease – *Washington Irving*

Small cheer and great welcome makes a merry feast – *William Shakespeare*

Let not the emphasis of hospitality lie in bed and board, but let truth, love, honour, and courtesy flow in all thy deeds – *Ralph Waldo Emerson*

If a man be gracious to strangers, it shows that he is a citizen of the
world – *Francis Bacon*

Provision is the foundation of hospitality, and thrift the fuel of mag-
nificence – *Sir Philip Sidney*

Like many other virtues hospitality is practised, in its perfection, by the
poor.

See also GUESTS.

HOUSE

My precept to all who build is that the owner should be an ornament to
the house, and not the house to the owner – *Cicero*

A house is never perfectly furnished for enjoyment unless there is a
child in it rising three years old, and a kitten of six weeks – *Robert
Southey*

Make your dwelling tasteful and attractive, both within and without; the
associations of the home of our early days have a strong influence on
the future life.

See also BUILDING, DOMESTICITY, HOME.

HUMILITY

Sense shines with a double lustre when it is set in humility – *William Penn*

The doctrines of grace humble man without degrading, and exalt
without inflating him – *Charles Hodge*

Be wise; soar not too high to fall, but stoop to rise – *Philip Massinger*

They that know God will be humble; they that know themselves cannot
be proud – *John Flavel*

It is the witness still of excellency / To put a strange face on his own
perfection – *William Shakespeare*

Heaven's gates are not so highly arched as princes' palaces; they that
enter there must go upon their knees – *John Webster*

Humility is to make a right estimate of one's self – *Charles Haddon
Spurgeon*

Forgive thyself little and others much – *Robert Leighton*

I believe the first test of a truly great man is his humility – *John Ruskin*

After crosses and losses men grow humbler and wiser – *Benjamin Franklin*

Humility is the solid foundation of all the virtues – *Confucius*

Humbleness is always grace; always dignity – *J. R. Lovell*

To be humble to superiors is duty; to equals is courtesy; to inferiors is
nobleness; and to all safety; it being a virtue that, for all its lowliness,
commandeth those it stoops to – *Thomas More*

Humility enforces where neither virtue, nor strength, nor reason can prevail – *Francis Quarles*

The fullest and best ears of corn hang lowest toward the ground – *Walter Reynolds*

Truly, this world can get on without us, if we would but think so – *Henry Wadsworth Longfellow*

Nothing sets a person so much out of the devil's reach as humility – *Jonathan Edwards*

He that places himself neither higher nor lower than he ought to do exercises the truest humility – *Charles Caleb Colton*

Humility, that low sweet root, / From which all heavenly virtues shoot.

It is easy to look down on others; to look down on ourselves is the difficulty.

It was pride that changed angels into devils; it is humility that makes men as angels.

The sufficiency of my merit is to know that my merit is not sufficient.

It is no great thing to be humble when you are brought low; but to be humble when you are praised is a great and rare attainment.

The Christian is like the ripening corn; the riper he grows the more lowly he bends his head.

The richest pearl in the Christian's crown of graces is humility.

Humility is the eldest born of virtue, and claims the birthright at the throne of heaven.

Humility – a prudent care not to overdue ourselves.

HUMOUR

Every time a man smiles – but much more so when he laughs – it adds something to this fragment of life – *Laurence Sterne*

Good humour is one of the best articles of dress one can wear in society – *William Makepeace Thackeray*

Don't put too fine a point to your wit for fear it should get blunted – *Miguel de Cervantes Saavedra*

Good humour is the clear blue sky of the soul, highly favourable to the discoveries and progress of genius.

All the wit in the world is thrown away upon the man who has none.

Impromptu is the touchstone of wit.

Everything is funny as long as it is happening to somebody else.

See also LAUGHTER, MIRTH, WIT.

HUNGER

No clock is more regular than the belly – *François Rabelais*

A hungry stomach has no ears.

If you give a man a fish you give him a meal. If you give him a net you
   feed him for life.

HYPOCRISY

A bad man is worse when he pretends to be a saint – *Francis Bacon*

O, what authority and show of truth, / Can cunning sin cover itself
   withal! – *William Shakespeare*

No man is a hypocrite in his pleasures – *Samuel Johnson*

He would say untruths, and be ever double / Both in his words and
   meaning. He was never, / But where he meant to ruin, pitiful –
   Shakespeare

Hypocrisy is the homage that vice pays to virtue – *François de La
   Rochefoucauld*

Hypocrisy is the necessary burden of villainy – *Johnson*

Hypocrites do the devil's drudgery in Christ's livery – *Matthew Henry*

False face must hide what the false heart doth know – *Shakespeare*

Saint abroad and devil at home – *John Bunyan*

With devotion's visage / And pious action we do sugar o'er / The devil
   himself – *Shakespeare*

One may smile, and smile, and be a villain – *Shakespeare*

The hypocrite was a man who stole the livery of the court of heaven to
   serve the devil in.

The most terrible of lies is not that which is uttered but that which is
   lived.

See also DECEIT.

IDEALS

A large portion of human beings live not so much in themselves as in
   what they desire to be – *E. P. Whipple*

Ideals are the world's masters – *Josiah Gilbert Holland*

Ideal beauty is a fugitive which is never located – *Mme Sévigné*

We build statues of snow, and weep to see them melt – *Walter Scott*

A man's ideal, like his horizon, is constantly receding from him as he
   advances toward it – *W. G. T. Shedd*

Words without actions are the assassins of idealism – *Herbert Hoover*

The attainment of an ideal is often the beginning of a disillusion – *Stanley
   Baldwin*

No folly is more costly than the folly of intolerant idealism – *Winston
   Churchill*

No ideal is as good as a fact – *Richard C. Cabot*

The best and noblest lives are those which are set toward high ideals.

What we need most is not so much to realize the ideal as to idealize the real.

Great objects form great minds.

IDEAS

Ideas control the world – *James Abram Garfield*

A healthful hunger for a great idea is the beauty and blessedness of life – *Jean Ingelow*

In these days we fight for ideas, and newspapers are our fortresses – *Heinrich Heine*

Many ideas grow better when transplanted into another mind than in the one where they sprung up – *Oliver Wendell Holmes*

Ideas are the great warriors of the world, and a war that has no idea behind it is simply a brutality – *Garfield*

Ideas are like beards; men do not have them until they grow up – *Voltaire*

Ideas are the factors that lift civilization – *Bishop Vincent*

Thoughts are mightier than armies – *W. M. Paxton*

A soul occupied with great ideas best performs small duties – *Harriet Martineau*

If the ancients left us ideas, to our credit be it spoken, we moderns are building houses for them – *Amos Bronson Alcott*

Ideas, though vivid and real, are often indefinite, and are shy of the close furniture of words – *Martin Farquhar Tupper*

To have ideas is to gather flowers; to think is to weave them into garlands – *Mme Swetchine*

An idea, like a ghost, according to the common notion of ghosts, must be spoken to a little before it will explain itself – *Charles Dickens*

Ideas make their way in silence like the waters that, filtering behind the rocks of the Alps, loosen them from the mountains on which they rest – *Jean Henri Merle D'Aubigné*

Ideas in the mind are the transcript of the world; words are the transcript of ideas; and writing and printing are the transcript of words – *Joseph Addison*

New ideas can be good or bad, just the same as old ones – *Franklin D. Roosevelt*

Alter ideas and you alter the world – *H. G. Wells*

Our ideas, like orange plants, spread out in proportion to the size of the box which imprisons the roots.

Old ideas are prejudices, and new ones caprices.

A great idea is usually original to more than one discoverer.

Great ideas come when the world needs them.

By what strange law of mind is it, that an idea long overlooked, and trodden underfoot as a useless stone, suddenly sparkles out in new light as a discovered diamond?

Our land is not more the recipient of the men of all countries than of their ideas.

Most of man's inventions have been time-savers – then came television.

IDLENESS

The idle man is the devil's cushion, on which he taketh his free ease – *Bishop Hall*

Idleness is the key of beggary, and the root of all evil – *Charles Haddon Spurgeon*

In idleness there is perpetual despair – *Thomas Carlyle*

If idleness do not produce vice or malevolence, it commonly produces melancholy – *Sydney Smith*

Idleness is only the refuge of weak minds, and the holiday of fools – *Lord Chesterfield*

Too much idleness fills up a man's time much more completely, and leaves him less his own master, than any sort of employment whatsoever – *Edmund Burke*

If you are idle you are on the way to ruin, and there are few stopping places upon it. It is rather a precipice than a road – *Henry Ward Beecher*

Life is a short day; but it is a working day. Activity may lead to evil, but inactivity cannot lead to good – *Hannah More*

Not only is he idle who is doing nothing, but he that might be better employed – *Socrates*

Laziness grows on people; it begins in cobwebs and ends in iron chains. The more business a man has to do the more he is able to accomplish, for he learns to economize his time – *Sir Matthew Hale*

Idleness among children, as among men, is the root of all evil, and leads to no other evil more certain than ill temper – *Hannah More*

Much bending breaks the bow; much unbending the mind – *Francis Bacon*

People who have nothing to do are quickly tired of their own company – *Jeremy Collier*

Idleness is many gathered miseries in one name – *Jean Paul Richter*

Idleness is the burial of a living man – *Jeremy Taylor*

Absence of occupation is not rest; / A mind quite vacant is a mind distressed – *William Cowper*

Do not allow idleness to deceive you; for while you give him today he steals tomorrow from you – *Alfred Crowquill*

Ten thousand harms, more than the ills I know / My idleness doth hatch – *William Shakespeare*

Idleness is leisure gone to seed – *Eli Schleifer*

The busy man is troubled with but one devil; the idle man by a thousand
  – *Spanish proverb*
An idle brain is the devil's workshop – *English proverb*
Idleness is the devil's home for temptation.
By nature's laws, immutable and just, enjoyment stops where indolence
  begins.
Indolence is considered as the mother of misery.
The way to be nothing is to do nothing.
Idleness is the stupidity of the body, and stupidity is the idleness of the
  mind.
Stagnation is something worse than death; it is corruption also.
Idleness travels very slowly, and poverty soon overtakes her.
An idle man is like a house that hath no walls; the devils may enter on
  every side.
I would not waste the springtime of my youth in idle dalliance; I would
  plant rich seeds to blossom in my manhood, and bear fruit when I am
  old.
See also INACTIVITY, INDOLENCE, SLOTH.

IGNORANCE

Better be unborn than untaught, for ignorance is the root of misfortune –
  Plato
Have the courage to be ignorant of a great number of things, in order to
  avoid the calamity of being ignorant of everything – *Sydney Smith*
He that does not know those things which are of use and necessity for
  him to know is but an ignorant man, whatever he may know besides
  – *John Tillotson*
Nothing is so indicative of deepest culture as a tender consideration of
  the ignorant – *Ralph Waldo Emerson*
To be ignorant of one's ignorance is the malady of ignorance – *Amos
  Bronson Alcott*
It is impossible to make people understand their ignorance; for it
  requires knowledge to perceive it, and therefore he that can perceive
  it hath it not – *Jeremy Taylor*
Ignorance, which in behaviour mitigates a fault, is, in literature, a capital
  offence – *Joseph Joubert*
The ignorant hath an eagle's wings and an owl's eyes – *George Herbert*
It is with nations as with individuals, those who know the least of others
  think the highest of themselves – *Charles Caleb Colton*
Ignorance, when voluntary, is criminal, and a man may be properly
  charged with that evil which he neglected or refused to learn how to
  prevent – *Samuel Johnson*
So long as thou art ignorant be not ashamed to learn. Ignorance is the

greatest of all infirmities, and, when justified, the chiefest of all follies – *Izaak Walton*

Ignorance gives a sort of eternity to prejudice, and perpetuity to error – *Robert Hall*

If thou art wise thou knowest thine own ignorance; and thou art ignorant if thou knowest not thyself – *Martin Luther*

He that is not aware of his ignorance will be only misled by his knowledge – *Richard Whately*

Ignorance is the curse of God, / Knowledge the wing wherewith we fly to heaven – *William Shakespeare*

Ignorance is the night of the mind, but a night without moon or star – *Confucius*

A wise man in the company of those who are ignorant has been compared to a beautiful girl in the company of blind men – *Sádi*

Ignorance is a prolonged infancy, only deprived of its charm – *Marquis de Boufflers*

There are times when ignorance is bliss, indeed – *Charles Dickens*

Nothing is so haughty and assuming as ignorance where self-conceit sets up to be infallible – *Robert South*

Ignorance lies at the bottom of all human knowledge, and the deeper we penetrate the nearer we come to it – *Colton*

Too much attention cannot be bestowed on that important, yet much neglected branch of learning, the knowledge of man's ignorance – *Whately*

Where ignorance is bliss / 'Tis folly to be wise – *Thomas Gray*

The highest reach of human science is the scientific recognition of human ignorance – *Sir William Hamilton*

There is nothing makes a man suspect much, more than to know little – *Francis Bacon*

It is as great a point of wisdom to hide ignorance as to discover knowledge.

It is not wisdom but ignorance that teaches men presumption. Genius may sometimes be arrogant, but nothing is so diffident as knowledge.

Be ignorance thy choice, where knowledge leads to woe.

ILLS

It is better to try to bear the ills we have than to anticipate those which may never come – *François de La Rochefoucauld*

Philosophy easily triumphs over past and future ills; but present ills triumph over philosophy – *La Rochefoucauld*

We trust that somehow good will be the final goal of ill – *Alfred, Lord Tennyson*

Think of the ills from which you are exempt, and it will aid you to bear patiently those which now you may suffer.

The fear of ill exceeds the ill we fear.

IMAGINATION

We are all of us imaginative in some form or other, for images are the brood of desire – *George Eliot*

He who has imagination without learning has wings and not feet – *Joseph Joubert*

Imagination rules the world – *Napoleon Bonaparte*

The soul without imagination is what an observatory would be without a telescope – *Henry Ward Beecher*

The world of reality has its limits; the world of imagination is boundless – *Jean Jacques Rousseau*

Thought convinces; feeling persuades – *Theodore Parker*

Imagination is mere fantasy – the image-making power, common to all who have the gift of dreams – *James Russell Lowell*

Imagination is the eye of the soul – *Joubert*

Imagination ennobles appetites which in themselves are low, and spiritualizes acts which, else, are only animal. But the pleasures which begin in the senses only sensualize – *Frederick William Robertson*

Our griefs, as well as our joys, owe their strongest colours to our imaginations – *Jane Porter*

Solitude is as needful to the imagination as society is wholesome for the character – *Lowell*

An uncommon degree of imagination constitutes poetical genius – *Dugald Stewart*

The lunatic, the lover, and the poet, / Are of imagination all compact – *William Shakespeare*

It is the divine attribute of the imagination, that when the real world is shut out it can create a world for itself – *Washington Irving*

Imagination is the ruler of our dreams; let reason be the ruler of our waking thoughts.

The great instrument of moral good is the imagination.

IMITATION

Man is an imitative creature, and whoever is foremost leads the herd – *Johann Christoph Friedrich von Schiller*

It is by imitation, far more than by precept, that we learn everything – *Edmund Burke*

He who imitates evil always goes beyond the example that is set; he who imitates what is good always falls short – *Francesco Guicciardini*

It is a poor wit who lives by borrowing the words, decisions, mien, inventions, and actions of others – *Johann Kaspar Lavater*

Men are so constituted that everyone undertakes what he sees another successful in, whether he has aptitude for it or not – *Johann Wolfgang von Goethe*

Every kind of imitation speaks the person that imitates inferior to him whom he imitates, as the copy is to the original – *Robert South*

Imitators are a servile race – *Jean de La Fontaine*

We imitate only what we believe and admire.

Precepts are useful, but practice and imitation go far beyond them.

Imitation belittles.

I hardly know so true a mark of a little mind as the servile imitation of others.

IMMORTALITY

Those who hope for no other life are dead even for this – *Johann Wolfgang von Goethe*

The seed dies into a new life, and so does man – *George Macdonald*

What springs from earth dissolves to earth again, and heaven-born things fly to their native beat – *Aurelius*

We do not believe in immortality because we have proved it, but, we forever try to prove it because we believe it – *James Martineau*

We are much better believers in immortality than we can give grounds for – *Ralph Waldo Emerson*

Without a belief in personal immortality, religion is like an arch resting on one pillar – *Max Miller*

As often as I hear of some undeserved wretchedness, my thoughts rest on that world where all will be made straight, and where the labours of sorrow will end in joy – *Johann Gottlieb Fichte*

Immortality is the glorious discovery of Christianity – *William Ellery Channing*

The monuments of the nations are all protests against nothingness after death; so are statues and inscriptions; so is history – *Lew Wallace*

One short sleep past, we wake eternally, / And death shall be no more – *John Donne*

It is not a question whether we shall live forever; the real question is whether we are worthy to live forever – *John Haynes Holmes*

Those who live in the Lord never see each other for the last time – *German motto*

The belief that we shall never die is the foundation of our dying well.

Immortality, which is the spiritual desire, is the intellectual necessity.

Immortality is the greatness of our being; the scene for attaining the fullness and perfection of our existence.

Man only of all earthly creatures asks, 'Can the dead die forever?' – and the instinct that urges the question is God's answer to man, for no instinct is given in vain.

It is immortality, and that alone, which amid life's pains, abasements, the soul can comfort, elevate, and fill.

There is no greater immortality than to occupy a place you cannot fill.

The soul is not where it lives, but where it loves.

IMPATIENCE

Impatience turns an ague into a fever, a fever to the plague, fear into despair, anger into rage, loss into madness, and sorrow to amazement – *Jeremy Taylor*

Adversity borrows its sharpest sting from our impatience – *Bishop Horne*

In that worthiest of all struggles, the struggle for self-mastery and goodness, we are far less patient with ourselves than God is with us – *Josiah Gilbert Holland*

Whoever is out of patience is out of possession of his soul – *Francis Bacon*

Impatience dries the blood sooner than age or sorrow.

IMPERFECTION

He censures God who quarrels with the imperfection of men – *Edmund Burke*

No human face is exactly the same in its lines on each side: no leaf is perfect in its lobes, and no branch in its symmetry. All admit irregularity, as they imply change. To banish imperfection is to destroy expression, to check exertion, to paralyse vitality. All things are better, lovelier, and more beloved for the imperfections which have been divinely appointed, that the law of human judgement may be mercy – *John Ruskin*

It is only imperfection that complains of what is imperfect. The more perfect we are, the more gentle and quiet we become toward the defects of others – *François de Fénelon*

The finer the nature, the more flaws will show through the clearness of it – *Ruskin*

What an absurd thing it is to pass over all the valuable parts of a man, and fix our attention on his infirmities – *Joseph Addison*

Great men are very apt to have great faults; and the faults appear the greater by their contrast with their excellencies.

See also FAULTS.

IMPOSSIBILITY

Few things are impossible in themselves. It is not so much means, as
   perseverance, that is wanting to bring them to a successful issue –
   François de La Rochefoucauld
One great difference between a wise man and a fool is the former
   only wishes for what he may possibly obtain; the latter desires
   impossibilities – *Democritus*
'Impossible!' That is not good French – *Napoleon Bonaparte*
It is not a lucky word, this same 'impossible'; no good comes of those
   who have it so often in their mouth – *Thomas Carlyle*
Impossible is a word only to be found in the dictionary of fools – *Napoleon
   Bonaparte*
Nothing is impossible; there are ways that lead to everything, and if we
   had sufficient will we should always have sufficient means – *La
   Rochefoucauld*

IMPRESSIONS

The mind unlearns with difficulty what has long been impressed on it –
   Seneca
If you would stand well with a great mind, leave him with a favourable
   impression of yourself; if with a little mind, leave him with a
   favourable opinion of himself – *Samuel Taylor Coleridge*
Do not all impressions made in life continue immortal as the soul itself?
Our first impression, whether of persons or things, have great influence
   on all our future estimates and opinions.

IMPROVEMENT

Slumber not in the tents of your fathers. The world is advancing.
   Advance with it – *Giuseppe Mazzini*
People seldom improve when they have no other model but themselves
   to copy after – *Oliver Goldsmith*
It is necessary to try to surpass oneself always; this occupation ought to
   last as long as life – *Queen Christina*
If a better system is thine, import it; if not make use of mine – *Horace*
All of us, who are worth anything, spend our manhood in unlearning
   the follies, or expiating the mistakes of our youth – *Percy Bysshe
   Shelley*
To hear always, to think always, to learn always, it is thus that we live
   truly; he who aspires to nothing, and learns nothing, is nothing.
Much of the wisdom of one age is the folly of the next.
If you want a better world get busy in your own little corner.

IMPROVIDENCE

Waste not, want not; wilful waste makes woeful want – *Benjamin Franklin*

What maintains one vice would bring up two children. Remember, many a little makes a mickle; and further, beware of little expenses; a small leak will sink a great ship – *Franklin*

Hundreds would never have known want, if they had not first known waste – *Charles Haddon Spurgeon*

There are men born under that constellation which maketh them as unapt to enrich themselves as they are ready to impoverish others.

How full or how empty our lives depends, we say, on Providence. Suppose we say, more or less on improvidence.

IMPULSE

The first impulse of conscience is apt to be right; the first impulse of appetite or passion is generally wrong. We should be faithful to the former, but suspicious of the latter – *Tryon Edwards*

Since the generality of persons act from impulse much more than from principle, men are neither so good nor so bad as we are apt to think them.

A true history of human events would show that a far larger proportion of our acts are the results of sudden impulses and accident, than of that reason of which we so much boast.

Our first impulses are good, generous, heroical; reflection weakens and kills them.

INACTIVITY

The mightiest powers by deepest calms are fed – *Bryan Waller Procter*

There are many times and circumstances in life when 'Our strength is to sit still.' – *Tryon Edwards*

Nature knows no pause in her progress and development, and attaches her curse on all inaction – *Johann Wolfgang von Goethe*

The keenest pangs the wretched find / Are rapture to the dreary void – / The leafless desert of the mind – / The waste of feelings unemployed – *Lord Byron*

Thoughtful, disciplined, intended inaction – *John Randolph*

The Commons, faithful to their system, remained in a wise and masterly inactivity.

Washington, it was said, knew how to conquer by delay.

He that takes time to think and consider will act more wisely than he that acts hastily and on impulse.

See also IDLENESS, SLOTH.

INCONSTANCY

Clocks will go as they are set; but man, irregular man, is never constant,
never certain – *Thomas Otway*

Were man / But constant, he were perfect; that one error / Fills him with
faults; makes him run through all the sins; / Inconstancy falls off ere it
begins – *William Shakespeare*

Inconstancy is but a name to fright poor lovers from a better choice.

INCREDULITY

The incredulous are of all men the most credulous; they believe the
miracles of Vespasian, in order not to believe those of Moses – *Blaise
Pascal*

Nothing is so contemptible as that affectation of wisdom which some
display by universal incredulity – *Oliver Goldsmith*

Incredulity robs us of many pleasures, and gives us nothing in return –
James Russell Lowell

Some men will believe nothing but what they can comprehend; and
there are but few things that such are able to comprehend – *Seigneur
de Saint-Evremond*

Of all the signs of a corrupt heart and a feeble head, the tendency of
incredulity is the surest. Real philosophy seeks rather to solve than to
deny.

A sceptical young man said to Dr Parr that he would belive nothing
which he could not understand. 'Then,' said the Doctor, 'your creed
will be the shortest of any man's I know.'

The amplest knowledge has the largest faith. Ignorance is always
incredulous.

INDECISION

The wavering mind is but a base possession – *Euripides*

It is a miserable thing to live in suspense; it is the life of a spider – *Jonathan
Swift*

There is nothing in the world more pitiable than an irresolute man –
Johann Wolfgang von Goethe

When a man has not a good reason for doing a thing, he has one good
reason for letting it alone – *Thomas Scott*

A man without decision can never be said to belong to himself; he is as a
feather in the air which every breeze blows about as it listeth – *John
Foster*

It is a great evil, as well as a misfortune, to be unable to utter a prompt
and decided 'No'.

INDEPENDENCE

It is not the greatness of a man's means that makes him independent, so much as the smallness of his wants – *William Cobbett*

Two things, contradictory as they may seem, must go together – humble dependence and manly independence, humble dependence on God and manly reliance on self – *William Wordsworth*

The greatest of all human benefits, that, at least, without which no other benefit can be truly enjoyed, is independence – *Parke Godwin*

Happy the man to whom heaven has given a morsel of bread without laying him under the obligation of thanking any other for it than heaven itself – *Miguel de Cervantes Saavedra*

The word independence is united to the ideas of dignity and virtue; the word dependence to the ideas of inferiority and corruption – *Jeremy Bentham*

No man can lift up his head with manly calmness and peace who is the slave of other men's judgements – *John White Alexander*

There is often as much independence in not being led as in not being driven – *Tryon Edwards*

The moral progression of a people can scarcely begin till they are independent.

See also FREEDOM.

INDIFFERENCE

Set honour in one eye, and death i' the other, / And I will look on both indifferently – *William Shakespeare*

Nothing for preserving the body like having no heart – *J. P. Senn*

Indifference is the invincible giant of the world – *Ouida*

Indifference never wrote great works, nor thought out striking inventions, nor reared the solemn architecture that awes the soul, nor breathed sublime music, nor painted glorious pictures, nor undertook heroic philanthropies. All these grandeurs are born of enthusiasm, and are done heartily.

INDISCRETION

An indiscreet man is more hurtful than an ill-natured one; for the latter will only attack his enemies, the other injures indifferently both friends and foes – *Joseph Addison*

Indiscretion and wickedness, be it known, are first cousins – *Ninon de Lenclos*

For good and evil in our actions meet ; / Wicked is not much worse than indiscreet – *John Donne*

The generality of men expend the early part of their lives in contributing
to render the latter part miserable – *Jean de La Bruyère*

Indiscretion, rashness, falsehood, levity, and malice produce each other
– *Johann Kaspar Lavater*

We waste our best years in distilling the sweetest flowers of life into
potions, which, after all, do not immortalize, but only intoxicate –
Henry Wadsworth Longfellow

Three things too much, and three too little are pernicious to man; to
speak much, and know little; to spend much, and have little; to
presume much, and be worth little – *Miguel de Cervantes Saavedra*

We may outrun, / By violent swiftness, that which we run at, / And lose
by over-running – *William Shakespeare*

INDIVIDUALITY

Every individual nature has its own beauty – *Ralph Waldo Emerson*

Individuality is everywhere to be spared and respected as the root of
everything good – *Jean Paul Richter*

You are tried alone; alone you pass into the desert; alone you are sifted by
the world – *Frederick William Robertson*

Every great man is a unique man – *Emerson*

The worth of a state, in the long run, is the worth of the individuals
composing it – *John Stuart Mill*

Not armies, not nations, have advanced the race; but here and there, in
the course of ages, an individual has stood up and cast his shadow
over the world – *E. H. Chapin*

It is said that if Noah's ark had had to be built by a company, they would
not have laid the keel yet; and it may be so. What is many men's
business is nobody's business. The greatest things are accomplished
by individual men – *Charles Haddon Spurgeon*

Everything without tells the individual that he is nothing; everything
within persuades him that he is everything.

That life only is truly free which rules and suffices for itself.

INDOLENCE

Indolence is the sleep of the mind – *Marquis de Vauvenargues*

What is often called indolence is, in fact, the unconscious consciousness
of incapacity – *Henry Crabb Robinson*

Indolence and stupidity are first cousins – *Antoine Rivarol*

The darkest hour in the history of any young man is when he sits down
to study how to get money without honestly earning it – *Horace
Greeley*

Laziness grows on people; it begins in cobwebs, and ends in iron chains.
 The more one has to do the more he is able to accomplish.
Nothing ages like laziness.
What men want is not talent; it is purpose.
See also IDLENESS.

INDULGENCE

Those who love dainties are likely soon to be beggars – *Benjamin Franklin*
Too many wish to be happy before becoming wise – *Mme Neckar*
Sensual indulgences are costly at both ends.
Live only for today, and you ruin tomorrow.
See also LENITY, LUXURY.

INDUSTRY

Sloth makes all things difficult, but industry all things easy – *Benjamin Franklin*

Like the bee, we should make our industry our amusement – *Oliver Goldsmith*

One loses all the time which he might employ to better purpose – *Jean Jacques Rousseau*

In every rank, both great and small, / It is industry that supports us all – *John Gay*

If you have great talents, industry will improve them; if but moderate abilities, industry will supply their deficiencies – *Joshua Reynolds*

There is always hope in a man who actually and earnestly works. In idleness alone is there perpetual despair – *Thomas Carlyle*

The more we do, the more we can do; the more busy we are, the more leisure we have – *William Hazlitt*

Mankind are more indebted to industry than ingenuity; the gods set up their favours at a price, and industry is the purchaser – *Joseph Addison*

No man is born into the world whose work is not born with him – *James Russell Lowell*

Excellence is never granted to man, but as a reward of labour – *Reynolds*

A man who gives his children habits of industry provides for them better than by giving them a fortune – *Richard Whately*

Industrious wisdom often doth prevent what lazy folly thinks inevitable.
It is better to wear out than to rust out.
Fortune may find a pot, but your own industry must make it boil.
Industry is not only the instrument of improvement, but the foundation of pleasure.
Application is the price to be paid for mental acquisition. To have the harvest we must sow the seed.

Industry keeps the body healthy, the mind clear, the heart whole, and
the purse full.

An hour's industry will do more to produce cheerfulness, suppress evil
humours, and retrieve one's affairs, than a month's moaning.

The chiefest action for a man of spirit is never to be out of action; the soul
was never put into the body to stand still.

See also LABOUR, OCCUPATION.

INFAMY

Infamy is where it is received. If thou art a mud wall, it will stick; if
marble it will rebound – *Francis Quarles*

What grief can there be that time doth not make less? / But infamy, time
never can suppress.

The most infamous are fond of fame; and those who fear not guilt, yet
start at shame.

INFLUENCE

It is the age that forms the man, not the man that forms the age – *Thomas
Babington Macaulay*

A word or a nod from the good has more weight than the eloquent
speeches of others – *Plutarch*

The least movement is of importance to all nature. The entire ocean is
affected by a pebble – *Blaise Pascal*

He who wishes to exert a useful influence must be careful to insult
nothing – *Johann Wolfgang von Goethe*

There are nine chances in ten that every man who goes with me will lose
his life in the undertaking. But there are times when dead men are
worth more than living ones – *John Brown*

Let him that would move the world first move himself – *Socrates*

Men are won, not so much by being blamed, as by being encompassed
with love – *William Ellery Channing*

The words that a father speaks to his children in the privacy of home are
not heard by the world, but, as in whispering galleries, they are
clearly heard at the end, and by posterity – *Jean Paul Richter*

Often the elements that move and mould society are the results of the
sister's counsel, and the mother's prayer – *E. H. Chapin*

Good words do more than hard speeches – *Robert Leighton*

The career of a great man remains an enduring monument of human
energy – *Samuel Smiles*

Blessed is the influence of one true, loving human soul on another –
George Eliot

When a great man dies, for years the light he leaves behind him lies on
  the paths of men – *Henry Wadsworth Longfellow*
Influence is the exhalation of character.
There is little influence where there is not great sympathy.
A good man does good merely by living.
The influence of individual character extends from generation to gener-
  ation. The world is moulded by it.

INGRATITUDE

He that calls a man ungrateful sums up all the evil of which one can be
  guilty – *Jonathan Swift*
An ungrateful man is like a hog under a tree eating acorns, but never
  looking up to see where they come from – *Timothy Dexter*
We can be thankful to a friend for a few acres, or a little money; and yet
  for the freedom and command of the whole earth, and for the great
  benefits of our being, our life, health, and reason, we look upon
  ourselves as under no obligation – *Seneca*
Flints may be melted – we see it daily – but an ungrateful heart cannot be;
  not by the strongest and noblest flame – *Robert South*
How sharper than a serpent's tooth it is / To have a thankless child! –
  William Shakespeare
One ungrateful man does an injury to all who stand in need of aid –
  Publius Syrus
We seldom find people ungrateful as long as we are in a condition to
  render them services – *François de La Rochefoucauld*
We often fancy we suffer from ingratitude, while in reality we suffer
  from self-love – *Walter Savage Landor*
Filial ingratitude! / Is it not as this mouth should tear this hand / For lifting
  food t' it? – *Shakespeare*
A grateful dog is better than an ungrateful man – *Sádi*
Blow, blow, thou winter wind, / Thou art not so unkind / As man's
  ingratitude . . . / Freeze, freeze, thou bitter sky, / That dost not bite so
  nigh, / As benefits forgot – *Shakespeare*
He that is ungrateful has no guilt but one; all other crimes may pass for
  virtues in him.
Ingratitude is treason to mankind.

INHERITANCE

What madness is it for a man to starve himself to enrich his heir, and so
  turn a friend into an enemy! For his joy at your death will be
  proportioned to what you leave him – *Seneca*
They who provide much wealth for their children but neglect to improve

them in virtue, do like those who feed their horses high, but never train them to be useful – *Socrates*

The mother knows best, whether the child be like the father.

No man is any good because his grandfather was.

INJURY

No man is hurt but by himself – *Diogenes*

To wilful men, / The injuries they themselves procure / Must be their schoolmasters – *William Shakespeare*

Christianity commands us to pass by injuries; policy, to let them pass by us – *Benjamin Franklin*

He who has injured thee was either stronger or weaker than thee. If weaker, spare him; if stronger spare thyself – *Seneca*

The public has more interest in the punishment of an injury than the one who receives it – *Charles Caleb Colton*

There is no ghost so difficult to lay as the ghost of an injury – *Alexander Smith*

The injuries we do, and those we suffer, are seldom weighed in the same balance.

Slight small injuries, and they will become none at all.

In life it is difficult to say who do you the most mischief – enemies with the worst intentions, or friends with the best.

INJUSTICE

If thou suffer injustice, console thyself; the true unhappiness is in doing it – *Democritus*

He who commits injustice is ever made more wretched than he who suffers it – *Plato*

No one will dare maintain that it is better to do injustice than to bear it – *Aristotle*

Anyone entrusted with power will abuse it if not also animated with the love of truth and virtue, no matter whether he be a prince, or one of the people – *Jean de La Fontaine*

Did the mass of men know the actual selfishness and injustice of their rulers, not a government would stand a year – *Theodore Parker*

Men endure the losses that befall them by mere casualty with more patience than the damages they sustain by injustice – *Walter Raleigh*

INK

My ways are as broad as the king's high road, and my means lie in an inkstand – *Robert Southey*

O! she is fallen / Into a pit of ink, that the wide sea / Hath drops too few to wash her clean again – *William Shakespeare*

A small drop of ink, falling like dew upon a thought, produces that which makes thousands, perhaps millions, think – *Lord Byron*

The coloured slave that waits upon thy thought, and sends that thought, without a voice, to the ends of the earth.

INNOCENCE

He is armed without who is innocent within – *Horace*

What stronger breastplate than a heart untainted! – *William Shakespeare*

To be innocent is to be not guilty but to be virtuous is to overcome our evil inclinations – *William Penn*

The innocent seldom find an uneasy pillow – *William Cowper*

The innocence that feels no risk and is taught no caution is more vulnerable than guilt, and oftener assailed – *Nathaniel Parker Willis*

Innocence and mystery never dwell long together – *Mme Neckar*

Innocence is like polished armour; it adorns and defends – *Robert South*

Unstain'd thoughts do seldom dream on evil – *Shakespeare*

There is no man so good, who, were he to submit all his thoughts and actions to the law, would not deserve hanging ten times in his life – *Michel Eyquem de Montaigne*

The silence often of pure innocence / Persuades when speaking fails – *Shakespeare*

They that know no evil will suspect none – *Ben Jonson*

Innocence is but a poor substitute for experience.

There is no courage but in innocence; no constancy but in an honest cause.

INQUISITIVENESS

Inquisitive people are the funnels of conversation; they do not take anything for their own use, but merely to pass it on to others – *Richard Steele*

An inquisitive man is a creature naturally very vacant of thought itself, and therefore forced to apply to foreign assistance – *Steele*

Shun the inquisitive, for you will be sure to find him leaky – *Horace*

Inquisitiveness or curiosity is a kernel of the forbidden fruit, which still sticketh in the throat of a natural man, and sometimes to the danger of his choking.

See also CURIOSITY.

INSANITY

All power of fancy over reason is a degree of insanity – *Samuel Johnson*

Now see that noble and most sovereign reason, / Like sweet bells
    jangled, out of tune and harsh – *William Shakespeare*

O judgement! thou art fled to brutish beasts, / And men have lost their
    reason – *Shakespeare*

Insane people easily detect the nonsense of other people – *John Hallam*

Every sense hath been o'erstrung, and each frail fibre of the brain sent
    forth her thoughts all wild and wide – *Lord Byron*

Insanity destroys reason, but not wit.

Those who are insane generally reason correctly, but they reason from
    false assumptions and on wrong principles.

This wretched brain gave way, and I became a wreck, at random driven,
    without one glimpse of reason, or of heaven.

INSENSIBILITY

Who can all sense of others' ills escape, / Is but a brute, at best, in human
    shape – *Juvenal*

A thorough and mature insensibility is rarely to be acquired but by a
    steady perseverance in infamy – *Junius*

INSTABILITY

A rolling stone can gather no moss – *Publius Syrus*

Some have at first for wits, then poets passed; / Turned critics next, and
    proved plain fools at last – *Alexander Pope*

Everything by starts, and nothing long – *John Dryden*

It will be found that they are the weakest-minded and the hardest-
    hearted men, that most love change – *John Ruskin*

He who begins many things finishes nothing.

INSTINCT

A goose flies by a chart which the Royal Geographical Society could not
    mend – *Oliver Wendell Holmes*

Though reason is progressive, instinct is stationary. Five thousand years
    have added no improvement to the hive of the bee, or the house of
    the beaver – *Charles Caleb Colton*

The instinctive feeling of a great people is often wiser than its wisest
    men – *Lajos Kossuth*

By a divine instinct men's minds mistrust / Ensuing danger; as, by proof,
    we see / The waters swell before a boisterous storm – *William
    Shakespeare*

Raise reason over instinct as you can; / In this 'tis God directs; in that 'tis
    man – *Alexander Pope*

Improvable reason is the distinction between man and the animal.
Swift instinct leaps; slow reason feebly climbs.

INSTRUCTION

The wise are instructed by reason; ordinary minds, by experience; the
stupid, by necessity; and brutes by instinct – *Cicero*

A good newspaper and Bible in every house, a good schoolhouse in
every district, and a church in every neighbourhood, all appreciated
as they deserve, are the chief support of virtue, morality, civil liberty,
and religion – *Benjamin Franklin*

Life is but one continual course of instruction. The hand of the parent
writes on the heart of the child the first faint characters which time
deepens into strength so that nothing can efface them.

The great business of the moral teacher is to make the best moral
impressions and excite the best feelings, by giving the clearest, fullest
and most accurate instruction as to truth and duty.

In moral lessons the understanding must be addressed before the
conscience, and the conscience before the heart, if we would make
the deepest impressions.

See also EDUCATION, LEARNING.

INSULT

Whatever be the motive of an insult it is always best to overlook it; for
folly scarcely can deserve resentment, and malice is punished by
neglect – *Samuel Johnson*

The way to procure insults is to submit to them. A man meets with no
more respect than he exacts – *William Hazlitt*

Injuries may be atoned for and forgiven; but insults admit of no compensation; they degrade the mind in its own esteem, and force it to
recover its level by revenge – *Junius*

The greater part of mankind are more sensitive to contemptuous
language than to unjust acts; they can less easily bear insult than
wrong – *Plutarch*

What insult is so keenly felt, as the polite insult which it is impossible to
resent? – *Julia Kavanagh*

Oppression is more easily borne than insult – *Junius*

Fate never wounds more deeply the generous heart / Than when a
blockhead's insult points the dart – *Samuel Johnson*

It is often better not to see an insult than to attempt to revenge it – *Seneca*

He who puts up with insult invites injury.

I once met a man who had forgiven an injury. I hope some day to meet
the man who has forgiven an insult.

INTEGRITY

Nothing more completely baffles one who is full of tricks and duplicity than straightforward and simple integrity – *Charles Caleb Colton*

Nothing is at last sacred but the integrity of your own mind – *Ralph Waldo Emerson*

Integrity without knowledge is weak and useless.

Integrity is the first step to true greatness.

A man of integrity will never listen to any plea against conscience.

See also HONESTY.

INTELLECT

Intellect is the simple power, anterior to all action or construction – *Ralph Waldo Emerson*

Intellect is brain force – *Johann Christoph Friedrich von Schiller*

The intellect has only one failing. It has no conscience. Napoleon is the readiest instance of this. If his heart had borne any proportion to his brain, he had been one of the greatest men in all history – *James Russell Lowell*

Every man should use his intellect not as he uses his lamp in the study, only for his own seeing, but as the lighthouse uses its lamps, that those afar off on the sea may see the shining, and learn their way – *Henry Ward Beecher*

Brains well prepared are the monuments where human knowledge is most surely engraved – *Jean Jacques Rousseau*

A man of intellect is lost unless he unites to it energy of character. When we have the lantern of Diogenes we must have his staff – *Nicolas Sébastian Roch Chamfort*

Intellect – the starlight of the brain – *Nathaniel Parker Willis*

Times of general calamity and confusion have ever been productive of the greatest minds. The purest ore is produced from the hottest furnace, and the brightest thunderbolt is elicited from the darkest storm – *Charles Caleb Colton*

The more we know of any one ground of knowledge, the further we see into the general domains of intellect – *James Henry Leigh Hunt*

Mind is the great lever of all things; human thought is the process by which human ends are answered – *Daniel Webster*

The men of action are, after all, only the unconscious instruments of the men of thought – *Heinrich Heine*

The intellect of the wise is like glass; it admits the light of heaven and reflects it.

Don't despair of a student if he has one clear idea.

Intellect, talent, and genius, like murder, 'will out'.

While the world lasts, the sun will gild the mountain-tops before it shines upon the plain.

INTELLIGENCE

Intelligence is a luxury, sometimes useless, sometimes fatal. It is a torch or firebrand according to the use one makes of it – *Fernán Caballero*

'Tis the mind that makes the body rich; / And as the sun breaks through the darkest clouds, / So honour peereth in the meanest habit – *William Shakespeare*

The superior man is he who develops, in harmonious proportions, his moral, intellectual, and physical nature – *Douglas William Jerrold*

Intelligence increases mere physical ability one half. The use of the head abridges the labour of the hands – *Henry Ward Beecher*

God multiplies intelligence, which communicates itself like fire, infinitely. Light a thousand torches at one torch, and the flame of the latter remains the same – *Joseph Joubert*

A man cannot leave a better legacy to the world than a well-educated family – *Thomas Scott*

INTEMPERANCE

I never drink – I cannot do it on equal terms with others. It costs them only one day; but it costs me three; the first in sinning, the second in suffering, and the third in repenting – *Laurence Sterne*

When the cup of any sensual pleasure is drained to the bottom, there is always poison in the dregs – *Jane Porter*

He that is a drunkard is qualified for all vice – *Francis Quarles*

He that tempts me to drink beyond my measure, civilly invites me to a fever – *Jeremy Taylor*

Greatness of any kind has no greater foe than the habit of drinking – *Walter Scott*

Every inordinate cup is unblessed and the ingredient is a devil – *William Shakespeare*

Of all the causes of crime, intemperance stands out the unapproachable chief – *Noah Davis*

The body, overcharged with the excess of yesterday, weighs down the mind together with itself – *Horace*

Touch the goblet no more; / It will make thy heart sore, / To its very core – *Henry Wadsworth Longfellow*

If we could sweep intemperance out of the country, there would be hardly poverty enough left to give healthy exercise to the charitable impulses – *Phillips Brooks*

Drunkenness takes away the man, and leaves only the brute.

In our world death deputes intemperance to do the work of age.

The drunkard, says Seneca, is a voluntary madman, and someone has added 'a necessary fool'.

There is no vice in nature more debasing and destructive to men than intemperance.

The youth who stands with a glass of liquor in his hand would do well to consider which he had best throw away – the liquor or himself.

See also DRUNKENNESS.

INTENTIONS

The innocence of the intention abates nothing of the mischief of the example – *Robert Hall*

Many good purposes and intentions lie in the churchyard – *Philip Henry*

Right intention is to the actions of a man what the soul is to the body, or the root to the tree – *Jeremy Taylor*

Good intentions are very mortal and perishable things; like very mellow and choice fruit they are difficult to keep.

The failures of life come from resting in good intentions, which are in vain unless carried out in wise action.

Good intentions will no more make a truth, than a good mark will make a good shot.

JEALOUSY

Trifles light as air / Are to the jealous confirmations strong / As proofs of holy writ – *William Shakespeare*

In jealousy there is more of self-love than of love to another – *François de La Rochefoucauld*

What frenzy dictates, jealousy believes – *John Gay*

Jealousy sees things always with magnifying glasses which make little things large – *Miguel de Cervantes Saavedra*

'Tis a monster / Begot upon itself, born on itself – *Shakespeare*

Jealousy is the injured lover's hell – *John Milton*

Women detest a jealous man whom they do not love, but it angers them when a man they do love is not jealous – *Ninon de Lenclos*

A jealous man always finds more than he looks for – *Madeleine de Scudéry*

Oh! beware . . . of jealousy; / It is the green-ey'd monster which doth mock / The meat it feeds on – *Shakespeare*

All jealousy must be strangled in its birth, or time will soon make it strong enough to overcome the truth – *William Davenant*

Jealousy is always born with love, but does not die with it – *La Rochefoucauld*

Jealousy is the fear or apprehension of superiority; envy our uneasiness under it – *William Shenstone*

He who is next heir to supreme power is always suspected and hated by him who actually wields it – *Tacitus*

We are more jealous of frivolous accomplishments with brilliant success, than of the most estimable qualities without – *William Hazlitt*

The jealous man poisons his own banquet, and then eats it.

See also ENVY.

JESTING

The jest loses its point when he who makes it is the first to laugh – *Johann Christoph Friedrich von Schiller*

Wit loses its respect with the good when seen in company with malice; and to smile at the jest which plants a thorn in another's breast is to become a principal in the mischief – *Richard Brinsley Sheridan*

Never risk a joke even the least offensive in its nature with a person who is not possessed of sense to comprehend it – *Jean de La Bruyère*

This fellow's wise enough to play the fool, / And to do that well craves a kind of wit; / He must observe their mood on whom he jests, / The quality of persons, and the time – *William Shakespeare*

The jest which is expected is already destroyed – *Samuel Johnson*

We have a right to resent injuries, but it is ridiculous to be angry at a jest – *François de La Rochefoucauld*

A jest's prosperity lies in the ear / Of him that hears it, never in the tongue / Of him that makes it – *Shakespeare*

Judge of a jest when you have done laughing.

Laughter should dimple the cheek, not furrow the brow.

It is good to make a jest, but not to make a trade of jesting.

Wanton jests make fools laugh, and wise men frown.

He that will lose his friend for a jest deserves to die a beggar by the bargain.

Joking often loses a friend, and never gains an enemy.

JOURNALISM

Did Charity prevail, the press would prove a vehicle of virtue, truth and love – *William Cowper*

Great is journalism. Is not every able editor a ruler of the world, being the persuader of it? – *Thomas Carlyle*

Get your facts first, and then you can distort 'em as you please – *Mark Twain*

Burke said there were Three Estates in Parliament; but, in the Reporters' Gallery yonder, there sat a fourth estate more important far than they all – *Carlyle*

We live under a government of men and morning newspapers – *Wendell Phillips*
See also NEWSPAPERS, PRESS.

JOY

It is better that joy should be spread over all the day in the form of strength, than that it should be concentrated into ecstasies, full of danger, and followed by reactions – *Ralph Waldo Emerson*

The most profound joy has more of gravity than of gaiety in it – *Michel Eyquem de Montaigne*

He who can conceal his joys is greater than he who can hide his griefs – *Johann Kaspar Lavater*

Joys are our wings; sorrows our spurs – *Jean Paul Richter*

The soul's calm sunshine, and the heartfelt joy – *Alexander Pope*

Joy never feasts so high as when the first course is of misery – *Sir John Suckling*

There is not a joy the world can give like that it takes away – *Lord Byron*

Joy is more divine than sorrow, for joy is bread and sorrow is medicine – *Henry Ward Beecher*

Great joy, especially after a sudden change of circumstances, is apt to be silent, and dwells rather in the heart than on the tongue – *Henry Fielding*

There is a sweet joy that comes to us through sorrow – *Charles Haddon Spurgeon*

True joy is only hope put out of fear.

We lose the peace of years when we hunt after the rapture of moments.

Tranquil pleasures last the longest; we are not fitted to bear long the burden of great joys.

To pursue joy is to lose it.

We can do nothing well without joy, and a good conscience which is the ground of joy.

Joy is not in things; it is in us.

See also DELIGHT.

JUDGEMENT

Men are not to be judged by their looks, habits, and appearances; but by the character of their lives and conversations, and by their works – *Sir Roger L'Estrange*

Judgement is forced upon us by experience – *Samuel Johnson*

A man has generally the good or ill qualities which he attributes to mankind – *William Shenstone*

It is with our judgements as with our watches: no two go just alike, yet each believes his own – *Alexander Pope*

How little do they see what really is, who frame their hasty judgement upon that which seems – *Robert Southey*

We judge ourselves by what we feel capable of doing; others judge us by what we have done – *Henry Wadsworth Longfellow*

Men's judgements are / A parcel of their fortunes, and things outward / Do draw the inward quality after them – *William Shakespeare*

It is a maxim received in life that, in general, we can determine more wisely for others than for ourselves – *Junius*

Everyone complains of his memory, nobody of his judgement – *François de La Rochefoucauld*

Lynx-eyed to our neighbours, and moles to ourselves – *Jean de La Fontaine*

The seat of knowledge is in the head; of wisdom, in the heart. We are sure to judge wrong if we do not feel right – *William Hazlitt*

We do not judge men by what they are in themselves, but by what they are relatively to us – *Mme Swetchine*

Think wrongly, if you please; but in all cases think for yourself – *Gotthold Ephraim Lessing*

I mistrust the judgement of every man in a case in which his own wishes are concerned – *Duke of Wellington*

You take all the experience and judgement of men over fifty out of the world and there wouldn't be enough left to run it – *Henry Ford*

Judge thyself with the judgement of sincerity, and thou wilt judge others with the judgement of charity.

JUSTICE

To be perfectly just is an attribute of the divine nature; to be so to the utmost of our abilities is the glory of man – *Joseph Addison*

Judges ought to be more learned than witty, more reverent than plausible, and more advised than confident. Above all things, integrity is their portion and proper virtue – *Francis Bacon*

Justice discards party, friendship, and kindred, and is therefore represented as blind – *Addison*

One man's word is no man's word; we should quietly hear both sides – *Johann Wolfgang von Goethe*

Justice is the constant desire and effort to render to every man his due – *Justinian*

Justice without wisdom is impossible – *James Anthony Froude*

The only way to make the mass of mankind see the beauty of justice is by showing them, in pretty plain terms, the consequences of injustice – *Sydney Smith*

Be just, and fear not. / Let all the ends thou aim'st at be thy country's, / Thy God's, and truth's – *William Shakespeare*

Justice delayed is justice denied – *William Gladstone*

When Infinite Wisdom established the rule of right and honesty, He saw to it that justice should be always the highest expediency – *Wendell Phillips*

What is in conformity with justice should also be in conformity to the laws – *Socrates*

Were he my brother, nay, my kingdom's heir, – / . . . Such neighbour nearness to our sacred blood / Should nothing privilege him, nor partialize / The unstooping firmness of my upright soul – *Shakespeare*

How can a people be free that has not learned to be just? – *Comte Sieyès*

He who is only just is cruel. Who on earth could live were all judged justly? – *Lord Byron*

Justice and power must be brought together, so that whatever is just may be powerful and whatever is powerful may be just – *Blaise Pascal*

Justice is to give to every man his own – *Aristotle*

Justice without strength, or strength without justice – fearful misfortunes! – *Joseph Joubert*

Use every man after his desert, and who should 'scape whipping? – *Shakespeare*

Justice is the first virtue of those who command, and stops the complaints of those who obey – *Denis Diderot*

Justice is the insurance we have on our lives and property, and obedience is the premium we pay for it – *William Penn*

Justice is the bread of the nation; it is always hungry for it – *François de Chateaubriand*

An honest man nearly always thinks justly – *Jean Jacques Rousseau*

Justice is the great and simple principle which is the secret of success in all government, as essential to the training of an infant as to the control of a mighty nation.

He who goes no further than bare justice stops at the beginning of virtue.

If judges would make their decisions just, they should behold neither plaintiff, defendant, nor pleader, but only the cause itself.

Impartiality is the life of justice, as justice is of all good government.

All are not just because they do no wrong; but he who will not wrong me when he may, he is truly just.

Justice, like lightning, ever should appear to few men's ruin, but to all men's fear.

Never judge your neighbour until you have been in the same situation.

KINDNESS

Kindness is the golden chain by which society is bound together – *Johann Wolfgang von Goethe*

The drying up a single tear has more of honest fame than shedding seas of gore – *Lord Byron*

Kindness in women, not their beauteous looks, / Shall win my love – *William Shakespeare*

Kind looks, kind words, kind acts, and warm handshakes – these are secondary means of grace when men are in trouble and are fighting their unseen battles – *John Hall*

The best portion of a good man's life is his little, nameless, unremembered acts of kindness and of love – *William Wordsworth*

A kind heart is a fountain of gladness, making everything in its vicinity freshen into smiles – *Washington Irving*

He hath a tear for pity and a hand / Open as day for melting charity – *Shakespeare*

You may find people ready enough to do the Samaritan without the oil and twopence – *Sydney Smith*

Paradise is open to all kind hearts – *Pierre Jean de Béranger*

Kindness in ourselves is the honey that blunts the sting of unkindness in another – *Walter Savage Landor*

An effort made for the happiness of others lifts us above ourselves – *Lydia Maria Child*

Kindness is the only charm permitted to the aged – *Octave Feuillet*

Sow good services; sweet remembrances will grow from them – *Mme de Staël*

To cultivate kindness is a valuable part of the business of life – *Samuel Johnson*

The one who will be found in trial capable of great acts of love is ever the one who is always doing considerate small ones – *Frederick William Robertson*

Kind hearts are more than coronets, and simple faith than Norman blood – *Alfred, Lord Tennyson*

I have sped much by land, and sea, and mingled with much people, but never yet could find a spot unsunned by human kindness – *Martin Farquhar Tupper*

Heaven in sunshine will requite the kind – *Byron*

Make a rule, and pray to God to help you to keep it, never, if possible, to lie down at night without being able to say: 'I have made one human being at least a little wiser, or a little happier, or at least a little better this day' – *Charles Kingsley*

We cannot be just unless we are kind-hearted – *Marquis de Vauvenargues*

Kindness is a language the dumb can speak and the deaf can hear and understand.

Win hearts and you have all men's hands and purses.

A word of kindness is seldom spoken in vain, while witty sayings are as easily lost as the pearls slipping from a broken string.

Kindness is wisdom; there is none in life but needs it, and may learn.

Both man and womankind belie their nature when they are not kind.

KINGS

Uneasy lies the head that wears a crown – *William Shakespeare*

Kings, in this chiefly, should imitate God; their mercy should be above all their works – *William Penn*

He on whom Heaven confers a sceptre knows not the weight till he bears it – *Pierre Corneille*

The people are fashioned according to the example of their king; and edicts are of less power than the model which his life exhibits – *Claudian*

Royalty consists not in vain pomp, but in great virtues – *Agesilaus*

Wise kings generally have wise counsellors; and he must be a wise man himself who is capable of distinguishing one – *Diogenes*

A crown, golden in show, is but a wreath of thorns; brings danger, troubles, cares, and sleepless nights, to him who wears a regal diadem – *John Milton*

The example of a vicious prince will corrupt an age, but that of a good one will not reform it – *Jonathan Swift*

A sovereign's great example forms a people; the public breast is noble or vile as he inspires it – *David Mallett*

Princes are never without flatterers to seduce them; ambition to deprave them; and desires to corrupt them – *Plato*

The king will best govern his realm who reigneth over his people as a father doth over his children – *Agesilaus*

He who reflects attentively upon the duties of a king trembles at the sight of a crown.

Happy the kings whose thrones are founded on their people's hearts.

The king who delegates his power to others' hands but ill deserves the crown he wears.

KISSES

A long, long kiss – the kiss of youth and love – *Lord Byron*

Stolen kisses are always sweetest – *James Henry Leigh Hunt*

Leave a kiss but in the cup, / And I'll not look for wine – *Ben Jonson*

Eden revives in the first kiss of love – *Byron*

And steal immortal blessing from her lips, / Who, even in pure and vestal modesty, / Still blush, as thinking their own kisses sin – *William Shakespeare*

That farewell kiss which resembles greeting, that last glance of love which becomes the sharpest pang of sorrow – *George Eliot*

Upon thy cheek lay I this zealous kiss, / As seal to this indenture of my love – *Shakespeare*

A soft lip would tempt you to eternity of kissing – *Jonson*

Now, by the jealous queen of heaven, that kiss / I carried from thee, dear, my true lip / Hath virgin'd it e'er since – *Shakespeare*

I felt the while a pleasing kind of smart; / The kiss went tingling to my panting heart. / When it was gone, the sense of it did stay; / The sweetness cling'd upon my lips all day. / Like drops of honey, loth to fall away – *John Dryden*

Some say kissing is a sin; but if it was na lawful, lawyers would na allow it; if it was na holy, ministers would na do it; if it was na modest, maidens would na take it; if it was na plenty, puir folk would na get it – *Robert Burns*

Blush, happy maiden, when you feel the lips that press love's glowing seal. But as the slow years darker roll, grown wiser, the experienced soul will own the lips which kiss the tears away – *Elizabeth Akers*

His kissing is as full of sanctity as the touch of holy bread – *Shakespeare*

Once he drew, with one long kiss, my whole soul through my lips – *Alfred, Lord Tennyson*

Then kiss'd me hard, / As if he pluck'd up kisses by the roots, / That grew upon my lips – *Shakespeare*

It is the passion that is in a kiss that gives to it its sweetness; it is the affection in a kiss that sanctifies it.

Four sweet lips, two pure souls, and one undying affection – those are love's pretty ingredients for a kiss.

And with a velvet lip, print on his brow such language as tongue hath never spoken.

A woman is invincible whose armoury consists of kisses, smiles, sighs, and tears.

KNAVERY

After long experience in the world, I affirm, before God, that I never knew a rogue who was not unhappy – *Junius*

The worst of all knaves are those who can mimic their former honesty – *Johann Kaspar Lavater*

Knaves will thrive where honest plainness knows not how to live – *James Shirley*

A very honest man, and a very good understanding, may be deceived by a knave – *Junius*

A knave thinks himself a fool all the time he is not making a fool of some other person – *William Hazlitt*

By fools knaves fatten.

Take head of an ox before, an ass behind, and a knave on all sides.

There is nothing seems so like an honest man as an artful knave.

KNOWLEDGE

We know accurately only when we know little; with knowledge doubt increases – *Johann Wolfgang von Goethe*

The essence of knowledge is having it, to apply it; not having it, to confess your ignorance – *Confucius*

He that would make real progress in knowledge must dedicate his age as well as youth; the latter grows as well as the first fruits on the altar of truth – *George Berkeley*

Knowledge of our own ignorance is the first step toward true knowledge – *Socrates*

We cannot make another comprehend our knowledge until we first comprehend his ignorance – *Samuel Taylor Coleridge*

I envy no man that knows more than myself, but pity them that know less – *Sir Thomas Browne*

Knowledge, like religion, must be 'experienced' in order to be known – *E. P. Whipple*

The desire of knowledge, like the thirst of riches, increases ever with the acquisition of it – *Laurence Sterne*

The seeds of knowledge may be planted in solitude, but must be cultivated in public – *Samuel Johnson*

Knowledge dwells in heads replete with thoughts of other men; wisdom, in minds attentive to their own – *William Cowper*

Man is not born to solve the problem of the universe, but to find out what he has to do; and to restrain himself within the limits of his comprehension – *Goethe*

If you would thoroughly know anything, teach it to others – *Tryon Edwards*

Most men want knowledge not for itself, but for the superiority which knowledge confers – *Sydney Smith*

There is nothing makes a man suspect much, more than to know little – *Francis Bacon*

A grain of real knowledge will outweigh a bushel of adroitness; and to produce persuasion there is one golden principle – to understand what you are talking about – *John Robert Seeley*

There is nothing so minute, or inconsiderable, that I would not rather know it than not – *Johnson*

There is a limit to the work that can be got out of a human body or a human brain, and he is a wise man who wastes no energy on pursuits for which he is not fitted – *William Gladstone*

The love of knowledge in a young mind is almost a warrant against the infirm excitement of passions and vices – *Henry Ward Beecher*

Seldom ever was any knowledge given to keep, but to impart; the grace of this rich jewel is lost in concealment – *Bishop Hall*

A taste of every sort of knowledge is necessary to form the mind, and is the only way to give the understanding its due improvement to the full extent of its capacity – *John Locke*

The more extensive a man's knowledge of what has been done, the greater will be his power of knowing what to do – *Benjamin Disraeli*

Nothing in this life, after health and virtue, is more estimable than knowledge – nor is there anything so easily attained, or so cheaply purchased – the labour, only sitting still, and the expense but time, which if we do not spend, we cannot save – *Laurence Sterne*

The learning thou gettest by thine own observation and experience is far beyond that thou gettest by precept, as the knowledge of a traveller exceeds that which is got by reading – *Thomas à Kempis*

Knowledge conquered by labour becomes a possession – *Thomas Carlyle*

The more we have read, the more we have learned, and the more we have meditated, the better conditioned we are to affirm that we know nothing – *Voltaire*

Knowledge is the treasure, but judgement is the treasurer of a wise man – *William Penn*

Knowledge and timber should not be much used until they are seasoned – *Oliver Wendell Holmes*

What we know here is very little, but what we are ignorant of is immense – *Marquis de Laplace*

The end of all knowledge should be in virtuous action – *Sir Philip Sidney*

A great deal of knowledge, which is not capable of making a man wise, has a natural tendency to make him vain and arrogant – *Joseph Addison*

All wish to possess knowledge, but few, comparatively speaking, are willing to pay the price – *Juvenal*

As soon as a true thought has entered our mind, it gives a light which makes us see a crowd of other objects which we have never perceived before – *François de Chateaubriand*

If a man empties his purse into his head, no one can take it away from him. An investment in knowledge always pays the best interest – *Benjamin Franklin*

Knowledge always desires increase; it is like fire, which must first be kindled by some external agent, but which will afterward propagate itself – *Johnson*

Imparting knowledge is only lighting other men's candles at our lamp, without depriving ourselves of any flame – *Jane Porter*

The word knowledge, strictly employed, implies three things, viz., truth, proof, and conviction – *Richard Whately*

Knowledge is the eye of desire, and can become the pilot of the soul – *Will Durant*

I had six honest serving men – / They taught me all I knew: / Their names were Where and What and When – / And Why and How and Who – *Rudyard Kipling*

The greatest undeveloped territory in the world lies under your hat.

A small town is one where the postmaster knows more than the schoolmaster.

The first step to knowledge is to know that we are ignorant.

They who know the most must mourn the deepest o'er the fatal truth that the tree of knowledge is not the tree of life.

The more you practise what you know, the more shall you know what to practise.

Accurate knowledge is the basis of correct opinions.

He fancies himself enlightened, because he sees the deficiencies of others; he is ignorant, because he has never reflected on his own.

'Knowledge', says Bacon, 'is power', but mere knowledge is not power; it is only possibility. Action is power; and its highest manifestation is when it is directed by knowledge.

The wise carry their knowledge, as they do their watches, not for display, but for their own use.

The brightest blaze of intelligence is of incalculably less value than the smallest spark of charity.

Knowledge is but folly unless it is guided by grace.

What a man knows should find its expression in what he does; the value of superior knowledge is chiefly in that it leads to a performing manhood.

Real knowledge, like everything else of value, is not to be obtained easily. It must be worked for, studied for, thought for.

Knowledge is realizing one's own ignorance and not being afraid to ask questions.

All the knowledge that we mortals can acquire is not knowledge positive, but knowledge comparative, and subject to the errors and passions of humanity.

Knowledge once gained casts a light beyond its own immediate boundaries.

If you have knowledge, let others light their candles at it.

Man often acquires just so much knowledge as to discover his ignorance, and attains so much experience as to see and regret his follies, and then dies.

Every man of sound brain whom you meet knows something worth knowing better than yourself.

One part of knowledge consists in being ignorant of such things as are not worthy to be known.

It's not what you know but who you know.

Knowledge of human nature teaches us not to expect too much.

Knowledge comes but wisdom lingers.

See also SCIENCE.

LABOUR

Nothing is denied to well directed labour, and nothing is ever to be attained without it – *Joshua Reynolds*

Without labour nothing prospers – *Sophocles*

The fruit derived from labour is the sweetest of all pleasures – *Marquis de Vauvenargues*

A man's best friends are his ten fingers – *Robert Collyer*

Labour rids us of three great evils – irksomeness, vice, and poverty – *Voltaire*

No race can prosper till it learns that there is as much dignity in tilling the field, as in writing a poem – *Booker T. Washington*

It is only by labour that thought can be made healthy, and only by thought that labour can be made happy – *John Ruskin*

If you divorce capital from labour, capital is hoarded, and labour starves – *Daniel Webster*

No abilities, however splendid, can command success without intense labour and persevering application – *Alexander Turney Stewart*

The guard of virtue is labour, and ease her sleep – *Torquato Tasso*

Do what thou dost as if the earth were heaven, and thy last day the day of judgement – *Charles Kingsley*

The labour of the body relieves us from the fatigues of the mind – *François de La Rochefoucauld*

Genius begins great works; labour alone finishes them – *Joseph Joubert*

Toil and pleasure, in their nature opposites, are yet linked together in a kind of necessary connection – *Livy*

There are many ways of being frivolous, only one way of being intellectually great; that is honest labour – *Sydney Smith*

Labour is the great producer of wealth; it moves all other causes – *Daniel Webster*

Excellence in any department can be attained only by the labour of a lifetime; it is not to be purchased at a lesser price – *Samuel Johnson*

Labour – the expenditure of vital effort in some form – is the measure, nay, it is the maker of values – *Josiah Gilbert Holland*

Nothing is impossible to the man who can will, and then do; this is the only law of success – *Comte de Mirabeau*

Men seldom die of hard work; activity is God's medicine.

From labour, health; from health, contentment springs.

Work is a great blessing; after evil came into the world, it was given as an antidote, not as a punishment.

Hard workers are usually honest; industry lifts them above temptation.

See also INDUSTRY, OCCUPATION.

LANGUAGE

Language as well as the faculty of speech was the immediate gift of God –
   Noah Webster

Language is the dress of thought – *Samuel Johnson*

Language is not only the vehicle of thought, it is a great and efficient
   instrument in thinking – *Humphrey Davy*

Language is the armoury of the human mind, and at once contains the
   trophies of its past and the weapons of its future conquests – *Samuel
   Taylor Coleridge*

One great use of words is to hide our thoughts – *Voltaire*

As a hawk flieth not high with one wing, even so a man reacheth not to
   excellence with one tongue – *Roger Ascham*

A man who is ignorant of foreign languages is ignorant of his own –
   Johann Wolfgang von Goethe

In the commerce of speech use only coin of gold and silver – *Joseph Joubert*

Felicity, not fluency, of language, is a merit – *E. P. Whipple*

Every language is a temple in which the soul of those who speak it is
   enshrined – *Oliver Wendell Holmes*

There was speech in their dumbness, language in their very gesture –
   William Shakespeare

Language is only the instrument of science, and words are but the signs
   of ideas – *Johnson*

Language was given us that we might say pleasant things to each
   other.

Words are the leaves of the tree of language, of which, if some fall away,
   a new succession takes their place.

To acquire a few tongues is the task of a few years; to be eloquent in one is
   the labour of a life.

The language denotes the man; a coarse or refined character finds its
   expression naturally in a coarse or refined phraseology.

Language is properly the servant of thought, but not unfrequently
   becomes its master.

LAUGHTER

A laugh is worth a hundred groans in any market – *Charles Lamb*

It is a good thing to laugh, at any rate; and if a straw can tickle a man, it is
   an instrument of happiness. Beasts can weep when they suffer, but
   they cannot laugh – *John Dryden*

Laughter is a most healthful exertion – *Christoph Wilhelm Hufeland*

I like the laughter that opens the lips and the heart, that shows at the
   same time pearls and the soul – *Victor Hugo*

No man who has once heartily and wholly laughed can be altogether and irreclaimably depraved – *Thomas Carlyle*

O, glorious laughter! thou man-loving spirit, that for a time doth take the burden from the weary back – *Douglas William Jerrold*

Laugh if you are wise – *Martial*

I am persuaded that every time a man smiles, but much more when he laughs, it adds something to this fragment of life – *Laurence Sterne*

God made both tears and laughter and both for kind purposes; for as laughter enables mirth and surprise to breathe freely, so tears enable sorrow to vent itself patiently – *James Henry Leigh Hunt*

Beware of him who hates the laugh of a child – *Johann Kaspar Lavater*

If we consider the frequent reliefs we receive from laughter, and how often it breaks the gloom which is apt to depress the mind, one would take care not to grow too wise for so great a pleasure of life – *Joseph Addison*

The laughter of girls is, and ever was, among the delightful sounds of earth – *Thomas De Quincey*

The most utterly lost of all days is that in which you have not once laughed – *Nicolas Sébastian Roch Chamfort*

Though laughter is looked upon by philosophers as the property of reason, the excess of it has always been considered the mark of folly – *Addison*

That laughter costs too much which is purchased by the sacrifice of decency – *Quintilian*

Men show their character in nothing more clearly than by what they think laughable – *Johann Wolfgang von Goethe*

A laugh, to be joyous, must flow from a joyous heart, for without kindness there can be no true joy – *Carlyle*

The horse-laugh indicates coarseness or brutality of character – *Lavater*

How inevitably does an immoderate laughter end in a sigh! – *Robert South*

No one is more profoundly sad than he who laughs too much – *Jean Paul Richter*

True wit never made a man laugh – *Lord Chesterfield*

A good laugh is sunshine in a house – *William Makepeace Thackeray*

Man is the only creature endowed with the power of laughter; is he not also the only one that deserves to be laughed at?

Next to a good soul-stirring prayer is a good laugh, when it is promoted by what is pure in itself.

The life that has grown up and developed without laughter becomes heavy and unsympathetic, if not harsh and morose.

He who laughs, lasts.

See also HUMOUR, MIRTH.

LAW

The plaintiff and defendant in an action at law are like two men ducking their heads in a bucket, and daring each other to remain longest under water – *Samuel Johnson*

These written laws are just like spiders' webs; the small and feeble may be caught and entangled in them, but the rich and mighty force through and despise them – *Anacharsis*

A countryman between two lawyers is like a fish between two cats – *Benjamin Franklin*

In law nothing is certain but the expense – *Samuel Butler*

The law, which is past depth / To those that without heed do plunge into 't – *William Shakespeare*

Use law only in cases of necessity; they that use it otherwise abuse themselves into weak bodies and light purses – *Francis Quarles*

A natural law is a process, not a power; it is a method of operation, not an operator. A natural law, without God behind it, is no more than a glove without a hand in it – *Joseph Cook*

Laws are like cobwebs, which may catch small flies, but let wasps and hornets break through – *Jonathan Swift*

Laws are generally found to be nets of such a texture, as the little creep through, the great break through, and the middle size are alone entangled in – *William Shenstone*

The English laws punish vice; the Chinese laws do more, they reward virtue – *Oliver Goldsmith*

A fish hangs in the net, like a poor man's right in the law; 'twill hardly come out – *Shakespeare*

Law is the embodiment of the moral sentiment of the people – *William Blackstone*

Good laws make it easier to do right and harder to do wrong – *William Gladstone*

The severity of laws often prevents their execution. When the penalty is excessive, one is often obliged to prefer impunity – *Charles de Montesquieu*

There is no country in the world in which everything can be provided for by the laws, or in which political institutions can prove a substitute for common sense and public morality – *Alexis de Tocqueville*

The science of jurisprudence – the pride of human intellect, with all its defects, redundancies, and errors – is the collected reason of ages, combining the principles of original justice with the infinite variety of human concerns – *Edmund Burke*

Law kept is only law; law broken is both law and execution – *Menander*

When laws, customs, or institutions cease to be beneficial to man, or are contrary to the will of God, they cease to be obligatory on us – *Lyman Beecher*

God is a law to men of sense; but pleasure is a law to the fool – *Plato*

The science of legislation is like that of medicine in one respect, viz.: that it is far more easy to point out what will do harm than what will do good – *Charles Caleb Colton*

Laws are silent in the midst of arms – *Cicero*

Equity judges with lenity; laws with extremity. In all moral cases the reason of the law is the law – *Walter Scott*

When I hear any man talk of an unalterable law, the only effect it produces on me is to convince me that he is an unalterable fool – *Sydney Smith*

Pity is the virtue of the law, / And none but tyrants use it cruelly – *Shakespeare*

The people's safety is the law of God – *James Otis*

Law and equity are two things that God hath joined together, but which man has put asunder – *Colton*

A law is valuable not because it is law, but because there is right in it – *Henry Ward Beecher*

When the state is most corrupt, then the laws are most multiplied – *Tacitus*

Law should be like death, which spares no one – *Montesquieu*

Laws are the silent assessors of God – *William Rounseville Alger*

We should never create by law what can be accomplished by morality – *Montesquieu*

A multitude of laws in a country is like a great number of physicians, a sign of weakness and malady – *Voltaire*

Laws grind the poor, and rich men rule the law – *Goldsmith*

To make an empire durable, the magistrates must obey the laws, and the people the magistrates – *Solon*

Reason is the life of law; nay, the common law itself is nothing else but reason – *Edward Coke*

The good need fear no law; / It is his safety, and the bad man's awe – *Philip Massinger*

Law is often spoken of as uncertain; but the uncertainty is not so much in the law as in the evidence – *Tryon Edwards*

Where law ends, tyranny begins – *William Pitt*

Laws are the very bulwarks of liberty; they define every man's rights, and defend the individual liberties of all men – *Josiah Gilbert Holland*

Ignorance of the law excuses no man; not that all men know the law, but because it is an excuse every man will plead, and no man can tell how to confute him – *John Selden*

War has its laws as well as peace – *David Hume*

Laws can discover sin, but not remove it – *John Milton*

No individual has the right to determine what law shall be obeyed and what law shall be enforced – *Herbert Hoover*

Laws should be like clothes. They should be made to fit the people they are meant to serve – *Clarence Darrow*

Going to law is losing a cow for the sake of a cat – *Chinese proverb*

The Jews ruin themselves at their passover; the Moors, at their marriages; and the Christians, in their lawsuits – *Spanish proverb*

To seek the redress of grievances by going to law is like sheep running for shelter to a bramble bush.

Law is a bottomless pit; it is a cormorant, a harpy that devours everything.

No people were ever better than their laws, though many have been worse.

The law is a sort of hocus-pocus science that smiles in your face while it picks your pockets.

A mouse-trap: easy to enter but not easy to get out of.

To go to law is for two persons to kindle a fire, at their own cost, to warm others and singe themselves to cinders.

We have no right to say that the universe is governed by natural laws, but only that it is governed according to natural laws.

Laws are not invented; they grow out of circumstances.

Law that shocks equity is reason's murder.

A prince who falleth out with laws breaketh with his best friends.

The best way to get a bad law repealed is to enforce it strictly.

The forms of law have always been the graves of buried liberties.

Consider the reason of the case, for nothing is law that is not reason.

'I never', says Voltaire, 'was ruined but twice – once when I gained a lawsuit, and once when I lost one.'

LAWYERS

If he would be a great lawyer, he must first consent to become a great drudge – *Daniel Webster*

Do as adversaries do in law, / Strive mightily, but eat and drink as friends – *William Shakespeare*

If there were no bad people there would be no good lawyers.

Lawyers on opposite sides of a case are like the two parts of shears; they cut what comes between them, but not each other.

LEARNING

Learning passes for wisdom among those who want both – *William Temple*

Learning is like mercury, one of the most powerful and excellent things in the world in skilful hands; in unskilful, the most mischievous – *Alexander Pope*

Learning is an ornament in prosperity, a refuge in adversity and a provision in old age – *Aristotle*

Learning by study must be won; / 'Twas ne'er entailed from sire to son – *John Gay*

I attribute the little I know to my not having been ashamed to ask for information, and to my rule of conversing with all descriptions of men on those topics that form their own peculiar professions and pursuits – *John Locke*

A little learning is a dang'rous thing; / Drink deep, or taste not the Pierian spring; / There shallow draughts intoxicate the brain, / And drinking largely sobers us again – *Pope*

Wear your learning, like your watch, in a private pocket. Do not pull it out merely to show that you have one. If asked what o'clock it is, tell it; but do not proclaim it hourly and unasked, like the watchman – *Lord Chesterfield*

That learning is most requisite which unlearns evil – *Antisthenes*

We should not ask who is the most learned, but who is the best learned – *Michel Eyquem de Montaigne*

The great art of learning is to undertake but little at a time – *Locke*

He might have been a very clever man by nature, but he had laid so many books on his head that his brain could not move – *Robert Hall*

The learning and knowledge that we have is, at the most, but little compared with that of which we are ignorant – *Plato*

He who knoweth not what he ought to know is a brute beast among men; he that knoweth no more than he hath need of is a man among brute beasts; and he that knoweth all that may be known is as a God among men – *Pythagoras*

Learning teaches how to carry things in suspense, without prejudice, till you resolve – *Francis Bacon*

Seeing much, suffering much, and studying much are the three pillars of learning – *Benjamin Disraeli*

It is a little learning, and but a little, which makes men conclude hastily. Experience and humility teach modesty and fear – *Jeremy Taylor*

Some will never learn anything because they understand everything too soon.

Learning is wealth to the poor, an honour to the rich, an aid to the young, and a support and comfort to the aged.

The true order of learning should be first, what is necessary; second, what is useful; and third, what is ornamental.

He who has no inclination to learn more will be very apt to think that he knows enough.

Swallow all your learning in the morning, but digest it in company at night.

Much learning shows how little mortals know; much wealth, how little
    worldlings enjoy.
There are three classes of people in the world. The first learn from their
    own experience – these are wise; the second learn from the experi-
    ence of others – these are happy; the third neither learn from their
    own experience nor the experience of others – these are fools.
Learning makes a man fit company for himself.
He is a learned man that understands one subject; a very learned man
    who understands two.
It is easy to learn something about everything, but difficult to learn
    everything about anything.
See also EDUCATION, INSTRUCTION.

LEISURE

The end of labour is to gain leisure – *Aristotle*
Leisure and solitude are the best effect of riches, because the mother of
    thought. Both are avoided by most rich men, who seek company and
    business, which are signs of being weary of themselves – *William
    Temple*
Leisure is gone; gone where the spinning-wheels are gone, and the
    pack-horses, and the slow wagons, and the peddlers who brought
    bargains to the door on sunny afternoons – *George Eliot*
Leisure for men of business and business for men of leisure would cure
    many complaints – *Hester Thrale*
Leisure is a beautiful garment, but it will not do for constant wear.
Spare minutes are the gold-dust of time; the portions of life most fruitful
    in good or evil; the gaps through which temptations enter.
See also HOLIDAYS, RECREATION, REPOSE.

LENDING

Lend not beyond thy ability, nor refuse to lend out of thy ability;
    especially when it will help others more than it can hurt thee. If thy
    debtor be honest and capable, thou hast thy money again, if not with
    increase, with praise. If he prove insolvent do not ruin him to get that
    which it will not ruin thee to lose; for thou art but a steward, and
    another is thy owner, master, and judge – *William Penn*
See also BORROWING.

LENITY

It is only necessary to grow old to become more indulgent. I see no fault
    committed that I have not committed myself – *Johann Wolfgang von
    Goethe*

Lenity is a part of mercy, but she must not speak too loud for fear of waking justice – *Joseph Joubert*

When lenity and cruelty play for a kingdom, the gentler gamester is the soonest winner – *William Shakespeare*

Man may dismiss compassion from his heart, but God will never – *William Cowper*

See also CLEMENCY, INDULGENCE, MERCY.

LETTERS

It is by the benefit of letters that absent friends are, in a manner, brought together – *Seneca*

The best time to frame an answer to the letters of a friend is the moment you receive them; then the warmth of friendship and the intelligence received most forcibly co-operate – *William Shenstone*

A letter shows the man it is written to as well as the man it is written by – *Lord Chesterfield*

To write a good love-letter, you ought to begin without knowing what you mean to say, and to finish without knowing what you have written – *Jean Jacques Rousseau*

Letters are those winged messengers that can fly from east to west on embassies of love.

Our thoughts are much alike, but female correspondence has a charm in it, of which that of the other sex is always devoid.

LEVELLERS

Your levellers wish to level down as far as themselves, but they cannot bear levelling up to themselves – *Samuel Johnson*

Those who attempt to level never equalize – *Edmund Burke*

Death and the cross are the two great levellers; kings and their subjects, masters and slaves, find a common level in two places – at the foot of the cross, and in the silence of the grave – *Charles Caleb Colton*

See also COMMUNISM, EQUALITY.

LIARS

All that one gains by falsehood is not to be believed when he speaks the truth – *Aristotle*

He who tells a lie is not sensible how great a task he undertakes; for he must be forced to invent twenty more to maintain one – *Alexander Pope*

One ought to have a good memory when he has told a lie – *Pierre Corneille*

Past all shame . . . so past all truth – *William Shakespeare*

Thou canst not better reward a liar than in not believing whatever he speaketh – *Aristippus*

They begin with making falsehood appear like truth, and end with making truth itself appear like falsehood – *William Shenstone*

The hell that a lie would keep a man from is doubtless the very best place for him to go – *George Macdonald*

Who dares think one thing, and another tell, / My soul detests him as the gates of hell – *Pope*

One lie must be thatched with another or it will soon rain through.

See also DECEIT, FALSEHOOD, LYING.

LIBERALITY

The riches we impart are the only wealth we shall always retain – *Matthew Henry*

Be rather bountiful than expensive; do good with what thou hast, or it will do thee no good – *William Penn*

No communications can exhaust genius; no gifts impoverish charity – *Johann Kaspar Lavater*

Proportion thy charity to the strength of thine estate, lest God in anger proportion thine estate to the weakness of thy charity – *Francis Quarles*

Liberality consists rather in giving seasonably than much – *Jean de La Bruyère*

He who is not liberal with what he has does but deceive himself when he thinks he would be liberal if he had more – *W. S. Plumer*

Some are unwisely liberal, and more delight to give presents than to pay debts – *Sir Philip Sidney*

The way to have nothing to give is to give nothing.

He that lays out for God lays up for himself.

See also CHARITY, GENEROSITY.

LIBERTY

Reason and virtue alone can bestow liberty – *Lord Shaftesbury*

Give me the liberty to know, to think, to believe, and to utter freely, according to conscience, above all other liberties – *John Milton*

What is life? It is not to stalk about, and draw fresh air, or gaze upon the sun; it is to be free – *Joseph Addison*

Oh, give me liberty! for even were paradise my prison, still I should long to leap the crystal walls – *John Dryden*

There are two freedoms, the false where one is free to do what he likes, and the true where he is free to do what he ought – *Charles Kingsley*

Liberty will not descend to a people; a people must raise themselves to

liberty; it is a blessing that must be earned before it can be enjoyed –
Charles Caleb Colton

A country cannot subsist well without liberty, nor liberty without
virtue – *Jean Jacques Rousseau*

It is impossible to enslave, mentally or socially, a Bible-reading people.
The principles of the Bible are the groundwork of human freedom –
Horace Greeley

The human race is in the best condition when it has the greatest degree of
liberty – *Dante Alighieri*

Liberty and union, one and inseparable, now and forever – *Daniel
Webster*

Interwoven is the love of liberty with every ligament of the heart – *George
Washington*

O liberty, how many crimes are committed in thy name! – *Mme Roland*

The people never give up their liberties but under some delusion –
Edmund Burke

A day, an hour of virtuous liberty is worth a whole eternity of bondage –
Addison

The true danger is, when liberty is nibbled away, for expedients, and by
parts – *Burke*

He is the free man whom the truth makes free, and all are slaves beside –
William Cowper

Liberty has restraints but no frontiers – *David Lloyd George*

Liberty is not merely a privilege to be conferred; it is a habit to be
acquired – *Lloyd George*

There is no liberty worth anything which is not a liberty under law.

Personal liberty is the paramount essential to human dignity and human
happiness.

Personal liberty is the right to act without interference within the limits of
the law.

Man's liberty ends, and it ought to end, when that liberty becomes the
curse of his neighbour.

If liberty with law is fire on the hearth, liberty without law is fire on the
floor.

Liberty cannot be established without morality, nor morality without
faith.

Liberty is the right to elect people to make restrictions for you to
overlook.

See also FREEDOM.

LIBRARIES

Let us pity those poor rich men who live barrenly in great bookless
houses – *Henry Ward Beecher*

A library is not a luxury, but one of the necessaries of life – *Beecher*

The student has his Rome, his Florence, his whole glowing Italy, within the four walls of his library. He has in his books the ruins of an antique world and the glories of a modern one – *Henry Wadsworth Longfellow*

My library / Was dukedom large enough – *William Shakespeare*

The true university of these days is a collection of books – *Thomas Carlyle*

Libraries are the wardrobes of literature, whence men, properly informed, may bring forth something for ornament, much for curiosity, and more for use.

A great library contains the diary of the human race. The great consulting room of a wise man is a library.

See also BOOKS.

LIFE

Life is a fatal complaint, and an eminently contagious one – *Oliver Wendell Holmes*

The secret of life is in art – *Oscar Wilde*

One life; a little gleam of time between two eternities; no second chance for us forever more – *Thomas Carlyle*

The shortest life is long enough if it lead to a better, and the longest life is short if it do not – *Charles Caleb Colton*

The retrospect of life swarms with lost opportunities – *Henry Taylor*

Death treats alike the fool and the philosopher – *David Hume*

When we are born we cry, that we are come / To this great stage of fools – *William Shakespeare*

A useless life is only an earthly death – *Johann Wolfgang von Goethe*

Life is rather a state of embryo, a preparation for life; a man is not completely born till he has passed through death – *Benjamin Franklin*

We never live; we are always in the expectation of living – *Voltaire*

Life is fruitful in the ratio in which it is laid out in noble action or patient perseverance – *Henry Parry Liddon*

We never live, but we ever hope to live – *Blaise Pascal*

Life is the childhood of our immortality – *Goethe*

Life is thick sown with thorns, and I know no other remedy than to pass quickly through them. The longer we dwell on our misfortunes, the greater is their power to harm us – *Voltaire*

A man should live with his superiors as he does with his fire; not too near, lest he burn, not too far off, lest he freeze – *Diogenes*

It is an infamy to die and not be missed – *Carlos Wilcox*

Life does not count by years. Some suffer a lifetime in a day, and so grow old between the rising and the setting of the sun – *Augusta Evans*

The vanity of human life is like a rivulet, constantly passing away, and yet constantly coming on – *Alexander Pope*

We are immortal till our work is done – *George Whitefield*

It is the bounty of nature that we live, but of philosophy that we live well; which is, in truth, a greater benefit than life itself – *Seneca*

Fleeting as were the dreams of old, / Remembered like a tale that's told, / We pass away – *Henry Wadsworth Longfellow*

The time of life is short; / To spend that shortness basely were too long – *Shakespeare*

Bestow thy youth so that thou mayst have comfort to remember it, when it hath forsaken thee, and not sigh and grieve at the account thereof. Whilst thou art young thou wilt think it will never have an end; but behold, the longest day hath his evening, and thou shalt enjoy it but once; it never turns again; use it therefore as the spring-time, which soon departeth, and wherein thou oughtest to plant and sow all provisions for a long and happy life – *Walter Raleigh*

Nor love thy life, nor hate; but what thou livest, live well; how long or short permit to heaven – *John Milton*

Dost thou love life? Then do not squander time, for that is the stuff life is made of – *Benjamin Franklin*

That man lives twice who lives the first life well – *Robert Herrick*

A sacred burden is this life ye bear; look on it; lift it; bear it solemnly; fail not for sorrow; falter not for sin; but onward, upward, till the goal ye win – *Frances Ann Kemble*

Thy life is no idle dream, but a solemn reality; it is thine own, and it is all thou hast to front eternity – *Carlyle*

He that lives to live forever never fears dying – *William Penn*

Our grand business in life is not to see what lies dimly at a distance, but to do what lies clearly at hand – *Carlyle*

We wish for more in life rather than more of it – *Jean Ingelow*

The man who has lived longest is not the man who has counted most years, but he who has enjoyed life most. Such a one was buried a hundred years old, but he was dead from his birth. He would have gained by dying young; at least he would have lived till that time – *Jean Jacques Rousseau*

Live as if you expected to live an hundred years, but might die tomorrow – *Ann Lee*

Be such a man, and live such a life, that if every man were such as you, and every life like yours, this earth would be God's Paradise – *Phillips Brooks*

Age and youth look upon life from the opposite ends of the telescope; to the one it is exceedingly long, to the other exceedingly short – *Henry Ward Beecher*

With most men life is like backgammon – half skill and half luck – *Holmes*

There is no cure for birth and death save to enjoy the interval – *George Santayana*

In seed time learn, in harvest teach, in winter enjoy – *William Blake*

There is more to life than increasing its speed – *Mohandas Karamchand Gandhi*

Live as if you were to die tomorrow.

Everything is funny as long as it is happening to somebody else.

To be born a gentleman is an accident, but to die a gentleman is an achievement.

As long as you live, keep learning how to live.

The whole of my family has been passed like a razor – in hot water or a scrape.

The earth produces all things, and receives all again.

It doesn't matter where we live as long as we live where we are.

Life is what happens to us while we are making other plans.

Much as we deplore our condition in life, nothing would make us more satisfied with it than the changing of places, for a few days, with our neighbours.

There appears to exist a greater desire to live long than to live well! Measure by man's desires, he cannot live long enough; measure by his good deeds, and he has not lived long enough; measure by his evil deeds, and he has lived too long.

As long as you live, keep learning how to live.

Life, according to an Arabic proverb, is composed of two parts: that which is past – a dream; and that which is to come – a wish.

How great a pity that we should not feel for what end we are born into this world, till just as we are leaving it.

They who are most weary of life – and yet are most unwilling to die – are such who have lived to no purpose; who have rather breathed than lived.

Life is a journey, not a home; a road, not a city of habitation; and the enjoyments and blessings we have are but little inns on the roadside of life, where we may be refreshed for a moment, that we may with new strength press on to the end.

Life's evening will take its character from the day that preceded it.

Live virtuously, my lord, and you cannot die too soon, nor live too long.

There is pleasure enough in this life to make us wish to live, and pain enough to reconcile us to death when we can live no longer.

The greatest results in life are usually attained by simple means and the exercise of ordinary qualities. These may for the most part be summed up in these two – common sense and perseverance.

To make good use of life, one should have in youth the experience of advanced years, and in old age the vigour of youth.

Life is not a matter of holding good cards, but playing a poor hand well.

Too many people go through life running from something that isn't after them.

The only thing most people get out of life is experience.

The purpose of life is not to be happy, but to matter.

Tomorrow, life is too late; live today.

If you want life to be plain sailing, then don't get the wind up.

As the wind blows you must set your sail.

Nothing is more precious than a day well lived.

The great thing is not what we get out of life, it is what we put into life.

See also DEATH.

LITERATURE

Literature happens to be the only occupation in which wages are not given in proportion to the goodness of the work done – *James Anthony Froude*

Literature is a great staff, but a sorry crutch – *Walter Scott*

If I might control the literature of the household, I would guarantee the well-being of the church and state – *Francis Bacon*

The decline of literature indicates the decline of a nation; the two keep pace in their downward tendency – *Johann Wolfgang von Goethe*

I never knew a man of letters ashamed of his profession – *William Makepeace Thackeray*

The study of literature nourishes youth, entertains old age, adorns prosperity, solaces adversity, is delightful at home and unobstrusive abroad – *Cicero*

In literature today there are plenty of good masons but few good architects – *Joseph Joubert*

Literary history is the great morgue where all seek the dead ones whom they love, or to whom they are related – *Heinrich Heine*

The literature of an age is but the mirror of its prevalent tendencies.

Literature is the immortality of speech.

Literature in many of its branches is no other than the shadows of good talk.

When literature is the sole business of life, it becomes a drudgery. When we are able to resort to it only at certain hours, it is a charming relaxation.

Books only partially represent their authors; the writer is always greater than his work.

The great standard of literature, as to purity and exactness of style, is the Bible.

See also BOOKS.

LITTLE THINGS

The smallest hair throws its shadow – *Johann Wolfgang von Goethe*

There is nothing too little for so little a creature as man. It is by studying little things that we attain the great art of having as little misery and as much happiness as possible – *Samuel Johnson*

Little things are great to little men – *Oliver Goldsmith*

Little things console us, because little things afflict us – *Blaise Pascal*

Most persons would succeed in small things if they were not troubled with great ambitions – *Henry Wadsworth Longfellow*

We blame others for slight things, and overlook greater in ourselves – *Thomas à Kempis*

Do little things now; so shall big things come to thee by and by asking to be done – *Persian proverb*

Most of the critical things in life, which become the starting points of human destiny, are little things.

Minute events are the hinges on which magnificent results turn. In a watch the smallest link, chain, ratchet, cog, or crank is as essential as the mainspring itself. If one falls out the whole will stand still.

Small things are not small if great results come of them.

The power to do great things generally arises from the willingness to do small things.

LOGIC

Assertion is the logic of ignorance and prejudice; argument, the logic of wisdom and truth – *Tryon Edwards*

Logic works; metaphysics contemplates – *Joseph Joubert*

Logic is the art of convincing us of some truth – *Jean de La Bruyère*

Ethics make one's soul mannerly and wise, but logic is the armoury of reason, furnished with all offensive and defensive weapons.

See also REASON.

LOOKS

Looks are more expressive and reliable than words – *Tryon Edwards*

Looks kill love and love by looks reviveth; / A smile recures the wounding of a frown – *William Shakespeare*

Cheerful looks make every dish a feast, and that it is which crowns a welcome – *Philip Massinger*

How in the looks does conscious guilt appear – *Ovid*

Features – the great soul's apparent seat.

If a good face is a letter of recommendation, a good heart is a letter of credit.

Coldness and aversion are in your looks, and tell no pity is concealed within.

There are looks and tones that dart an instant sunshine to the heart.

See also COUNTENANCE, FACE.

LOQUACITY

Speaking much is a sign of vanity, for he that is lavish in words is a niggard in deed – *Walter Raleigh*

Nature has given us two ears, two eyes, and but one tongue, to the end that we should hear and see more than we speak – *Socrates*

Those who have few affairs to attend to are great speakers. The less men think the more they talk – *Charles de Montesquieu*

Every absurdity has a champion to defend it, for error is always talkative – *Oliver Goldsmith*

You cram these words into mine ears, against / The stomach of my sense – *William Shakespeare*

A gentlemen . . . that loves to hear himself talk, and will speak more in a minute than he will stand to in a month – *Shakespeare*

What thou speakest thou givest. It is more glorious to give, but more profitable to receive – *Francis Quarles*

Many a man's tongue shakes out his master's undoing – *Shakespeare*

They only babble who practise not reflection – *Richard Brinsley Sheridan*

He draweth out the thread of his verbosity finer than the staple of his argument – *Shakespeare*

They always talk who never think, and who have the least to say.

Learn to hold thy tongue; five words cost Zacharias forty weeks of silence.

Of a great and wise statesman it is said, 'that he can hold his tongue in ten different languages'.

Thou may'st esteem a man of many words and many lies much alike.

See also BABBLERS.

LOSSES

Wise men ne'er sit and wail their loss, / But cheerly seek how to redress their harms – *William Shakespeare*

Losses are comparative, imagination only makes them of any moment – *Blaise Pascal*

The greatness of a loss is determinable, not so much by what we have lost, as by what we have left.

We never seem to know what anything means till we have lost it.

When wealth is lost, nothing is lost; when health is lost, something is lost; when character is lost, all is lost – *German motto*

LOVE

Man's love is of man's life a thing apart. 'Tis woman's whole existence –
   Lord Byron

Who ever loved that loved not at first sight? – *Christopher Marlowe*

The greatest pleasure of life is love – *William Temple*

Love gives itself; it is not bought – *Henry Wadsworth Longfellow*

We are shaped and fashioned by what we love – *Johann Wolfgang von
   Goethe*

Absence in love is like water upon fire; a little quickens, but much
   extinguishes it – *Hannah More*

The motto of chivalry is also the motto of wisdom; to serve all, but love
   only one – *Honoré de Balzac*

I have enjoyed the happiness of the world; I have lived and loved –
   Johann Christoph Friedrich von Schiller

Man while he loves is never quite depraved – *Charles Lamb*

Mutual love, the crown of all our bliss – *John Milton*

'Tis better to have loved and lost / Than never to have loved at all – *Alfred,
   Lord Tennyson*

Corporal charms may indeed gain admirers, but there must be mental
   ones to retain them – *Charles Caleb Colton*

Friendship often ends in love, but love in friendship never – *Colton*

Solid love, whose root is virtue, can no more die than virtue itself –
   Desiderius Erasmus

True love's the gift which God hath given / To man alone beneath the
   heaven – *Walter Scott*

Love looks not with the eyes, but with the mind – *Shakespeare*

Love that has nothing but beauty to keep it in good health is short-lived –
   Erasmus

But love is blind, and lovers cannot see / The pretty follies that themselves commit – *Shakespeare*

It is in love as in war, we are often more indebted for success to the
   weakness of the defence, than to the energy of the attack – *Colton*

Love sought is good, but given unsought is better – *Shakespeare*

The greatest happiness of life is the conviction that we are loved, loved
   for ourselves, or rather loved in spite of ourselves – *Victor Hugo*

As love increases, prudence diminishes – *François de La Rochefoucauld*

As soon go kindle fire with snow / As seek to quench the fire of love with
   words – *Shakespeare*

Never self-possessed, or prudent, love is all abandonment – *Ralph Waldo
   Emerson*

Love is love's reward – *John Dryden*

Love is a canvas furnished by nature and embroidered by imagination –
   Voltaire

Nuptial love maketh mankind; friendly love perfecteth it; but wanton love corrupteth and embaseth it – *Francis Bacon*

Life is a flower of which love is the honey – *Hugo*

Love is strongest in pursuit; friendship in possession – *Emerson*

Base men being in love have then a nobility in their natures more than is native to them – *Shakespeare*

Love reckons hours for months, and days for years; and every little absence is an age – *Dryden*

Two things create love, perfection and usefulness, to which answer, on our part, admiration and desire; and both these are centred in love – *Jeremy Taylor*

A man of sense may love like a madman, but not as a fool – *La Rochefoucauld*

Love lessens woman's delicacy, and increases man's – *Jean Paul Richter*

Love makes obedience lighter than liberty – *William Rounseville Alger*

Love is to the moral nature what the sun is to the earth – *Balzac*

A woman cannot love a man she feels to be her inferior – *George Sand*

They love least that let men know their love – *Shakespeare*

To love is to place our happiness in the happiness of another – *Gottfried Wilhelm Leibniz*

Oh, why should man's success remove the very charms that wake his love! – *Scott*

Love with old men is as the sun upon the snow, it dazzles more than it warms them – *J. P. Senn*

Love's like the measles, all the worse when it comes late in life – *Douglas William Jerrold*

The blood of youth burns not with such excess / As gravity's revolt to wantonness – *Shakespeare*

Love, and you shall be loved – *Emerson*

In peace, love tunes the shepherd's reed; / In war, he mounts the warrior's steed; / In halls, in gay attire is seen; / In hamlets, dances on the green. / Love rules the court, the camp, the grove, / And men below, and saints above; / For love is heaven, and heaven is love – *Scott*

The first symptom of love in a young man is timidity; in a girl it is boldness – *Hugo*

Love takes away the sight; matrimony restores it – *Greek saying*

Love lives in cottages as well as in courts.

Love makes all hearts gentle.

A man has choice to begin love, but not to end it.

Love makes one fit for any work.

They love too much that die for love.

How much better is the love that is ready to die than the zeal that is ready to kill.

Love starts when she sinks in your arms and ends with her arms in the sink.

Love is an ocean of emotion entirely surrounded by expenses.

All true love is grounded on esteem.

The heart of him who truly loves is a paradise on earth; he has God in himself, for God is love.

I am not one of those who do not believe in love at first sight, but I believe in taking a second look.

The soul of woman lives in love.

The treasures of the deep are not so precious as are the concealed comforts of a man locked up in a woman's love.

As love without esteem is volatile and capricious, esteem without love is languid and cold.

Love is an egotism of two.

No cord or cable can draw so forcibly, or bind so fast, as love can do with a single thread.

The heart of a woman is never so full of affection that there does not remain a little corner for flattery and love.

Our first love, and last love, is self-love.

Love and a cough cannot be hid.

Where there is room in the heart there is always room in the house.

One expresses well only the love he does not feel.

Love is like the moon; when it does not increase it decreases.

It is astonishing how little one feels poverty when one loves.

We attract hearts by the qualities we display: we retain them by the qualities we possess.

Of all the paths leading to a woman's love, pity is the straightest.

If nobody loves you, be sure it is your own fault.

Divine love is a sacred flower, which in its early bud is happiness, and in its full bloom is heaven.

Love is friendship set to music.

The love we give away is the only love we keep.

See also COURTSHIP.

LUCK

If you have had bad luck, don't lie down and let it kick you – *David Harum*

I never knew an early-rising, hard-working, prudent man, careful of his earnings, and strictly honest, who complained of bad luck – *Joseph Addison*

Ill luck is, in nine cases out of ten, the result of saying pleasure first and duty second, instead of duty first and pleasure second – *T. T. Munger*

Pitch a lucky man into the Nile, says the Arabian proverb, and he will come up with a fish in his mouth – *Nathaniel Parker Willis*

Shallow men believe in luck, wise and strong men in cause and effect –
  Ralph Waldo Emerson
Luck is for ever waiting for something to turn up. Labour will turn up
  something.
'Luck' is a very good word if you put a P before it.
He that dares not venture must not complain of ill luck.
Luck is knowing when to take the risks.
See also CHANCE.

LUXURY

Avarice and luxury, those pests which have ever been the ruin of every
  great state – *Livy*
Superfluity comes sooner by white hairs, but competency lives longer –
  William Shakespeare
He repents on thorns that sleeps in beds of roses – *Francis Quarles*
War destroys men, but luxury destroys mankind; at once corrupts the
  body and the mind.
Luxury makes a man so soft, that it is hard to please him, and easy to
  trouble him.
On the soft bed of luxury most kingdoms have expired.
Luxury may possibly contribute to give bread to the poor; but if there
  were no luxury, there would be no poor.
Where necessity ends, luxury begins.
A status symbol is anything you can't afford, but did.
See also INDULGENCE.

LYING

After a tongue has once got the knack of lying, 'tis not to be imagined
  how impossible almost it is to reclaim it – *Michel Eyquem de Montaigne*
Never chase a lie. Let it alone, and it will run itself to death – *Henry Ward
  Beecher*
Sin has many tools, but a lie is the handle that fits them all – *Oliver
  Wendell Holmes*
The gain of lying is not to be trusted of any, nor to be believed when we
  speak the truth – *Walter Raleigh*
A lie, though it be killed and dead, can sting sometimes – like a dead
  wasp – *Anna Jameson*
Falsehoods not only disagree with truths, but they usually quarrel
  among themselves – *Daniel Webster*
White lies are but the ushers to black ones.
Lying is a certain mark of cowardice.
A great lie is like a great fish on dry land; it may fret and fling, and make a

frightful bother, but it cannot hurt you. You have only to keep still and it will die of itself.
See also DECEIT, FALSEHOOD, LIARS.

MAGNANIMITY

Of all virtues magnanimity is the rarest; there are a hundred persons of merit for one who willingly acknowledges it in another – *William Hazlitt*

A brave man knows no malice; but forgets, in peace, the injuries of war, and gives his direst foe a friend's embrace – *William Cowper*

A great mind will neither give an affront, nor bear it.

MAGNET

That trembling vessel of the pole, / The feeling compass, navigation's soul – *Lord Byron*

The obedient steel with living instinct moves, / And veers forever to the pole it loves.

Instinct with life, it safely points the way through trackless seas, which else were never sailed.

MAIDENHOOD

Nature has thrown a veil of modest beauty over maidenhood and moss roses – *Nathaniel Parker Willis*

The blushing beauties of a modest maid – *John Dryden*

A maiden never bold; / Of spirit so still and quiet, that her motion / Blush'd at herself – *William Shakespeare*

A child no more; a maiden now; / A graceful maiden with a gentle brow, / And cheek tinged lightly, and a dove-like eye; /And all hearts bless her, as she passes by – *Mary Howitt*

The honour of a maid is her name, and no legacy is so rich as honesty – *Shakespeare*

No padlock, bolts, or bars can secure a maiden so well as her own reserve – *Miguel de Cervantes Saavedra*

A loving maiden grows unconsciously more bold – *Jean Paul Richter*

MAJORITY

The voice of the majority is no proof of justice – *Johann Christoph Friedrich von Schiller*

There is one body that knows more than anybody, and that is everybody – *Charles Maurice de Talleyrand-Périgord*

It never troubles the wolf how many the sheep may be – *Virgil*

We go by the major vote, and if the majority are insane, the sane must go to the hospital – *Horace Mann*

One and God make a majority – *Frederick Douglass*

MALICE

Malice drinks one half of its own poison – *Seneca*

Malice sucks up the greater part of her own venom, and poisons herself – *Michel Eyquem de Montaigne*

There is no malice like the malice of the renegade – *Thomas Babington Macaulay*

Malice scorned, puts out itself; but argued, gives a kind of credit to a false accusation – *Philip Massinger*

MAN

Indisputably a great, good, handsome man is the first of created things – *Charlotte Brontë*

The test of every religious, political, or educational system is the man that it forms – *Henri Frédéric Amiel*

Count what is in man, not what he is worth – *Henry Ward Beecher*

Men, in general, are but great children – *Napoleon Bonaparte*

Man is the highest product of his own history – *Theodore Parker*

Man is an animal that makes bargains; no other animal does this – one dog does not change a bone with another – *Adam Smith*

Man is an animal that cooks his victuals – *Edmund Burke*

Man is a reasoning rather than a reasonable animal – *Alexander Hamilton*

Do you know what a man is? Is not birth, beauty, good shape, discourse, manhood, learning, gentleness, virtue, youth, liberality, and so forth, the spice and salt that season a man? – *William Shakespeare*

No man is so great as mankind – *Parker*

Man perfected by society is the best of all animals; he is the most terrible of all when he lives without law, and without justice – *Aristotle*

Show me the man you honour, and I will know what kind of a man you are – *Thomas Carlyle*

Man is to be trained chiefly by studying and by knowing man – *William Gladstone*

Manhood must come with years – *Beecher*

The way of a superior man is threefold; virtuous, he is free from anxieties; wise, he is free from perplexities; bold, he is free from fear – *Confucius*

One cannot always be a hero, but one can always be a man – *Johann Wolfgang von Goethe*

Every man is valued in this world as he shows by his conduct he wishes
  to be valued – *Jean de La Bruyère*
He is but the counterfeit of a man who hath not the life of a man –
  Shakespeare
The soul of man createth its own destiny of power – *Nathaniel Parker
  Willis*
The highest manhood resides in disposition, not in mere intellect –
  Beecher
I dare do all that may become a man; / Who dares do more is none –
  Shakespeare
It is not a question how much a man knows, but what use he makes of
  what he knows – *Josiah Gilbert Holland*
An honest man is the noblest work of God – *Alexander Pope*
When faith is lost, and honour dies, the man is dead – *John Greenleaf
  Whittier*
The proud man hath no God; the envious man hath no neighbour; the
  angry man hath not himself. Earth holds up to her master no fruit like
  the finished man.
Of all crafts, to be an honest man is the mastercraft.
It is not what he has, or even what he does which expresses the worth of
  a man, but what he is.
In my youth I thought of writing a satire on mankind; but now in my age I
  think I should write an apology for them.
A man wrapped up in himself makes a very small parcel.
A man is never too tired to tell how hard he has worked.
Man is the only animal that blushes, or needs to.
The great man is he who does not lose his child's heart.
Man is not always the fly caught in the web of life; he is often the spider
  who spins it.
Three things come unawares upon a man; sleep, sin and old age.
A noble man is led far by a woman's gentle words.
The ablest man I ever met is the man you think you are.

MANNERS

Good manners is the art of making those people easy with whom we
  converse; whoever makes the fewest persons uneasy, is the best bred
  man in company – *Jonathan Swift*
Manners are minor morals – *William Paley*
Grace is to the body what good sense is to the mind – *François de La
  Rochefoucauld*
Manner is everything with some people, and something with everybody
  – *Bishop Middleton*
Good manners are made up of petty sacrifices – *Ralph Waldo Emerson*

Better were it to be unborn than to be ill bred – *Walter Raleigh*

A well bred man is always sociable and complaisant – *Michel Eyquem de Montaigne*

A man's own good breeding is the best security against other people's ill manners – *Lord Chesterfield*

Fine manners are a stronger bond than a beautiful face. The former binds; the latter only attracts – *Alphonse Marie Louis de Lamartine*

Hail! ye small sweet courtesies of life, for smooth do ye make the road of it, like grace and beauty which beget inclinations to love at first sight; 'tis ye who open the door and let the stranger in – *Laurence Sterne*

Good breeding is the result of much good sense, some good nature, and a little self-denial for the sake of others, and with a view to obtain the same indulgence from them – *Chesterfield*

Coolness, and absence of heat and haste, indicate fine qualities. A gentleman makes no noise; a lady is serene – *Emerson*

The manner of a vulgar man has freedom without ease; the manner of a gentleman, ease without freedom – *Chesterfield*

To be always thinking about your manners is not the way to make them good; the very perfection of manners is not to think about yourself – *Richard Whately*

In manners, tranquillity is the supreme power – *Marquise de Maintenon*

Good breeding consists in having no particular mark of any profession, but a general elegance of manners – *Samuel Johnson*

We cannot always oblige, but we can always speak obligingly – *Voltaire*

Men are like wine; not good before the lees of clownishness be settled – *Owen Feltham*

Prepare yourself for the world, as the athletes used to do for their exercise; oil your mind and your manners, to give them the necessary suppleness and flexibility; strength alone will not do – *Chesterfield*

Virtue itself offends when coupled with forbidding manners – *Middleton*

What better school for manners than the company of virtuous women – *David Hume*

Civility costs nothing, and buys everything – *Lady Mary Wortley Montagu*

A man's fortune is frequently decided by his first impression. If pleasing, others at once conclude he has merit; but if ungraceful, they decide against him – *Chesterfield*

A man's own manner and character is what most becomes him – *Cicero*

Good breeding shows itself most where to an ordinary eye it appears least – *Joseph Addison*

Manners easily and rapidly mature into morals – *Horace Mann*

Manners are the shadows of virtues, the momentary display of those qualities which our fellow creatures love and respect – *Sydney Smith*

The test of good manners is being able to put up with bad ones.

Good manners are the happy way of doing things.

Good manners are the small coin of virtue.

Cultured and fine manners are everywhere a passport to regard.

Good manners are the blossom of good sense and good feeling.

Good manners and good morals are sworn friends and fast allies.

No manners are finer than even the most awkward manifestations of good will to others.

There is no policy like politeness; and a good manner is the best thing in the world either to get a good name, or to supply the want of it.

Nothing, except what flows from the heart, can render even external manners truly pleasing.

Manners are stronger than laws.

Bad manners are a species of bad morals; a conscientious man will not offend in that way.

Truth, justice, and reason lose all their force, and all their lustre, when they are not accompanied with agreeable manners.

One of the most important rules of the science of manners is an absolute silence in regard to yourself.

Better late than never, but better never late.

Manner is one of the greatest engines of influence ever given to man.

There is certainly something of exquisite kindness and thoughtful benevolence in that rarest of gifts – fine breeding.

I don't believe in the goodness of disagreeable people.

Good manners are a part of good morals; and it is as much our duty as our interest to practise both.

Unbecoming forwardness oftener proceeds from ignorance than impudence.

Praise loudly, blame softly.

A company attitude is rarely anybody's best.

Better for a man to possess manners than to have wealth, beauty, or talent; they will more than supply all.

The age of chivalry has gone and one of calculators and economics succeeded.

Merit and good breeding will make their way everywhere.

See also CIVILITY, COURTESY, POLITENESS.

MARRIAGE

A man may be cheerful and contented in celibacy, but I do not think he can ever be happy; it is an unnatural state, and the best feelings of his nature are never called into action – *Robert Southey*

If you would marry suitably, marry your equal – *Ovid*

Men that marry women very much superior to themselves are not so truly husbands to their wives, as they are unawares made slaves to their portions – *Plutarch*

I chose my wife, as she did her wedding gown, for qualities that would wear well – *Oliver Goldsmith*

The bloom or blight of all men's happiness – *Lord Byron*

Married in haste, we repent at leisure – *William Congreve*

Of all the actions of a man's life, his marriage does least concern other people, yet of all actions of our life, 'tis most meddled with by other people – *John Selden*

The reason why so few marriages are happy is because young ladies spend their time in making nets, not in making cages – *Jonathan Swift*

Men are generally more careful of the breed of their horses and dogs than of their children – *William Penn*

Humble wedlock is far better than proud virginity – *Augustine*

There is no disparity in marriage like unsuitability of mind and purpose – *Charles Dickens*

Hasty marriage seldom proveth well – *Shakespeare*

Fathers their children and themselves abuse, / That wealth a husband for their daughters choose – *James Shirley*

For any man to match above his rank is but to sell his liberty – *Philip Massinger*

Let still the woman take / An elder than herself, so wears she to him, / So sways she level in her husband's heart – *Shakespeare*

Wedlock's like wine, not properly judged of till the second glass – *Douglas William Jerrold*

A husband is a plaster that cures all the ills of girlhood – *Molière*

A man finds himself seven years older the day after his marriage – *Francis Bacon*

Men dream in courtship, but in wedlock wake – *Alexander Pope*

The kindest and the happiest pair / Will find occasion to forbear; / And something, every day they live, / To pity and perhaps forgive – *William Cowper*

Marriage with a good woman is a harbour in the tempest of life; with a bad woman, it is a tempest in the harbour – *J. P. Senn*

A good marriage is that in which each appoints the other guardian of his solitude – *Rainer Maria Rilke*

A man is incomplete until he's married – then he's finished.

In some marriages problems are all relative.

Take the daughter of a good mother.

A person's character is but half formed till after wedlock.

In choosing a wife, a nurse, or a schoolteacher, look to the breed. There is as much blood in men as in horses.

Men marry to make an end; women to make a beginning.

The man, at the head of the house, can mar the pleasure of the household, but he cannot make it. That must rest with the woman, and it is her greatest privilege.

When a man and woman are married their romance ceases and their history commences.

For a young man to marry a young woman is of the Lord; for an old man to marry a young woman is of man; but for a young man to marry an old woman is of the devil!

Men should keep their eyes wide open before marriage, and half shut afterward.

If you would have the nuptial union last, / Let virtue be the bond that ties it fast.

If you wish to ruin yourself, marry a rich wife.

Old bachelors always look under 'Marriages' for the news of the week.

Marriage: An investment that pays you dividends if you pay interest.

Alimony: A case of a man going from a co-starring spot to a supporting role.

Marriage by making us more contented often causes us to be less enterprising.

Marriage is a romance in which the hero dies in the first chapter.

See also DOMESTICITY.

MARTYRS

It is the cause and not merely the death that makes the martyr – *Napoleon Bonaparte*

Christianity has made martyrdom sublime, and sorrow triumphant – *E. H. Chapin*

It is admirable to die the victim of one's faith; it is sad to die the dupe of one's ambition – *Alphonse Marie Louis de Lamartine*

It is more difficult, and calls for higher energies of soul, to live a martyr than to die one – *Horace Mann*

For some not to be martyred is a martyrdom – *John Donne*

Who falls for the love of God shall rise a star – *Ben Jonson*

The blood of the martyrs is the seed of the church.

The way of the world is to praise dead saints, and persecute living ones.

MASTER

The eye of the master will do more work than both of his hands; not to oversee workmen is to leave your purse open – *Benjamin Franklin*

The measure of a master is his success in bringing all men round to his opinion twenty years later – *Ralph Waldo Emerson*

Men at some time are masters of their fates – *William Shakespeare*

If thou art a master, sometimes be blind; if a servant, sometimes be deaf.

MAXIMS

Maxims are the condensed good sense of nations – *James Mackintosh*

Pithy sentences are like sharp nails which force truth upon our memory – *Denis Diderot*

Precepts or maxims are of great weight; and a few useful ones at hand do more toward a happy life than whole volumes that we know not where to find – *Seneca*

Coin wisdom into maxims, proverbs, sentences, that can easily be retained and transmitted – *Joseph Joubert*

General observations drawn from particulars are the jewels of knowledge, comprehending great store in a little room – *John Locke*

See also APOTHEGMS, PROVERBS.

MEANNESS

Superior men, and yet not always virtuous, there have been; but there never has been a mean man, and at the same time virtuous – *Confucius*

Whoever is mean in his youth runs a great risk of becoming a scoundrel in riper years – *Victor Cherbuliez*

I have great hope of a wicked man; slender hope of a mean one – *Henry Ward Beecher*

To dally much with subjects mean and low, / Proves that the mind is weak or makes it so – *William Cowper*

See also MISERS.

MEANS

How oft the sight of means to do ill deeds / Makes ill deeds done! – *William Shakespeare*

The end must justify the means.

See also OPPORTUNITY.

MEDICINE

Physic is, for the most part, only a substitute for temperance and exercise – *Joseph Addison*

The disease and its medicine are like two factions in a besieged town; they tear one another to pieces, but both unite against their common enemy, Nature – *Francis Jeffrey*

The best of all medicines are rest and fasting – *Benjamin Franklin*

Doctor, no medicine. We are machines made to live – organized expressly for that purpose. Such is our nature. Leave it at liberty to defend itself, and it will do better than your drugs – *Napoleon Bonaparte*

Over the door of a library in Thebes is the inscription 'Medicine for the
    soul' – *Diodorus Siculus*
Medicine has been defined to be the art or science of amusing a sick man
    with frivolous speculations about his disorder, and of tampering
    ingeniously, till nature either kills or cures him.

MEDIOCRITY

Minds of moderate calibre ordinarily condemn everything which is
    beyond their range – *François de La Rochefoucauld*
The art of putting into play mediocre qualities often begets more
    reputation than is achieved by true merit – *La Rochefoucauld*
Mediocrity can talk; but it is for genius to observe – *Benjamin Disraeli*
There are certain things in which mediocrity is not to be endured, such as
    poetry, music, painting, public speaking – *Jean de La Bruyère*
Nothing in the world is more haughty than a man of moderate capacity
    when once raised to power.

MEDITATION

Meditation is the life of the soul – *Francis Quarles*
A man of meditation is happy, not for an hour or a day, but quite round
    the circle of all his years – *Isaac Taylor*
Meditation is the soul's perspective glass.
Meditation is the nurse of thought, and thought the food of meditation.
See also REFLECTION.

MEETING

The joy of meeting, not unmixed with pain – *Henry Wadsworth Longfellow*
Absence, with all its pains, is, by this charming moment, wiped away.
The joy of meeting pays the pangs of absence; else who could bear it?

MEMORY

Memory is the receptacle and sheath of all knowledge – *Cicero*
We rarely forget that which has made a deep impression on our minds –
    Tryon Edwards
We consider ourselves as defective in memory, either because we
    remember less than we desire, or less than we suppose others to
    remember – *Samuel Johnson*
Joy's recollection is no longer joy, while sorrow's memory is sorrow still –
    Lord Byron
Everyone complains of his memory; nobody of his judgement – *François
    de La Rochefoucauld*

⌐ offices of memory are collection and distribution – *Johnson*

⌐ry is not wisdom; idiots can by rote repeat volumes. Yet what is
⌐wisdom without memory! – *Martin Farquhar Tupper*

O, Memory, thou bitter-sweet both a joy and a scourge – *Mme de Staël*

Memory, the daughter of attention, is the teeming mother of knowledge
– *Tupper*

Memory can glean, but never renew – *Henry Ward Beecher*

Memory seldom fails when its office is to show us the tombs of our
buried hopes – *Lady Blessington*

The true art of memory is the art of attention – *Johnson*

How can such deep-imprinted images sleep in us at times, till a word, a
sound, awake them? – *Gotthold Ephraim Lessing*

Of all the faculties of the mind, memory is the first that flourishes, and
the first that dies – *Charles Caleb Colton*

Recollection is the only paradise from which we cannot be turned out –
Jean Paul Richter

Memory tempers prosperity, mitigates adversity, controls youth, and
delights old age – *Lactantius*

There are many books that owe their success to two things – the good
memory of those who write them, and the bad memory of those who
read them – *Colton*

What we learn with pleasure we never forget – *Alfred Mercier*

My memory is the thing I forget with – *child's definition*

The memory is a treasurer to whom we must give funds, if we would
draw the assistance we need.

Memory is the treasure-house of the mind wherein the monuments
thereof are kept and preserved.

Memory is the cabinet of imagination, the treasury of reason, the registry
of conscience, and the council chamber of thought.

Memory is as much of a curse as a blessing.

MEN

Men are but children, too, though they have grey hairs; they are only of a
larger size – *Seneca*

God divided man into men, that they might help each other – *Seneca*

All great men are in some degree inspired – *Cicero*

Great men stand like solitary towers in the city of God, and secret
passages, running deep beneath external nature, give their thoughts
intercourse with higher intelligence, which strengthens and consoles
them, and of which the labourers on the surface do not even dream –
Henry Wadsworth Longfellow

It is far easier to know men than to know man – *François de La
Rochefoucauld*

Lives of great men all remind us, we can make our lives sublime –
  Longfellow
Men are the sport of circumstances, when the circumstances seem the
  sport of men – *Lord Byron*
We do not commonly find men of superior sense amongst those of the
  highest fortune – *Juvenal*
The real difference between men is energy. A strong will, a settled
  purpose, an invincible determination, can accomplish almost any-
  thing; and in this lies the distinction between great men and little
  men.
We may judge of men by their conversation toward God, but never by
  God's dispensations toward them.
A bachelor is a man who never makes the same mistake once.
Many a groom has been taken for a ride along the bridal path.
Husbands are slow at remembering – their speed is four knots per
  hanky.

MERCY

The greatest attribute of heaven is mercy – *Francis Beaumont and John
  Fletcher*
Wilt thou draw near the nature of the gods? / Draw near them then
  in being merciful; / Sweet mercy is nobility's true badge – *William
  Shakespeare*
Among the attributes of God, although they are all equal, mercy
  shines with even more brilliancy than justice – *Miguel de Cervantes
  Saavedra*
The quality of mercy is not strain'd, / It droppeth as the gentle rain from
  heaven / Upon the place beneath; it is twice bless'd; / It blesseth him
  that gives and him that takes: / 'Tis mightiest in the mightiest; it
  becomes / The throned monarch better than his crown . . . / It is an
  attribute to God himself; / And earthly power doth then show likest
  God's / When mercy seasons justice . . . / consider this, / That in the
  course of justice none of us / Should see salvation: we do pray for
  mercy, / And that same prayer doth teach us all to render / The deeds
  of mercy – *Shakespeare*
Mercy turns her back to the unmerciful – *Francis Quarles*
Nothing emboldens sin so much as mercy – *Shakespeare*
Mercy more becomes a magistrate than the vindictive wrath which men
  call justice – *Henry Wadsworth Longfellow*
We hand folks over to God's mercy, and show none ourselves – *George
  Eliot*
Mercy to him that shows it is the rule – *William Cowper*
Hate shuts her soul when dove-eyed Mercy pleads – *Charles Sprague*

Who will not mercy unto others show, how can he mercy ever hope to have? – *Edmund Spenser*

Teach me to feel another's woe, / To hide the fault I see: / That mercy I to others show, / That mercy show to me – *Alexander Pope*

A God all mercy were a God unjust.

He that has tasted the bitterness of sin fears to commit it; and he that hath felt the sweetness of mercy will fear to offend it.

Least said soonest mended.

See also CLEMENCY, LENITY, PARDON.

MERIT

Charms strike the sight but merit wins the soul – *Alexander Pope*

Nature creates merit, and fortune brings it into play – *François de La Rochefoucauld*

There is merit without elevation, but there is no elevation without some merit – *La Rochefoucauld*

True merit, like a river, the deeper it is, the less noise it makes.

Elevation is to merit what dress is to a handsome person – *La Rochefoucauld*

Contemporaries appreciate the man rather than his merit; posterity will regard the merit rather than the man – *Charles Caleb Colton*

The mark of extraordinary merit is to see those most envious of it constrained to praise – *La Rochefoucauld*

It never occurs to fools that merit and good fortune are closely united – *Johann Wolfgang von Goethe*

The force of his own merit makes his way; / A gift that heaven gives for him – *William Shakespeare*

I will not be concerned at other men's not knowing me; I will be concerned at my own want of ability – *Confucius*

O! that estates, degrees, and offices / Were not deriv'd corruptly, and that clear honour / Were purchas'd by the merit of the wearer – *Shakespeare*

If you wish your merit to be known, acknowledge that of other people – *oriental proverb*

Good actions crown themselves with lasting bays; / Who deserves well, needs not another's praise.

Remedy your deficiencies and your merits will take care of themselves.

Among the sons of men how few are known, / Who dare be just to merit not their own!

METHOD

Methods are the masters of masters – *Charles Maurice de Talleyrand-Périgord*

Method will teach you to win time – *Johann Wolfgang von Goethe*
The shortest way to do many things is to do only one thing at a time.
Dispatch is the life of business, and method is the soul of dispatch.
Method and dispatch govern the world.
Method is like packing things in a box; a good packer will get in half as
    much again as a bad one.

MIND

The more accurately we search into the human mind, the stronger traces
    we everywhere find of the wisdom of Him who made it – *Edmund
    Burke*
The mind grows narrow in proportion as the soul grows corrupt – *Jean
    Jacques Rousseau*
As the firefly only shines when on the wing, so it is with the human mind
    – when at rest, it darkens – *L. E. Landon*
There is nothing so elastic as the human mind. The more we are obliged
    to do the more we are able to accomplish – *Tryon Edwards*
We find means to cure folly, but none to reclaim a distorted mind –
    François de La Rochefoucauld
A wise man is never less alone than when he is alone – *Jonathan Swift*
The defects of the mind, like those of the face, grow worse as we grow
    old – *La Rochefoucauld*
The mind is its own place, and in itself can make a heaven of hell, a
    hell of heaven – *John Milton*
A weak mind is like a microscope, which magnifies trifling things, but
    cannot receive great ones – *Lord Chesterfield*
Old minds are like old horses; you must exercise them if you wish to keep
    them in working order – *John Adams*
It is with diseases of the mind as with diseases of the body; we are half
    dead before we understand our disorder, and half cured when we do
    – *Charles Caleb Colton*
As the mind must govern the hands, so in every society the man of
    intelligence must direct the man of labour – *Samuel Johnson*
My mind to me a kingdom is; such present joys therein I find, that it
    excels all other bliss that earth affords – *Geoffrey Chaucer*
Narrow minds think nothing right that is above their own capacity – *La
    Rochefoucauld*
The mind is ever ingenious in making its own distress.
The blessing of an active mind is that it not only employs itself, but is
    almost sure to be the means of giving wholesome employment to
    others.
Few minds wear out; more rust out.

A mind once cultivated will not lie fallow for half an hour.
Your mind is your mint. What are you coining?

MINORITIES

Votes should be weighed, not counted – *Johann Christoph Friedrich von Schiller*
The smallest number, with God and truth on their side, are weightier than thousands.

MIRTH

Man is the merriest species of the creation; all above or below him are serious – *Joseph Addison*
Frame your mind to mirth and merriment, / Which bars a thousand harms and lengthens life – *William Shakespeare*
I love such mirth as does not make friends ashamed to look upon one another next morning – *Izaak Walton*
Fun gives you a forcible hug, and shakes laughter out of you, whether you will or not – *David Garrick*
Care to our coffin adds a nail, no doubt, and every grin, so merry, draws one out.
Harmless mirth is the best cordial against the consumption of the spirit.
There is nothing like fun, is there? I haven't any myself, but I do like it in others. We need all the counterweights we can muster to balance the sad relations of life. God has made sunny spots in the heart; why should we exclude the light from them?
Mirth should be the embroidery of conversation.
What more than mirth would mortals have? The cheerful man is a king.
See also LAUGHTER, HUMOUR.

MISANTHROPY

Man delights not me; no, nor woman neither – *William Shakespeare*
There cannot live a more unhappy creature than an ill-natured old man, who is neither capable of receiving pleasures, nor sensible of doing them to others – *William Temple*

MISCHIEF

O mischief, thou art swift / To enter in the thoughts of desperate men! – *William Shakespeare*
The opportunity to do mischief is found a hundred times a day, and that of doing good once a year – *Voltaire*

The sower of the seed is assuredly the author of the whole harvest of
mischief – *Demosthenes*

Few men are so clever as to know all the mischief they do – *François de La
Rochefoucauld*

He that may hinder mischief, yet permits it, is an accessory – *Edward
Augustus Freeman*

It is difficult to say who do you the most mischief, enemies with the
worst intentions, or friends with the best.

MISERS

The prodigal robs his heir; the miser robs himself – *Jean de La Bruyère*

The miser is as much in want of that which he has, as of that which he has
not – *Publius Syrus*

A miser grows rich by seeming poor; an extravagant man grows poor by
seeming rich – *William Shenstone*

Misers mistake gold for good, whereas it is only a means of obtaining it –
François de La Rochefoucauld

Gold is the God, the wife, the friend of the money-monger of the world –
William Penn

There is a perpetual frost in the pockets of some rich people; as soon as
they put their hands into them, they are frozen so they cannot draw
out their purses – *Rowland Hill*

A mere madness – to live like a wretch that he may die rich.

Groan under gold, yet weep for want of bread.

See also MEANNESS.

MISERY

Twins, even from the birth, are misery and man – *Homer*

Man is only miserable so far as he thinks himself – *Jacopo Sannazaro*

If you wish to be miserable, think about yourself; you will be as wretched
as you choose – *Charles Kingsley*

There are a good many real miseries in life that we cannot help smiling at,
but they are the smiles that make wrinkles and not dimples – *Oliver
Wendell Holmes*

Misery acquaints a man with strange bedfellows – *William Shakespeare*

A misery is not to be measured from the nature of the evil, but from the
temper of the sufferer – *Joseph Addison*

Notwithstanding the sight of all the miseries which wring us and
threaten our destruction, we have still an instinct that we cannot
repress, which elevates us above our sorrows – *Blaise Pascal*

The true recipe for a miserable existence is to quarrel with Providence.

MISFORTUNE

Misfortune serves to make us wise – *John Gay*

Who hath not known ill-fortune, never knew himself, or his own virtue – *David Mallet*

I never knew a man who could not bear the misfortunes of another perfectly like a Christian – *Alexander Pope*

By struggling with misfortunes, we are sure to receive some wounds in the conflict; but a sure method to come off victorious is by running away – *Oliver Goldsmith*

A soul exasperated by its ills falls out with everything, with its friend and itself – *Joseph Addison*

Rats and conquerors must expect no mercy in misfortune – *Charles Caleb Colton*

Our bravest and best lessons are not learned through success, but through misadventure – *Amos Bronson Alcott*

He that is down needs fear no fall – *John Bunyan*

There is a chill air surrounding those who are down in the world, and people are glad to get away from them, as from a cold room – *George Eliot*

Men shut their doors against the setting sun – *William Shakespeare*

After all, our worst misfortunes never happen, and most miseries lie in anticipation – *Honoré de Balzac*

Most of our misfortunes are more supportable than the comments of our friends upon them – *Colton*

Little minds are tamed and subdued by misfortune; but great minds rise above it – *Washington Irving*

When I was happy I thought I knew men, but it was fated that I should know them only in misfortune – *Napoleon Bonaparte*

It is seldom that God sends such calamities upon man as men bring upon themselves and suffer willingly – *Jeremy Taylor*

We exaggerate misfortune and happiness alike. We are never either so wretched or so happy as we say we are – *Balzac*

The greatest misfortune of all is not to be able to bear misfortune – *Bias of Priene*

Ovid finely compares a man of broken fortune to a falling column; the lower it sinks, the greater weight it is obliged to sustain – *Goldsmith*

Sorrow's crown of sorrow is remembering happier things – *Alfred, Lord Tennyson*

Misfortune does not always wait on vice; nor is success the constant guest of virtue.

The less we parade our misfortunes, the more sympathy we command.

Of fortune's sharp adversity, the worst kind of misfortune is this, that a man hath been in prosperity and it remembers when it passed is.

MISTAKE

Any man may make a mistake, but none but a fool will continue in it – *Cicero*

No man ever became great or good except through many and great mistakes – *William Gladstone*

When you make a mistake, don't look back at it long – *Hugh White*

The only people who make no mistakes are dead people – *H. L. Wayland*

We learn wisdom from failure much more than from success – *Samuel Smiles*

Show us the man who never makes a mistake and we will show you a man who never makes anything – *Wayland*

Some of the best lessons we ever learn we learn from our mistakes and failures. The error of the past is the wisdom and success of the future – *Tryon Edwards*

No persons are more frequently wrong than those who will not admit they are wrong – *François de La Rochefoucauld*

The Providence that watches over the affairs of men works out their mistakes, at times, to a healthier issue than could have been accomplished by their wisest forethoughts – *James Anthony Froude*

A mistake is evidence that someone has tried to do something.

Wise men learn by other men's mistakes; fools, by their own.

MOB

A mob is the scum that rises upmost when the nation boils – *John Dryden*

A crowd always thinks with its sympathy, never with its reason – *William Rounseville Alger*

Let there be an entire abstinence from intoxicating drinks throughout this country during the period of a single generation, and a mob would be as impossible as combustion without oxygen – *Horace Mann*

Licence they mean, when they cry liberty – *John Milton*

It is the proof of a bad cause when it is applauded by the mob – *Seneca*

The blunt monster with uncounted heads, / The still-discordant wavering multitude – *William Shakespeare*

The mob is man, voluntarily descending to the nature of the beast – *Ralph Waldo Emerson*

As a goose is not alarmed by hissing, nor a sheep by bleating; so neither be you terrified by the voice of a senseless multitude.

A mob is a monster, with heads enough, but no heart, and little brains.

MODERATION

The pursuit, even of the best things, ought to be calm and tranquil – *Cicero*

To climb steep hills / Requires slow pace at first – *William Shakespeare*

To live long it is necessary to live slowly – *Cicero*

Moderation is the inseparable companion of wisdom, but with it genius has not even a nodding acquaintance – *Charles Caleb Colton*

Only actions give life strength; only moderation gives it a charm – *Jean Paul Richter*

In adversity assume the countenance of prosperity, and in prosperity moderate the temper and desires – *Livy*

Everything that exceeds the bounds of moderation has an unstable foundation – *Seneca*

Moderation resembles temperance. We are not so unwilling to eat more, as afraid of doing ourselves harm by it – *François de La Rochefoucauld*

It is a little stream which flows softly but it freshens everything along its course – *Mme Swetchine*

The superior man wishes to be slow in his words, and earnest in his conduct – *Confucius*

Moderation is a fatal thing. Nothing succeeds like excess.

Moderate desires constitute a character fitted to acquire all the good which the world can yield.

There is a German proverb which says that 'Take it easy' and 'Live long' are brothers.

Tranquil pleasures last the longest. We are not fitted to bear long the burden of great joys.

The true boundary of man is moderation. When once we pass that pale, our guardian angel quits his charge of us.

MODESTY

The first of all virtues is innocence; the next is modesty – *Joseph Addison*

Modesty is the conscience of the body – *Honoré de Balzac*

Modesty is the chastity of merit – *Emile de Girardin*

A false modesty is the meanest species of pride – *Edward Gibbon*

False modesty is the refinement of vanity – It is a lie – *Jean de La Bruyère*

Experience and humility teach modesty and fear – *Jeremy Taylor*

Modesty is to merit as shades to figures in a picture, giving it strength and beauty – *La Bruyère*

In the modesty of fearful duty / I read as much as from the rattling tongue / Of saucy and audacious eloquence – *William Shakespeare*

Modesty, when she goes, is gone forever – *Walter Savage Landor*

Modesty seldom resides in a breast that is not enriched with nobler virtues – *Oliver Goldsmith*

Modesty is the colour of virtue – *Diogenes*

Modesty is not only an ornament, but also a guard to virtue – *Addison*

The greatest ornament of an illustrious life is modesty and humility, which go a great way in the character even of the most exalted princes – *Napoleon Bonaparte*

Modesty was designed by Providence as a guard to virtue – *Jeremy Collier*

True modesty avoids everything that is criminal; false modesty everything that is unfashionable – *Addison*

Modesty is the citadel of beauty and virtue – *Demades*

Modesty once extinguished knows not how to return – *Seneca*

True modesty is a discerning grace, / And only blushes in the proper place – *William Cowper*

On their own merits modest men are dumb.

Modesty and humility are the sobriety of the mind, as temperance and chastity are of the body.

The crimson glow of modesty o'erspread her cheek and gave new lustre to her charms.

MONEY

Money is a handmaiden, if thou knowest how to use it; a mistress, if thou knowest not – *Horace*

Put not your trust in money, but put your money in trust – *Oliver Wendell Holmes*

A wise man should have money in his head, not in his heart – *Jonathan Swift*

Make money your god, it will plague you like the devil – *Henry Fielding*

Money is like manure, of very little use except to be spread – *Francis Bacon*

Make all you can, save all you can, give all you can – *John Wesley*

He that wants money, means, and content is without three good friends – *William Shakespeare*

Money is not required to buy one necessity of the soul – *Henry David Thoreau*

O, what a world of vile ill-favour'd faults / Looks handsome in three hundred pounds a year! – *Shakespeare*

Ready money is Aladdin's lamp – *Lord Byron*

Money is the life blood of the nation – *Swift*

Mammon has enriched his thousands, and has damned his ten thousands – *Robert South*

The use of money is all the advantage there is in having it – *Benjamin Franklin*

Our incomes are like our shoes; if too small, they gall and pinch us; but if too large, they cause us to stumble and to trip – *Charles Caleb Colton*

No friend like the penny – *Spanish proverb*

The rich never want for kindred.

When we have gold we are in fear; when we have none we are in danger.

When money burns your pocket, you will not be alone at the fire.

Money may not buy friends but it does attract the better class of enemy.

A budget is a method of worrying before you spend instead of afterwards.

Money is a good servant, but a poor master.

Money spent on myself may be a millstone about my neck; money spent on others may give me wings like the angels.

It is not money, but the love of money that is the root of all evil.

Money is a bottomless sea, in which honour, conscience, and truth may be drowned.

There is a vast difference in one's respect for the man who has made himself, and the man who has only made his money.

Mammon is the largest slave-holder in the world.

Wealth is a very dangerous inheritance, unless the inheritor is trained to active benevolence.

Money has little value to its possessor unless it also has value to others.

Gold is the fool's curtain, which hides all his defects from the world.

Money is like an arm or leg – use it or lose it.

There are much more important things in life than money. Trouble is, they all cost money.

Never marry for money – you can borrow it cheaper.

MONUMENTS

No man who needs a monument ever ought to have one – *Nathaniel Hawthorne*

If I have done any deed worthy of remembrance, that deed will be my monument – *Agesilaus*

They only deserve a monument who do not need one; that is, who have raised themselves a monument in the minds and memories of men – *William Hazlitt*

Tombs are the clothes of the dead; a grave is but a plain suit; a rich monument is an embroidered one.

MORALE

Morale is when your hands and feet keep on working when your head says it can't be done.

MORALITY

All sects are different, because they come from men; morality is everywhere the same, because it comes from God – *Voltaire*

Piety and morality are but the same spirit differently manifested. Piety is religion with its face toward God; morality is religion with its face toward the world – *Tryon Edwards*

Morality does not make a Christian, yet no man can be a Christian
without it – *Bishop Wilson*

In this life, ten men have failed from defect in morals where one has
failed from defect in intellect – *Horace Mann*

In matters of prudence last thoughts are best; in matters of morality, first
thoughts – *Robert Hall*

There can be no high civility without deep morality – *Ralph Waldo
Emerson*

A straight line is the shortest in morals as well as in geometry.

Morality is religion in practice; religion is morality in principle.

The health of a community is an almost unfailing index of its morals.

Morality without religion is a tree without roots.

Nothing really immoral is ever permanently popular.

Moral indignation is usually jealousy with a halo.

MORNING

The morning hour has gold in its mouth – *Benjamin Franklin*

Sweet is the breath of morn; her rising sweet with charm of earliest
birds – *John Milton*

The morning steals upon the night, / Melting the darkness – *William
Shakespeare*

The morn is up again, the dewy morn, / With breath all incense, and with
cheek all bloom, / Laughing the clouds away with playful scorn, /
And glowing into day – *Lord Byron*

The silent hours steal on, / And flaky darkness breaks within the east –
Shakespeare

Let your sleep be necessary and healthful, not idle and expensive of time
beyond the needs and conveniences of nature – *Jeremy Taylor*

Night is in her wane; day's early flush glows like a hectic on her fading
cheek, wasting its beauty – *Henry Wadsworth Longfellow*

Nor is a day lived, if the dawn is left out of it, with the prospects it opens –
Amos Bronson Alcott

The cock, that is the trumpet to the morn, / Doth with his lofty and
shrill-sounding throat / Awake the god of day – *Shakespeare*

Morn in the white-wake of the morning star, came furrowing all the
Orient into gold – *Alfred, Lord Tennyson*

The morning, pouring everywhere, / Its golden glory on the air –
Longfellow

Darkness is fled. Now flowers unfold their beauties to the sun, and,
blushing, kiss the beam he sends to wake them – *Richard Brinsley
Sheridan*

The first hour of the morning is the rudder of the day – *Henry Ward
Beecher*

MORTALITY

Lo! as the wind is, so is mortal life; / a moan, a sigh, a sob, or a storm, a strife – *Edwin Arnold*

The mortality of mankind is but a part of the process of living – a step on the way to immortality – *Tryon Edwards*

The boast of heraldry, the pomp of pow'r, / And all that beauty, all that wealth e'er gave, / Awaits alike th' inevitable hour, / The paths of glory lead but to the grave – *Thomas Gray*

All men think all mortal but themselves.

See also DEATH.

MOTHERS

I think it must somewhere be written, that the virtues of mothers shall be visited on their children, as well as the sins of the fathers – *Charles Dickens*

The future destiny of the child is always the work of the mother – *Napoleon Bonaparte*

Children are what the mothers are; no fondest father's fondest care can so fashion the infant's heart, or so shape the life – *Walter Savage Landor*

All that I am, or hope to be, I owe to my angel mother – *Abraham Lincoln*

Unhappy is the man for whom his own mother has not made all other mothers venerable – *Jean Paul Richter*

No joy in nature is so sublimely affecting as the joy of a mother at the good fortune of her child – *Richter*

Men are what their mothers made them – *Ralph Waldo Emerson*

The babe at first feeds upon the mother's bosom, but is always on her heart – *Henry Ward Beecher*

A man never sees all that his mother has been to him till it's too late to let her know that he sees it – *William Dean Howells*

The mother's heart is the child's schoolroom – *Beecher*

Let France have good mothers, and she will have good sons – *Napoleon Bonaparte*

God could not be everywhere, and therefore he made mothers – *Jewish saying*

An ounce of mother is worth a pound of clergy – *Spanish proverb*

Nature's loving proxy, the watchful mother.

If you would reform the world from its errors and vices, begin by enlisting the mothers.

But one thing on earth is better than the wife, and that is the mother.

The future of society is in the hands of the mothers. If the world was lost through woman, she alone can save it.

It is the general rule, that all superior men inherit the elements of superiority from their mothers.

I would desire for a friend the son who never resisted the tears of his
  mother.
If there be aught surpassing human deed or word or thought, it is a
  mother's love!
A mother's love is indeed the golden link that binds youth to age.

MOTIVES

The two great movers of the human mind are the desire of good, and the
  fear of evil – *Samuel Johnson*
It is motive alone that gives character to the actions of men – *Jean de La
  Bruyère*
It is not the incense, or the offering which is acceptable to God, but the
  purity and devotion of the worshipper – *Seneca*
He that does good for God's sake, seeks neither praise nor reward, but
  he is sure of both in the end – *William Penn*
If a man speaks or acts with pure thought, happiness follows him like a
  shadow that never leaves him – *Buddha*
However brilliant an action, it should not be esteemed great unless the
  result of a great and good motive – *François de La Rochefoucauld*
The morality of an action depends upon the motive from which we act –
  Johnson
The noblest motive is the public good – *Virgil*
Many actions, like the Rhône, have two sources: one pure, the other
  impure.
Let the motive be in the deed and not in the event.

MURDER

One murder makes a villain; millions, a hero; numbers sanctify the
  crime – *Bielby Porteus*
To murder character is as truly a crime as to murder the body; the tongue
  of the slander is brother to the dagger of the assassin – *Tryon Edwards*
Every unpunished murder takes away something from the security of
  every man's life – *Daniel Webster*
Blood, though it sleep a time, yet never dies.
Nor cell, nor chain, nor dungeon speaks to the murderer like the voice of
  solitude.

MUSIC

Music is the mediator between the spiritual and the sensual life – *Ludwig
  van Beethoven*
Music is almost the only innocent and unpunished passion – *Sydney
  Smith*

Music can noble hints impart, engender fury, kindle love, with unsuspected eloquence can move and manage all the man with secret art – *Joseph Addison*

Music, in the best sense, does not require novelty; nay, the older it is, and the more we are accustomed to it, the greater its effect – *Johann Wolfgang von Goethe*

The man that hath no music in himself, / Nor is not mov'd with concord of sweet sounds, / Is fit for treasons, stratagems, and spoils; / . . . Let no such man be trusted – *William Shakespeare*

Music is the only sensual gratification in which mankind may indulge to excess without injury to their moral or religious feelings – *Addison*

Music, of all the liberal arts, has the greatest influence over the passions, and is that to which the legislator ought to give the greatest encouragement – *Napoleon Bonaparte*

Music is the only one of the fine arts in which not only man, but all other animals, have a common property – *Jean Paul Richter*

Music is a prophecy of what life is to be; the rainbow of promise translated out of seeing into hearing – *Lydia Maria Child*

We love music for the buried hopes, the garnered memories, the tender feelings it can summon at a touch – *L. E. Landon*

Music has charms to soothe a savage breast – *William Congreve*

Both music and painting add a spirit to devotion, and elevate the ardour – *Laurence Sterne*

Lord, what music hast thou provided for thy saints in heaven, when thou affordest bad men such music on earth! – *Izaak Walton*

Music is the child of prayer, the companion of religion – *François de Chateaubriand*

Let me have music dying, and I seek no more delight – *John Keats*

When griping grief the heart doth wound, / And doleful dumps the mind oppress, / Then music with her silver sound/, / With speedy help doth lend redress – *Shakespeare*

Music is well said to be the speech of angels – *Thomas Carlyle*

Yea, music is the prophet's art; / Among the gifts that God hath sent, / One of the most magnificent – *Henry Wadsworth Longfellow*

Music is the fourth great material want of our nature – first food, then raiment, then shelter, then music.

The highest graces of music flow from the feelings of the heart.

It is in learning music that many youthful hearts learn to love.

The direct relation of music is not to ideas, but to emotions – in the works of its greatest masters, it is more marvellous, more mysterious than poetry.

Music is the medicine of the breaking heart.

Music washes away from the soul the dust of everyday life.

MYSTERY

Mystery is but another name for our ignorance; if we were omniscient, all would be perfectly plain – *Tryon Edwards*

There are more things in heaven and earth . . . / Than are dreamt of in your philosophy – *William Shakespeare*

It is the dim haze of mystery that adds enchantment to pursuit – *Antoine Rivarol*

Many things God reserves to himself, and many are reserved for the unfoldings of the future life – *Edwards*

Most men take least notice of what is plain, as if that was of no use, but puzzle their thoughts with those vast depths and abysses which no human understanding can fathom – *Bishop Sherlock*

As defect of strength in us makes some weights to be immovable, so likewise, defect of understanding makes some truths to be mysterious – *Sherlock*

He had lived long enough to know that it is unwise to wish everything explained.

A religion without mystery must be a religion without God.

NAMES

Who hath not owned, with rapture-smitten frame, / The power of grace, the magic of a name – *William Cowper*

Some to the fascination of a name surrender judgement hoodwinked – *Cowper*

What's in a name? that which we call a rose / By any other name would smell as sweet – *William Shakespeare*

Some men do as much begrudge others a good name, as they want one themselves; and perhaps that is the reason of it – *William Penn*

Good name in man or woman . . . / Is the immediate jewel of their souls – *Shakespeare*

A good name lost is seldom regained.

No better heritage can a father bequeath to his children than a good name.

A handle to your name will open many doors.

A good life hath but a few days, but a good name endureth for ever.

A name is a kind of face whereby one is known.

With the vulgar and the learned, names have great weight; the wise use a writ of inquiry into their legitimacy when they are advanced as authorities.

A person with a bad name is already half hanged.

NATIONS

Individuals may form communities, but it is institutions alone that can create a nation – *Benjamin Disraeli*

The best protection of a nation is its men; towns and cities cannot have a surer defence than the prowess and virtue of their inhabitants – *François Rabelais*

Territory is but the body of a nation. The people who inhabit its hills and valleys are its soul, its spirit, its life – *James Abram Garfield*

No nation can be destroyed while it possesses a good home life – *Josiah Gilbert Holland*

In the youth of a state, arms do flourish; in the middle age, learning; and then both of them together for a time; in the declining age, mechanical arts and merchandise – *Francis Bacon*

A nation's character is the sum of its splendid deeds – *Henry Clay*

The true grandeur of nations is in those qualities which constitute the true greatness of the individual – *Charles Sumner*

The commandments of God are the bread of life for the nations.

NATURE

Nature is but a name for an effect whose cause is God – *William Cowper*

Nature has perfections, in order to show that she is the image of God; and defects, to show that she is only his image – *Blaise Pascal*

Nature knows no pause in progress and development, and attaches her curse on all inaction – *Johann Wolfgang von Goethe*

Study nature as the countenance of God – *Charles Kingsley*

Nature is the time-vesture of God that reveals him to the wise, and hides him from the foolish – *Thomas Carlyle*

Nature and wisdom always say the same – *Juvenal*

Nature is commanded by obeying her – *Francis Bacon*

Nature is the living, visible garment of God – *Goethe*

In contemplation of created things, by steps we may ascend to God – *John Milton*

The laws of nature are but the thoughts and agencies of God – the modes in which he works and carries out the designs of his providence and will – *Tryon Edwards*

Nature gives to every time and season some beauties of its own – *Charles Dickens*

In nature, all is managed for the best with perfect frugality and just reserve – *Lord Shaftesbury*

In nature things move violently to their place, and calmly in their place – *Bacon*

Nature is a frugal mother, and never gives without measure. When she

has work to do, she qualifies men for that and sends them equipped –
Ralph Waldo Emerson

He that follows nature is never out of his way. Nature is sometimes
subdued, but seldom extinguished – *Bacon*

Whatever you are by nature, keep to it; never desert your own line of
talent. Be what nature intended you for, and you will succeed –
Sydney Smith

Nothing is rich but the inexhaustible wealth of nature – *Emerson*

All nature is a vast symbolism; every material fact has sheathed within it
a spiritual truth – *E. H. Chapin*

Nature imitates herself. A grain thrown into good ground brings forth
fruit; a principle thrown into a good mind brings forth fruit – *Pascal*

Sympathy with nature is a part of the good man's religion.

Nature is the most thrifty thing in the world; she never wastes anything.

If we did not take great pains to corrupt our nature, our nature would
never corrupt us.

Epicureanism is human nature drunk, cynicism is human nature mad,
and stoicism is human nature in despair.

The ignorant man marvels at the exceptional; the wise man marvels at
the common; the greatest wonder of all is the regularity of nature.

Nature is man's teacher.

Nature hath nothing made so base, but can read some instruction to the
wisest man.

NECESSITY

Necessity is the argument of tyrants; it is the creed of slaves – *William Pitt
the Younger*

What fate imposes, that men must needs abide; / It boots not to resist
both wind and tide – *William Shakespeare*

Necessity, that great refuge and excuse for human frailty, breaks
through all law; and he is not to be accounted in fault whose crime is
not the effect of choice, but force – *Blaise Pascal*

And with necessity, the tyrant's plea excused his devilish deeds – *John
Milton*

Necessity of action takes away the fear of the act, and makes bold
resolution the favourite of fortune – *Francis Quarles*

We cannot conquer fate and necessity, yet we can yield to them in such a
manner as to be greater than if we could – *Walter Savage Landor*

Necessity may render a doubtful act innocent, but it cannot make it
praiseworthy – *Joseph Joubert*

Necessity is the mother of invention – *George Farquhar*

The argument of necessity is not only the tyrant's plea but the patriot's
defence, and the safety of the state – *James Wilson*

Necessity never made a good bargain.

A people never fairly begins to prosper till necessity is treading on its heels.

The worth of anything is best known by the want of it.

What more of us need is to need less.

We live not as we would, but as need drives us.

Circumstances and necessity are infallible masters.

NEGLECT

A little neglect may breed great mischief – *Benjamin Franklin*

He that thinks he can afford to be negligent is not far from being poor – *Samuel Johnson*

The best ground untilled and neglected soonest runs out into rank weeds – *Bishop Hall*

Self-love . . . is not so vile a sin / As self-neglecting – *William Shakespeare*

Negligence is the rust of the soul, that corrodes through all her best resolves.

NEUTRALITY

Neutral men are the devil's allies – *E. H. Chapin*

Neutrality, as a lasting principle, is an evidence of weakness – *Lajos Kossuth*

A wise neuter joins with neither, but uses both as his honest interest leads him – *William Penn*

The cold neutrality of an impartial judge – *Edmund Burke*

NEWSPAPERS

A newspaper is the history for one day of the world in which we live – *Bishop Horne*

I read the newspaper to see how God governs the world – *John Newton*

A newspaper should be the maximum of information, and the minimum of comment – *Richard Cobden*

Newspapers are the schoolmaster of the common people – a greater treasure to them than uncounted millions of gold – *Henry Ward Beecher*

Newspapers are the world's cyclopaedia of life. They are a universal whispering gallery for mankind, only their whispers are sometimes thunders – *Tryon Edwards*

A journalist is a grumbler, a censurer, a giver of advice, a regent of sovereigns, a tutor of nations. Four hostile newspapers are more to be feared than a thousand bayonets – *Napoleon Bonaparte*

The newspaper press is the people's university – *James Parton*

The careful reader of a few good newspapers can learn more in a year than most scholars do in their great libraries.

Newspapers should be news-carriers, not news-makers.

The press is good or evil according to the character of those who direct.

If a dog bites a man it is not news; if a man bites a dog it is.

The most thought-provoking item in a newspaper is the one your wife cut out before you saw it.

See also JOURNALISM, PRESS.

NICKNAMES

A nickname is the heaviest stone the devil can throw at a man.

A good name will wear out; a bad one may be turned; a nickname lasts forever.

Nicknames stick to people, and the most ridiculous are the most adhesive.

Names alone mock destruction; they survive the doom of all creation.

NIGHT

The day is done, and darkness falls from the wings of night – *Henry Wadsworth Longfellow*

In her starry shade of dim and solitary loveliness, I learn the language of another world – *Lord Byron*

Quiet night, that brings rest to the labourer, is the outlaw's day, in which he rises early to do wrong, and when his work is ended, dares not sleep – *Philip Massinger*

How sweet and soothing is this hour of calm! I thank thee, night! – *Byron*

The worm of conscience is the companion of the owl. The light is shunned by sinners and evil spirits only – *Johann Christoph Friedrich von Schiller*

Earth, turning from the sun, brings night to man.

Oh, treacherous night! thou lendest thy ready veil to every treason, and teeming mischiefs thrive beneath thy shade.

NOBILITY

The origin of all men is the same, and virtue is the only nobility – *Seneca*

Nobility, without virtue, is a fine setting without a gem – *Jane Porter*

All nobility, in its beginnings, was somebody's natural superiority – *Ralph Waldo Emerson*

I can make a lord, but only the Almighty can make a gentleman – *James VI/I*

If a man be endued with a generous mind, this is the best kind of nobility – *Plato*

He who is lord of himself, and exists upon his own resources, is a noble
but a rare being – *Sir Samuel Egerton Brydges*
It is better to be nobly remembered, than nobly born – *John Ruskin*
Virtue is the first title of nobility – *Molière*
It seems to me 'tis only noble to be good – *Alfred, Lord Tennyson*
It is not wealth, nor ancestry, but honourable conduct and a noble
disposition that make men great – *Ovid*
True nobility is indicated by one's heart and not by one's social position –
Bede Jarrett
Nobility should be elective, not hereditary.
Titles of honour add not to his worth, who is an honour to his title.
The best school of nobility is the imitation of Christ.
True nobility is derived from virtue, not from birth. Title may be
purchased, but virtue is the only coin that makes the bargain valid.
See also ARISTOCRACY.

NONSENSE

I find that nonsense, at times, is singularly refreshing – *Charles Maurice de
Talleyrand-Périgord*
A careless song, with a little nonsense in it, now and then, does not
misbecome a monarch – *Horace Walpole*
Nonsense and noise will oft prevail, / When honour and affection fail.
Nonsense is to sense, as shade to light; it heightens effect.
A little nonsense, now and then, / Is relished by the wisest men.
Those who best know human nature will acknowledge most fully what a
strength light-hearted nonsense gives to a hard-working man.

NOVELS

The habitual indulgence in such reading is a silent, ruining mischief –
Hannah More
To the composition of novels and romances, nothing is necessary but
paper, pens, and ink, with the manual capacity of using them – *Henry
Fielding*
A little grain of the romance is no ill ingredient to preserve and exalt the
dignity of human nature, without which it is apt to degenerate into
everything that is sordid, vicious, and low – *Jonathan Swift*
The novel, in its best form, I regard as one of the most powerful engines
of civilization ever invented – *Sir John Herschel*
Novels may teach us as wholesome a moral as the pulpit. There are
'sermons in stones', in healthy books, and 'good in everything' –
Charles Caleb Colton
Lessons of wisdom have never such power over us as when they are

wrought into the heart through the groundwork of a story which
engages the passions – *Laurence Sterne*

We gild our medicines with sweets; why not clothe truth and morals in
pleasant garments as well? – *Nicolas Sébastian Roch Chamfort*

Novels are mean imitations of literature. They devour much precious
time, and have a bad effect upon mind and morals. Their fanciful,
distorted, and exaggerated sketches of life tend to vitiate and corrupt
the taste, and to excite expectations that can never be fulfilled.

Fiction is a potent agent for good in the hands of the good; and so it may
be a potent agent for evil, according to its character and the character
of its readers.

A good novel should be, and generally is, a magnifying or diminishing
glass of life.

Novels do not force their readers to sin, but only instruct them how to
sin.

To the romance writers of his time, Pierre Nicole gave the title of public
poisoners, and the same title might well be applied to a large class of
modern novels.

See also BOOKS, FICTION.

NOVELTY

Novelty is the great parent of pleasure – *Robert South*

It is not only old and early impressions that deceive us; the charms of
novelty have the same power – *Blaise Pascal*

All with one consent praise new-born gawds, / Though they are made
and moulded of things past – *William Shakespeare*

New customs, / Though they be never so ridiculous, / Nay, let 'em be
unmanly, yet are follow'd – *Shakespeare*

Of all the passions that possess mankind, / The love of novelty rules most
the mind; / In search of this from realm to realm we roam, / Our fleets
come fraught with every folly home.

Novelty is short lived. After four days all respect for it is gone.

OATHS

Nay, but weigh well what you presume to swear – *Sir Thomas Overbury*

Rash oaths, whether kept or broken, frequently lead to guilt – *Samuel
Johnson*

It is a great sin to swear unto a sin, / But greater sin to keep a sinful oath –
William Shakespeare

Not . . . for all the sun sees or / The close earth wombs or the profound
sea hides / In unknown fathoms, will I break my oath – *Shakespeare*

OBEDIENCE

No man doth safely rule but he that hath learned gladly to obey – *Thomas à Kempis*

Obedience is the mother of success, and is wedded to safety – *Aeschylus*

Let them obey that know not how to rule – *William Shakespeare*

We are born subjects, and to obey God is perfect liberty. He that does this shall be free, safe and happy – *Seneca*

Wicked men obey from fear; good men, from love – *Aristotle*

Obedience is not truly performed by the body, if the heart is dissatisfied – *Sádi*

Command is anxiety; obedience is ease – *William Paley*

No principle is more noble than that of a true obedience.

Let thy child's first lesson be obedience, and the second may be what thou wilt.

OBLIGATION

To owe an obligation to a worthy friend is a happiness – *Pierre Charron*

We are always much better pleased to see those whom we have obliged than those who have obliged us – *François de La Rochefoucauld*

It is well known to all great men that by conferring an obligation they do not always procure a friend but are certain of creating many enemies – *Henry Fielding*

An extraordinary haste to discharge an obligation is a sort of ingratitude – *La Rochefoucauld*

In some there is a kind of graceless modesty that makes a man ashamed of requiting an obligation, because it is a confession that he has received one – *Seneca*

Man owes not only his services but himself to God.

To feel oppressed by obligation is only to prove that we are incapable of a proper sentiment of gratitude.

Most men remember obligations, but not often to be grateful; the proud are made sour by the remembrance and the vain silent.

OBLIVION

What's past and what's to come is strew'd with husks / And formless ruin of oblivion – *William Shakespeare*

Oblivion is the flower that grows best on graves – *George Sand*

In the swallowing gulf / Of dark forgetfulness and deep oblivion – *Shakespeare*

Oblivion is a second death, which great minds dread more than the first – *Marquis de Boufflers*

Fame is a vapour; popularity an accident; riches take wings; the only
   certainty is oblivion – *Horace Greeley*
Oblivion is the rule and fame the exception of humanity – *Antoine Rivarol*
How soon men and events are forgotten! Each generation lives in a
   different world.

OBSCURITY

The obscurity of a writer is generally in proportion to his incapacity –
   Quintilian
Objects imperfectly discerned take forms from the hope or fear of the
   beholder – *Samuel Johnson*
Lost in the dreary shades of dull obscurity – *William Shenstone*
Thus let me live, unseen, unknown, / Thus unlamented let me die, / Steal
   from the world, and not a stone / Tell where I lie – *Alexander Pope*
Unintelligible language is a lantern without a light.

OBSERVATION

He alone is an acute observer, who can observe minutely without being
   observed – *Johann Kaspar Lavater*
It is the close observation of little things which is the secret of success in
   business, in art, in science, and in every pursuit in life – *Samuel Smiles*
Each one sees what he carries in his heart – *Johann Wolfgang von Goethe*

OBSTINACY

Obstinacy is the strength of the weak – *Johann Kaspar Lavater*
Obstinacy is ever most positive when it is most in the wrong – *Mme
   Neckar*
There are few, very few, that will own themselves in a mistake – *Jonathan
   Swift*
An obstinate man does not hold opinions, but they hold him.
Obstinacy and contradiction are like a paper kite: they are kept up only
   so long as you pull against them.
Obstinacy and vehemency in opinion are the surest proofs of stupidity.

OCCUPATION

Indolence is a delightful but distressing state; we must be doing something to be happy – *William Hazlitt*
The great happiness of life consists in the regular discharge of some
   mechanical duty – *Johann Christoph Friedrich von Schiller*
No thoroughly occupied man was ever yet very miserable – *L. E. Landon*

The prosperity of a people is proportionate to the number of hands and minds usefully employed. Every being that continues to be fed, and ceases to labour, takes away something from the public stock – *Samuel Johnson*

The crowning fortune of a man is to be born with a bias to some pursuit which finds him in employment and happiness – *Ralph Waldo Emerson*

Occupation is the scythe of time – *Napoleon Bonaparte*

Occupation is the necessary basis of all enjoyment – *James Henry Leigh Hunt*

The want of occupation is no less the plague of society than of solitude – *Jean Jacques Rousseau*

The busy have no time for tears – *Lord Byron*

Cheerfulness is the daugher of employment – *Bishop Horne*

Absence of occupation is not rest; / A mind quite vacant is a mind distressed – *William Cowper*

He that does not bring up his son to some honest calling and employment, brings him up to be a thief – *Jewish maxim*

Employment, which Galen calls 'nature's physician', is essential to human happiness.

Temptation rarely comes in working hours. It is in their leisure time that men are made or marred.

Idleness is the mother of mischief.

Nature has made occupation a necessity to us; society makes it a duty; habit may make it a pleasure.

See also INDUSTRY, LABOUR.

OFFENCE

Who fears to offend takes the first step to please – *Colley Cibber*

At every trifle scorn to take offence; / That always shows great pride, or little sense – *Alexander Pope*

Offences ought to be pardoned, for few offend willingly, but only as led by some excitement – *Hegesippus*

When anyone has offended me, I try to raise my soul so high that the offence cannot reach it – *René Descartes*

All's not offence that indiscretion finds / And dotage terms so – *William Shakespeare*

OFFICE

When a king creates an office, Providence at once creates a fool to buy it – *Jean Baptiste Colbert*

Five things are requisite to a good officer – ability, clean hands, dispatch, patience, and impartiality – *William Penn*

'Tis the curse of service, / Preferment goes by letter and affection, / Not by
the old gradation, where each second / Stood heir to the first –
William Shakespeare

High office is like a pyramid; only two kinds of animals reach the
summit, reptiles and eagles – *Jean le Rond D'Alembert*

If ever this free people, if this government itself is ever utterly demoral-
ized, it will come from this incessant human wriggle and struggle for
office, which is but a way to live without work – *Abraham Lincoln*

The gratitude of place to expectants is a lively sense of future favours.

OLD AGE

We hope to grow old, yet we fear old age; that is, we are willing to live,
and afraid to die – *Jean de La Bruyère*

Some men are born old, and some never seem so – *Tryon Edwards*

When men grow virtuous only in old age, they are merely making a
sacrifice to God of the devil's leavings – *Jonathan Swift*

Old age is a tyrant who forbids, at the penalty of life, all the pleasures of
youth – *François de La Rochefoucauld*

To know how to grow old is the master-work of wisdom, and one of the
most difficult chapters in the great art of living – *Henri Frédéric Amiel*

A man isn't old when his hair turns grey, / A man isn't old when his teeth
decay, / But a man is ready for his last long sleep / The day his mind
makes appointments his body can't keep.

A comfortable old age is the reward of a well-spent youth.

There is not a more repulsive spectacle than an old man who will not
forsake the world which has already forsaken him.

OMNISCIENCE

We cannot too often think there is a never-sleeping eye, which reads the
heart, and registers our thoughts – *Francis Bacon*

In all thy actions, think God sees thee; and in all his actions labour to see
him – *Francis Quarles*

What can escape the eye of God, all seeing, or deceive his heart,
omniscient! – *John Milton*

OPINION

All power, even the most despotic, rests ultimately on opinion – *David
Hume*

A man's opinions are generally of much more value than his arguments –
Oliver Wendell Holmes

The world is governed much more by opinion than by laws – *William
Ellery Channing*

Our system of thought and opinion is often only the history of our heart – *Johann Gottlieb Fichte*

Popular opinion is the greatest lie in the world – *Thomas Carlyle*

The feeble tremble before opinion, the foolish defy it, the wise judge it, the skilful direct it – *Mme Roland*

As our inclinations, so our opinions – *Johann Wolfgang von Goethe*

He that never changes his opinions, never corrects his mistakes, will never be wiser on the morrow than he is today – *Tryon Edwards*

Predominant opinions are generally the opinions of the generation that is vanishing – *Benjamin Disraeli*

Public opinion is, with multitudes, a second conscience; with some, the only one – *William Rounseville Alger*

A statesman should follow public opinion as a coachman follows his horses; having firm hold on the reins, and guiding them – *Julius Charles Hare*

Error of opinion may be tolerated where reason is left free to combat it – *Thomas Jefferson*

The eyes of other people are the eyes that ruin us. If all but myself were blind, I should want neither fine clothes, fine houses, nor fine furniture – *Benjamin Franklin*

Wind puffs up empty bladders; opinion, fools – *Socrates*

The men of the past had convictions, while we moderns have only opinions – *Heinrich Heine*

Private opinion is weak, but public opinion is almost omnipotent – *Henry Ward Beecher*

Those who never retract their opinions love themselves more than they love truth – *Joseph Joubert*

The history of human opinion is scarcely anything more than the history of human errors – *Voltaire*

The free expression of opinion, as experience has taught us, is the safety-valve of passion – *William Gladstone*

Change of opinion is often only the progress of sound thought and growing knowledge – *Edwards*

We think very few people sensible, except those who are of our opinion – *François de La Rochefoucauld*

No liberal man would impute a charge of unsteadiness to another for having changed his opinion – *Cicero*

It is not only arrogant but profligate for a man to disregard the world's opinion of himself – *Cicero*

The opinions of men who think are always growing and changing, like living children – *Philip Gilbert Hamerton*

Conscience in most men is but the anticipation of the opinions of others.

No errors of opinion can possibly be dangerous in a country where opinion is left free to grapple with them.

What I admire in Columbus is not his having discovered a world, but his having gone to search for it on the faith of an opinion.

A wise man alters his opinions, a fool never.

Opinion in good men is but knowledge in the making.

Every new opinion at its starting is precisely a minority one.

He who has no opinion of his own but depends upon the opinion and taste of others is a slave.

They must first judge themselves, that presume to censure others.

Opinion is a medium between knowledge and ignorance.

Opinion is private property which the law cannot seize.

Men are never so good or so bad as their opinions.

See also PREJUDICE.

OPPORTUNITY

There is a tide in the affairs of men, / Which, taken at the flood, leads on to fortune; / Omitted, all the voyage of their life / Is bound in shallows and in miseries. / On such a full sea are we now afloat / And we must take the current when it serves, / Or lose our ventures – *William Shakespeare*

Chance opportunities make us known to others, and still more to ourselves – *François de La Rochefoucauld*

The secret of success in life is for a man to be ready for his opportunity when it comes – *Benjamin Disraeli*

Opportunity is rare, and a wise man will never let it go by him – *Bayard Taylor*

If you want to succeed in the world you must make your own opportunities – *John B. Gough*

Next to knowing when to seize an opportunity, the most important thing in life is to know when to forgo an advantage – *Disraeli*

There are no times in life when opportunity, the chance to be and do, gathers so richly about the soul as when it has to suffer – *Phillips Brooks*

Who makes quick use of the moment is a genius of prudence – *Johann Kaspar Lavater*

Turning, for them who pass, the common dust of servile opportunity to gold – *William Wordsworth*

Everyone has a fair turn to be as great as he pleases – *Jeremy Collier*

You will never 'find' time for anything. If you want time you must make it – *Charles Buxton*

Take all the swift advantage of the hours – *Shakespeare*

Miss not the occasion; by the forelock take that subtle power, the never-halting time – *Wordsworth*

A wise man will make more opportunities than he finds – *Francis Bacon*

Opportunity to statesmen is as the just degree of heat to chemists; it perfects all the work – *Sir John Suckling*

Do not wait for extraordinary circumstances to do good; try to use ordinary situations – *Jean Paul Richter*

The May of life blooms only once – *Johann Christoph Friedrich von Schiller*

Who seeks, and will not take when once 'tis offer'd, / Shall never find it more – *Shakespeare*

When one door shuts another opens – *Spanish proverb*

A pessimist is one who complains of the noise when opportunity knocks.

Nothing will ever be attempted if all objectors must first be overcome.

An opportunist is one who does just what you were going to do.

Our opportunities to do good are our talents.

The sure way to miss success is to miss the opportunity.

A philosopher, being asked what was the first thing necessary to win the love of a woman, answered 'Opportunity'.

Opportunity, sooner or later, comes to all who work and wish.

The public man needs but one patron, namely, the lucky moment.

Opportunity comes in vain to the man who is unprepared.

Two men look out between the same bars: / One sees the mud, and one the stars.

See also MEANS.

OPPOSITION

The coldest bodies warm with opposition; the hardest sparkle in collision – *Junius*

He that wrestles with us strengthens our nerves and sharpens our skill. Our antagonist is our helper – *Edmund Burke*

The greater the obstacle the more glory in overcoming it – *Molière*

It is not ease but effort – not facility, but difficulty – that makes men – *Samuel Smiles*

A strenuous soul hates cheap success; it is the ardour of the assailant that makes the vigour of the defendant – *Ralph Waldo Emerson*

Opposition inflames the enthusiast, never converts him – *Johann Christoph Friedrich von Schiller*

OPPRESSION

A desire to resist oppression is implanted in the nature of man – *Tacitus*

The smallest worm will turn being trodden on, / And doves will peck in safeguard of their brood – *William Shakespeare*

There is no happiness for him who oppresses and persecutes – *Johann Heinrich Pestalozzi*

Oppression makes wise men mad; but the distemper is still the madness of the wise, which is better than the sobriety of fools – *Edmund Burke*

I never could believe that Providence had sent a few men into the world, ready booted and spurred to ride, and millions ready saddled and bridled to be ridden – *Richard Rumbold*

An extreme rigour is sure to arm everything against it – *Burke*

I marvel how the fishes live in the sea. – Why, as men do a-land; the great ones eat up the little ones – *Shakespeare*

The camomile, the more it is trodden on the faster it grows – *Shakespeare*

Oppression is but another name for irresponsible power.

See also PERSECUTION, TYRANNY.

ORATORY

It is the first rule in oratory that a man must appear such as he would persuade others to be; and that can be accomplished only by the force of his life – *Jonathan Swift*

List his discourse of war, and you shall hear / A fearful battle render'd you in music – *William Shakespeare*

What too many orators want in depth, they give you in length – *Charles de Montesquieu*

In oratory, the greatest art is to conceal art – *Swift*

An orator without judgement is a horse without a bridle – *Theophrastus*

The effective public speaker receives from his audience in vapour what he pours back on them in a flood – *William Gladstone*

The passions are the only orators that always succeed. Simplicity, with the aid of the passions, persuades more than the utmost eloquence without it – *François de La Rochefoucauld*

Suit the action to the word, the word to the action – *Shakespeare*

An orator or author is never successful till he has learned to make his words smaller than his ideas – *Ralph Waldo Emerson*

It is a sign of ignorance not to know that long speeches, though they may please the speaker, are the torture of the hearer.

Eloquence is vehement simplicity.

It is not by the compositions he learns, but by the memory of the effects he has produced that an orator is to be judged.

The language of the heart which comes from the heart and goes to the heart is always simple, but no art of rhetoric can teach it.

See also ELOQUENCE.

ORDER

Order is heaven's first law – *Alexander Pope*

A place for everything, everything in its place – *Benjamin Franklin*

Order means light and peace, inward liberty and free command over oneself; order is power – *Henri Frédéric Amiel*

Set all things in their own peculiar place, / And know that order is the greatest grace – *John Dryden*

Good order is the foundation of all good things – *Edmund Burke*

ORIGINALITY

Originality is nothing but judicious imitation – *Voltaire*

Originality is simply a pair of fresh eyes – *Thomas Wentworth Higginson*

The merit of originality is not novelty, it is sincerity – *Thomas Carlyle*

Every human being is intended to have a character of his own; to be what no other is, and to do what no other can do – *William Ellery Channing*

He who thinks for himself, and rarely imitates, is a free man – *Friedrich Gottlieb Klopstock*

Great things cannot have escaped former observations – *Samuel Johnson*

If you would create something, you must be something – *Johann Wolfgang von Goethe*

Those who are ambitious of originality, and aim at it, are necessarily led by others, since they seek to be different from them – *Richard Whately*

They who have light in themselves will not revolve as satellites.

One of the best uses of originality is to say common things in an uncommon way.

It is better to create than to be learned; creating is the true essence of life.

I would rather be the author of one original thought than the conqueror of a hundred battles.

Every man is an original and solitary character.

ORNAMENT

All finery is a sign of littleness – *Johann Kaspar Lavater*

Ornaments were invented by modesty – *Joseph Joubert*

Modern education too often covers the fingers with rings, and at the same time cuts the sinews at the wrists – *John Sterling*

Excess in apparel is another costly folly. The very trimming of the vain world would clothe all the naked ones – *William Penn*

Show is not substance; realities govern wise men – *Penn*

The true ornament of matrons is virtue, not apparel.

PAIN

Pain may be said to follow pleasure, as its shadow – *Charles Caleb Colton*

Pain adds rest unto pleasure, and teaches the luxury of health – *Martin Farquhar Tupper*

Pain and pleasure, like light and darkness, succeed each other – *Laurence Sterne*

There was never yet philosopher / That could endure the toothache patiently – *William Shakespeare*

They talk of short-lived pleasures: be it so; / Pain dies as quickly, and lets her weary prisoner go; / The fiercest agonies have shortest reign.

The heart can ne'er a transport know that never feels a pain.

The same refinement which brings us new pleasures exposes us to new pains.

A man of pleasure is a man of pains.

Swift run the sands of time except in the hour of pain.

See also SUFFERING.

PAINTING

Painting is silent poetry, and poetry is a speaking picture – *Simonides of Ceos*

A picture is a poem without words – *Horace*

The love of gain never made a painter, but it has marred many – *Washington Allston*

A room hung with pictures is a room hung with thoughts – *Joshua Reynolds*

A picture is an intermediate something between a thought and a thing – *Samuel Taylor Coleridge*

The best portraits are those in which there is a slight mixture of caricature – *Thomas Babington Macaulay*

Style in painting is the same as in writing – a power over materials, whether words or colours, by which conceptions or sentiments are conveyed – *Reynolds*

The first merit of pictures is the effect they produce on the mind – *Henry Ward Beecher*

PANIC

A panic is the stampede of our self-possession – *Antoine Rivarol*

A panic is a sudden desertion of us, and a going over to the enemy of our imagination.

PARDON

The man who pardons easily courts injury – *Pierre Corneille*

Mercy is not itself, that oft looks so; / Pardon is still the nurse of second woe – *William Shakespeare*

Pardon others often, thyself never – *Publius Syrus*

Forgive thyself little, and others much – *Robert Leighton*
Pardon is the virtue of victory – *Giuseppe Mazzini*
They who forgive most shall be most forgiven.
See also CLEMENCY, MERCY.

PARENTS

Next to God thy parents – *William Penn*
We never know the love of the parent till we become parents ourselves –
   Henry Ward Beecher
Parents wonder why the streams are bitter, when they themselves have
   poisoned the fountain – *John Locke*
Whoever makes his father's heart to bleed, / Shall have a child that will
   revenge the deed – *F. Randolph*
Sins of the parents may be visited upon their children.
Parents who wish to train up their children in the way they should go,
   must go in the way in which they would have their children go.
A suspicious parent makes an artful child.
When our parents are living we feel that they stand between us and
   death; when they are gone, we ourselves are in the forefront of the
   battle.

PARTING

In every parting there is an image of death – *George Eliot*
I have no parting sigh to give, so take my parting smile – *L. E. Landon*
Never part without loving words – *Jean Paul Richter*
Adieu! I have too grieved a heart / To take a tedious leave – *William
   Shakespeare*
Let us not unman each other; part at once; all farewells should be
   sudden, when forever – *Lord Byron*
What! gone without a word? / Ay, so true love should do: it cannot speak;
   / For truth hath better deeds than words to grace it – *Shakespeare*
Farewell! God knows when we shall meet again. / I have a faint cold fear
   thrills through my veins, / That almost freezes up the heat of life –
   Shakespeare
To die and part is a less evil; but to part and live, there, there is the
   torment.

PARTY

Party is the madness of many, for the gain of a few – *Alexander Pope*
He knows very little of mankind, who expects, by any facts or reasoning,
   to convince a determined party-man – *Johann Kaspar Lavater*

The political parties that I would call great are those which cling more to principles than to consequences – *Alexis de Tocqueville*

If we mean to support the liberty and independence which have cost us so much blood and treasure to establish, we must drive far away the demon of party spirit and local reproach – *George Washington*

He that aspires to be the head of a party will find it more difficult to please his friends than to perplex his foes – *Charles Caleb Colton*

Men in a party have liberty only for their motto; in reality they are greater slaves than anybody else would care to make them.

PASSION

The passionate are like men standing on their heads; they see all things the wrong way – *Plato*

Men spend their lives in the service of their passions, instead of employing their passions in the service of their life – *Richard Steele*

There are moments when our passions speak and decide for us, and we seem to stand by and wonder – *George Eliot*

A vigorous mind is as necessarily accompanied with violent passions as a great fire with great heart – *Edmund Burke*

Passions makes us feel, but never see clearly – *Charles de Montesquieu*

He submits to be seen through a miscroscope who suffers himself to be caught in a fit of passion – *Johann Kaspar Lavater*

Passions are likened best to floods and streams: the shallow murmur, but the deep are dumb – *Walter Raleigh*

Passion is the drunkenness of the mind – *Robert South*

Passion, though a bad regulator, is a powerful spring – *Ralph Waldo Emerson*

The only praiseworthy indifference is an acquired one; we must feel as well as control our passions – *Jean Paul Richter*

The brain may devise laws for the blood, but a hot temper leaps o'er a cold decree – *William Shakespeare*

The passions are the winds that fill the sails of the vessel – *Voltaire*

It is the passions of men that both do and undo everything – *Bernard de Fontenelle*

Passion often makes fools of the ablest men, and able men of the most foolish – *François de La Rochefoucauld*

If we resist our passions, it is more through their weakness than from our strength – *La Rochefoucauld*

He only employs his passion who can make no use of his reason – *Cicero*

A man is by nothing so much himself, as by his temper and the character of his passions and affections – *Lord Shaftesbury*

When passion rules, how rare the hours that fall to virtue's share – *Walter Scott*

Give me that man / That is not passion's slave, and I will wear him / In my heart's core, ay, in my heart of hearts – *Shakespeare*

Our headstrong passions shut the door of our souls against God – *Confucius*

We use up in our passions the stuff that was given us for happiness – *Joseph Joubert*

The ruling passion, be it what it will, / The ruling passion conquers reason still – *Alexander Pope*

May I govern my passions with absolute sway, / And grow wiser and better as life wears away – *Walter Pope*

Sudden passions are hard to be managed.

The worst of slaves is he whom passion rules.

Passion looks not beyond the moment of its existence.

The passions are like fire, useful in a thousand ways and dangerous only in one, through their excess.

Alas! too well, too well they know / The pain, the penitence, the woe, / That passion brings down on the best, / The wisest, and the loveliest.

What a mistake to suppose that the passions are strongest in youth! The passions are not stronger, but the control over them is weaker!

PAST

So sad, so fresh, the days that are no more – *Alfred, Lord Tennyson*

No hand can make the clock strike for me the hours that are passed – *Lord Byron*

It is to live twice, when we can enjoy the recollections of our former life – *Martial*

I desire no future that will break the ties of the past – *George Eliot*

Things without all remedy / Should be without regard; what's done is done – *William Shakespeare*

We ought not to look back unless it is to derive useful lessons from past errors, and for the purpose of profiting by dear bought experience – *George Washington*

Nor deem the irrevocable past / As wholly wasted, wholly vain, / If rising on its wrecks, at last / To something nobler we attain – *Henry Wadsworth Longfellow*

Study the past if you would divine the future – *Confucius*

What's gone and what's past help / Should be past grief – *Shakespeare*

Our reverence for the past is just in proportion to our ignorance of it – *Theodore Parker*

The past is the sepulchre of our dead emotions.

Age and sorrow have the gift of reading the future by the sad past.

PATIENCE

Everything comes if a man will only wait – *Tancred*

He that can have patience can have what he will – *Benjamin Franklin*

It is not necessary for all men to be great in action. The greatest and sublimest power is often simple patience – *Horace Bushnell*

How poor are they that have not patience! / What wound did ever heal but by degrees? – *William Shakespeare*

For patience lies at the root of all pleasures as well as of all powers – *John Ruskin*

Patience is the art of hoping – *Marquis de Vauvenargues*

It's easy finding reasons why other folks should be patient – *George Eliot*

Patience is the key of content – *Muhammad*

Accustom yourself to that which you bear ill, and you will bear it well – *Seneca*

They also serve who only stand and wait – *John Milton*

Patience and time do more than strength or passion – *Jean de La Fontaine*

A patient humble temper gathers blessings that are marred by the peevish, and overlooked by the aspiring – *E. H. Chapin*

Endurance is the crowning quality, and patience all the passion of great hearts – *James Russell Lowell*

That which in mean men we intitle patience / Is pale cold cowardice in noble breasts – *Shakespeare*

Beware the fury of a patient man – *John Dryden*

Patience is bitter, but its fruit is sweet – *Jean Jacques Rousseau*

Patience is so like fortitude that she seems either her sister or her daughter – *Aristotle*

Patience is the support of weakness; impatience is the ruin of strength – *Charles Caleb Colton*

He surely is most in need of another's patience, who has none of his own – *Johann Kaspar Lavater*

No honours are too distant for the man who prepares himself for them with patience – *Jean de La Bruyère*

Patience is power; with time and patience the mulberry leaf becomes silk – *Chinese proverb*

Steady, patient, persevering thinking, will generally surmount every obstacle in the search after truth.

To know how to wait is the great secret of success.

Patience is not passive: on the contrary it is active; it is concentrated strength.

Patience is a virtue, possess it if you can, / You find it in a woman but seldom in a man.

PATRIOTISM

The noblest motive is the public good – *Virgil*

Be just, and fear not. / Let all the ends thou aim'st at be thy country's, / Thy God's, and truth's – *William Shakespeare*

Let our object be our country, our whole country, and nothing but our country – *Daniel Webster*

Had I a dozen sons, each in my love alike . . . I had rather had eleven die nobly for their country than one voluptuously surfeit out of action – *Shakespeare*

There can be no affinity nearer than our country – *Plato*

The love of country produces good manners; and good manners, love of country – *Charles de Montesquieu*

The proper means of increasing the love we bear to our native country is to reside some time in a foreign one – *William Shenstone*

The patriot's boast, where'er we roam, / His first, best country ever is at home – *Oliver Goldsmith*

I do love / My country's good with a respect more tender, / More holy and profound, than mine own life – *Shakespeare*

Liberty and union, now and forever, one and inseparable – *Daniel Webster*

Patriotism is the last refuge of a scoundrel! – *Samuel Johnson*

He who loves not his country can love nothing.

National enthusiasm is the great nursery of genius.

PEACE

Peace is such a precious jewel that I would give anything for it but truth – *Matthew Henry*

'Tis death to me to be at enmity; / I hate it, and desire all good men's love – *William Shakespeare*

If we have not peace within ourselves, it is in vain to seek it from outward sources – *François de La Rochefoucauld*

Peace is rarely denied to the peaceful – *Johann Christoph Friedrich von Schiller*

Peace is the proper result of the Christian temper – *Bishop Patrick*

Nothing can bring you peace but yourself – *Ralph Waldo Emerson*

Peace hath her victories, no less renowned than war – *John Milton*

Peace, / Dear nurse of arts, plenties and joyful birth – *Shakespeare*

A peace is of the nature of a conquest; / For then both parties nobly are subdu'd, / And neither party loser – *Shakespeare*

We love peace, but not peace at any price. Chains are worse than bayonets – *Douglas William Jerrold*

To be prepared for war is one of the most effectual means of preserving peace – *George Washington*

I am a man of peace. God knows how I love peace. But I hope I shall never be such a coward as to mistake oppression for peace – *Lajos Kossuth*

Peace is the happy, natural state of man; war, his corruption, his disgrace.

Peace rules the day, where reason rules the mind.

PEDANTRY

Pedantry crams our heads with learned lumber, and takes out our brains to make room for it – *Charles Caleb Colton*

The vacant skull of a pedant generally furnishes out a throne and temple for vanity – *William Shenstone*

Deep versed in books, and shallow in himself – *John Milton*

Pedantry prides herself on being wrong by rules; while common sense is contented to be right without them – *Colton*

Pedantry and taste are as inconsistent as gaiety and melancholy – *Johann Kaspar Lavater*

Brimful of learning, see the pedant stride, / Bristling with horrid Greek, and puffed with pride! / A thousand authors he in vain has read, / And with their maxims stuffed his empty head; / And thinks that without Aristotle's rules, / Reason is blind, and common sense a fool! – *Nicolas Boileau*

A well-read fool is the most pestilent of blockheads.

PEN

There are only two powers in the world, the sword and the pen; and in the end the former is always conquered by the latter – *Napoleon Bonaparte*

I had rather stand in the shock of a basilisk than in the fury of a merciless pen – *Sir Thomas Browne*

Oh, nature's noblest gift, – my grey goose-quill! – *Lord Byron*

Take away the sword; states can be saved without it; bring the pen!

PEOPLE

When judging a friend remember he is judging you with the same godlike and superior impartiality – *Arnold Bennett*

People seldom improve when they have no other model but themselves to copy – *Oliver Goldsmith*

There are three kinds of people in the world, the wills, the won'ts and the can'ts. The first accomplish everything; the second oppose everything; the third fail in everything – *Eclectic Magazine*

You can fool all the people some of the time, and some of the people all
the time, but you cannot fool all the people all of the time – *Abraham
Lincoln*

Most people judge others either by the company they keep, or by their
fortune – *François de La Rochefoucauld*

If you can't be a star, you needn't be a cloud.

A frequent disappointment is meeting someone we have heard so much
about.

He that serves everybody is paid by nobody.

There are people who make things happen, people who watch things
happen and people who don't know anything did happen.

It's odd how people waiting for you stand out far less clearly than people
you are waiting for.

People who give themselves away are not always charitable.

PERCEPTION

So weak a thing is reason in competition with inclination – *Bishop Berkeley*

To see what is right, and not do it, is want of courage, or of principle –
Confucius

Penetration seems a kind of inspiration.

The heart has eyes that the brain knows nothing of.

PERFECTION

Perfection is attained by slow degrees; it requres the hand of time –
Voltaire

Bachelor's wives and old maid's children are always perfect – *Nicolas
Sébastian Roch Chamfort*

Perfection consists not in doing extraordinary things, but in doing
ordinary things extraordinarily well – *Angélique Arnauld*

Aim at perfection in everything, though in most things it is unattainable
– *Lord Chesterfield*

Every rose has its thorns, and every day its night – *Charles Haddon
Spurgeon*

Faultily faultless, icily regular, splendidly null, / Dead perfection, no
more – *Alfred, Lord Tennyson*

Whoever thinks a faultless piece to see, / Thinks what ne'er was, nor is,
nor ever shall be – *Alexander Pope*

This is the very perfection of a man, to find out his own imperfection –
Augustine

He that seeks perfection on earth leaves nothing new for the saints to
find in heaven.

The more a thing is perfect, the more it feels pleasure and likewise pain.
We are what we are; we cannot be truly other than ourselves.
The more perfect the sight is the more delightful the beautiful object. The
    more perfect the appetite, the sweeter the food. The more musical the
    ear, the more pleasant the melody.

PERSECUTION

Persecution is not wrong because it is cruel, but cruel because it is wrong
    – *Richard Whately*
In all places, and in all times, those religionists who have believed too
    much have been more inclined to violence and persecution than
    those who have believed too little – *Charles Caleb Colton*
Wherever you see persecution, there is more than a probability that truth
    is on the persecuted side – *Bishop Latimer*
Persecution often does in this life what the last great day will do
    completely, separate the wheat from the tares.
The blood of the martyrs is the seed of the church.
The way of the world is to praise dead saints, and persecute living ones.
See also OPPRESSION.

PERSEVERANCE

The falling drops at last will wear the stone – *Lucretius*
Great works are performed, not by strength, but by perseverance –
    Samuel Johnson
Much rain wears the marble – *William Shakespeare*
Do not, for one repulse, forgo the purpose / That you resolv'd to effect –
    Shakespeare
Nothing is so hard, but search will find it out – *Robert Herrick*
No road is too long to the man who advances deliberately and without
    undue haste – *Jean de La Bruyère*
By gnawing through a dyke, even a rat may drown a nation – *Edmund
    Burke*
That which grows slowly endures – *Josiah Gilbert Holland*
Perseverance . . . / Keeps honour bright – *Shakespeare*
Every noble work is at first impossible – *Thomas Carlyle*
There are two ways of attaining an important end – force and persever-
    ance – *Mme Swetchine*
The nerve that never relaxes, the eye that never blenches, the thought
    that never wanders – these are the masters of victory – *Burke*
Hasten slowly, and without losing heart put your work twenty times
    upon the anvil – *Nicolas Boileau*
Victory belongs to the most persevering – *Napoleon Bonaparte*

Hard pounding, gentlemen; but we will see who can pound the longest –
Duke of Wellington

Perseverance gives power to weakness, and opens to poverty the
world's wealth – *Samuel Griswold Goodrich*

Even in social life, it is persistency which attracts confidence more than
talents and accomplishments – *E. P. Whipple*

No rock so hard but that a little wave may beat admission in a thousand
years – *Alfred, Lord Tennyson*

Persistent people begin their success where others end in failure –
Edward Eggleston

Whoever perseveres will be crowned – *Johann Gottfried Herder*

The difference between perseverance and obstinacy is that one often
comes from a strong will and the other from a strong won't – *Henry
Ward Beecher*

The tree falls not at the first stroke.

Every man who observes vigilantly, and resolves steadfastly, grows
unconsciously into genius.

The virtue lies in the struggle, not in the prize.

PHILOSOPHY

To be a philosopher is so to love wisdom as to live according to its dictates
– *Henry David Thoreau*

Philosophy is the art and law of life – *Seneca*

Philosophy is nothing but discretion – *John Selden*

The discovery of what is true and the practice of that which is good are
the two most important objects of philosophy – *Voltaire*

The sum of philosophy is to learn what is just in society, and beautiful in
nature and the order of the world – *Lord Shaftesbury*

Philosophy triumphs easily over past and over future evils, but present
evils triumph over philosophy – *François de La Rochefoucauld*

Adversity's sweet milk, philosophy – *William Shakespeare*

Philosophy is a longing after heavenly wisdom – *Plato*

The greater the philosopher, the harder it is for him to answer the
questions of the average man – *Henryk Sienkiewicz*

A man of business may talk of philosophy, a man who has none may
practise it – *Jonathan Swift*

It is not a head merely, but a heart and resolution, which complete the
real philosopher – *Shaftesbury*

Philosophy is the science which considers truth – *Aristotle*

Christianity is a philosophy of principles rather than of rules – *Tryon
Edwards*

It is the bounty of nature that we live, but of philosophy that we live
well; which is, in truth, a greater benefit than life itself – *Seneca*

True philosophy is that which makes us to ourselves and to all about us
better – *Johann Kaspar Lavater*
All philosophy lies in two words, sustain and abstain – *Epictetus*
The idea of philosophy is truth; the idea of religion is life – *Peter Bayne*
To study philosophy is nothing but to prepare oneself to die – *Cicero*
The first business of a philosopher is to part with self-conceit – *Epictetus*
Philosophy, when superficially studied, excites doubt; when thoroughly
explored, it dispels it – *Francis Bacon*
Philosophy alone makes the mind invincible, and places us out of the
reach of fortune, so that all her arrows fall short of us – *Seneca*
Be a philosopher; but amid all your philosophy, be still a man – *David
Hume*
Philosophy, if rightly defined, is nothing but the love of wisdom – *Cicero*
Philosophy is a goddess, whose head indeed is in heaven, but whose feet
are upon earth – *Charles Caleb Colton*
Philosophy goes no further than probabilities and in every assertion
keeps a doubt in reserve – *James Anthony Froude*
You cannot strengthen the weak by weakening the strong.
A philosopher may despise riches; but I'll bet his wife doesn't.

PHYSICIANS

God heals, and the doctor takes the fee – *Benjamin Franklin*
Physicians mend or end us; / But though in health we sneer, / When sick
we call them to attend us, / Without the least propensity to jeer – *Lord
Byron*
We have not only multiplied diseases, but we have made them more
fatal.
Everyone is a physician or a fool at forty.
Exercise, temperance, fresh air, and needful rest are the best of all
physicians.
Never argue with your doctor – he has inside information.

PITY

Pity is not natural to man. Children and savages are always cruel. Pity is
acquired and improved by the cultivation of reason – *Samuel Johnson*
The truly brave are soft of heart and eyes, and feel for what their duty
bids them do – *Lord Byron*
Pity is best taught by fellowship in woe – *Samuel Taylor Coleridge*
Of all the paths that lead to a woman's love, pity is the straightest –
Francis Beaumont and John Fletcher
Pity is sworn servant unto love.
Pity is akin to love.

Pity swells the tide of love.
No pity is wasted except self-pity.
See also COMPASSION.

PLACE

Where you are is of no moment, but only what you are doing there –
    Petrarch
It is not the place that maketh the person, but the person that maketh the
    place honourable – *Cicero*
The place is dignified by the doer's deed – *William Shakespeare*
He who thinks his place below him will certainly be below his place.
See also RANK, STATION.

PLEASURE

If you wish to please people, you must begin by understanding them –
    Charles Reade
Enjoy present pleasures in such a way as not to injure future ones –
    Seneca
The seeds of repentance are sown in youth by pleasure, but the harvest is
    reaped in age by suffering – *Charles Caleb Colton*
A man that knows how to mix pleasures with business is never entirely
    possessed by them – *Seigneur de Saint-Evremond*
The most delicate, the most sensible of all pleasures, consists in pro-
    moting the pleasure of others – *Jean de La Bruyère*
The worst of enemies are flatterers, and the worst of flatterers are
    pleasures – *Jacques Bénigne Bossuet*
The greatest pleasure I know is to do a good action by stealth, and have it
    found out by accident – *Charles Lamb*
Consider pleasures as they depart, not as they come – *Aristotle*
Pleasure is very seldom found where it is sought – *Samuel Johnson*
To make pleasures pleasant shortens them – *Charles Buxton*
He that is violent in the pursuit of pleasure will not mind turning villain
    for the purchase – *Aurelius*
In diving to the bottom of pleasures we bring up more gravel than pearls
    – *Honoré de Balzac*
There is no sterner moralist than pleasure – *Lord Byron*
What leads to unhappiness is making pleasure the chief aim – *William
    Shenstone*
The man of pleasure little knows the perfect joy he loses for the
    disappointing gratifications which he pursues – *Joseph Addison*
If the soul be happily disposed, everything becomes capable of affording

entertainment, and distress will almost want a name – *Oliver Gold-smith*

Though a taste of pleasure may quicken the relish of life, an un-restrained indulgence leads to inevitable destruction – *Robert Dodsley*

Pleasure is to woman what the sun is to the flower; if moderately enjoyed, it beautifies, refreshes and improves; but if immoderately, it withers, deteriorates and destroys – *Colton*

When pleasure rules the life, mind, sensibility, and health shrivel and waste, till at last, and not tardily, no joy in earth or heaven can move the worn-out heart to response.

Fly the pleasure that bites tomorrow.

A life of pleasure makes even the strongest mind frivolous at last.

Choose such pleasures as recreate much and cost little.

He buys honey too dear who licks it from thorns.

The sweetest pleasures are those which do not exhaust hope.

Pleasure's couch is virtue's grave.

Most pleasures, like flowers, when gathered die.

All earthly delights are sweeter in expectation than enjoyment.

Pleasure is far sweeter as a recreation than a business.

See also ENJOYMENT.

POETRY

The office of poetry is not to make us think accurately, but feel truly – *Frederick William Robertson*

You will find poetry nowhere, unless you bring some with you – *Joseph Joubert*

Sad is his lot, who, once at least in his life, has not been a poet – *Alphonse Marie Louis de Lamartine*

Truth shines the brighter clad in verse – *Alexander Pope*

Poets utter great and wise things which they do not themselves under-stand – *Plato*

Poetry is the utterance of deep and heart-felt truth – *E. H. Chapin*

Superstition is the poetry of life – *Johann Friedrich von Goethe*

Some scrap of a childish song hath often been a truer alms than all the benevolent societies could give – *James Russell Lowell*

You arrive at truth through poetry; I arrive at poetry through truth – *Joubert*

Poetry is in itself strength and joy, whether it be crowned by all mankind, or left alone in its own magic hermitage – *John Sterling*

In poetry, which is all fable, truth still is the perfection – *Lord Shaftesbury*

How different is the poet from the mystic. The former uses symbols, knowing they are symbols; the latter mistakes them for realities – *Robertson*

Poetry is the record of the best and happiest moments of the happiest and best minds – *Percy Bysshe Shelley*

He who finds elevated and lofty pleasure in the feeling of poetry is a true poet, though he never composed a line of verse in his entire lifetime – *George Sand*

All that is best in the great poets of all countries is not what is national in them but what is universal – *Henry Wadsworth Longfellow*

Poetry comes nearer to vital truth than history – *Plato*

One merit of poetry few persons will deny; it says more, and in fewer words, than prose – *Voltaire*

They learn in suffering what they teach in song – *Shelley*

Poets are all who love and feel great truths and tell them.

Poetry is the music of thought, conveyed to us in the music of language.

Poetry is the sister of sorrow; every man that suffers and weeps is a poet; every tear is a verse; and every heart a poem.

As nightingales feed on glow-worms, so poets live upon the living light of nature and beauty.

Poetry is the intellect coloured by feelings.

Thoughts that breathe, and words that burn.

POLICY

To manage men one ought to have a sharp mind in a velvet sheath – *George Eliot*

The devil knew not what he did when he made man politic; he crossed himself by't – *William Shakespeare*

Measurers, not men, have always been my mark – *Oliver Goldsmith*

By a kind of fashionable discipline, the eye is taught to brighten, the lip to smile, and the whole countenance to emanate with the semblance of friendly welcome, while the bosom is unwarmed by a single spark of genuine kindness and goodwill – *Washington Irving*

Men must learn now with pity to dispense; / For policy sits above conscience – *Shakespeare*

A statesman makes the occasion, but the occasion makes the politician.

At court one becomes a sort of human ant-eater, and learns to catch one's prey by one's tongue.

POLITENESS

Politeness smoothes wrinkles – *Joseph Joubert*

Politeness is good nature regulated by good sense – *Sydney Smith*

Politeness has been well defined as benevolence in small things – *Thomas Babington Macaulay*

The true effect of genuine politeness seems to be rather ease than
pleasure – *Samuel Johnson*

Men, like bullets, go farthest when they are smoothest – *Jean Paul Richter*

The wise are polite all the world over; fools are polite only at home –
Francis Bacon

To be over-polite is to be rude – *Japanese proverb*

Whoever pays you more court than he is accustomed to pay, either
intends to deceive you or finds you necessary to him.

As charity covers a multitude of sins before God, so does politeness
before men.

Politeness is like an air-cushion; there may be nothing in it, but it eases
our jolts wonderfully.

Politeness is as natural to delicate natures as perfume is to flowers.

There is no policy like politeness, since a good manner often succeeds
where the best tongue has failed.

A polite man is one who listens with interest to things he knows all
about, when they are told him by a person who knows nothing about
them.

The only true source of politeness is considerattion.

There are few defects in our nature so glaring as not to be veiled from
observation by politeness and good breeding.

Great talent and success render a man famous; great merit procures
respect; great learning, veneration; but politeness alone ensures love
and affection.

See also CIVILITY, COURTESY, MANNERS.

POLITICS

If ever this free people, if this government itself is ever utterly demoral-
ized, it will come from this incessant human wriggle and struggle for
office, which is but a way to live without work – *Abraham Lincoln*

There is no gambling like politics – *Benjamin Disraeli*

Nothing is politically right which is morally wrong – *Daniel O'Connell*

How little do politics affect the life, the moral life of a nation. One
single good book influences the people a vast deal more – *William
Gladstone*

A politician . . . one that would circumvent God – *William Shakespeare*

To be a politician you need only to study your own interests – *Max O'Rell*

Politics is the science of exigencies – *Theodore Parker*

The politics of courts are so mean that private people would be ashamed
to act in the same way; all is trick and finesse, to which the common
cause is sacrificed – *Horatio Nelson*

Political friendships are so well understood that we can hardly pity the
simplicity they deceive – *Junius*

Abundance of political lying is a sure sign of true English liberty – *Jonathan Swift*

Politics is perhaps the only profession for which no preparation is thought necessary – *Robert Louis Stevenson*

Politics is the science of how who gets what, when and why – *Sidney Hillman*

No country can rise higher than its wage level. The people are both producers and consumers – *Henry Ford*

You can't run a government solely on a business basis . . . Government should be human. It should have a heart – *Herbert H. Lehman*

Our purpose is to build in this nation a human society, not an economic system – *Herbert Hoover*

There is no more independence in politics than there is in gaol – *William Pierce Rogers*

Dictatorship is always merely an aria, never an opera – *Emil Ludwig*

Socialism is the European theory of Despair – *Hoover*

Politics is the art of being wise for others – policy of being wise for self.

Politics in practice too often means all for party, nothing for the people; all for policy, nothing for principle; all for office, nothing for honour; all for power, nothing for progress.

There is an infinity of political errors which, being once adopted, become principles.

Two kinds of men generally best succeed in political life; men of no principle, but of great talent; and men of no talent, but of one principle – that of obedience to their superiors.

A politician thinks of the next election; a statesman of the next generation.

In politics, merit is rewarded by the possessor being raised, like a target, to a position to be fired at.

Liberty is the right to elect people to make restrictions for you to overlook.

You cannot make the poor rich by making the rich poor.

Diplomacy is the art of letting someone have your own way.

Adversity makes socialists of us all.

POPULACE

The multitude which is not brought to act in unity is confusion. That unity which has not its origin in the multitude is tyranny – *Blaise Pascal*

I will not choose what many men desire, / Because I will not jump with common spirits / And rank me with the barbarous multitude – *William Shakespeare*

The rabble gather round the man of news, and listen with their mouths

wide open; some tell, some hear, some judge of news, some make it,
and he that lies most loud, is most believed – *John Dryden*
Nothing is so uncertain as the minds of the multitude.
The multitude is always in the wrong.

POPULARITY

Popular opinion is the greatest lie in the world – *Thomas Carlyle*
Avoid popularity; it has many snares, and no real benefit – *William Penn*
An habitation giddy and unsure / Hath he that buildeth on the vulgar
heart – *William Shakespeare*
As inclination changes, thus ebbs and flows the unstable tide of public
judgement – *Johann Christoph Friedrich von Schiller*
The love of popularity seems little else than the love of being beloved –
William Shenstone
O popular applause! what heart of man is proof against thy sweet
seducing charms? – *William Cowper*
A popular man soon becomes more powerful than power itself.
True popularity is not the popularity which is followed after, but the
popularity which follows after.
The secret of popularity is always to remember what to forget.

POVERTY

Poverty is no disgrace to a man but it is confoundedly inconvenient –
Sydney Smith
Poverty is not dishonourable in itself, but only when it comes from
idleness, intemperance, extravagance, and folly – *Plutarch*
When it is not despicable to be poor, we want fewer things to live in
poverty with satisfaction than to live magnificently with riches –
Seigneur de Saint-Evremond
Of all the advantages which come to any young man, I believe it to be
demonstrably true that poverty is the greatest – *Josiah Gilbert Holland*
An avowal of poverty is no disgrace to any man; to make no effort to
escape it is indeed disgraceful – *Thucydides*
Poor and content is rich and rich enough; / But riches fineless is as poor as
winter / To him that ever fears he shall be poor – *William Shakespeare*
He travels safe and not unpleasantly who is guarded by poverty and
guided by love – *Sir Philip Sidney*
Few save the poor feel for the poor – *L. E. Landon*
If poverty is the mother of crimes, want of sense is the father of them –
Jean de La Bruyère
There is on earth no more powerful advocate for vice than poverty –
Oliver Goldsmith

Poverty often deprives a man of all spirit and virtue; it is hard for an empty bag to stand upright – *Benjamin Franklin*

Not to be able to bear poverty is a shameful thing; but not to know how to chase it away by work is a more shameful thing yet – *Pericles*

To be poor, and seem to be poor, is a certain way never to rise – *Goldsmith*

He is poor whose expenses exceed his income – *La Bruyère*

Poverty is the test of civility and the touchstone of friendship – *William Hazlitt*

Nature makes us poor only when we want necessaries, but custom gives the name of poverty to the want of superfluities – *Samuel Johnson*

No man is poor who does not think himself so – *Jeremy Taylor*

The poor are always considered under the peculiar care of the gods – *Menander*

A man isn't poor if he can still laugh – *Raymond Hitchcock*

It's very seldom that stark ambition can talk as convincingly as an empty stomach – *Norma Shearer*

Poverty is the sixth sense – *German proverb*

A wise man poor / Is like a sacred book that's never read; / To himself he lives and to all else seems dead.

He is not poor that has little, but he that desires much.

We should not so much esteem our poverty as a misfortune, were it not that the world treats it so.

You cannot help the poor by destroying the rich.

Laziness travels so slowly that poverty soon overtakes him.

God loves the poor – that's why he made so many of them.

The slum mind as well as the slum dwelling requires to be converted.

POWER

I know of nothing sublime which is not some modification of power – *Edmund Burke*

Even in war moral power is to physical as three parts out of four – *Napoleon Bonaparte*

The greater a man is in power above others, the more he ought to excel them in virtue – *Publius Syrus*

All human power is a compound of time and patience – *Honoré de Balzac*

Arbitrary power is the natural object of temptation to a prince; as wine or women to a young fellow, or a bride to a judge, or avarice to old age, or vanity to a woman – *Jonathan Swift*

Power will intoxicate the best hearts, as wine the strongest heads – *Charles Caleb Colton*

Power, like the diamond, dazzles the beholder, and also the wearer – *Colton*

A king is never powerful that has not power on the sea – *Spanish proverb*
Power and liberty are like heat and moisture; where they are well mixt,
    everything prospers; where they are single, they are destructive.
Power loses nothing of its effect by being silent.
Power admits no equal and dismisses friendship for flattery.
A position of eminence makes a great man greater and a little man less.
Glory not in what you are, but in what you have the power to become.
If you think you have someone eating out of your hand it's a good idea to
    count your fingers.
See also AUTHORITY.

PRAISE

We are all excited by the love of praise, and it is the noblest spirits that
    feel it most – *Cicero*
Praise, like gold and diamonds, owes its value only to its scarcity –
    Samuel Johnson
It is not he that searches for praise that finds it – *Antoine Rivarol*
It is a great happiness to be praised of them who are most praiseworthy –
    Sir Philip Sidney
Those who are greedy of praise prove that they are poor in merit –
    Plutarch
Expect not praise without envy until you are dead – *Charles Caleb Colton*
One good deed, dying tongueless, / Slaughters a thousand waiting upon
    that. / Our praises are our wages – *William Shakespeare*
They are the most frivolous and superficial of mankind, who can be
    much delighted with that praise which they themselves know to be
    altogether unmerited – *Adam Smith*
As the Greek said, many men know how to flatter; few know to praise –
    Wendell Phillips
Praise no man too liberally before his face, nor censure him too lavishly
    behind his back – *Francis Quarles*
Think not those faithful who praise all thy words and actions, but those
    who kindly reprove thy faults – *Socrates*
There's not one wise man among twenty that will praise himself –
    Shakespeare
Praising what is lost / Makes the remembrance dear – *Shakespeare*
Praise undeserved is satire in disguise.
The praises of others may be of use in teaching us not what we are but
    what we ought to be.
Praise, more divine than prayer; prayer points our ready path to heaven;
    praise is already there.
Praise loudly, blame softly.
None have less praise than those who hunt after it.
See also APPLAUSE.

PRAYER

Heaven is never deaf but when man's heart is dumb – *Francis Quarles*

Certain thoughts are prayers. There are moments when, whatever be the attitude of the body, the soul is on its knees – *Victor Hugo*

I have been driven many times to my knees by the overwhelming conviction that I had nowhere else to go – *Abraham Lincoln*

A prayer in its simplest definition is merely a wish turned God-ward – *Phillips Brooks*

Whatsoever we beg of God, let us also work for it – *Jeremy Taylor*

God dwells far off from us, but prayer brings him down to our earth, and links his power with our efforts – *Mme de Gasparin*

The fewer words the better prayer – *Martin Luther*

He who runs from God in the morning will scarcely find Him the rest of the day – *John Bunyan*

Practise in life whatever you pray for, and God will give it to you more abundantly – *Edward Bouverie Pusey*

We, ignorant of ourselves, / Beg often our own harms, which the wise powers / Deny us for our good; so we find profit / By losing of our prayers – *William Shakespeare*

The deepest wishes of the heart find expression in secret prayer – *George E. Rees*

The Lord's Prayer contains the sum total of religion and morals – *Duke of Wellington*

He prayeth best who loveth best – *Samuel Taylor Coleridge*

The greatest prayer is patience – *Buddha*

Every man can build a chapel in his breast, himself the priest, his heart the sacrifice, and the earth he treads on, the altar – *Jeremy Taylor*

The simplest heart that freely asks in love obtains – *John Greenleaf Whittier*

It is good for us to keep some account of our prayers, that we may not unsay them in our practice – *Matthew Henry*

In prayer it is better to have a heart without words, than words without a heart – *Bunyan*

They never sought in vain that sought the Lord aright – *Robert Burns*

Prayer and provender hinder no man's journey.

Our prayer and God's mercy are like two buckets in a well; while the one ascends, the other descends.

Human life is a constant want, and ought to be a constant prayer.

If you would have God hear you when you pray, you must hear him when he speaks.

God hears no more than the heart speaks; and if the heart be dumb, God will certainly be deaf.

A single grateful thought raised to heaven is the most perfect prayer.

See also DEVOTION.

PREACHING

A strong and faithful pulpit is no mean safeguard of a nation's life – *John Hall*

The Christian ministry is the worst of all trades, but the best of all professions – *John Newton*

Men of God have always, from time to time, walked among men, and made their commission felt in the heart and soul of the commonest hearer – *Ralph Waldo Emerson*

It is not a minister's wisdom but his conviction which imparts itself to others – *Frederick William Robertson*

A preacher should have the skill to teach the unlearned simply, for teaching is of more importance than exhorting – *Martin Luther*

To preach more than half an hour, a man should be an angel himself or have angels of hearers – *George Whitefield*

Many a meandering discourse one hears, in which the preacher aims at nothing, and – hits it – *Richard Whately*

He who the sword of heaven will bear / Should be as holy as severe – *William Shakespeare*

It is a good divine that follows his own instructions – *Shakespeare*

The pulpit is the clergyman's parade; the parish is his field of active service – *Robert Southey*

To love to preach is one thing – to love those to whom we preach, quite another.

The world looks at ministers out of the pulpit to know what they mean when in it.

Genius is not essential to good preaching, but a live man is.

PREJUDICE

He who knows only his own side of the case knows little of that – *John Stuart Mill*

Prejudice, which sees what it pleases, cannot see what is plain – *Aubrey de Vere*

Never try to reason the prejudice out of a man. It was not reasoned into him, and cannot be reasoned out – *Sydney Smith*

All looks yellow to the jaundiced eye – *Alexander Pope*

Prejudice is the reason of fools – *Voltaire*

Ignorance is less remote from the truth than prejudice – *Denis Diderot*

The prejudiced and obstinate man does not so much hold opinions, as his opinions hold him – *Tryon Edwards*

Prejudice and self-sufficiency naturally proceed from inexperience of the world, and ignorance of mankind – *Joseph Addison*

Every period of life has its peculiar prejudice; whoever saw old age that did not applaud the past, and condemn the present times? – *Michel Eyquem de Montaigne*

He that never leaves his own country is full of prejudices – *Carlo Goldoni*

Prejudices, it is well known, are most difficult to eradicate from the heart whose soil has never been loosened or fertilized by education; they grow there, firm as weeds among rocks – *Charlotte Brontë*

To lay aside all prejudices is to lay aside all principles. He who is destitute of principles is governed by whims – *Friedrich Heinrich Jacobi*

When we destroy an old prejudice we have need of a new virtue – *Mme de Staël*

Prejudices are what rule the vulgar crowd – *Voltaire*

Prejudice is never easy unless it can pass itself off for reason – *William Hazlitt*

The great obstacle to progress is prejudice.

Beware of prejudices. They are like rats, and men's minds are like traps; prejudices get in easily, but it is doubtful if they ever get out.

Opinions grounded on prejudice are always sustained with the greatest violence.

When the judgement is weak the prejudice is strong.

Even when we fancy we have grown wiser, it is only, it may be, that new prejudices have displaced old ones.

Moral prejudices are the stop-gaps of virtue.

See also OPINION.

PRESENT

Every man's life lies within the present; for the past is spent and done with, and the future is uncertain – *Aurelius*

Devote each day to the object then in time, and every evening will find something done – *Johann Wolfgang von Goethe*

Live this day as if it were the last – *Bishop Kerr*

If I am faithful to the duties of the present, God will provide for the future – *William Bedell*

Man, living, feeling man, is the easy sport of the over-mastering present – *Johann Christoph Friedrich von Schiller*

Since Time is not a person we can overtake when he is gone, let us honour him with mirth and cheerfulness of heart while he is passing – *Goethe*

Look upon every day as the whole of life – *Jean Paul Richter*

Duty and today are ours, results and futurity belong to God – *Horace Greeley*

The future is purchased by the present – *Samuel Johnson*

To eternity itself there is no other handle than the present moment.

PRESS

The press is the foe of rhetoric, but the friend of reason – *Charles Caleb Colton*

What gunpowder did for the war, the printing-press has done for the mind; the statesman is no longer clad in the steel of special education, but every reading man is his judge – *Wendell Phillips*

When the press is the echo of sages and reformers, it works well; when it is the echo of turbulent cynics, it merely feeds political excitement – *Alphonse Marie Louis de Lamartine*

An enslaved press is doubly fatal; it not only takes away the true light, for in that case we might stand still, but it sets up a false one that decoys us to our destruction – *Colton*

This country is not priest-ridden, but press-ridden – *Henry Wadsworth Longfellow*

The liberty of the press is a blessing when we are inclined to write against others, and a calamity when we find ourselves overborne by the multitude of our assailants – *Samuel Johnson*

The Reformation was cradled in the printing-press and established by no other instrument – *Agnes Strickland*

Let it be impressed upon your minds, let it be installed into your children, that the liberty of the press is the palladium of all the civil, political, and religious rights – *Junius*

See also JOURNALISM, NEWSPAPERS.

PRETENSION

He who gives himself airs of importance exhibits the credentials of impotence – *Johann Kaspar Lavater*

The desire of appearing clever often prevents our becoming so – *François de La Rochefoucauld*

Who makes the fairest show means most deceit – *William Shakespeare*

There is a false modesty, which is vanity; a false glory, which is levity; a false grandeur, which is meanness; a false virtue, which is hypocrisy, and a false wisdom, which is prudery – *Jean de La Bruyère*

The more honesty a man has, the less he affects the air of a saint – *Lavater*

Pretences go a great way with men that take fair words and magisterial looks for current payment – *Sir Roger L'Estrange*

The higher the character or rank, the less the pretence, because there is less to pretend to.

PREVENTION

Preventives of evil are far better than remedies; cheaper and easier of application, and surer in result – *Tryon Edwards*

Prevention is the best bridle.

Laws act after crimes have been committed; prevention goes before them both.

Who would not give a trifle to prevent what he would give a thousand worlds to cure?

PRIDE

Pride, the first peer and president of hell – *Daniel Defoe*

Pride, like the magnet, constantly points to one object – *Charles Caleb Colton*

Pride is increased by ignorance; those assume the most who know the least – *John Gay*

If a proud man makes me keep my distance, the comfort is that he keeps his at the same time – *Jonathan Swift*

Pride defeats its own end, by bringing the man who seeks esteem and reverence into contempt – *Henry St John Bolingbroke*

Pride is a vice, which pride itself inclines every man to find in others, and to overlook in himself – *Samuel Johnson*

Pride is as loud a beggar as want and a great deal more saucy – *Benjamin Franklin*

Pride – that never failing vice of fools – *Alexander Pope*

If a man has a right to be proud of anything, it is of a good action done as it ought to be, without any base interest lurking at the bottom of it – *Laurence Sterne*

Pride helps us; and pride is not a bad thing when it only urges us to hide our own hurts – not to hurt others – *George Eliot*

There is this paradox in pride – it makes some men ridiculous, but prevents others from becoming so – *Colton*

Men are sometimes accused of pride merely because their accusers would be proud themselves if they were in their places – *William Shenstone*

Pride is the master sin of the devil – *E. H. Chapin*

There is a certain noble pride, through which merits shine brighter than through modesty – *Jean Paul Richter*

None have more pride than those who dream that they have none – *Charles Haddon Spurgeon*

To be proud of learning is the greatest ignorance – *Bishop Taylor*

Pride breakfasted with plenty, dined with poverty, and supped with infamy – *Franklin*

The proud are ever most provoked by pride – *William Cowper*

A beggar's rags may cover as much pride as an alderman's gown – *Spurgeon*

Nature has given us pride to spare us the pain of being conscious of our imperfections – *François de La Rochefoucauld*

To acknowledge our faults when we are blamed is modesty; to discover them to one's friends is confidence; but to preach them to all the world, if one does not take care, is pride – *Confucius*

When pride and presumption walk before, shame and loss follow very closely – *Louis XI*

O world, how apt the poor are to be proud! – *William Shakespeare*

Pride, which inspires us with so much envy, serves also to moderate it – *La Rochefoucauld*

A proud man is seldom a grateful man, for he never thinks he gets as much as he deserves – *Henry Ward Beecher*

The infinitely little have a pride infinitely great – *Voltaire*

The devil did grin, / For his darling sin / Is pride that apes humility – *Samuel Taylor Coleridge*

Pride is to the character like the attic to the house – the highest part, and generally the most empty.

A proud man never shows his pride so much as when he is civil.

The proud never have friends; not in prosperity, for then they know nobody; and not in adversity, for then nobody knows them.

To be proud and inaccessible is to be timid and weak.

We rise in glory as we sink in pride.

It is hardly possible to overvalue ourselves but by undervaluing our neighbours.

Pride, the most dangerous of all faults, proceeds from want of sense, or want of thought.

Pride is at the bottom of all great mistakes.

See also ARROGANCE.

PRINCIPLES

He who merely knows right principles is not equal to him who loves them – *Confucius*

Principle is a passion for truth and right – *William Hazlitt*

Expedients are for the hour; principles for the ages – *Henry Ward Beecher*

Many men do not allow their principles to take root, but pull them up every now and then, as children do the flowers they have planted, to see if they are growing – *Henry Wadsworth Longfellow*

Better be poisoned in one's blood, than to be poisoned in one's principles.

The principles now implanted in thy bosom will grow, and one day reach maturity; and in that maturity thou wilt find thy heaven or thy hell.

PROCRASTINATION

By the streets of 'by and by' one arrives at the house of 'never' – *Miguel de Cervantes Saavedra*

Never put off till tomorrow that which you can do today – *Benjamin Franklin*

We pass our life in deliberation, and we die upon it – *Pasquier Quesnel*

The next advantage / Will we take throughly – *William Shakespeare*

The man who procrastinates struggles with ruin – *Hesiod*

There is, by God's grace, an immeasurable distance between late and too late – *Mme Swetchine*

Delay not till tomorrow to be wise; / Tomorrow's sun to thee may never rise – *William Congreve*

When a fool has made up his mind the market has gone by – *Spanish proverb*

Undue procrastination indicates that a man does not see his way clearly.

Tomorrow is the day when idlers work, and fools reform.

A procrastinator is one who puts off until tomorrow the things he's already put off until today.

See also DELAY.

PROGRESS

All that is human must retrograde if it do not advance – *Edward Gibbon*

Progress is the activity of today and the assurance of tomorrow – *Ralph Waldo Emerson*

Every age has its problem, by solving which, humanity is helped forward – *Heinrich Heine*

The world is full of hopeful analogies and handsome dubious eggs called possibilities – *George Eliot*

Revolutions never go backwards – *Emerson*

We ought not to be over-anxious to encourage innovation for an old system must ever have two advantages over a new one; it is established and it is understood – *Charles Caleb Colton*

He that is good will infallibly become better, and he that is bad will as certainly become worse; for vice, virtue, and time, are three things that never stand still – *Colton*

He is only advancing in life, whose heart is getting softer, his blood warmer, his brain quicker, and his spirit entering into living peace – *John Ruskin*

If a man is not rising upward to be an angel, depend upon it, he is sinking downward to be a devil – *Samuel Taylor Coleridge*

All our progress is an unfolding, like the vegetable bud – *Emerson*

We are never present with, but always beyond ourselves. Fear, desire, and hope are still pushing us on toward the future – *Michel Eyquem de Montaigne*

Some falls are means the happier to arise – *William Shakespeare*

Mankind never loses any good thing, physical, intellectual, or moral, till it finds a better, and then the loss is a gain – *Theodore Parker*

The world owes all its onward impulses to men ill at ease. The happy man inevitably confines himself within ancient limits – *Nathaniel Hawthorne*

Progress is the real cure for an overestimate of ourselves – *George Macdonald*

Progress is the law of life; man is not man as yet – *Robert Browning*

All things wax and roll onwards – arts, establishments, opinions; nothing is ever completed, but completing – *Thomas Carlyle*

Nature knows no pause in progress and development, and attaches her curse on all inaction – *Johann Wolfgang von Goethe*

Works of true merit are seldom very popular in their own day; for knowledge is on the march and men of genius are far in advance of their comrades – *Colton*

Progress – the onward stride of God – *Victor Hugo*

All growth that is not toward God, is growing to decay – *Macdonald*

I find the great thing in this world is not so much where we stand, as in what direction we are moving – *Oliver Wendell Holmes*

The grandest of all laws is the law of progressive development.

Intellectually, as well as politically, the direction of all true progress is toward greater freedom.

Nothing will ever be attempted if all objections must first be overcome.

Horse-power was a lot safer when the horses had it.

PROMISES

He who promises runs in debt – *Talmud*

It is easy to promise, and alas! how easy to forget! – *Alfred de Musset*

He who is most slow in making a promise is the most faithful in its performance – *Jean Jacques Rousseau*

A mind conscious of integrity scorns to say more than it means to perform – *Robert Burns*

Magnificent promises are always to be suspected – *Theodore Parker*

Every brave man is a man of his word – *Pierre Corneille*

Unclaimed promises are like uncashed cheques; they will keep us from bankruptcy, but not from want.

I had rather do and not promise, than promise and not do.

An acre of performance is worth the whole world of promise.

PROMPTNESS

Promptness is the soul of business – *Lord Chesterfield*

Deliberate with caution, but act with decision and promptness – *Charles Caleb Colton*

The keen spirit seizes the prompt occasion; makes the thought start into instant action, and at once plans and performs, resolves, and executes ! – *Hannah More*

'How', said one to Sir Walter Raleigh, 'do you accomplish so much, and in so short a time?' 'When I have anything to do, I go and do it,' was the reply.

Celerity is never more admired / Than by the negligent – *William Shakespeare*

If it were done when 'tis done, then 'twere well / It were done quickly – *Shakespeare*

See also PUNCTUALITY.

PROSPERITY

Everything in the world may be endured, except continual prosperity – *Johann Wolfgang von Goethe*

Prosperity is the touchstone of virtue; for it is less difficult to bear misfortunes than to remain uncorrupted by pleasure – *Tacitus*

Prosperity too often has the same effect on its possessor that a calm at sea has on the Dutch mariner, who frequently, it is said, in these circumstances, ties up the rudder, gets drunk, and goes to sleep – *Bishop Horne*

The virtue of prosperity is temperance, but the virtue of adversity is fortitude – *Francis Bacon*

The good things which belong to prosperity may be wished; but the good things which belong to adversity are to be admired – *Seneca*

As full ears load and lay down corn, so does too much fortune bend and break the mind – *Pierre Charron*

No man is prosperous whose immortality is forfeited – *Henry Ward Beecher*

Watch lest prosperity destroy generosity – *Beecher*

He that swells in prosperity will be sure to shrink in adversity – *Charles Caleb Colton*

It is the bright day that brings forth the adder; / And that craves wary walking – *William Shakespeare*

They who lie soft and warm in a rich estate seldom come to heat themselves at the altar – *Robert South*

While prosperous you can number many friends; but when the storm comes you are left alone – *Ovid*

All sunshine makes the desert – *Arab proverb*

A smooth sea never made a skilful mariner; neither do uninterrupted prosperity and success qualify men for usefulness and happiness.

If adversity hath killed his thousands, propserity hath killed his ten thousands.

Take care to be an economist in prosperity: there is no fear of your being
one in adversity.

Prosperity's right hand is industry, and her left hand is frugality.

In prosperity prepare for a change; in adversity hope for one.

A weak mind sinks under prosperity as well as under adversity.

To rejoice in the prosperity of another is to partake of it.

There is a glare about worldly success which is very apt to dazzle men's
eyes.

When the heart has no more to wish, it yawns over its possessions, and
the energy of the soul goes out like a flame that has no more to
devour.

Prosperity makes friends; adversity tests them.

See also GOLD, RICHES, WEALTH.

PROVERBS

The wisdom of many, and the wit of one – *John Russell*

Jewels five words long, that on the stretched forefinger of all times
sparkle forever – *Alfred, Lord Tennyson*

Proverbs are the literature of reason, or the statements of absolute truth,
without qualification – *Ralph Waldo Emerson*

The genius, wit, and spirit of a nation are discovered in its proverbs –
Francis Bacon

Short sentences drawn from long experiences – *Miguel de Cervantes
Saavedra*

Sense, brevity, and point are the elements of a good proverb – *Tryon
Edwards*

The study of proverbs may be more instructive and comprehensive than
the most elaborate scheme of philosophy – *William Motherwell*

Proverbs may be said to be the abridgements of wisdom – *Joseph Joubert*

Proverbs are the condensed wisdom of long experience.

The sanctuary of intuitions.

See also APOTHEGMS, MAXIMS.

PROVIDENCE

There's a divinity that shapes our ends, / Rough-hew them how we will –
William Shakespeare

To doubt the providence of God is presently to wax impatient with his
commands – *Edward Garrett*

Who finds not Providence all good and wise, / Alike in what it gives and
what denies? – *Alexander Pope*

All nature is but art, unknown to thee; / All chance, direction which thou
canst not see; / All discord, harmony not understood; / All partial evil,
universal good – *Pope*

We are not to lead events, but follow them – *Epictetus*

Happy the man who sees a God employed in all the good and ill that
chequer life – *William Cowper*

God hangs the greatest weights upon the smallest wings – *Francis Bacon*

God tempers the wind to the shorn lamb – *Laurence Sterne*

The longer I live, the more faith I have in Providence, and the less faith in
my interpretation of Providence.

Providence is a greater mystery than revelation.

See also DESTINY, FATE, FORTUNE.

PRUDENCE

Prudence is the necessary ingredient in all the virtues, without which
they degenerate into folly and excess – *Jeremy Collier*

Want of prudence is too frequently the want of virtue – *Oliver Goldsmith*

The one prudence in life is concentration; the one evil is dissipation –
Ralph Waldo Emerson

There is nothing more imprudent than excessive prudence – *Charles Caleb
Colton*

The bounds of a man's knowledge are easily concealed if he has but
prudence – *Goldsmith*

The rich endowments of the mind are temperance, prudence, and
fortitude. Prudence is a universal virtue, which enters into the
composition of all the rest; and where she is not, fortitude loses its
name and nature – *Voltaire*

The prudence of the best heads is often defeated by the tenderness of the
best of hearts – *Henry Fielding*

Prudence is a conformity to the rules of reason, truth, and decency, at all
times and in all circumstances.

Let prudence always attend your pleasures; it is the way to enjoy the
sweets of them, and not be afraid of the consequences.

Prudence keeps life safe, but does not always make it happy.

PUBLIC

Private opinion is weak, but public opinion is almost omnipotent – *Henry
Ward Beecher*

The public wishes itself to be managed like a woman; one must say
nothing to it except what it likes to hear – *Johann Wolfgang von Goethe*

Public sentiment is a battery which protects the city behind it, but
sweeps with destruction all in the plain before it – *Beecher*

Public opinion, or public sentiment, is able to sustain or to pull down any
law of the commonwealth.

The public is wiser than the wisest critic.

People are like sheep: a flock is more easily driven than a single one.

PUNCTUALITY

I have always been a quarter of an hour before my time, and it has made a
man of me – *Horatio Nelson*

Better three hours too soon than a minute too late – *William Shakespeare*

It is of no use running; to set out betimes is the main point – *Jean de La
Fontaine*

Strict punctuality is, perhaps, the cheapest virtue which can give force to
an otherwise utterly insignificant character.

Nothing inspires confidence in a business man sooner than punctuality.

Punctuality is the stern virtue of men of business, and the graceful
courtesy of princes.

The most indispensable qualification of a cook is punctuality. The same
must be said of guests.

Want of punctuality is a want of virtue.

When a secretary of Washington, excusing himself for being late, said
that his watch was too slow, the reply of Washington was, 'You must
get a new watch, or I must get a new secretary.'

'Better later than never' is not half so good a maxim as 'Better never
late'.

See also PROMPTNESS.

PUNISHMENT

Penalties may be delayed, but they are sure to come – *Henry Ward Beecher*

It is as expedient that a wicked man be punished as that a sick man be
cured by a physician; for all chastisement is a kind of medicine – *Plato*

The certainty of punishment, even more than its severity, is the preven-
tive of crime – *Tryon Edwards*

The work of eradicating crimes is not by making punishment familiar,
but formidable – *Oliver Goldsmith*

If punishment makes not the will supple it hardens the offender – *John
Locke*

The public have more interest in the punishment of an injury than he
who receives it – *Cato*

The punishment of criminals should be of use; when a man is hanged he
is good for nothing – *Voltaire*

We do not aim to correct the man we hang; we correct and warn others by
him – *Michel Eyquem de Montaigne*

The object of punishment is threefold: for just retribution; for the protection of society; for the reformation of the offender – *Edwards*

Gaols and prisons are the complement of schools; so many less as you have of the latter, so many more you must have of the former – *Horace Mann*

Punishment is justice for the unjust – *Augustine*

The seeds of our punishment are sown at the same time we commit the sin – *Hesiod*

Faults of the head are punished in this world; those of the heart in another – *Charles Caleb Colton*

There is no future pang can deal that justice on the self-condemned, that he deals on his own soul – *Lord Byron*

God is on the side of virtue; for whoever dreads punishment suffers it, and whoever deserves it dreads it – *Colton*

There is no greater punishment than that of being abandoned to oneself – *Pasquier Quesnel*

Never was the voice of conscience silenced without retribution – *Anna Jameson*

Wickedness, when properly punished, is disgraceful only to the offender; unpunished, it is disgraceful to the whole community.

See also RETRIBUTION.

PURITY

I pray thee, O God, that I may be beautiful within – *Socrates*

The chaste mind, like a polished plane, may admit foul thoughts without receiving their tincture – *Laurence Sterne*

There's nothing ill can dwell in such a temple: / If the ill spirit have so fair a house, / Good things will strive to dwell with 't – *William Shakespeare*

Evil into the mind of God or man, may come and go, and yet, if unapproved, still without sin – *John Milton*

See also CHASTITY.

PURPOSE

The secret of success is constancy to purpose – *Benjamin Disraeli*

The flighty purpose never is o'ertook / Unless the deed go with it – *William Shakespeare*

Man proposes, but God disposes – *Thomas à Kempis*

The man without a purpose is like a ship without a rudder – *Thomas Carlyle*

It is the old lesson – a worthy purpose, patient energy for its accomplishment, a resoluteness undaunted by difficulties, and then success.

A purpose underlies character, culture, position, attainment of every sort.

QUALITIES

Wood burns because it has the proper stuff in it; and a man becomes
    famous because he has the proper stuff in him – *Johann Wolfgang von
    Goethe*

We should not judge of a man's merits by his great qualities but by the
    use he makes of them – *François de La Rochefoucauld*

It is not enough to have great qualities, we must also have the manage-
    ment of them – *La Rochefoucauld*

Good nature and evenness of temper will give you an easy companion
    for life; virtue and good sense an agreeable friend; love and constancy
    a good wife or husband – *Spectator*

Hearts may be attracted by assumed qualities, but the affections are only
    to be fixed by those which are real.

The qualities we possess never make us as ridiculous as those we
    pretend to have.

QUARRELS

I consider your very testy and quarrelsome people as I do a loaded gun,
    which may, by accident, at any time, go off and kill people – *William
    Shenstone*

Quarrels would never last long if the fault was only on one side – *François
    de La Rochefoucauld*

Beware / Of entrance to a quarrel; but, being in, / Bear't that th' opposer
    may beware of thee – *William Shakespeare*

He that blows the coals in quarrels he has nothing to do with has no right
    to complain if the sparks fly in his face – *Benjamin Franklin*

The quarrels of lovers are like summer storms. Everything is more
    beautiful when they have passed – *Mme Neckar*

If you cannot avoid a quarrel with a blackguard, let your lawyer manage
    it rather than yourself – *Charles Caleb Colton*

In a false quarrel there is no true valour – *Shakespeare*

Thrice is he arm'd that hath his quarrel just, / And he but naked, though
    lock'd up in steel, / Whose conscience with injustice is corrupted –
    Shakespeare

No quarrel ought ever to be converted into a policy – *David Lloyd George*

When worthy men fall out, only one of them may be faulty at first; but if
    the strife continue long, both commonly become guilty.

See also ARGUMENT, CONTENTION.

QUESTIONS

Judge a man by his questions rather than by his answers – *Voltaire*

A child can ask a thousand questions that the wisest man cannot answer.

'How do you know so much about everything?' was asked of a very wise
and intelligent man; and the answer was, 'By never being afraid or
ashamed to ask questions as to anything of which I was ignorant.'

QUOTATIONS

Quotation is the highest compliment you can pay to an author – *Samuel
Johnson*

Next to the originator of a good sentence is the first quoter of it – *Ralph
Waldo Emerson*

A thing is never too often repeated which is never sufficiently learned –
Seneca

Full of wise saws and modern instances – *William Shakespeare*

When we would prepare the mind by a forcible appeal, an opening
quotation is a symphony preluding on the chords whose tones we are
about to harmonize – *Benjamin Disraeli*

The art of quotation requires more delicacy in the practice than those
conceive who can see nothing more in a quotation than an extract –
Disraeli

Quotations are the honey collected from the nectar of many flowers –
Vivien Foster

The wisdom of the wise and the experience of ages may be preserved by
quotation – *Disraeli*

Every quotation contributes something to the stability or enlargement of
the language – *Johnson*

An apt quotation is as good as an original remark.

To select well among old things is almost equal to inventing new ones.

A verse may find him who a sermon flies.

RAGE

In rage deaf as the sea, hasty as fire – *William Shakespeare*

When passion is on the throne, reason is out of doors – *Matthew Henry*

When transported by rage, it is best to observe its effects on those who
deliver themselves up to the same passion – *Plutarch*

Rage is essentially vulgar, and never more vulgar than when it proceeds
from mortified pride, disappointed ambition, or thwarted wilfulness
– *Hartley Coleridge*

See also ANGER.

RANK

There are no persons more solicitous about the preservation of rank than
those who have no rank at all – *William Shenstone*

Every error of the mind is the more conspicuous, and culpable, in proportion to the rank of the person who commits it – *Juvenal*

Rank and riches are chains of gold, but still chains – *Giovanni Domenico Ruffini*

I weigh the man, not his title, 'tis not the king's stamp can make the metal better – *William Wycherly*

The rank is but the guinea's stamp; the man's the gold for all that – *Robert Burns*

To be vain of one's rank or place is to show that one is below it.

Rank is a great beautifier.

See also PLACE, STATION.

RASHNESS

Rashness is the characteristic of ardent youth, and prudence that of mellowed age – *Cicero*

We may outrun, / By violent swiftness, that which we run at, / And lose by over-running – *William Shakespeare*

Some act first, think afterward, and then repent forever.

Rashness is the faithful but unhappy parent of misfortune.

None are rash when they are not seen by anybody.

Rashness and haste make all things insecure.

See also RECKLESSNESS.

READING

No entertainment is so cheap as reading, nor any pleasure so lasting – *Lady Mary Wortley Montagu*

The foundation of knowledge must be laid by reading – *Samuel Johnson*

Happy is he who has laid up in his youth, and held fast in all fortune, a genuine and passionate love for reading – *Rufus Choate*

Reading maketh a full man; conference a ready man; and writing an exact man – *Francis Bacon*

Read not books alone, but men, and amongst them chiefly thyself – If thou find anything, there is more profit in a distasteful truth than in deceitful sweetness – *Francis Quarles*

What is twice read is commonly better remembered than what is transcribed – *Johnson*

To read without reflecting is like eating without digesting – *Edmund Burke*

Some read to think, these are rare; some to write, these are common; some to talk, and these are the great majority – *Charles Caleb Colton*

The love of reading enables a man to exchange the wearisome hours of life, which come to everyone, for hours of delight – *Charles de Montesquieu*

Deep versed in books, but shallow in himself – *John Milton*

Some books are to be tasted, others to be swallowed, and some few to be chewed and digested – *Bacon*

We should accustom the mind to keep the best company by introducing it only to the best books – *Sydney Smith*

Exceedingly well read, and profited / In strange concealments – *William Shakespeare*

He picked something valuable out of everything he read – *Pliny the Younger*

No man can read with profit that which he cannot learn to read with pleasure – *Noah Porter*

A page digested is better than a volume hurriedly read – *Thomas Babington Macaulay*

How well he's read, to reason against reading! – *Shakespeare*

We should be as careful of the books we read as of the company we keep – *Tryon Edwards*

There are three classes of readers: some enjoy without judgement; others judge without enjoyment; and some there are who judge while they enjoy, and enjoy while they judge – *Johann Wolfgang von Goethe*

One ought to read just as inclination takes him, for what he reads as a task will do him little good – *Johnson*

One may as well be asleep as to read for anything but to improve his mind and morals, and regulate his conduct – *Laurence Sterne*

Reading furnishes the mind only with materials of knowledge; it is thinking makes what we read ours – *John Locke*

You may glean knowledge by reading, but you must separate the chaff from the wheat by thinking.

It is well to read everything of something, and something of everything.

Imprint the beauties of authors upon your imagination, and their good morals upon your heart.

Reading without purpose is sauntering, not exercise.

It is not what people eat but what they digest that makes them strong. It is not what they gain but what they save that makes them rich. It is not what they read but what they remember that makes them learned.

Never read a book through merely because you have begun it.

See also BOOKS.

REASON

There are few things reason can discover with so much certainty and ease as its own insufficiency – *Jeremy Collier*

Reason cannot show itself more reasonable, than to cease reasoning on things above reason – *Sir Philip Sidney*

He is next to the gods whom reason, and not passion, impels – *Claudian*

What men want of reason for their opinions, they usually supply and make up in prejudice or wilfulness – *John Tillotson*

It is useless to attempt to reason a man out of a thing he was never reasoned into – *Jonathan Swift*

What or how can we reason but from what we know? – *Alexander Pope*

The soundest argument will produce no more conviction in an empty head than the most superficial declamation; a feather and a guinea fall with equal velocity in a vacuum – *Charles Caleb Colton*

Good reasons must, of force, give place to better – *William Shakespeare*

Neither great poverty nor great riches will hear reason – *Henry Fielding*

When a man has not a good reason for doing a thing, he has one good reason for letting it alone – *Walter Scott*

Wise men are instructed by reason; men of less understanding by experience; the most ignorant by necessity; and beasts by nature – *Cicero*

Strong reasons make strong actions – *Shakespeare*

An idle reason lessens the weight of the good ones you gave before – *Swift*

He that speaketh against his own reason speaks against his own conscience – *Jeremy Taylor*

Human reason is like a drunken man on horseback; set it up on one side, and it tumbles over on the other – *Martin Luther*

Your giving a reason for it will not make it right. You may have a reason why two and two should make five, but they will still make but four – *Samuel Johnson*

The heart has reasons that reason does not understand – *Jacques Bénigne Bossuet*

Thou shalt govern many if reason govern thee – *Francis Quarles*

If reasons were as plenty as blackberries I would give no man a reason upon compulsion – *Shakespeare*

We can only reason from what is; we can reason on actualities, but not on possibilities – *Henry St John Bolingbroke*

I have no other but a woman's reason; / I think him so, because I think him so – *Shakespeare*

Sure he that made us with such large discourse, / Looking before and after, gave us not / That capability and god-like reason / To fust in us unus'd – *Shakespeare*

Reason is the glory of human nature, and one of the chief eminences whereby we are raised above the beasts, in this lower world.

Reasoning implies doubt and uncertainty; and therefore God does not reason.

He that will not reason is a bigot; he that cannot reason is a fool; and he that dares not reason is a slave.

Revelation is a telescope kindly given us, through which reason should look up to the heavens.

Reason is our intellectual eye, and like the bodily eye it needs light to see; and to see clearly and far it needs the light of heaven.

Reason is progressive; instinct is complete; swift instinct leaps; slow reason feebly climbs.

See also LOGIC.

REBELLION

Rebellion against tyrants is obedience to God – *Benjamin Franklin*

There is little hope of equity where rebellion reigns – *Sir Philip Sidney*

This word, rebellion, it had froze them up, / As fish are in a pond – *William Shakespeare*

Men seldom, or rather never for a length of time, and deliberately, rebel against anything that does not deserve rebelling against – *Thomas Carlyle*

RECKLESSNESS

Who falls from all he knows of bliss, / Cares little into what abyss – *Lord Byron*

I am one . . . / Whom the vile blows and buffets of the world / Have so incens'd that I am reckless what / I do to spite the world – *William Shakespeare*

Beware of desperate steps; the darkest day, live till tomorrow, will have passed away – *William Cowper*

See also RASHNESS.

RECOMPENSE

Recompense injury with justice, and unkindness with kindness – *Confucius*

There never was a person who did anything worth doing that did not receive more than he gave – *Henry Ward Beecher*

Mercy to him that shows it is the rule – *William Cowper*

Forever from the hand that takes one blessing from us, others fall; / And soon or late, our Father makes his perfect recompense to all – *John Greenleaf Whittier*

RECREATION

The bow cannot possibly always stand bent, nor can human nature or human frailty subsist without some lawful recreation – *Miguel de Cervantes Saavedra*

Make thy recreation servant to thy business, lest thou become a slave to thy recreation – *Francis Quarles*

He that will make a good use of any part of his life must allow a large part of it to recreation – *John Locke*

Amusements are to virtue like breezes of air to the flame; gentle ones will fan it, but strong ones will put it out.

Recreation is not being idle; it is easing the wearied part by change of occupation.

See also LEISURE.

RE-CREATION

To re-create strength, rest. To re-create mind, repose. To re-create cheerfulness hope in God.

RECTITUDE

If you would convince a man that he does wrong, do right – *Henry David Thoreau*

Nothing more completely baffles one who is full of tricks and duplicity than straightforward and simple integrity – *Charles Caleb Colton*

A straight line is the shortest in morals as in mathematics – *Maria Edgeworth*

See also GOODNESS.

REFLECTION

The reflections on a day well spent furnish us with joys more pleasing than ten thousand triumphs – *Thomas à Kempis*

They only babble who practise not reflection. I shall think; and thought is silence – *Seneca*

Think twice before you speak, or act once, and you will speak or act the more wisely for it – *Benjamin Franklin*

He that will not reflect is a ruined man.

Evil is wrought by want of thought as well as by want of heart.

See also MEDITATION.

REFORM

One vicious habit each year rooted out, in time might make the worst man good – *Benjamin Franklin*

Necessity reforms the poor, and satiety the rich – *Tacitus*

It is easier to enrich ourselves with a thousand virtues than to correct ourselves of a single fault – *Jean de La Bruyère*

They say best men are moulded out of faults, / And, for the most, become much more the better / For being a little bad – *Shakespeare*

To reform a man, you must begin with his grandmother – *Victor Hugo*

What you dislike in another, take care to correct in yourself.

Many hope the tree may be felled that they may gather chips by the fall.

How important, often, is the pain of guilt, as a stimulant to amendment and reformation.

The true reformer will not only hate evil, but will earnestly endeavour to fill its place with good.

Reformer – one who insists upon his conscience being your guide.

See also SELF-IMPROVEMENT.

RELIGION

The pious man and the atheist always talk of religion; the one of what he loves, and the other of what he fears – *Charles de Montesquieu*

It is a great dishonour to religion to imagine that it is an enemy to mirth and cheerfulness, and a severe exacter of pensive looks and solemn faces – *Walter Scott*

It is no good reason for a man's religion that he was born and brought up in it – *William Chillingworth*

The writers against religion, while they oppose every system, are wisely careful never to set up any of their own – *Edmund Burke*

Religion is the best armour in the world, but the worst cloak – *John Newton*

If our religion is not true, we are bound to change it; if it is true, we are bound to propagate it – *Richard Whately*

What I want is not to possess religion but to have a religion that shall possess me – *Charles Kingsley*

The call to religion is not a call to be better than your fellows, but to be better than yourself – *Henry Ward Beecher*

If men are so wicked with religion, what would they be without it! – *Benjamin Franklin*

Nothing can be hostile to religion which is agreeable to justice – *William Gladstone*

Where true religion has prevented one crime, false religions have afforded a pretext for a thousand – *Charles Caleb Colton*

I have now disposed of all my property to my family. There is one thing more I wish I could give them, and that is the Christian religion. If they had that, and I had not given them one shilling, they would have been rich, and if they had not that, and I had given them all the world, they would be poor – *Patrick Henry*

You have no security for a man who has no religious principle – *Richard Cobden*

When religion is made a science there is nothing more intricate; when it is made a duty, there is nothing more easy.

If we make religion our business, God will make it our blessedness.

Religion presents few difficulties to the humble; many to the proud; insuperable ones to the vain.

Measure not men by Sundays, without regarding what they do all the week after.

Religion's home is the conscience. Its watchword is the word 'ought'.

Men will wrangle for religion, write for it, fight for it, anything but live for it.

Nature teaches us to love our friends, but religion our enemies.

It were better to be no Church than to be bitter toward any.

If people will not come to the church, then the church must go to the people.

See also ATHEISM, CHRISTIANITY, THE CHURCH, GOD, HOLINESS.

REMEMBRANCE

Remembrance is the only paradise out of which we cannot be driven away – *Jean Paul Richter*

The world does not require so much to be informed as reminded – *Hannah More*

Praising what is lost / Makes the remembrance dear – *Shakespeare*

Pleasure is the flower that fades; remembrance is the lasting perfume – *Marquis de Boufflers*

Sorrows remembered sweeten present joy.

REMORSE

There is no future pang can deal that justice on the self-condemned he deals on his own soul – *Lord Byron*

I am afraid to think what I have done; / Look on't again I dare not – *William Shakespeare*

To be left alone, and face to face with my own crime, had been just retribution – *Henry Wadsworth Longfellow*

This is the bitterest of all, to wear the yoke of our own wrong-doing – *George Eliot*

Not sharp revenge, nor hell itself, can find a fiercer torment than a guilty mind – *John Dryden*

Remorse is the echo of a lost virtue.

Remorse is beholding heaven and feeling hell.

REPENTANCE

To do so no more is the truest repentance – *Martin Luther*

True repentance is to cease from sinning – *Ambrose*

Right actions for the future are the best apologies for wrong ones in the past – *Tryon Edwards*

God hath promised pardon to him that repenteth, but he hath not promised repentance to him that sinneth – *Anselm*

Repentance may begin instantly, but reformation often requires a sphere of years – *Henry Ward Beecher*

Nothing but heart-sorrow / And a clear life ensuing – *William Shakespeare*

Our greatest glory consists not in never falling, but in rising every time we may fall – *Oliver Goldsmith*

The vain regret that steals above the wreck of squandered hours – *John Greenleaf Whittier*

If you would be good, first believe you are bad – *Epictetus*

Whatever stress some may lay upon it, a death-bed repentance is but a weak and slender plank to trust our all upon – *Laurence Sterne*

Great is the difference betwixt a man's being frightened at, and humbled for, his sins – *Fuller*

The best part of repentance is little sinning – *Arabian proverb*

Mere sorrow, which weeps and sits still, is not repentance.

Repentance is sorrow converted into action.

Repentance, without amendment, is like continually pumping without mending the leak.

You cannot repent too soon, because you do not know how soon it may be too late.

REPOSE

Our foster-nurse of nature is repose – *William Shakespeare*

These should be hours for necessities, / Not for delights; times to repair our nature / With comforting repose, and not for us / To waste these times – *Shakespeare*

There is no mortal truly wise and restless at once; wisdom is the repose of minds – *Johann Kaspar Lavater*

Repose without stagnation is the state most favourable to happiness.

If we find not repose in ourselves, it is in vain to seek it elsewhere.

See also REST, SLEEP.

REPROOF

He that cleanses a blot with blotted fingers makes a greater blur – *Francis Quarles*

Reproof is a medicine like mercury or opium; if it be improperly administered, it will do harm instead of good – *Horace Mann*

Ill deeds are doubled with an evil word – *William Shakespeare*

Reprove thy friend privately; commend him publicly – *Solon*

Few love to hear the sins they love to act – *Shakespeare*

Better a little chiding than a great deal of heart-break – *Shakespeare*

Chide him for faults, and do it reverently, / When you perceive his blood
inclin'd to mirth – *Shakespeare*

I will chide no breather in the world but myself, against whom I know
most faults – *Shakespeare*

Confront improper conduct, not by retaliation, but by example.

No reproach is like that we clothe in a smile, and present with a bow.

The silent upbraiding of the eye is the very poetry of reproach; it speaks
at once to the imagination.

The reproof of a good man resembles fuller's earth; it not only removes
the spots from our character, but it rubs off when it is dry.

REPUTATION

The way to gain a good reputation is to endeavour to be what you desire
to appear – *Socrates*

A proper self-regard becomes improper as soon as we begin to value
reputation more than real character – *Morning Star*

The purest treasure mortal times afford / Is spotless reputation; that
away, / Men are but gilded loam or painted clay – *William Shakespeare*

Reputation, reputation, reputation! O, I have lost my reputation. I have
lost the immortal part of myself, and what remains is bestial –
Shakespeare

The reputation of a man is like his shadow, gigantic when it precedes
him, and pigmy in its proportions when it follows – *Charles Maurice de
Talleyrand-Périgord*

One may be better than his reputation, but never better than his
principles – *Latena*

The blaze of reputation cannot be blown out, but it often dies in the
socket – *Samuel Johnson*

In all the affairs of this world, so much reputation is, in reality, so much
power – *John Tillotson*

There are two modes of establishing our reputation: to be praised by
honest men, and to be abused by rogues – *Charles Caleb Colton*

Character is what one really is; reputation what others believe him to be –
Henry Ward Beecher

Reputation is an idle and most false imposition; oft got without merit,
and lost without deserving – *Shakespeare*

Associate with men of good quality, if you esteem your own reputation; it is better to be alone than in bad company – *George Washington*

When a man has once forfeited the reputation of his integrity, he is set fast; nothing will then serve his turn, neither truth nor falsehood – *Tillotson*

O! reputation, dearer far than life, thou precious balsam, lovely, sweet of smell, whose cordial drops once spilt by some rash hand, not all thy owner's care, nor the repenting toil of the rude spiller, ever can collect to its first purity and native sweetness – *Walter Raleigh*

Reputation is what men and women think of us; character is what God and angels know of us.

See that your character is right, and in the long run your reputation will be right.

Good will, like a good name, is got by many actions, and lost by one.

No man was ever written out of reputation but by himself.

A reputation once broken may possibly be repaired, but the world will always keep their eyes on the spot where the crack was.

Honest confession may be good for the soul, but it's often bad for the reputation.

Always begin somewhere. You can't build a reputation on what you intend to do.

See also CREDIT.

RESERVE

Reserve may be pride fortified in ice; dignity is worth reposing on truth – *William Rounseville Alger*

There is nothing more allied to the barbarous and savage character than sullenness, concealment, and reserve – *Park Godwin*

Reserve is the truest expression of respect toward those who are its objects – *Thomas De Quincey*

Persons extremely reserved and diffident are like old enamelled watches, which had painted covers that hindered your seeing what o'clock it was.

RESOLUTION

He who is firm and resolute in will moulds the world to himself – *Johann Wolfgang von Goethe*

The block of granite which is an obstacle in the pathway of the weak becomes a stepping-stone in the pathway of the strong – *Thomas Carlyle*

To think we are able is almost to be so – *Samuel Smiles*

Do not, for one repulse, forgo the purpose / That you resolv'd to effect – *William Shakespeare*

A good intention clothes itself with power – *Ralph Waldo Emerson*
The fearful are the failing – *Sarah J. Hale*
Either I will find a way, or I will make one – *Sir Philip Sidney*
Good resolutions are a pleasant crop to sow.
If we have need of a strong will in order to do good, it is still more necessary for us in order not to do evil.
The fatality of good resolutions is that they are always too late.

RESPONSIBILITY

Responsibility educates – *Wendell Phillips*
Much misconstruction and bitterness are spared to him who thinks naturally upon what he owes to others rather than what he ought to expect from them – *Mme Guizot*
Responsibility walks hand in hand with capacity and power – *Josiah Gilbert Holland*
Sin with the multitude, and your responsibility and guilt are as great and as truly personal, as if you alone had done the wrong – *Tryon Edwards*
If the master takes no account of his servants, they will make small account of him.

REST

Rest is the sweet sauce of labour – *Plutarch*
Absence of occupation is not rest; / A mind quite vacant is a mind distressed – *William Cowper*
Too much rest itself becomes a pain – *Homer*
Alternate rest and labour long endure – *Ovid*
Some seek bread; and some seek wealth and ease; and some seek fame, but all are seeking rest.
Rest is valuable only so far as it is a contrast.
All work and no rest takes the spring and bound out of the most vigorous life.
Rest is not quitting the busy career; / Rest is the fitting of self to its sphere.
See also LEISURE, REPOSE, SLEEP.

RETIREMENT

To judge rightly of our own worth we should retire from the world so as to see both its pleasures and pains in their proper light and dimensions – *Laurence Sterne*
This our life, exempt from public haunt, / Finds tongues in trees, books in the running brooks, / Sermons in stones, and good in every thing – *William Shakespeare*

Depart from the highway, and transplant thyself in some enclosed ground, for it is hard for a tree that stands by the wayside to keep its fruit until it be ripe – *St John Chrysostom*

Don't think of retiring from the world until the world will be sorry that you retire – *Samuel Johnson*

How use doth breed a habit in a man! / This shadowy desert, unfrequented woods, / I better brook than flourishing peopled towns – *Shakespeare*

He whom God hath gifted with the love of retirement, possesses, as it were, an extra sense.

Let me often to these solitudes retire, and in their presence reassure my feeble virtue.

Before you think of retiring from the world, be sure you are fit for retirement.

RETRIBUTION

God is a sure paymaster. He may not pay at the end of every week, or month, or year, but remember he pays in the end – *Anne of Austria*

Life resembles the banquet of Damocles; the sword is ever suspended – *Voltaire*

Old age seizes upon an ill-spent youth like fire upon a rotten house – *Robert South*

'One soweth and another reapeth' is a verity that applies to evil as well as good – *George Eliot*

He that sows the wind ought to reap the whirlwind.

God's mill grinds slow but sure.

See also PUNISHMENT.

RETROSPECTION

The thought of our past years in me doth breed perpetual benediction – *William Wordsworth*

A man advanced in years, who thinks fit to look back upon his former life, and call that only life which was passed with satisfaction and enjoyment will find himself very young, if not in his infancy – *Richard Steele*

To look back to antiquity is one thing; to go back to it another – *Charles Caleb Colton*

REVENGE

Revenge is the abject pleasure of an abject mind – *Juvenal*

By taking revenge, a man is but even with his enemy; but in passing over it, he is superior – *Francis Bacon*

He that studieth revenge keepeth his own wounds green, which otherwise would heal and do well – *Bacon*

Revenge, at first, though sweet, bitter, ere long, back on itself recoils –
John Milton

Pleasure and revenge / Have ears more deaf than adders to the voice / Of
any true decision – *William Shakespeare*

Revenge is an act of passion; vengeance of justice. Injuries are revenged;
crimes are avenged – *Joseph Joubert*

To revenge is no valour, but to bear – *Shakespeare*

Hath any wronged thee? Be bravely revenged. Slight it, and the work is
begun; forgive it, and it is finished. He is below himself that is not
above any injury – *Francis Quarles*

Heat not a furnace for your foe so hot / That it do singe thyself –
Shakespeare

Revenge is a much more punctual paymaster than gratitude.

Revenge is a common passion; it is the sin of the uninstructed.

It is a work of prudence to prevent injury, and of a great mind.

The noblest revenge is forgiveness.

See also VENGEANCE.

REVOLUTION

Revolution is the larva of civilization – *Victor Hugo*

Political convulsions, like geological upheavings, usher in new epochs of
the world's progress – *Wendell Phillips*

Too long denial of guaranteed right is sure to lead to revolution – bloody
revolution, where suffering must fall upon the innocent as well as the
guilty – *Ulysses Simpson Grant*

All experience hath shown that mankind are more disposed to suffer,
while evils are sufferable, than to right themselves by abolishing the
forms to which they are accustomed – *Thomas Jefferson*

Times and occasions and provocations will teach their own lessons. But
with or without right, a revolution will be the very last resource of the
thinking and the good – *Edmund Burke*

Let them call it mischief; when it's past and prospered, it will be virtue –
Ben Jonson

Revolutions are like the most noxious dung-heaps, which bring into life
the noblest vegetables – *Napoleon Bonaparte*

The whirlpool of the hour engulfs the growth of centuries! – *Sir Thomas
Noon Talfourd*

REWARD

He who wishes to secure the good of others has already secured his
own – *Confucius*

Blessings ever wait on virtuous deeds, / And though a late, a sure reward succeeds – *William Congreve*

RHETORIC

Rhetoric is nothing but reason well dressed, and argument put in order – *Jeremy Collier*

The best rules of rhetoric are to speak intelligently; speak from the heart; have something to say; say it; and stop when you've done – *Tryon Edwards*

There is truth and beauty in rhetoric; but it oftener serves ill turns than good ones – *William Penn*

Mere rhetoric, in serious discourses, is like flowers in corn, pleasing to those who look only for amusement, but prejudical to him who would reap profit from it – *Jonathan Swift*

All a rhetorician's rules teach nothing but to name his tools – *Samuel Butler*

RICHES

He is rich whose income is more than his expenses; and he is poor whose expenses exceed his income – *Jean de Là Bruyère*

Riches are not an end of life, but an instrument of life – *Henry Ward Beecher*

The pride of dying rich raises the loudest laugh in hell – *John Foster*

He hath riches sufficient, who hath enough to be charitable – *Sir Thomas Browne*

The larger the income, the harder it is to live within it – *Richard Whately*

Riches without charity are nothing worth – *Henry Fielding*

He is richest who is content with the least, for content is the wealth of nature – *Socrates*

Wealth is not his that has it, but his that enjoys it – *Benjamin Franklin*

Riches are apt to betray a man into arrogance – *Joseph Addison*

If thou art rich, thou'rt poor; / For, like an ass whose back with ingots bows, / Thou bear'st thy heavy riches but a journey, / And death unloads thee – *William Shakespeare*

Riches, honours and pleasures are the sweets which destroy the mind's appetite for heavenly food; poverty, disgrace, and pain are the bitters which restore it – *Bishop Horne*

Every man is rich or poor according to the proportion between his desires and his enjoyments – *Samuel Johnson*

Riches amassed in haste will diminish, but those collected by little and little will multiply – *Johann Wolfgang von Goethe*

If a rich man is proud of his wealth, he should not be praised until it is
known how he employs it – *Socrates*

As riches and favour forsake a man we discover him to be a fool, but
nobody could find it out in his prosperity – *Jean de La Bruyère*

Nothing is so hard for those who abound in riches as to conceive how
others can be in want – *Jonathan Swift*

My riches consist not in the extent of my possessions, but in the fewness
of my wants.

A man that hoards up riches and enjoys them not is like an ass that
carries gold and eats thistles.

Riches, though they may reward virtue, cannot cause it.

There are two things needed in these days: first, for rich men to find out
how poor men live; and second, for poor men to know how rich men
work.

A fortune is usually the greatest of misfortunes to children. It takes the
muscle out of the limbs, the brain out of the head, and virtue out of
the heart.

Man was born to be rich, or grows rich by the use of his faculties, by the
union of thought with nature.

Worldly riches are like nuts; many clothes are torn in getting them, many
a tooth broke in cracking them, but never a belly filled with eating
them.

Much learning shows how little mortals know; much wealth, how little
worldlings can enjoy.

Riches do not delight us so much with their possession, as torment us
with their loss.

Never respect men merely for their riches, but rather for their philanthropy; we do not value the sun for its height, but for its use.

See also FORTUNE, GOLD, PROSPERITY, WEALTH.

RIDICULE

Man learns more readily and remembers more willingly what excites his
ridicule than what deserves esteem and respect – *Horace*

Reason is the test of ridicule – not ridicule the test of truth – *William
Warburton*

Ridicule is a weak weapon when levelled at strong minds – *Martin
Farquhar Tupper*

Ridicule is the first and last argument of fools.

Vices, when ridiculed, first lose the horror they ought to raise, / Grow by
degrees approved, and almost aim at praise.

RIGHT

Let us have faith that right makes might – *Abraham Lincoln*

No man has a right to do as he pleases, except when he pleases to do right.

The fears of one class of men are not the measure of the rights of another.

RIVALRY

Two stars keep not their motion in one sphere – *William Shakespeare*

Nothing is ever done beautifully which is done in rivalship; or nobly, which is done in pride – *John Ruskin*

ROGUERY

After long experience of the world, I affirm before God, that I never knew a rogue who was not unhappy – *Junius*

Make yourself an honest man, and then you may be sure there is one rascal less in the world – *Thomas Carlyle*

A rogue is a roundabout fool – *Samuel Taylor Coleridge*

ROMANCE

Romance is the poetry of literature – *Mme Neckar*

Lessons of wisdom have never such power over us as when they are wrought into the heart through the groundwork of a story which engages the passions – *Laurence Sterne*

In this commonplace world every one is said to be romantic who either admires a fine thing or does one – *Alexander Pope*

Romance has been elegantly defined as the offspring of fiction and love – *Benjamin Disraeli*

In the meanest hut is a romance, if you but knew the hearts there.

To the romance writers, and comparatively decorous dramatists of his own time Pierre Nicole gave the title of public poisoners.

See also FICTION.

RUINS

The legendary tablets of the past – *Walter Scott*

Black-letter record of the ages – *Denis Diderot*

Cicero was not so eloquent as thou, thou nameless column with the buried base – *Lord Byron*

Mile-stones on the road of time – *Nicolas Sébastian Roch Chamfort*

Historic records of the past, but each, also, an index of the world's progress.

RUMOUR

Stuffing the ears of men with false reports – *William Shakespeare*

Upon my tongues continual slanders ride – *Shakespeare*

Rumour is a pipe / Blown by surmises, jealousies, conjectures, / And of so easy and plain a stop / That the blunt monster with uncounted heads, / The still-discordant wavering multitude, / Can play upon it – *Shakespeare*

Rumour was the messenger of defamation, and so swift, that none could be first to tell an evil tale.

Curse the tongue whence slanderous rumour, like the adder's drop, distils her venom, withering friendship's faith, turning love's favour.

See also GOSSIP, SCANDAL.

SABBATH

He who ordained the Sabbath loves the poor – *James Russell Lowell*

Sunday is the golden clasp that binds together the volume of the week – *Henry Wadsworth Longfellow*

I feel as if God had, by giving the Sabbath, given fifty-two springs in every year – *Samuel Taylor Coleridge*

Sunday is like a stile between the fields of toil, where we can kneel and pray, or sit and meditate – *Longfellow*

There are many persons who look on Sunday as a sponge to wipe out the sins of the week – *Henry Ward Beecher*

I never knew a man escape failures, in either mind or body, who worked seven days in a week – *Sir Robert Peel*

Perpetual memory of the Maker's rest.

The Sabbath is the link between the paradise which has passed away, and the paradise which is yet to come.

The savings bank of human existence is the weekly Sabbath.

SADNESS

A feeling of sadness that is not akin to pain resembles sorrow only as the mist resembles rain – *Henry Wadsworth Longfellow*

Every heart has its secret sorrows, which the world knows not; and often times we call a man cold when he is only sad – *Longfellow*

Of all the sad words of tongue or pen, / The saddest are these: 'It might have been.' – *John Greenleaf Whittier*

The saddest thing under the sky is a soul incapable of sadness.

See also GRIEF, SORROW.

SARCASM

Sarcasm is the language of the devil – *Thomas Carlyle*
A sneer is the weapon of the weak – *James Russell Lowell*
Sarcasm poisons reproof.
The arrows of sarcasm are barbed with contempt.

SATIETY

The sweetest honey / Is loathsome in his own deliciousness / And in the
taste confounds the appetite – *William Shakespeare*
With much we surfeit; plenty makes us poor – *Michael Drayton*
The flower that we do not pluck is the only one that never loses its beauty
or its fragrance – *William Rounseville Alger*
A surfeit of the sweetest things / The deepest loathing to the stomach
brings – *Shakespeare*
With pleasure drugged, he almost longed for woe – *Lord Byron*
Pleasure, when it is a man's chief purpose, disappoints itself – *Richard
Steele*

SATIRE

Lampoons and satires that are written with wit and spirit are like
poisoned darts, which not only inflict a wound but make it incurable
– *Joseph Addison*
Satire should, like a polished razor, keen, wound with a touch that is
scarcely felt or seen – *Lady Mary Wortley Montagu*
No sword bites so fiercely as an evil tongue – *Sir Philip Sidney*
By satire kept in awe, they shrink from ridicule, though not from law –
Lord Byron
Walls that have remained impenetrable to cannon have fallen before a
roar of laughter or a hiss of contempt – *E. P. Whipple*
We smile at the satire expended upon the follies of others, but we forget
to weep at our own – *Mme Neckar*
If satire charms, strike faults, but spare the man – *Young*
Satire should not be like a saw, but a sword, it should cut, and not
mangle.
Satire is a composition of salt and mercury; and it depends upon the
different mixture and preparation of those ingredients, that it comes
out a noble medicine, or a rank poison.
Satire! thou shining supplement of public laws.
Arrows of satire, feathered with wit, and wielded with sense, fly home to
their mark.
If evil be said of thee, and if it be true, correct thyself: if it be a lie, laugh at
it.

SCANDAL

Believe that story false that ought not to be true – *Richard Brinsley Sheridan*

Number among your worst enemies the hawker of malicious rumours and unexplored anecdote – *Johann Kaspar Lavater*

How large a portion of chastity is sent out of the world by distant hints – *Laurence Sterne*

The tale-bearer and the tale-hearer should be both hanged up, back to back, one by the tongue, the other by the ear – *Robert South*

Scandal breeds hatred; hatred begets division; division makes faction, and faction brings ruin – *Francis Quarles*

In scandal, as in robbery, the receiver is always as bad as the thief – *Lord Chesterfield*

A cruel story runs on wheels, and every hand oils the wheels as they run – *George Eliot*

Praise undeserved is scandal in disguise – *Alexander Pope*

For greatest scandal waits on greatest state – *William Shakespeare*

Scandal is like an egg; when it is hatched it has wings.

Never make your ear the grave of another's good name.

If there is any person of whom you feel dislike, that is the person of whom you ought never to speak.

Great numbers of moderately good people think it fine to talk scandal; they regard it as a sort of evidence of their own goodness – *Frederick William Faber*

If hours did not hang heavy what would become of scandal?

Scandal is the sport of its authors, the dread of fools, and the contempt of the wise.

There is a lust in a man no charm can tame / Of loudly publishing his neighbour's shame; / On eagle's wings immortal scandals fly, / While virtuous actions are but born and die.

See also GOSSIP, RUMOUR.

SCEPTICISM

Scepticism is slow suicide – *Ralph Waldo Emerson*

Free thinkers are generally those who never think at all – *Laurence Sterne*

I know not any crime so great a man could contrive to commit as poisoning the sources of eternal truth – *Samuel Johnson*

Imperfect knowledge is the parent of doubt: thorough and honest research dispels it – *Tryon Edwards*

The prejudices of sceptics are surpassed only by their ignorance – *Samuel Taylor Coleridge*

A foe to God was ne'er true friend to man.

See also DOUBT.

SCIENCE

Science is the topography of ignorance – *Oliver Wendell Holmes*

The highest reach of human science is the recognition of human ignorance – *Sir William Hamilton*

Science ever has been, and ever must be, the safeguard of religion – *David Brewster*

Science when well digested is nothing but good sense and reason – *Stanislaus*

Learning is the dictionary, but sense the grammar of science – *Laurence Sterne*

Science surpasses the old miracles of mythology – *Ralph Waldo Emerson*

When man seized the lodestone of science, the lodestar of superstition vanished in the clouds – *William Rounseville Alger*

Human science is an uncertain guess.

Art and science have their meeting point in method.

The person who thinks there can be any real conflict between science and religion must be either very young in science or very ignorant in religion.

Science is nothing but trained and organized common sense.

Science is but the statement of truth found out.

See also KNOWLEDGE.

SEA

Surely oak and threefold brass surrounded his heart who first trusted a frail vessel to the merciless ocean – *Horace*

There is society where none intrudes, by the deep sea, and music in its roar – *Lord Byron*

Whoever commands the sea, commands the trade, whoever commands the trade of the world, commands the riches of the world, and consequently the world itself – *Walter Raleigh*

Praise the sea, but keep on the land.

He that will learn to pray, let him go to sea.

SECRECY

A proper secrecy is only the mystery of able men; mystery is only the secrecy of weak and cunning ones – *Lord Chesterfield*

What is mine, even to my life, is hers I love; but the secret of my friend is not mine – *Sir Philip Sidney*

Two may keep counsel when the third's away – *William Shakespeare*

He who trusts secrets to a servant makes him his master – *John Dryden*

The truly wise man should have no keeper of his secret but himself – *François Pierre Guillaume Guizot*

Who shall be true to us, / When we are so unsecret to ourselves –
Shakespeare

Three may keep a secret, if two of them are dead – *Benjamin Franklin*

Secrecy is the chastity of friendship – *Jeremy Taylor*

When a secret is revealed, it is the fault of the man who has entrusted it –
Jean de La Bruyère

A secret in his mouth is like a wild bird put into a cage; whose door no
sooner opens, but it is out – *Ben Jonson*

Where secrecy or mystery begins, vice or roguery is not far off – *Samuel
Johnson*

Fire that's closest kept burns most of all – *Shakespeare*

Thou hast betrayed thy secret as a bird betrays her nest, by striving to
conceal it – *Henry Wadsworth Longfellow*

What thou seest speak of with caution – *Solon*

Trust him not with your secrets, who, when left alone in your room,
turns over your papers – *Johann Kaspar Lavater*

No one ever keeps a secret so well as a child – *Victor Hugo*

Washington, having been asked by an officer on the morning of a battle
what were his plans for the day, replied in a whisper, 'Can you keep a
secret?' On being answered in the affirmative, the general added, 'So
can I.'

He deserves small trust who is not privy counsellor to himself.

A secret is too little for one, enough for two, and too much for three.

Secrets with girls, like guns with boys, / Are never valued till they make a
noise.

I vow and protest there's more plague than pleasure with a secret.

When two friends part they should lock up one another's secrets, and
interchange their keys.

SELF-CONCEIT

There are few people who are more often in the wrong than those who
cannot endure to be thought so – *François de La Rochefoucauld*

Conceited men are a harmless kind of creatures, who, by their overweening self-respect, relieve others from the duty of respecting them
at all – *Henry Ward Beecher*

In one thing men of all ages are alike: they have believed obstinately in
themselves – *Friedrich Heinrich Jacobi*

The less a man thinks or knows about his virtues the better we like him –
Ralph Waldo Emerson

Prize not thyself by what thou hast, but by what thou art; he that values a
jewel by its golden frame, or a book by its silver clasps, or a man by
his vast estate, errs – *Francis Quarles*

Whenever nature leaves a hole in a person's mind, she generally plasters it over with a thick coat of self-conceit – *Henry Wadsworth Longfellow*

The weakest spot in every man is where he thinks himself to be the wisest.

He that fancies himself very enlightened, because he sees the deficiencies of others, may be very ignorant, because he has not studied his own.

A wise man knows his own ignorance; a fool thinks he knows everything.

He who is always his own counsellor will often have a fool for his client.

See also COMPLACENCY.

SELF-CONTROL

He who reigns within himself and rules his passions, desires and fears is more than a king – *John Milton*

Most powerful is he who has himself in his own power – *Seneca*

The best of all governments is that which teaches us to govern ourselves – *Johann Wolfgang von Goethe*

Those who can command themselves command others – *William Hazlitt*

He who would govern others should first be master of himself – *Philip Massinger*

A man must first govern himself, ere he be fit to govern a family; and his family, ere he be fit to bear the government in the commonwealth – *Walter Raleigh*

No conflict is so severe as his who labours to subdue himself – *Thomas à Kempis*

Do you want to know the man against whom you have most reason to guard yourself? Your looking-glass will give you a very fair likeness of his face – *Richard Whately*

No man is free who cannot command himself – *Pythagoras*

He is a fool who cannot be angry; but he is a wise man who will not – *proverb*

He who best governs himself is best fitted to govern others.

Humility is the antidote to this evil.

Real glory springs from the silent conquest of ourselves; without that the conqueror is only the first slave.

Better conquest never canst thou make, than warn thy constant and thy nobler parts against giddy, loose suggestions.

May I govern my passions with absolute sway, / And grow wiser and better as life wears away.

SELF-DECEPTION

Who has deceived thee so often as thyself? – *Benjamin Franklin*

No man was ever so much deceived by another as by himself.

The coward reckons himself cautious; the miser thinks himself frugal.

The first and worst of all frauds is to cheat oneself. All sin is easy after that.

We cheat ourselves in order to enjoy a quiet conscience, without possessing virtue.

SELF-DENIAL

Teach self-denial and make its practice pleasurable, and you can create for the world a destiny more sublime than ever issued from the brain of the wildest dreamer – *Walter Scott*

He who never sacrificed a present to a future good, or a personal to a general one, can speak of happiness only as the blind speak of colour – *Horace Mann*

Brave conquerors, – for so you are, / That war against your own affections / And the huge army of the world's desires – *William Shakespeare*

When you give, take to yourself no credit for generosity, unless you deny yourself something in order that you may give.

Shall we call ourselves benevolent, when the gifts we bestow do not cost us a single privation?

The secret of all success is to know how to deny yourself.

SELF-EXAMINATION

Observe thyself as thy greatest enemy would do, so shalt thou be thy greatest friend – *Jeremy Taylor*

The superior man will watch over himself when he is alone. He examines his heart there, and that he may have no cause of dissatisfaction with himself – *Confucius*

We should every night call ourselves to an account – *Seneca*

Let not sleep fall upon thy eyes till thou hast thrice reviewed the transactions of the past day – *Pythagoras*

I will chide no breather in the world but myself, against whom I know most faults – *William Shakespeare*

Inspect the neighbourhood of thy life; every shelf, every nook of thine abode – *Jean Paul Richter*

Go to your bosom; / Knock there, and ask your heart what it doth know / That's like my brother's fault – *Shakespeare*

You might as well fall flat on your face as lean over too far backwards – *James Thurber*

If any speak ill of thee, fly home to thy own conscience and examine thy heart. If thou art guilty, it is a just correction; if not guilty, it is a fair instruction.

SELF-IMPROVEMENT

You will find that the mere resolve not to be useless, and the honest desire to help other people, will, in the quickest and delicatest ways, improve yourself – *John Ruskin*

People seldom improve, when they have no other model but themselves to copy after – *Oliver Goldsmith*

One vicious habit each year rooted out, in time might make the worst man good – *Benjamin Franklin*

When a tradesman is about to weigh his goods, he first of all looks to his scales and sees that his weights are right – *Tryon Edwards*

Look back, and smile at perils past – *Walter Scott*

Self-inspection – the best cure for self-esteem.

See also REFORM.

SELFISHNESS

Selfishness is that detestable vice which no one will forgive in others, and no one is without in himself – *Henry Ward Beecher*

A man is called selfish, not for pursuing his own good, but for neglecting his neighbour's – *Richard Whately*

He who lives only to benefit himself confers on the world a benefit when he dies – *Tertullian*

The virtues are lost in self-interest as rivers are in the sea – *François de La Rochefoucauld*

Let us think often of our own sin, and we shall be lenient to the sins of others – *François de Fénelon*

The selfish man suffers more from his selfishness than he from whom that selfishness withholds some important benefit – *Ralph Waldo Emerson*

Whenever education and refinement grow away from the common people, they are growing toward selfishness, which is the monster evil of the world – *Beecher*

The world is governed only by self-interest – *Johann Christoph Friedrich von Schiller*

Beware of no man more than of yourself; we carry our worst enemies within us – *Charles Haddon Spurgeon*

Show me the man who would go to heaven alone, and I will show you one who will never be admitted there.

He who makes an idol of his self-interest will often make a martyr of his integrity.

We erect the idol self, and not only wish others to worship, but worship
   it ourselves.

As a man goes down in self, he goes up in God.

SELF-KNOWLEDGE

No one who has not a complete knowledge of himself will ever have a
   true understanding of another – *Novalis*

Self-knowledge is best learned, not by contemplation, but action – *Johann
   Wolfgang von Goethe*

Nothing will make us so charitable and tender to the faults of others,
   as, by self-examination, thoroughly to know our own – *François de
   Fénelon*

Trust not yourself, but your defects to know, / Make use of every friend
   and every foe – *Alexander Pope*

Other men's sins are before our eyes; our own are behind our back –
   Seneca

Our own opinion of ourselves should be lower than that formed by
   others, for we have a better chance at our imperfections – *Thomas à
   Kempis*

Man, know thyself; all wisdom centres there.

SELF-LOVE

Of all mankind each loves himself the best – *Terence*

The greatest of all flatterers is self-love – *François de La Rochefoucauld*

The most amiable people are those who least wound the self-love of
   others – *Jean de La Bruyère*

Self-love . . . is not so vile a sin / As self-neglecting – *William Shakespeare*

The cause of all the blunders committed by man arises from excessive
   self-love – *Plato*

Self-love leads men of narrow minds to measure all mankind by their
   own capacity – *Jane Porter*

Self-love is a cup without any bottom – *Oliver Wendell Holmes*

Self-love is the instrument of our preservation – *Voltaire*

One should always learn to love oneself, for that is the only life-long
   romance – *Gabriele d' Annunzio*

In all time self-love has blinded the wisest.

Offended self-love never forgives.

SELF-PRAISE

There's not one wise man among twenty that will praise himself –
   William Shakespeare

It is equally a mistake to hold oneself too high, or to rate oneself too cheap – *Johann Wolfgang von Goethe*

A man's accusations of himself are always believed; his praises of self never – *Michel Eyquem de Montaigne*

SELF-RELIANCE

If you would have a faithful servant, and one that you like, serve yourself – *Benjamin Franklin*

They can conquer who believe they can – *Virgil*

Let every eye negotiate for itself / And trust no agent – *William Shakespeare*

Our remedies oft in ourselves do lie, / Which we ascribe to heaven – *Shakespeare*

God gives every bird its food, but he does not throw it into the nest – *Josiah Gilbert Holland*

Time and I against any two – *Philip II*

Trust in God, and keep your powder dry – *Oliver Cromwell*

The man who cannot enjoy his own natural gifts in silence, and find his reward in the exercise of them, will generally find himself badly off – *Johann Wolfgang von Goethe*

God helps those that help themselves – *Franklin*

I carry my sovereignty under my hat – *William A. Prendergast*

Help thyself, and God will help thee.

Doubt whom you will, but never doubt yourself.

Call on God, but row away from the rocks.

Make the most of yourself for that is all there is of you.

SELF-RESPECT

When thou hast profited so much that thou respectest thyself, thou mayest let go thy tutor – *Seneca*

Everyone stamps his own value on himself – *Johann Christoph Friedrich von Schiller*

Above all things, reverence yourself – *Pythagoras*

Our own heart, and not other men's opinions of us, forms our true honour – *Schiller*

To have a respect for ourselves guides our morals; and to have a deference for others governs our manners – *Laurence Sterne*

Self-respect – that corner-stone of all virtue – *Sir John Herschel*

Self-respect is the noblest garment with which a man may clothe himself – *Samuel Smiles*

Self-reverence, self-knowledge, self-control, these three alone lead life to sovereign power – *Alfred, Lord Tennyson*

One self-approving hour whole years outweighs – *Alexander Pope*
Behaviour is a mirror in which everyone shows his image.

SENSIBILITY

Too much sensibility creates unhappiness; too much insensibility leads
    to crime – *Charles Maurice de Talleyrand-Périgord*
Sensibility is the power of woman – *Johann Kaspar Lavater*
Dearly bought the hidden treasure, / Finer feelings can bestow; / Chords
    that vibrate sweetest pleasure, / Thrill the deepest notes of woe –
    Robert Burns
Men's feelings are always purest and most glowing in the hour of
    meeting and of farewell – *Jean Paul Richter*
Laughter and tears are meant to turn the wheels of the same machinery
    of sensibility; one is wind-power, and the other water-power; that is
    all – *Oliver Wendell Holmes*
Sensibility is neither good nor evil in itself, but in its application – *Hannah
    More*
The heart that is soonest awake to the flowers is always the first to be
    touched with the thorns.

SENSITIVENESS

There are moments when petty slights are harder to bear than even a
    serious injury. Men have died of the festering of a gnat-bite – *Cecil
    Danby*
Quick sensitiveness is inseparable from a ready understanding – *Joseph
    Addison*
That chastity of honour which felt a stain like a wound – *Edmund Burke*
Sensitiveness is closely allied to egotism. Indeed excessive sensitiveness
    is only another name for morbid self-consciousness. The cure for it is
    to make more of our objects, and less of ourselves.

SENSUALITY

I have never known a man who was sensual in his youth, who was
    high-minded when old – *Charles Sumner*
What if one might have all the pleasures of the world for the asking? Who
    would so unman himself as by accepting them to desert his soul and
    become a perpetual slave to his senses? – *Seneca*
Sordid and infamous sensuality, the most dreadful evil that issued from
    the box of Pandora, corrupts the entire heart and eradicates every
    virtue – *François de Fénelon*
Sin the mother and shame the daughter of lewdness – *Sir Philip Sidney*

A youth of sensuality and intemperance delivers over a worn-out body to old age – *Cicero*

He that lives in the kingdom of sense, shall die in the kingdom of sorrow.

SHAME

I regard that man as lost who has lost his sense of shame – *Plautus*

Shame may restrain what law does not prohibit – *Seneca*

I never wonder to see men wicked, but I often wonder to see them not ashamed – *Jonathan Swift*

Shame is nature's hasty conscience – *Maria Edgeworth*

Be assured that when once a woman begins to be ashamed of what she ought not to be ashamed of, she will not be ashamed of what she ought – *Livy*

Of all evils to the generous, shame is the most deadly pang.

Those who fear not guilt yet start at shame.

SICKNESS

Disease, opening our eyes to the realities of life, is an indirect blessing – *Hosea Ballou*

In sickness the soul begins to dress herself for immortality – *Jeremy Taylor*

Sickness is a sort of early old age; it teaches us a diffidence in our earthly state – *Alexander Pope*

Sickness is the vengeance of nature for the violation of her laws.

That which is painful to the body may be profitable to the soul.

SILENCE

He can never speak well, who knows not how to hold his peace – *Plutarch*

True silence is the rest of the mind – *William Penn*

Silence is the understanding of fools, and one of the virtues of the wise – *Nicolas Boileau*

I do know of these / That therefore only are reputed wise / For saying nothing – *William Shakespeare*

The silence often of pure innocence / Persuades when speaking fails – *Shakespeare*

Silence is the highest wisdom of a fool as speech is the greatest trial of a wise man – *Francis Quarles*

Speech is great, but silence is greater – *Thomas Carlyle*

The silence of the place was like a sleep, so full of rest it seemed – *Henry Wadsworth Longfellow*

Silence is the perfectest herald of joy: I were but little happy if I could say how much – *Shakespeare*

The temple of our purest thoughts is silence – *Sarah Josepha Hale*
Silence in woman is like speech in men; deny it who can – *Ben Jonson*
The unspoken word never does harm – *Lajos Kossuth*
If thou desirest to be held wise, be so wise as to hold thy tongue – *Quarles*
Blessed is the man who, having nothing to say, abstains from giving
    wordy evidence of the fact – *George Eliot*
It is only reason that teaches silence; the heart teaches us to speak – *Jean
    Paul Richter*
None preaches better than the ant, and she says nothing – *Benjamin
    Franklin*
I think the first virtue is to restrain the tongue; he approaches nearest to
    the gods who knows how to be silent, even though he is in the right –
    Cato
Silence is one of the great arts of conversation; there is not only an art,
    but an eloquence in it – *Cicero*
Of all virtues, Zeno made choice of silence; for by it, said he, I hear other
    men's imperfections, and conceal my own.
Silence is a virtue in those who are deficient in understanding.
Silence, when nothing need be said, is the eloquence of discretion.
It is the wise head that makes the still tongue.
Fellows who have no tongues are often all eyes and ears.
Silence is the ornament and safeguard of the ignorant.
If you would pass for more than your value, say little. It is easier to look
    wise than to talk wisely.
Learn to hold thy tongue. Five words cost Zacharias forty weeks of
    silence.
A judicious silence is always better than truth spoken without
    charity.
If a word be worth one shekel, silence is worth two.
Silence does not mean contentment.
Silence is the gratitude of true affection.
If you keep your mouth shut, you won't put your foot in it.
Silence is a most perfect expression of scorn.
Silence is the one great art of conversation.

SIMPLICITY

Simplicity, of all things, is the hardest to be copied – *Richard Steele*
Whose nature is so far from doing harms, / That he suspects none –
    William Shakespeare
Simplicity of character is the natural result of profound thought – *William
    Hazlitt*
When thought is too weak to be simply expressed, it is a clear proof that it
    should be rejected – *Marquis de Vauvenargues*

A childlike mind, in its simplicity, practises that science of good to which the wise may be blind – *Johann Christoph Friedrich von Schiller*

Simplicity is Nature's first step, and the last of Art.

It is far more difficult to be simple than to be complicated.

The greatest truths are the simplest; and so are the greatest men.

SIN

Sin is, essentially, a departure from God – *Martin Luther*

If thou wouldst conquer thy weakness thou must never gratify it – *William Penn*

Few love to hear the sins they love to act – *William Shakespeare*

The deadliest sin were the consciousness of no sin – *Thomas Carlyle*

The wages that sin bargains for with the sinner are life, pleasure, and profit; but the wages it pays him are death, torment, and destruction – *Robert South*

When we think of death, a thousand sins, which we have trodden as worms beneath our feet, rise up against us as flaming serpents – *Walter Scott*

Sin may open bright as the morning, but it will end dark as night – *De Witt Talmage*

Whatever disunites man from God disunites man from man – *Edmund Burke*

It is not only what we do, but also what we do not do, for which we are accountable – *Molière*

No sin is small as no grain of sand is small in the mechanism of a watch – *Jeremy Taylor*

Man-like it is, to fall into sin; / Fiend-like it is, to dwell therein; / Christ-like it is, for sin to grieve; / God-like it is, all sin to leave – *Henry Wadsworth Longfellow*

Pleasure's a sin and sometimes sin's a pleasure – *Lord Byron*

He who sins against men may fear discovery, but he who sins against God is sure of it.

If you would be free from sin, fly temptation.

Sin writes history, goodness is silent.

SINCERITY

Inward sincerity will of course influence the outward deportment – *Laurence Sterne*

His words are bonds, his oaths are oracles, / His love sincere, his thoughts immaculate, / His tears pure messengers sent from his heart, / His heart as far from fraud as heaven from earth – *William Shakespeare*

Sincerity and truth are the basis of every virtue – *Confucius*
A silent address is the genuine eloquence of sincerity – *Oliver Goldsmith*
Sincerity is the face of the soul.
Sincerity, a deep, genuine, heartfelt sincerity is a trait of true and noble manhood.

SLANDER

The worthiest people are the most injured by slander, as it is the best fruit which the birds have been pecking at – *Jonathan Swift*

Slander is the revenge of a coward, and dissimulation his defence – *Samuel Johnson*

Slander, / Whose sting is sharper than the sword's – *William Shakespeare*

False and malicious reports which vex the spirit, and consequently impair health, is a degree of murder – *Walter Raleigh*

Slugs crawl and crawl over our cabbages, like the world's slander over a good name. You may kill them, it is true, but there is the slime – *Douglas William Jerrold*

There would not be so many open mouths if there were not so many open ears – *Bishop Hall*

He, who would free from malice pass his days, / Must live obscure, and never merit praise – *John Gay*

Oh! many a shaft at random sent, / Finds mark the archer little meant; / And many a word, at random spoken, / May soothe or wound a heart that's broken – *Walter Scott*

So thou be good, slander doth but approve / Thy worth the greater – *Shakespeare*

The slander of some people is as great a recommendation as the praise of others – *Henry Fielding*

We cannot control the evil tongues of others, but a good life enables us to despise them – *Cato*

Slander is a vice that strikes a double blow, wounding both him that commits, and him against whom it is committed.

When will talkers refrain from evil-speaking? When listeners refrain from evil-hearing.

Slanderers are like flies, that pass all over a man's good parts to light only on his sores.

See also GOSSIP.

SLEEP

Our foster-nurse of nature is repose – *William Shakespeare*
Sleep, to the homeless thou art home; the friendless find in thee a friend – *Ebenezer Elliott*

Sleep, the antechamber of the grave – *Jean Paul Richter*
One hour's sleep before midnight is worth two after – *Henry Fielding*
Downy sleep, death's counterfeit – *Shakespeare*
God gives sleep to the bad, in order that the good may be undisturbed – *Sádi*
When one turns over in bed, it is time to turn out – *Duke of Wellington*
Weariness / Can snore upon the flint, when resty sloth / Finds the down pillow hard – *Shakespeare*
An hour in the morning is worth two at night.
See also REPOSE, REST.

SLOTH

Sloth, like rust, consumes faster than labour wears, while the key often used is always bright – *Benjamin Franklin*
Sloth, if it has prevented many crimes, has also smothered many virtues – *Charles Caleb Colton*
Flee sloth, for the indolence of the soul is the decay of the body – *Cato*
Sloth makes all things difficult, but industry all easy – *Franklin*
Sloth never arrived at the attainment of a good wish – *Miguel de Cervantes Saavedra*
See also IDLENESS, INACTIVITY.

SMILES

A smile is the whisper of a laugh – *child's definition*
A face that cannot smile is never good – *Martial*
A smile is the light in the window of a face – *Henry Ward Beecher*
A smile is the colour which love wears – *Beecher*
A face that cannot smile is like a bud that cannot blossom – *Beecher*
A smile is something you can always wear without being old-fashioned.
A smile a day brings a friend your way.
The curve that can set a lot of things straight is a smile.

SNEERS

A sneer is the weapon of the weak.

SOCIETY

There are four varieties in society; the lovers, the ambitious, observers, and fools. The fools are the happiest – *Hippolyte Adolphe Taine*
We are more sociable, and get on better with people by the heart than the intellect – *Jean de La Bruyère*

Society is no comfort / To one not sociable – *William Shakespeare*
No company is preferable to bad company – *Charles Caleb Colton*

SOLITUDE

A wise man is never less alone than when he is alone – *Jonathan Swift*
Solitude is a good school, but the world is the best theatre – *Jeremy Taylor*
If from society we learn to live, it is solitude should teach us how to die –
    Lord Byron
Solitude, seeming a sanctuary, proves a grave; / A sepulchre in which the
    living lie, / Where all good qualities grow sick and die – *William
    Cowper*
Solitude is dangerous to reason without being favourable to virtue –
    Samuel Johnson
Solitude cherishes great virtues and destroys little ones – *Sydney Smith*
If the mind loves solitude, it has thereby acquired a loftier character.
One hour of thoughtful solitude may nerve the heart for days of conflict.
Through the wide world he only is alone who lives not for another.
Solitude bears the same relation to the mind that sleep does to the body.
Solitude shows us what we should be; society shows us what we are.
Solitude: a good place to visit, but a poor place to stay.

SORROW

Sorrow breaks seasons and reposing hours, / Makes the night morning,
    and the noontide night – *William Shakespeare*
Never morning wore to evening, but some heart did break – *Alfred, Lord
    Tennyson*
The deeper the sorrow the less tongue it has – *Talmud*
He that goes a-borrowing goes a-sorrowing – *Benjamin Franklin*
Give sorrow words; the grief that does not speak / Whispers the o'er-
    fraught heart and bids it break – *Shakespeare*
He that hath pity on another man's sorrow shall be free from it himself –
    Walter Raleigh
One can never be the judge of another's grief – *François de Chateaubriand*
One sorrow never comes but brings an heir, / That may succeed as his
    inheritor – *Shakespeare*
Social sorrow loses half its pain – *Samuel Johnson*
Sorrows humanize our race; tears are the showers that fertilize the world
    – *Owen Meredith*
Light griefs do speak, while sorrow's tongue is bound – *Seneca*
A small sorrow distracts; a great one makes us collected – *Jean Paul Richter*
Sorrow is only one of the lower notes in the oratorio of our blessedness.
Sorrows are our best educators. A man can see further through a tear
    than a telescope.

Earth hath no sorrow that heaven cannot heal.

Sorrows remembered sweeten present joy.

Whole years of joy glide unperceived away, while sorrow counts the minutes as they pass.

See also GRIEF, SADNESS.

SOUL

The wealth of a soul is measured by how much it can feel; its poverty by how little – *William Rounseville Alger*

Life is the soul's nursery – its training place for the destinies of eternity – *William Makepeace Thackeray*

The body, that is but dust; the soul, it is a bud of eternity.

SPEECH

Speech is a faculty given to man to conceal his thoughts – *Charles Maurice de Talleyrand-Périgord*

A superior man is modest in his speech, but exceeds in his actions – *Confucius*

There is a wide difference between speaking to deceive, and being silent to be impenetrable – *Voltaire*

Speech is silvern, silence is golden; speech is human, silence is divine – *German proverb*

Speeches cannot be made long enough for the speakers, nor short enough for the hearers.

A printed speech is like a dried flower, the colour is faded and the perfume gone.

Never rise to speak till you have something to say; and when you have said it, cease.

Think all you speak, but speak not all you think.

More have repented of speech than of silence.

One of the most important ingredients in a recipe of speech-making is plenty of shortening.

Speak softly, and carry a big stick.

The more you say, the less people remember.

Talking is sharing but listening is caring.

See also TALKING, TONGUE.

STARS

Ye stars, that are the poetry of heaven! – *Lord Byron*

The lovely stars, the forget-me-nots of angels – *Henry Wadsworth Longfellow*

The gems of heaven, that gild night's sable throne – *John Dryden*

The stars are mansions built by nature's hand – *William Wordsworth*

The evening star, love's harbinger, appeared – *John Milton*

The preachers of beauty, which light the world with their admonishing smile – *Ralph Waldo Emerson*

STATESMANSHIP

True statesmanship is the art of changing a nation from what it is into what it ought to be – *William Rounseville Alger*

The worth of a state, in the long run, is the worth of the individuals composing it – *John Stuart Mill*

Honest statemanship is the wise employment of individual meannesses for the public good – *Abraham Lincoln*

If I had wished to raise up a race of statesmen higher than politicians, animated not by greed or selfishness, by policy or party, I would familiarize the boys of the land with the characters of the Bible – *John Hall*

What morality requires, true statesmanship should accept – *Edmund Burke*

The three great ends for a statesman are security to possessors, facility to acquirers, and liberty and hope to the people – *Samuel Taylor Coleridge*

It is curious that we pay statesmen for what they say, not for what they do, and judge them from what they do, not from what they say – *Charles Caleb Colton*

A statesman, we are told, should follow public opinion as a coachman follows his horses, having firm hold on the reins, and guiding them.

STATION

Eminent stations make great men more great, and little ones less – *Jean de La Bruyère*

They that stand high have many blasts to shake them – *William Shakespeare*

The place should not honour the man, but the man the place – *Agesilaus*

True dignity is never gained by place, and never lost when honours are withdrawn – *Philip Massinger*

Our distinctions do not lie in the places we occupy, but in the grace and dignity with which we fill them.

He who thinks his place below him will certainly be below his place.

See also PLACE, RANK.

STRENGTH

It is excellent / To have a giant's strength; but it is tyrannous / To use it like a giant – *William Shakespeare*

Strength, wanting judgement and policy to rule, overturneth itself – *Horace*

Strength alone knows conflict; weakness is below even defeat, and is born vanquished – *Mme Swetchine*

Strength is in men as in soils, where sometimes there is a vein of gold which the owner knows not of – *Jonathan Swift*

Strength is born in the deep silence of long-suffering hearts; not amidst joy – *Felicia Dorothea Hemans*

The tree falls not at the first stroke.

STUDY

There are more men ennobled by study than by nature – *Cicero*

He that studies only men will get the body of knowledge without the soul; and he that studies only books, the soul without the body – *Charles Caleb Colton*

They are not the best students who are most dependent on books. What can be got out of them is at best only material; a man must build his house for himself – *George Macdonald*

As the turning of logs will make a dull fire burn, so change of studies will a dull brain – *Henry Wadsworth Longfellow*

A boy will learn more true wisdom in a public school in a year than by a private education in five. It is not from masters, but from their equals that youth learn a knowledge of the world – *Oliver Goldsmith*

There is an unspeakable pleasure attending the life of a voluntary student – *Goldsmith*

The more we study the more we discover our ignorance – *Percy Bysshe Shelley*

As land is improved by sowing it with various seeds, so is the mind by exercising it with different studies – *Pliny the Younger*

The understanding is more relieved by change of study than by total inactivity.

STYLE

Style may be defined, 'proper words in proper places' – *Jonathan Swift*

With many readers, brilliancy of style passes for affluence of thought – *Henry Wadsworth Longfellow*

Generally speaking, an author's style is a faithful copy of his mind – *Johann Wolfgang von Goethe*

Any style formed in imitation of some model must be affected and strait-laced – *E. P. Whipple*

A man's style is nearly as much a part of himself as his face – *François de Fénelon*

A pure style in writing results from the rejection of everything superfluous – *Mme Neckar*

Clear writers, like clear fountains, do not seem so deep as they are – *Walter Savage Landor*

A great writer possesses, so to speak, an individual and unchangeable style, which does not permit him easily to preserve the anonymous – *Voltaire*

Long sentences in a short composition are like large rooms in a little house – *William Shenstone*

In what he leaves unsaid I discover a master of style – *Johann Christoph Friedrich von Schiller*

When we meet with a natural style we are surprised and delighted, for we expected to find an author, and have found a man – *Blaise Pascal*

Obscurity and affectation are the two great faults of style – *Thomas Babington Macaulay*

The style shows the man.

Style is a man's own; it is a part of his nature.

When you doubt between words, use the plainest, the commonest, the most idiomatic. Eschew fine words as you would rouge, and love simple ones as you would native roses on your cheek.

SUBLIMITY

One source of sublimity is infinity – *Edmund Burke*

The sublime is the temple-step of religion. A great misfortune, a great blessing, a great crime, a noble action are building sites for a child's church – *Jean Paul Richter*

From the sublime to the ridiculous there is but one step – *Napoleon Bonaparte*

The sublimest thoughts are conceived by the intellect when it is excited by pious emotion.

SUBTLETY

Subtlety may deceive you; integrity never will – *Oliver Cromwell*

Cunning is the dwarf of wisdom – *William Rounseville Alger*

Cunning pays no regard to virtue, and is but the low mimic of wisdom – *Henry St John Bolingbroke*

SUCCESS

Moderation is commonly firm, and firmness is commonly successful – *Samuel Johnson*

He that would make sure of success should keep his passion cool, and his expectation low – *Jeremy Collier*

Nothing can seem foul to those that win – *William Shakespeare*

Success is full of promise till we get it, and then it is as a last year's nest, from which the bird has flown – *Henry Ward Beecher*

In most things success depends on knowing how long it takes to succeed – *Charles de Montesquieu*

Success soon palls. The joyous time is when the breeze first strikes your sails, and the waters rustle under your bows – *Charles Buxton*

Success has a great tendency to conceal and throw a veil over the evil deeds of men – *Demosthenes*

To know a man, observe how he wins his object, rather than how he loses it; for when we fail, our pride supports; when we succeed, it betrays us – *Charles Caleb Colton*

The surest way not to fail is to determine to succeed – *Richard Brinsley Sheridan*

Not what men do worthily but what they do successfully is what history makes haste to record – *Beecher*

Success serves men as a pedestal; it makes them look larger, if reflection does not measure them – *Joseph Joubert*

Nothing succeeds so well as success – *Charles Maurice de Talleyrand-Périgord*

Success produces confidence; confidence relaxes industry, and negligence ruins the reputation which accuracy had raised – *Samuel Johnson*

Let them call it mischief; when it is past and prospered, it will be virtue – *Ben Jonson*

It is not in mortals to command success, but we will do more, we will deserve it – *Joseph Addison*

Had I succeeded well, I had been reckoned among the wise; our minds are so disposed to judge from the event – *Euripides*

If you wish success in life, make perseverance your bosom friend, experience your wise counsellor, caution your elder brother, and hope your guardian genius – *Joseph Addison*

The men who are always fortunate cannot easily have a great reverence for virtue – *Cicero*

The talent of success is nothing more than doing what you can do well, and doing well whatever you do without a thought of fame. If it comes at all it will come because it is not sought after – *Henry Wadsworth Longfellow*

Success makes success, as money makes money – *Nicolas Sébastian Roch Chamfort*

Didst thou never hear / That things ill got had ever bad success? – *Shakespeare*

To character and success, two things, contradictory as they may seem, must go together – humble dependence and manly independence;

humble dependence on God, and manly reliance on self – *William Wordsworth*

Applause waits on success; the fickle multitude, like the light straw that floats along the stream, glide with the current still, and follow fortune – *Benjamin Franklin*

The secret of success is how you survive failure.

A man will not climb the ladder of success with his hands in his pockets.

There is only one road to success – work, method, discipline.

Usually success is not so much a question of ability as a question of applicability.

By working faithfully eight hours a day, you may become a boss and work twelve hours a day.

Success requires pains and brains.

The secret of success is hard work. Maybe that is why it has remained a secret to so many.

Success in life is a matter not so much of talent or opportunity as of concentration and perseverance.

If you wish your merit to be known acknowledge that of other people.

All the proud virtue of this vaunting world fawns on success and power, however acquired.

Everybody finds out, sooner or later, that all success worth having is founded on Christian rules of conduct.

Success at first doth many times undo men at last.

The greatest results in life are usually attained by simple means and the exercise of ordinary qualities. These may for the most part be summed in these two – common sense and perseverance.

To become an able and successful man in any profession three things are necessary: nature, study and practice.

Success to the strongest, who are always at last, the wisest and best.

Concentrate and the world is yours.

The only 'good time coming' we are justified in hoping for is that which we are capable of making for ourselves.

There is a glare about worldly success, which is very apt to dazzle men's eyes.

No crime's so great as daring to excel.

The secret of success is constancy to purpose.

The tree is known by its fruits; not by its roots.

SUFFERING

Suffering well borne is better than suffering removed – *Henry Ward Beecher*

Not being untutored in suffering, I learn to pity those in affliction –
   Virgil

The most massive characters are seamed with scars – *E. H. Chapin*

Know how sublime a thing it is to suffer and be strong – *Henry Wadsworth
   Longfellow*

Suffering is the surest means of making us truthful to ourselves – *Jean
   Charles de Sismondi*

We need to suffer that we may learn to pity – *L. E. Landon*

It requires more courage to suffer than to die – *Napoleon Bonaparte*

Out of suffering have emerged the strongest souls.

Night brings out stars, as sorrow shows us truths.

Forgiveness is rarely perfect except in the breasts of those who have
   suffered.

Swift run the sands of time except in the hour of pain.

See also PAIN.

SUICIDE

When all the blandishments of life are gone, the coward sneaks to death;
   the brave lives on – *Martial*

Against self-slaughter / There is a prohibition so divine / That cravens my
   weak hand – *William Shakespeare*

O deaf to nature and to Heaven's command, / Against thyself to lift the
   murdering hand! / Oh, damned despair, to shun the living light, /
   And plunge thy guilty soul in endless night! – *Lucretius*

True heroism consists in being superior to the ills of life in whatever
   shape they may challenge him to combat – *Napoleon Bonaparte*

He is not valiant that dares to die; but he that boldly bears calamity –
   Philip Massinger

Suicide sometimes proceeds from cowardice, but not always; for
   cowardice sometimes prevents it; since as many live because they are
   afraid to die, as die because they are afraid to live – *Charles Caleb Colton*

The dread of something after death / . . . puzzles the will, / And makes us
   rather bear those ills we have / Than fly to others that we know not of
   – *Shakespeare*

It is cowardice to shun the trials and crosses of life, not undergoing
   death because it is honourable, but to avoid evil – *Aristotle*

There are some vile and contemptible men who allowing themselves to
   be conquered by misfortune, seek a refuge in death.

The miserablest day we live there is many a better thing to do than
   die.

Those men who destroy a healthful constitution of body by intemperance kill themselves as those who hang, or poison, or drown
   themselves.

SUPERSTITION

Superstitions are, for the most part, but the shadows of great truths –
Tryon Edwards

Religion worships God, while superstition profanes that worship –
Seneca

Superstition is a senseless fear of God; religion the intelligent and pious
worship of the deity – *Cicero*

Superstition is the only religion of which base souls are capable – *Joseph
Joubert*

You cannot educate a man wholly out of the superstitious fears which
were implanted in his imagination, no matter how utterly his reason
may reject them – *Oliver Wendell Holmes*

A peasant can no more help believing in a traditional superstition than a
horse can help trembling when he sees a camel – *George Eliot*

Superstition is the poetry of life – inherent in man's nature – *Johann
Wolfgang von Goethe*

Superstition is not, as has been defined, an excess of religious feeling,
but a misdirection of it – *Richard Whately*

Superstition renders a man a fool, and scepticism makes him mad –
Henry Fielding

The master of superstition is the people, and in all superstition wise men
follow fools – *Francis Bacon*

Superstition is but the fear of belief; religion is confidence and trust.

Open biographical volumes wherever you please, and the man who has
no faith in religion is the one who hath faith in a nightmare and
ghosts.

SURETY

He that would be master of his own, must not be bound for another –
Benjamin Franklin

He that payeth another man's debt seeketh his own decay – *Lord Burleigh*

If thou force him for whom thou art bound to pay he will become thy
enemy; if thou pay it thyself, thou wilt become a beggar – *Walter
Raleigh*

Endorsing character is hazardous; endorsing credit, presumptuous –
C. Simmons

SUSPICION

To be suspicious is to invite treachery – *Voltaire*

There is no rule more invariable than that we are paid for our suspicions
by finding what we suspect – *Henry David Thoreau*

Suspicion always haunts the guilty mind; / The thief doth fear each bush an officer – *William Shakespeare*

Ignorance is the mother of suspicion – *William Rounseville Alger*

Whose own hard dealings teaches them suspect / The thoughts of others – *Shakespeare*

A brother noble, / Whose nature is so far from doing harms / That he suspects none – *Shakespeare*

At the gate which suspicion enters, love and confidence go out.

He that lives in perpetual suspicion lives the life of a sentinel never relieved, whose business it is to look out for and expect an enemy, which is an evil not very far short of perishing by him.

The virtue of a coward is suspicion.

Suspicion is the poison of true friendship.

One of the principal ingredients in the happiness of childhood is freedom from suspicion.

SYMPATHY

Next to love, sympathy is the divinest passion of the human heart – *Edmund Burke*

More helpful than all wisdom or counsel is one draught of simple human pity that will not forsake us – *George Eliot*

With a soul that ever felt the sting of sorrow, sorrow is a sacred thing – *William Cowper*

Our sympathy is never very deep unless founded on our own feelings – *L. E. Landon*

All sympathy not consistent with acknowledged virtue is but digested selfishness – *Samuel Taylor Coleridge*

Sympathy wanting, all is wanting. Personal magnetism is the conductor of the sacred spark that puts us in human communion, and gives us to company, conversation, and ourselves – *Amos Bronson Alcott*

A helping word to one in trouble is often like a switch on a railroad-track – an inch between wreck and smooth-rolling prosperity – *Henry Ward Beecher*

The world has no sympathy with any but positive griefs; it will pity you for what you lose, but never for what you lack – *Mme Swetchine*

Grief is a stone that bears one down, but two bear it lightly – *Wilhelm Hauff*

So long as you can sweeten another's pain, life is not in vain – *Helen Keller*

A trouble shared is a trouble halved.

The generous heart should scorn a pleasure which gives others pain.

He who bestows compassion communicates his own soul.

Open your hearts to sympathy, but close them to despondency.

Sympathy is like hair; a lot of it is not the real thing.
Sympathy is the gift of knowing without being told.

TACT

Never join with your friend when he abuses his horse or his wife, unless
    the one is to be sold, and the other to be buried – *Charles Caleb Colton*
Tact comes as much from goodness of heart as from fineness of taste.
Tact supplies the place of many talents.
A little tact and wise management may often evade resistance, and carry
    a point, where direct force might be in vain.
Talent is power; tact is skill.
Tact will take a person further than cleverness.
See also DISCRETION.

TALKING

It has been well observed, that the tongue discovers the state of the mind
    no less than that of the body; but, in either case, before the philo-
    sopher or the physician can judge, the patient must open his mouth –
    Charles Caleb Colton
The tongue of a fool is the key of his counsel, which, in a wise man,
    wisdom hath in keeping – *Socrates*
They think too little who talk too much – *John Dryden*
Such as thy words are, such will thy affections be esteemed; and such
    will thy deeds as thy affections, and such thy life as thy deeds –
    Socrates
Talkers are no good doers – *William Shakespeare*
Those who have but little business to attend to are great talkers. The less
    men think, the more they talk – *Charles de Montesquieu*
Speaking much is a sign of vanity; for he that is lavish in words is a
    niggard in deed – *Walter Raleigh*
As empty vessels make the loudest sound, so they that have least wit are
    the greatest babblers – *Plato*
The talkative listen to no one, for they are ever speaking. And the first
    evil that attends those who know not how to be silent is that they hear
    nothing – *Plutarch*
Does a man speak foolishly? Suffer him gladly, for you are wise. Does he
    speak erroneously? Stop such a man's mouth with sound words that
    cannot be gainsaid. Does he speak truly? Rejoice in the truth – *Oliver
    Cromwell*
Brisk talkers are usually slow thinkers – *Jonathan Swift*
There is the same difference between the tongues of some as between the

hour and the minute hand; one goes ten times as fast, and the other signifies ten times as much – *Sydney Smith*
A full tongue and an empty brain are seldom parted – *Francis Quarles*
What a spendthrift he is of his tongue! – *Shakespeare*
It is a sad thing when men have neither the wit to speak well, nor judgement to hold their tongues – *Jean de La Bruyère*
I have never been hurt by anything I didn't say – *Calvin Coolidge*
The silent bear no witness against themselves – *Aldous Huxley*
They talk most who have the least to say.
A wise man reflects before he speaks; a fool speaks, and then reflects on what he has uttered.
Great talkers are like leaky vessels; everything runs out of them.
A civil guest will no more talk all than eat all the feast.
Wise men talk because they have something to say; fools, because they would like to say something.
If thy words be too luxuriant, confine them, lest they confine thee.
Wise men never talk to make time; they talk to save it.
Your tongue can undo everything you do.
See also SPEECH, TONGUE.

TAXES

Taxes make vices very good patriots – *Napoleon Bonaparte*
Taxes are the sinews of the state – *Cicero*
We are taxed twice as much by our idleness, three times as much by our pride, and four times as much by our folly; and from these taxes the commissioners cannot ease or deliver us by allowing an abatement – *Benjamin Franklin*
Taxing is an easy business. Any projector can contrive new impositions; any bungler can add to the old; but is it altogether wise to have no other bounds to your impositions than the patience of those who are to bear them? – *Edmund Burke*
Kings and government ought to shear, not skin, their sheep – *Robert Herrick*
Millions for defence; not a cent for tribute.
Born to live – taxed to death.
Taxation without representation is injustice and oppression. It brought on the American Revolution, and gave birth to a free and mighty nation.

TEACHING

I am indebted to my father for living, but to my teacher for living well – *Alexander the Great*

To know how to suggest is the art of teaching – *Henri Frédéric Amiel*

The true aim of everyone who aspires to be a teacher should be not to impart his own opinions, but to kindle minds – *Frederick William Robertson*

In the education of children there is nothing like alluring the interest and affection; otherwise you only make so many asses laden with books – *Michel Eyquem de Montaigne*

Thoroughly to teach another is the best way to learn yourself – *Tryon Edwards*

The teacher who is attempting to teach without inspiring the pupil with a desire to learn is hammering on cold iron – *Horace Mann*

Those who educate children well are more to be honoured than even their parents, for those only give them life, those the art of living well – *Aristotle*

If ever I am a teacher, it will be to learn more than to teach – *Mme Deluzy*

To waken interest and kindle enthusiasm is the sure way to teach easily and successfully – *Tryon Edwards*

He that governs well, leads the blind; but he that teaches, gives them eyes – *Robert South*

It would be a great advantage to some schoolmasters if they would steal two hours a day from their pupils, and give their own minds the benefit of the robbery.

The teachings of youth make impressions on the mind and heart that are to last forever.

The highest function of the teacher consists not so much in imparting knowledge as in stimulating the pupil in its love and pursuit.

Whatever you would have your children become, strive to exhibit in your own lives and conversations.

If, in instructing a child, you are vexed with it for want of adroitness, try, if you have never tried before, to write with your left hand, and then remember that a child is all left hand.

TEARS

There is a sacredness in tears. They are not the mark of weakness, but of power – *Washington Irving*

Tears are the safety-valves of the heart – *Albert Smith*

Tears are sometimes the happiest smiles of love – *Stendhal*

Love is loveliest when embalmed in tears – *Walter Scott*

All my mother came into mine eyes / And gave me up to tears – *William Shakespeare*

My plenteous joys, / Wanton in fulness, seek to hide themselves / In drops of sorrow – *Shakespeare*

Tears hinder sorrow from becoming despair – *James Henry Leigh Hunt*

Tears are often the telescope through which men see far into heaven –
Henry Ward Beecher

Tears are the softening showers which cause the seed of heaven to spring
up in the human heart – *Scott*

What a hell of witchcraft lies / In the small orb of one particular tear! –
Shakespeare

Pride dries the tears of anger and vexation; humility those of grief – *Mme
Swetchine*

Weep for love, but not for anger; a cold rain will never bring flowers.

Tearless grief bleeds inwardly.

Blest tears of soul-felt penitence.

Hide not thy tears; it is nature's mark to know an honest heart by.

Beauty's tears are lovelier than her smiles.

Scorn the proud man that is ashamed to weep.

Those tender tears that humanize the soul.

TEMPER

Men who have had a great deal of experience learn not to lose their
tempers – *Victor Cherbuliez*

A tart temper never mellows with age; and a sharp tongue is the only
edged tool that grows keener with constant use – *Washington Irving*

Temper, if ungoverned, governs the whole man – *Lord Shaftesbury*

A man who cannot command his temper should not think of being a man
of business – *Lord Chesterfield*

A man's venom poisons himself more than his victim – *Charles Buxton*

If religion does nothing for your temper it has done nothing for your
soul.

The happiness and misery of men depend no less on temper than
fortune.

Those who are surly and imperious to their inferiors are generally
humble, flattering, and cringing to their superiors.

Of all bad things by which mankind are curst, / Their own bad tempers
surely are the worst.

With good temper in his wife, the earthly felicity of man is complete.

The artistic temperament is a disease that afflicts amateurs.

TEMPERANCE

Temperance is the lawful gratification of a natural and healthy appetite –
John B. Gough

Temperance puts wood on the fire, meal in the barrel, flour in the tub,
money in the purse, credit in the country, contentment in the house,

clothes on the children, vigour in the body, intelligence in the brain, and spirit in the whole constitution – *Benjamin Franklin*

Temperance and labour are the two best physicians; the one sharpens the appetite – the other prevents indulgence to excess – *Jean Jacques Rousseau*

Drinking water neither makes a man sick nor in debt nor his wife a widow – *John Neal*

Though I look old, yet I am strong and lusty; / For in my youth I never did apply / Hot and rebellious liquors in my blood – *William Shakespeare*

Great men should drink with harness on their throats – *Shakespeare*

Temperance is reason's girdle, and passion's bride – *Jeremy Taylor*

I have four good reasons for being an abstainer – my head is clearer, my health is better, my heart is lighter, and my purse is heavier.

I dare not drink for my own sake, I ought not to drink for my neighbour's sake.

If it is a small sacrifice to you to discontinue the use of wine, do it for the sake of others; if a great sacrifice, do it for your own.

TEMPTATION

Temptations are a file which rub off much of the rust of our self-confidence – *François de Fénelon*

No man is matriculated to the art of life till he has been well tempted – *George Eliot*

'Tis one thing to be tempted . . . / Another thing to fall – *William Shakespeare*

Every temptation is great or small according as the man is – *Jeremy Taylor*

The devil tempts us not. It is we tempt him, beckoning his skill with opportunity – *George Eliot*

Learn to say no; it will be of more use to you than to be able to read Latin – *Charles Haddon Spurgeon*

Occasions of adversity best discover how great virtue or strength each one hath. For occasions do not make a man frail, but show what he is – *Thomas à Kempis*

Most confidence has still most cause to doubt – *John Dryden*

Temptations without imply desires within – *Henry Ward Beecher*

Better shun the bait than struggle in the snare – *Dryden*

He who has no mind to trade with the devil should be so wise as to keep away from his shop – *Robert South*

Some temptations come to the industrious, but all temptations attack the idle – *Spurgeon*

It is the bright day that brings forth the adder; / And that craves wary walking – *Shakespeare*

How oft the sight of means to do ill deeds / Makes ill deeds done! – *Shakespeare*

Few men have virtue to withstand the highest bidder – *George Washington*

Sometimes we are devils to ourselves, / When we will tempt the frailty of our powers, / Presuming on their changeful potency – *Shakespeare*

Do not give dalliance / To much the rein: the strongest oaths are straw / To the fire i' the blood – *Shakespeare*

No degree of temptation justifies any degree of sin – *Nathaniel Parker Willis*

Most dangerous / Is that temptation that doth goad us on / To sin in loving virtue – *Shakespeare*

The absence of temptation is the absence of virtue – *Johann Wolfgang von Goethe*

One effort to resist temptation strengthens the will for the next encounter – *Walter M. Gallichan*

To pray against temptations, and yet to rush into occasions, is to thrust your fingers into the fire and then pray they might not be burnt!

Temptation is the fire that brings up the scum of the heart.

Opportunity often makes the thief.

Every moment of resistance to temptation is a victory.

I see the devil's hook, and yet cannot help nibbling at his bait.

A vacant mind invites dangerous inmates.

TENDERNESS

When death, the great reconciler, has come, it is never our tenderness that we repent of, but our severity – *George Eliot*

Tenderness is the repose of love – *Antoine Rivarol*

The less tenderness a man has in his nature the more he requires of others – *Rahel*

There never was any heart truly great and generous that was not also tender and compassionate – *Robert South*

Tenderness is the repose of passion – *Joseph Joubert*

THANKFULNESS

God has two dwellings: one in heaven, and the other in a meek and thankful heart – *Izaak Walton*

The worship most acceptable to God comes from a thankful and cheerful heart – *Plutarch*

God's goodness hath been great to thee: / Let never day nor night unhallow'd pass, / But still remember what the Lord hath done – *William Shakespeare*

A proud man is seldom a grateful man, for he never thinks he gets as much as he deserves – *Henry Ward Beecher*

Pride slays thanksgiving, but a humble mind is the soil out of which thanks naturally grow.

Old thanks pay not for a new debt.

See also GRATITUDE.

THOUGHT

Thinking is the talking of the soul with itself – *Plato*

All grand thoughts come from the heart – *Marquis de Vauvenargues*

They are never alone who are accompanied by noble thoughts – *Sir Philip Sidney*

Those who have finished by making all others think with them have usually been those who began by daring to think for themselves – *Charles Caleb Colton*

In matters of conscience first thoughts are best; in matters of prudence last thoughts are best – *Robert Hall*

Thought is the property of those only who can entertain it – *Ralph Waldo Emerson*

Only the light which we have kindled in ourselves can illuminate others – *Arthur Schopenhauer*

To cast the gift of a lovely thought into the heart of a friend is giving as the angels give – *George Macdonald*

Bad thoughts quickly ripen into bad actions – *Bielby Porteus*

All truly wise thoughts have been thought already thousands of times; but to make them truly ours, we must think them over again honestly, till they take root in our personal experience – *Johann Wolfgang von Goethe*

Our thoughts are ours, their ends none of our own – *Shakespeare*

Thoughts come into our minds by avenues which are left open, and thoughts go out of our minds through avenues which we never voluntarily opened – *Emerson*

Thoughts that do often lie too deep for tears – *William Wordsworth*

All that a man does outwardly is but the expression and completion of his inward thought – *William Ellery Channing*

Learning without thought is labour lost; thought without learning is perilous – *Confucius*

Though an inheritance of acres may be bequeathed, an inheritance of knowledge and wisdom cannot – *Samuel Smiles*

Good thoughts are blessed guests, and should be heartily welcomed, well fed, and much sought after – *Charles Haddon Spurgeon*

Our thoughts are epochs in our lives; all else is but as a journal of the winds that blow while we are here – *Henry David Thoreau*

Secret study, silent thought, is, after all, the mightiest agent in human affairs – *Channing*

When God lets loose a great thinker on this planet, then all things are at risk – *Emerson*

Nurture your mind with great thoughts; to believe in the heroic makes heroes – *Benjamin Disraeli*

It is the hardest thing in the world to be a good thinker without being a good self-examiner – *Lord Shaftesbury*

Thought means life. Thinking makes the man – *Amos Bronson Alcott*

A thought embodied and embrained in fit words walks the earth a living being – *E. P. Whipple*

The thoughts that are unsought for are commonly the most valuable, and should be secured, because they seldom return – *Francis Bacon*

Thinking leads man to knowledge – *Johann Heinrich Pestalozzi*

When a nation gives birth to a man who is able to produce a great thought, another is born who is able to understand and admire it – *Joseph Joubert*

Some people pass through life soberly and religiously enough, without knowing why, or reasoning about it, but, from force of habit merely, go to heaven like fools – *Laurence Sterne*

The men of action are, after all, only the unconscious instruments of the men of thought – *Heinrich Heine*

Garner up pleasant thoughts in your mind, for pleasant thoughts make pleasant lives.

The greatest events of an age are its best thoughts. Thought finds its way into action.

What we are afraid to do before men, we should be afraid to think before God.

Guard well thy thoughts; our thoughts are heard in Heaven.

Thoughts, even more than overt acts, reveal character.

The busiest of living agents are certain dead men's thoughts; they are forever influencing the opinions and destinies of men.

An arrow may fly through the air and leave no trace; but an ill thought leaves a trail like a serpent.

Some people study all their life, and at their death they have learned everything except to think.

It is much easier to think right without doing right, than to do right without thinking right.

Nothing is so practical as thought; our view of life moulds our life; our view of God moulds our souls.

Thought is deeper than speech; / Feeling deeper than thought; / Souls to souls can never teach / What to themselves was taught.

TIME

Time is the chrysalis of eternity – *Jean Paul Richter*

Lost time is never found again – *Benjamin Franklin*

Time will bring to light whatever is hidden – *Horace*

Time will discover everything to posterity; it is a bladder, and speaks even when no question is put – *Euripides*

One today is worth two tomorrow – *Francis Quarles*

Our yesterdays follow us; they constitute our life, and they give character and force and meaning to our present deeds – *Joseph Parker*

The hours of a wise man are lengthened by his ideas, as those of a fool are by his passions – *Joseph Addison*

Remember that time is money – *Franklin*

Minutes, hours, days, months, and years, / Pass'd over to the end they were created, / Would bring white hairs unto a quiet grave – *William Shakespeare*

Time, with all its celerity, moves slowly on to him whose whole employment is to watch its flight – *Samuel Johnson*

The end crowns all, / And that old common arbitrator, Time, / Will one day end it – *Shakespeare*

Time hath often cured the wound which reason failed to heal – *Seneca*

Time, the cradle of hope, but the grave of ambition – *Charles Caleb Colton*

It is better to be doing the most insignificant thing than to reckon even a half-hour insignificant – *Johann Wolfgang von Goethe*

We always have time enough, if we will but use it aright – *Goethe*

A man that is young in years may be old in hours, if he had lost no time – *Francis Bacon*

Time well employed is Satan's deadliest foe – *Carlos Wilcox*

All my possessions for a moment of time – *Elizabeth I* [last words]

I wasted time, and now doth time waste me – *Shakespeare*

Lost wealth may be replaced by industry, lost knowledge by study, lost health by temperance or medicine, but lost time is gone forever – *Samuel Smiles*

Those that dare lose a day are dangerously prodigal; those that dare misspend it are desperate – *Bishop Hall*

Dost thou love life? then do not squander time, for that is the stuff life is made of – *Franklin*

We sleep, but the loom of life never stops, and the pattern which was weaving when the sun went down is weaving when it comes up in the morning – *Henry Ward Beecher*

The greatest loss of time is delay – *Seneca*

All that time is lost which might be better employed – *Jean Jacques Rousseau*

Well arranged time is the surest mark of a well arranged mind – *Isaac Pitman*

No clock is more regular than the belly – *François Rabelais*

Better late than never, but better never late – *Charles Haddon Spurgeon*

Tomorrow we marvel at our short-sightedness of today – *Henry Ford*

Today is yesterday's plan put into action – *George Mathew Adams*

As every thread of gold is valuable so is every moment of time.

Time – what it's worth, ask death-beds; they can tell.

There is a time to be born, and a time to die, but there is an interval between these two times of infinite importance.

Time is the greatest of all tyrants. As we go on toward age, he taxes our health, limbs, faculties, strength, and features.

'Improve your opportunities,' said Bonaparte to a school of young men. 'Every hour lost now is a chance of future misfortune.'

Those who know the value of time use it in preparation for eternity.

Though we do nothing, time keeps his constant pace, and flies as fast in idleness as in employment.

Time is the warp of life; oh, tell the young, the fair, the gay, to weave it well.

The quarter of an hour before dinner is the worst suitors can choose.

Nay, dally not with time, the wise man's treasure, though fools are lavish of it.

He lives long that lives well, and time misspent is not lived, but lost.

Oh, time! the beautifier of the dead; adorner of the ruin; comforter and only healer when the heart hath bled.

Inscribed on the dial at All Souls, Oxford: Periunt et imputantur – the hours perish, and are laid to our charge; for time, like life, can never be recalled.

Each moment, as it passes, is the meeting place of two eternities.

Spare moments are the gold dust of time.

Counting that day lost whose slow descending sun views from thine hand no worthy action done.

Swift run the sands of time except in the hour of pain.

Lose an hour in the morning and you will spend all day looking for it.

TITLES

The three highest titles that can be given a man are those of a martyr, hero, saint – *William Gladstone*

Titles of honour are like the impressions on coin, which add no value to gold and silver, but only render brass current – *Laurence Sterne*

It is not titles that reflect honour on men, but men on their titles – *Niccolò Machiavelli*

Titles of honour add not to his worth, who is himself an honour to his title – *John Ford*

Virtue is the first title of nobility – *Molière*

Titles, indeed, may be purchased; but virtue is the only coin that makes the bargain valid.

A fool, indeed, has great need of a title; it teaches men to call him count and duke, and to forget his proper name of fool.

TOLERATION

The tolerance of all religions is a law of nature, stamped on the hearts of all men – *Voltaire*

Toleration is a good thing in its place; but you cannot tolerate what will not tolerate you, and is trying to cut your throat – *James Anthony Froude*

Tolerance comes with age; I see no fault committed that I myself could not have committed at some time or other – *Johann Wolfgang von Goethe*

Error tolerates, truth condemns – *Fernán Caballero*

The responsibility of tolerance lies with those who have the wider vision – *George Eliot*

There are those who believe something, and therefore will tolerate nothing; and on the other hand, those who tolerate everything, because they believe nothing.

See also FORBEARANCE.

TONGUE

The tongue is, at the same time, the best part of man, and his worst: with good government, none is more useful; without it, none is more mischievous – *Anarcharsis*

The chameleon, who is said to feed upon nothing but air, has of all animals the nimblest tongue – *Jonathan Swift*

When we advance a little into life, we find that the tongue of man creates nearly all the mischief of the world – *Paxton Hood*

Men's fortunes are oftener made by their tongues than by their virtues; and more men's fortunes overthrown thereby than by their vices – *Walter Raleigh*

Give not thy tongue too great liberty, lest it take thee prisoner – *Francis Quarles*

A wound from a tongue is worse than a wound from a sword; for the latter affects only the body, the former the spirit – *Pythagoras*

A tart temper never mellows with age; and a sharp tongue is the only edged tool that grows keener with constant use – *Washington Irving*

If thou desire to be wise, be so wise as to hold thy tongue – *Johann Kaspar Lavater*

A fool's heart is in his tongue; but a wise man's tongue is in his heart – *Quarles*

No sword bites so fiercely as an evil tongue – *Sir Philip Sidney*

The tongue is but three inches long, yet it can kill a man six feet high – *Japanese proverb*

The Chinese have a saying, that an unlucky word dropped from the tongue cannot be brought back again by a coach and six horses.

There are many men whose tongues might govern multitudes if they can govern their tongues.

By examining the tongue, physicians find out the diseases of the body; and philosophers the diseases of the mind and heart.

It is a great misfortune not to have sense enough to speak well and judgement enough to speak little.

If wisdom's ways you widely seek, / Five things observe with care: / Of whom you speak, to whom you speak, / And how, and when, and where.

See also SPEECH, TALKING.

TRAVEL

Travel is the frivolous part of serious lives, and the serious part of frivolous ones – *Mme Swetchine*

Men may change their climate, but they cannot change their nature – *Joseph Addison*

The use of travelling is to regulate imagination by reality, and, instead of thinking how things may be, to see them as they are – *Samuel Johnson*

To see the world is to judge the judges – *Joseph Joubert*

Rather . . . see the wonders of the world abroad / Than, living dully sluggardiz'd at home, / Wear out thy youth with shapeless idleness – *William Shakespeare*

The proper means of increasing the love we bear to our native country is to reside some time in a foreign one – *William Shenstone*

He travels safe, and not unpleasantly, who is guarded by poverty, and guided by love – *Sir Philip Sidney*

He who never leaves his own country is full of prejudices – *Carlo Goldoni*

A traveller without observation is a bird without wings – *Sádi*

To travel hopefully is better than to arrive – *Robert Louis Stevenson*

It is not fit that every man should travel; it makes a wise man better, and a fool worse.

Travel gives a character of experience to our knowledge.

The world is a great book, of which they who never stir from home read only a page.

TRIALS

The best people need afflictions for trial of their virtue – *John Tillotson*

We are always in the forge, or on the anvil; by trials God is shaping us for higher things – *Henry Ward Beecher*

Prosperity tries the fortunate, adversity the great – *Pliny the Younger*

A truly virtuous person is like good metal – the more he is fired, the more he is fined; the more he is opposed, the more he is approved – *Cardinal Richelieu*

God had one Son on earth without sin, but never one without suffering – *Augustine*

The brightest crowns that are worn in heaven have been tried, and smelted, and polished, and glorified through the furnaces of tribulation – *E. H. Chapin*

There are no crown-wearers in heaven that were not cross-bearers here below – *Charles Haddon Spurgeon*

The hardest trial of the heart is whether it can bear a rival's failure without triumph.

Reckon any matter of trial to thee among thy gains.

Great trials seem to be a necessary preparation for great duties.

It is rough treatment that gives souls, as well as stones, their lustre.

TRIFLES

Trifles make perfection, but perfection itself is no trifle – *Michelangelo Buonarroti*

There is nothing insignificant – nothing – *Samuel Taylor Coleridge*

It is in those acts which we call trivialities that the seeds of joy are forever wasted – *George Eliot*

Trifles discover character more than actions of seeming importance; what one is in little things he is also in great – *William Shenstone*

Trifles light as air / Are to the jealous confirmations strong / As proof of Holy Writ – *William Shakespeare*

The great moments of life are but moments like the others. Your doom is spoken in a word or two – *William Makepeace Thackeray*

Whoever shall review his life will find that the whole tenor of his conduct has been determined by some accident of no apparent moment – *Samuel Johnson*

The power of duly appreciating little things belongs to a great mind –
  Richard Whately

If the nose of Cleopatra had been a little shorter it would have changed
  the history of the world – *Blaise Pascal*

Men are led by trifles – *Napoleon Bonaparte*

A grain of sand leads to the fall of a mountain when the moment has
  come for the mountain to fall – *Ernest Renan*

The creation of a thousand forests is in one acorn – *Ralph Waldo Emerson*

A little and a little collected together become a great deal – *Sádi*

A stray hair, by its continued irritation, may give more annoyance than a
  smart blow.

Sands make the mountain, moments make the year, and trifles, life.

True greatness consists in being great in little things.

TROUBLE

If all men were to bring their miseries together in one place, most would
  be glad to take each his own home again rather than take a portion
  out of the common stock – *Solon*

Troubles are often the tools by which God fashions us for better things –
  Henry Ward Beecher

Heart troubles in God's husbandry are not wounds, but the putting in of
  the spade before planting the seeds – *Beecher*

Trouble is the next best thing to enjoyment; there is no fate in the world
  so horrible as to have no share in either its joys or sorrows – *Henry
  Wadsworth Longfellow*

There are many troubles which you cannot cure by the Bible and the
  hymn book, but which you can cure by a good perspiration and a
  breath of fresh air – *Beecher*

The true way of softening one's troubles is to solace those of others –
  Marquise de Maintenon

The little troubles and worries of life are stumbling blocks in our way, or
  stepping-stones to a noble character and to Heaven.

A trouble shared is a trouble halved.

Troubles are usually the brooms and shovels that smooth the road to a
  good man's fortune.

If you brood over troubles you'll have a perfect hatch.

Worry is interest paid on trouble before it falls due.

Trouble that is recognized is half cured.

You cannot keep out of trouble by spending more than you earn.

TRUST

The man who trusts men will make fewer mistakes than he who distrusts
  them – *Camillo Benso di Cavour*

To be trusted is a greater compliment than to be loved.
We trust as we love, and where we love.
Trust like the soul never returns once it has left.
Sudden trust brings sudden repentance.
See also CONFIDENCE.

TRUTH

Even though I am a minority of one, the truth is the truth – *Mohandas Karamchand Gandhi*
To thine own self be true, / And it must follow, as the night the day, / Thou canst not then be false to any man – *William Shakespeare*
While you live, tell the truth and shame the devil! – *Shakespeare*
He that would make real progress in knowledge must dedicate his age as well as youth; the latter grows as well as first fruits on the altar of knowledge – *George Berkeley*
He who truly knows has no occasion to shout.
Oil and truth will get uppermost at last.
Truth will be uppermost, one time or other like cork, though kept down in the water.
The first and last thing required of genius is the love of truth.
Do the truth you know and you shall learn all the truth you need.
It is better to hold back the truth than to speak it ungraciously.
If it is the truth what does it matter who says it?
The deepest truths are the simplest and the most common.
The door of truth never opens to the key of prejudice.
Truth is developed in the hour of need; time, and not man discovers it.
A way of joking is to tell the truth. It's the funniest joke in the world.
The greatest friend of truth is time; her greatest enemy is prejudice, and her constant companion is humility.
He that has truth on his side is a coward as well as a fool if he is afraid to own it because of other men's opinions.
Peace if possible but truth at any rate.
Truth needs to be cultivated as a talent as well as recommended as a virtue.
The way to truth is like a great road. It is not difficult to know it. The evil is that men will not seek it.
We must not let go manifest truths because we cannot answer all questions about them.
Receiving a new truth is adding a new sense.
We must never throw away a bushel of truth because it happens to contain a few grains of chaff; on the contrary, we may sometimes profitably receive a bushel of chaff for the few grains of truth it may contain.

Men must love truth before they thoroughly believe it.

Truth is the foundation of all knowledge and the cement of all societies.

You can prove anything by statistics except the truth.

One of the sublimest things in the world is the plain truth.

Everyone wishes to have the truth on his side, but it is not everyone that wishes to be on the side of truth.

Every violation of truth is a stab at the health of human society.

The greatest homage we can pay to truth is to use it.

TWILIGHT

The sun from the western horizon, like a magician, extended his golden wand o'er the landscape – *Henry Wadsworth Longfellow*

The weary sun hath made a golden set, / And, by the bright track of his fiery car, / Gives token of a goodly day tomorrow – *William Shakespeare*

Oh, how beautiful is the summer night, which is not night, but a sunless, yet unclouded, day, descending upon earth with dews, and shadows, and refreshing coolness! How beautiful the long mild twilight, which, like a silver clasp, unites today with yesterday! How beautiful the silent hour, when morning and evening thus sit together, hand in hand, beneath the starless sky of midnight! – *Longfellow*

Twilight grey hath in her sober livery all things clad – *John Milton*

What heart has not acknowledged the influence of this hour, the sweet and soothing hour of twilight – the hour of love – *Longfellow*

Nature hath appointed the twilight, as a bridge, to pass us out of night into day.

TYRANNY

Tyranny and anarchy are never far asunder – *Jeremy Bentham*

Free governments have committed more flagrant acts of tyranny than the most perfectly despotic governments we have ever known – *Edmund Burke*

Every wanton and causeless restraint of the will of the subject is a degree of tyranny – *William Blackstone*

Bad laws are the worst sort of tyranny – *Burke*

Power, unless managed with gentleness and discretion, does but make a man the more hated; no intervals of good humour, no starts of bounty, will atone for tyranny and oppression – *Jeremy Collier*

Tyranny is always weakness – *James Russell Lowell*

Hateful is the power, and pitiable is the life, of those who wish to be feared rather than to be loved – *Cornelius Nepos*

A tyrant never tasteth of true friendship, nor of perfect liberty – *Diogenes*

Kings will be tyrants from policy, when subjects are rebels from principle – *Burke*

And with necessity, the tyrant's plea excused his devilish deeds – *John Milton*

That sovereign is a tyrant who knows no law but his own caprice – *Voltaire*

Where law ends, tyranny begins – *William Pitt the Elder*

Rebellion to tyrants is obedience to God – *Benjamin Franklin*

Necessity is the argument of tyrants; it is the creed of slaves – *William Pitt the Younger*

Tyranny is far the worst of treasons.

See also OPPRESSION.

UNCERTAINTY

All that lies between the cradle and the grave is uncertain – *Seneca*

Uncertainty! fell demon of our fears! The human soul, that can support despair, supports not thee – *David Mallet*

A bitter and perplexed, 'What shall I do?' is worse to man than worst necessity – *Samuel Taylor Coleridge*

The torment of suspense is very great; and as soon as the wavering, perplexed mind begins to determine, be the determination which way soever, it will find itself at ease – *Robert South*

Our doubts are traitors / And make us lose the good we oft might win / By fearing to attempt – *William Shakespeare*

See also DOUBT.

UNDERSTANDING

It is a common fault never to be satisfied with our fortune, nor dissatisfied with our understanding – *François de La Rochefoucauld*

The eye of the understanding is like the eye of the sense; for as you may see great objects through small crannies or holes, so you may see great axioms of nature through small and contemptible instances – *Francis Bacon*

The defects of the understanding, like those of the face, grow worse as we grow old – *La Rochefoucauld*

A man of understanding finds less difficulty in submitting to a wrong-headed fellow than in attempting to set him right – *La Rochefoucauld*

The light of the understanding humility kindleth, and pride covereth – *Francis Quarles*

He who calls in the aid of an equal understanding doubles his own – *Edmund Burke*

I know no evil so great as the abuse of the understanding, and yet there is no one vice more common – *Richard Steele*

No one knows what strength of parts he has till he has tried them – *John Locke*

UNHAPPINESS

It is better not to be than to be unhappy – *John Dryden*

The most unhappy of all men is he who believes himself to be so – *David Hume*

A perverse temper, and a discontented, fretful disposition, wherever they prevail, render any state of life unhappy – *Cicero*

If we cannot live so as to be happy, let us at least live so as to deserve it.

O! how bitter a thing it is to look into happiness through another man's eyes. – *William Shakespeare*

What is earthly happiness? that phantom of which we hear so much and see so little – *Charles Caleb Colton*

We never enjoy perfect happiness; our most fortunate successes are mingled with sadness – *Pierre Corneille*

It is from the remembrance of joys we have lost that the arrows of affliction are pointed.

As the ivy twines around the oak, so do misery and misfortune encompass the happiness of man.

UNION AND UNITY

Men's hearts ought not to be set against one another, but set with one another, and all against evil only – *Thomas Carlyle*

By uniting we stand; by dividing we fall – *John Dickinson*

The multitude which does not reduce itself to unity is confusion; the unity which does not depend upon the multitude is tyranny – *Blaise Pascal*

What science calls the unity and uniformity of nature truth calls the fidelity of God.

UNKINDNESS

Rich gifts wax poor when givers prove unkind – *William Shakespeare*

As unkindness has no remedy at law, let its avoidance be with you a point of honour – *Hosea Ballou*

She hath tied / Sharp-tooth'd unkindness, like a vulture, here – *Shakespeare*

More hearts pine away in secret anguish for unkindness from those who should be their comforters than for any other calamity in life.

Hard unkindness mocks the tear it forced to flow.

USEFULNESS

There is but one virtue – the eternal sacrifice of self – *George Sand*

Doing good is the only certainly happy action of a man's life – *Sir Philip Sidney*

All the good things of this world are no further good than as they are of use – *Daniel Defoe*

I never knew a man that was bad fit for any service that was good – *Edmund Burke*

Try to make at least one person happy every day, and then in ten years you may have made three thousand, six hundred and fifty persons happy, or brightened a small town by your contribution to the fund of general enjoyment – *Sydney Smith*

Think that day lost, whose low descending sun / Views from thy hand no worthy action done.

Amid life's quests there seems but worthy one, to do men good.

VALOUR

The truly valiant dare everything except doing any other body an injury – *Sir Philip Sidney*

How strangely high endeavours may be blessed, where piety and valour jointly go – *John Dryden*

No man can answer for his own valour or courage, till he has been in danger – *François de La Rochefoucauld*

The better part of valour is discretion – *William Shakespeare*

The true valiant man dares nothing but what he may, and fears nothing but what he ought – *Francis Quarles*

There is no love-broker in the world can more prevail in man's commendation with woman than report of valour – *Shakespeare*

The mean of true valour lies between the extremes of cowardice and rashness – *Miguel de Cervantes Saavedra*

When valour preys on reason, / It eats the sword it fights with – *Shakespeare*

True valour, on virtue founded strong, meets all events alike – *David Mallet*

Valour would cease to be a virtue if there were no injustice – *Agesilaus*

Some men's valours are in the eyes of them that look on – *Francis Bacon*

Where life is more terrible than death it is then the truest valour to dare to live – *Sir Thomas Browne*

See also BOLDNESS, BRAVERY, COURAGE.

VANITY

Take away from mankind their vanity and their ambition, and there would be but few claiming to be heroes or patriots – *Seneca*

It is our own vanity that makes the vanity of others intolerable to us – *François de La Rochefoucauld*

The strongest passions allow us some rest, but vanity keeps us perpetually in motion – *Jonathan Swift*

When men will not be reasoned out of a vanity, they must be ridiculed out of it – *Sir Roger L'Estrange*

Vanity makes us do more things against inclination than reason – *La Rochefoucauld*

Of all our infirmities, vanity is the dearest to us; a man will starve his other vices to keep that alive – *Benjamin Franklin*

Ladies of fashion starve their happiness to feed their vanity, and their love to feed their pride – *Charles Caleb Colton*

Offended vanity is the great separator in social life – *Arthur Helps*

If you cannot inspire a woman with love of you, fill her above the brim with love of herself; all that runs over will be yours – *Colton*

Vanity is the quicksand of reason – *George Sand*

It is vanity which makes the rake at twenty, the worldly man at forty, and the retired man at sixty – *Alexander Pope*

In a vain man, the smallest spark may kindle into the greatest flame, because the materials are always prepared for it – *David Hume*

Vanity is the foundation of the most ridiculous and contemptible vices – the vices of affectation and common lying – *Adam Smith*

A golden mind stoops not to shows of dross – *William Shakespeare*

Virtue would not go far if vanity did not keep it company – *La Rochefoucauld*

Every man's vanity ought to be his greatest shame, and every man's folly ought to be his greatest secret – *Francis Quarles*

Vanity is the weakness of the ambitious man – *Joseph Addison*

She neglects her heart who studies her glass – *Johann Kaspar Lavater*

Vanity is as advantageous to a government as pride is dangerous – *Charles de Montesquieu*

There is no restraining men's tongues or pens when charged with a little vanity – *George Washington*

If vanity does not entirely overthrow the virtues, at least it makes them all totter – *La Rochefoucauld*

There is no arena in which vanity displays itself under such a variety of forms as in conversation – *Blaise Pascal*

Vanity is the poison of agreeableness; yet as poison, when properly applied, has a salutary effect in medicine, so has vanity in the commerce and society of the world.

Vanity is the very antidote to conceit; for while the former makes us all nerve to the opinion of others, the latter is perfectly satisfied with its opinion of itself.

Pride makes us esteem ourselves; vanity to desire the esteem of others.

Self-portraits are usually coloured.

VARIETY

Variety is the very spice of life, that gives it all its flavour – *William Cowper*

Order in variety we see; / Though all things differ, all agree – *Alexander Pope*

As land is improved by sowing it with various seeds, so is the mind by exercising it with different studies – *Pliny the Younger*

Nothing is pleasant that is not spiced with variety – *Francis Bacon*

Variety of mere nothings gives more pleasure than uniformity of something – *Jean Paul Richter*

Variety alone gives joy; / The sweetest meats the soonest cloy.

Countless the various species of mankind; / Countless the shades that separate mind from mind; / No general object of desire is known; / Each has his will, and each pursues his own.

VENGEANCE

If you have committed iniquity, you must expect to suffer; for vengeance with its sacred light shines upon you – *Sophocles*

Deep vengeance is the daughter of deep silence – *Vittorio Alfieri*

Is it to be thought unreasonable that the people, in atonement for the wrongs of a century, demanded the vengeance of a single day? – *Maximilien Marie Isidore de Robespierre*

Vengeance has no foresight – *Napoleon Bonaparte*

See also REVENGE.

VICE

Vice stings us even in our pleasures, but virtue consoles us even in our pains – *Charles Caleb Colton*

This is the essential evil of vice, that it debases a man – *E. H. Chapin*

We do not despise all those who have vices, but we do despise all those who have not a single virtue – *François de La Rochefoucauld*

Vice repeated is like the wandering wind, / Blows dust in others' eyes, to spread itself – *William Shakespeare*

No man ever arrived suddenly at the summit of vice – *Juvenal*

Experience tells us that each man most keenly and unerringly detects in others the vice with which he is most familiar himself – *Frederick William Robertson*

What maintains one vice would bring up two children – *Benjamin Franklin*

When our vices have left us we flatter ourselves that we had left them – *La Rochefoucauld*

One sin . . . another doth provoke – *Shakespeare*

There is no vice so simple but assumes / Some mark of virtue on his outward parts – *Shakespeare*

The gods are just and of our pleasant vices / Make instruments to plague us – *Shakespeare*
The vicious obey their passions as slaves do their masters – *Diogenes*
A few vices are sufficient to darken many virtues – *Plutarch*
Vice is but a nurse of agonies – *Sir Philip Sidney*
The most fearful characteristic of vice is its irresistible fascination – *Chapin*
Let thy vices die before thee – *Franklin*
Vices are often habits rather than passions – *Antoine Rivarol*
Vice – that digs her own voluptuous tomb – *Lord Byron*
One vice worn out makes us wiser than fifty tutors.
Many a man's vices have at first been nothing worse than good qualities run wild.
The hatred of the vicious will do you less harm than their conversation.
The end of a dissolute life is, most commonly, a desperate death.
Crimes sometimes shock us too much; vices almost always too little.
Misfortune does not always wait on vice, nor is success the constant guest of virtue.

VICTORY

Victories that are easy are cheap. Those only are worth having which come as a result of hard fighting – *Henry Ward Beecher*
The smile of God is victory – *John Greenleaf Whittier*
In victory the hero seeks the glory, not the prey – *Sir Philip Sidney*
A victory is twice itself when the achiever brings home full numbers – *William Shakespeare*
Who overcomes by force hath overcome but half his foe – *John Milton*
He who surpasses or subdues mankind must look down on the hate of those below – *Lord Byron*
Victory or Westminster Abbey – *Horatio Nelson*
Victory may be honourable to the arms, but shameful to the counsels of the nation – *Henry St John Bolingbroke*
Win without boasting. Lose without excuse – *Albert Payson Terhune*
Victory, simple for the sake of achieving it, is empty – *Alfred E. Smith*

VIGILANCE

It is the enemy who keeps the sentinel watchful – *Mme Swetchine*
Better three hours too soon than a minute too late – *William Shakespeare*
He is most free from danger, who, even when safe, is on his guard – *Publius Syrus*
Eternal vigilance is the price of liberty – *Thomas Jefferson*
See also WATCHFULNESS.

VILLAINY

The villainy you teach me I will execute, and it shall go hard but I will
  better the instruction – *William Shakespeare*
Villainy, when detected, never gives up, but boldly adds impudence to
  imposture – *Oliver Goldsmith*
Villainy that is vigilant will be an over-match for virtue, if she slumber at
  her post – *Charles Caleb Colton*
One murder made the villain; millions the hero – *Bielby Porteus*
It is the masterpiece of villainy to smooth the brow, and so outface
  suspicion.
See also WICKEDNESS.

VIOLENCE

Violent fires soon burn out themselves; / Small showers last long,
  but sudden storms are short; / He tires betimes that spurs too fast
  betimes – *William Shakespeare*
Nothing good ever comes of violence – *Martin Luther*
Violent delights have violent ends – *Shakespeare*
The violence done us by others is often less painful than that which we
  do to ourselves – *François de La Rochefoucauld*
Nothing violent, oft have I heard tell, can be permanent – *Christopher
  Marlowe*
If you must use a hammer, build something.

VIRTUE

To be innocent is to be not guilty; but to be virtuous is to overcome our
  evil feelings and intentions – *William Penn*
That virtue which requires to be ever guarded is scarce worth the sentinel
  – *Oliver Goldsmith*
Were there but one virtuous man in the world, he would hold up his
  head with confidence and honour; he would shame the world, and
  not the world him – *Robert South*
To be able under all circumstances to practise five things constitutes
  perfect virtue; these five are gravity, generosity of soul, sincerity,
  earnestness, and kindness – *Confucius*
I willingly confess that it likes me better when I find virtue in a fair
  lodging than when I am bound to seek it in an ill-favoured creature –
  Sir Philip Sidney
Virtue without talent is a coat of mail without a sword – *Charles Caleb
  Colton*

Wealth is a weak anchor, and glory cannot support a man; virtue only is firm, and cannot be shaken by a tempest – *Pythagoras*

Virtue is the only thing whose value must ever increase with the price it has cost us – *Colton*

I am no herald to inquire of men's pedigrees; it sufficeth me if I know their virtues – *Sidney*

He that is good will infallibly become better, and he that is bad will as certainly become worse; for vice, virtue, and time are three things that never stand still – *Colton*

The most virtuous of all men, says Plato, is he that contents himself with being virtuous without seeking to appear so – *François de Fénelon*

The virtue of a man ought to be measured not by his extraordinary exertions but by his everyday conduct – *Blaise Pascal*

Virtue is the dictate of reason – *Algernon Sidney*

If you can be well without health, you may be happy without virtue – *Edmund Burke*

Our virtues would be proud if our faults whipped them not; and our crimes would despair if they were not cherished by our virtues – *William Shakespeare*

When men grow virtuous in old age they are merely making an offering to God of the devil's leavings – *Jonathan Swift*

Virtue is not innocence, but the exertion of our faculties in doing good – *Bishop Butler*

Virtue has many preachers, but few martyrs – *Claude Adrien Helvétius*

A large part of virtue consists in good habits – *William Paley*

Virtue is a state of war, and to live in it we have always to combat with ourselves – *Jean Jacques Rousseau*

While shame keeps its watch virtue is not wholly extinguished in the heart – *Burke*

It has ever been my experience that folks who have no vices have very few virtues – *Abraham Lincoln*

Every vice was once a virtue, and may become respectable again, just as hatred becomes respectable in wartime – *Will Durant*

There is no virtue of any kind unless one feels temptation – *Richard C. Cabot*

Virtue is a nobility without heraldry.

All bow to virtue, and then walk away.

Many who have tasted all the pleasures of sin have forsaken it and come over to virtue; but there are few, if any, who having tried the sweets of virtue could ever be drawn off from it.

Live virtuously, and you cannot die too soon, nor live too long.

We are all born equal, and are distinguished alone by virtue.

The less a man thinks of his virtues the greater their value.

VOICE

How wonderful is the human voice! It is indeed the organ of the soul – *Henry Wadsworth Longfellow*

The sweetest of all sounds is that of the voice of the woman we love – *Jean de La Bruyère*

There is no index of character so sure as the voice – *Tancred*

The tones of human voices are mightier than strings or brass to move the soul – *Friedrich Gottlieb Klopstock*

How sweetly sounds the voice of a good woman! When it speaks it ravishes all senses – *Philip Massinger*

Thy voice is celestial melody – *Longfellow*

VOWS

Lovers' vows seem sweet in every whispered word – *Lord Byron*

Unheedful vows may heedfully be broken – *William Shakespeare*

Men's vows are women's traitors – *Shakespeare*

The vows that woman makes to her fond lover are fit only to be written on air, or on the swiftly passing stream – *Catullus*

Those mouth-made vows / Which break themselves in swearing! – *Shakespeare*

WAGERS

Most men, until by losing rendered sager, / Will back their opinions by a wager – *Lord Byron*

Fools for arguments use wagers.

WAITING

They also serve who only stand and wait – *John Milton*

All good abides with him who waiteth wisely – *Henry David Thoreau*

WANTS

It is not from nature, but from education and habits, that our wants are chiefly derived – *Henry Fielding*

We are ruined not by what we really want but by what we think we do – *Charles Caleb Colton*

Hundreds would never have known want if they had not first known waste – *Charles Haddon Spurgeon*

The fewer our wants, the nearer we resemble the gods – *Socrates*

Of all the enemies of idleness, want is the most formidable – *Samuel Johnson*

To men pressed by their wants all change is ever welcome – *Ben Jonson*

Supplying our wants by lopping off our desires is like cutting off our feet when we want shoes – *Jonathan Swift*

Choose rather to want less than to have more – *Thomas à Kempis*

The wants of women are an unknown quantity.

See also DESIRE.

WAR

War! that mad game the world so loves to play – *Jonathan Swift*

War makes thieves, and peace brings them to the gallows – *Niccolò Machiavelli*

There never was a good war, or a bad peace – *Benjamin Franklin*

War is the business of barbarians – *Napoleon Bonaparte*

Men who have nice notions of religion have no business to be soldiers – *Duke of Wellington*

War is a system out of which almost all the virtues are excluded, and in which nearly all the vices are included – *Robert Hall*

War is an instrument entirely inefficient toward redressing wrong; and multiplies, instead of indemnifying losses – *Thomas Jefferson*

The next dreadful thing to a battle lost is a battle won – *Wellington*

The feast of vultures, and the waste of life – *Lord Byron*

War is the sink of all injustice – *Henry Fielding*

Civil wars leave nothing but tombs – *Alphonse Marie Louis de Lamartine*

Even in war, moral power is to physical as three parts out of four – *Napoleon Bonaparte*

War is a game, which, were their subjects wise, kings would not play at – *William Cowper*

Even in a righteous cause force is a fearful thing; God only helps when man can help no more – *Johann Christoph Friedrich von Schiller*

War ought never to be accepted until it is forced upon us by the hand of necessity – *Sir Philip Sidney*

War is one of the greatest plagues that can afflict humanity; it destroys religion, it destroys states, it destroys families – *Martin Luther*

Mad wars destroy in one year the works of many years of peace – *Franklin*

The arms are fair, / When the intent of bearing them is just – *William Shakespeare*

O war! thou son of hell, / Whom angry heavens do make their minister, / Throw in the frozen bosoms of our part / Hot coals of vengeance – *Shakespeare*

To be prepared for war is one of the most effectual ways of preserving peace – *George Washington*

What is war but murder in uniform? – *Douglas William Jerrold*

Laws are commanded to hold their tongues among arms – *Edmund Burke*

It is a horrible fact that there is no great nation that has attained freedom
    except by war – *Susan Lawrence*

We shall never be able to effect physical disarmament until we
    have succeeded in effecting moral disarmament – *James Ramsay*
    MacDonald

Asking Europe to disarm is like asking a man in Chicago to give up his
    life insurance – *Will Rogers*

We have all taken risks in the making of war. Isn't it time that we should
    take risks to secure peace? – *MacDonald*

A great war leaves the country with three armies – an army of cripples,
    an army of mourners, and an army of thieves – *German proverb*

We cannot make a more lively representation and emblem to ourselves
    of hell than by the view of a kingdom in war.

Rash, fruitless war, from wanton glory waged, is only splendid murder.

War may save the state, but it destroys the citizen.

One to destroy is murder by the law; to murder thousands takes a
    specious name and gives immortal fame.

Success in war, like charity in religion, covers a multitude of sins.

Peace is the happy state of man; war is corruption and disgrace.

Unless people get busy and abolish wars, wars will abolish people.

WATCHFULNESS

Watchfulness and industry are natural virtues – *Bishop Conybeare*

Wise distrust and constant watchfulness are the parents of safety.

A soul without watchfulness is, like a city without walls, exposed to the
    inroads of all its enemies.

See also VIGILANCE.

WEAKNESS

Some of our weaknesses are born in us, others are the result of edu-
    cation; it is a question which of the two gives us most trouble – *Johann*
    Wolfgang von Goethe

Men are in general so tricky, so envious, and so cruel, that when we find
    one who is only weak, we are happy – *Voltaire*

The weak soul, within itself unblest, / Leans for all pleasure on another's
    breast – *Oliver Goldsmith*

The weakest spot with mankind is where they fancy themselves most
    wise.

To excuse our faults on the ground of our weakness is to quiet our fears at
    the expense of our hopes.

The weak may be joked out of anything but their weakness.

WEALTH

The wealth of man is the number of things which he loves and blesses which he is loved and blessed by – *Thomas Carlyle*

Our wealth is often a snare to ourselves, and always a temptation to others – *Charles Caleb Colton*

Gold, worse poison to men's souls, / Doing more murders in this loathsome world / Than these poor compounds – *William Shakespeare*

He is richest who is content with the least, for content is the wealth of nature – *Socrates*

He that will not permit his wealth to do any good to others while he is living prevents it from doing any good to himself when he is dead – *Colton*

As riches and favour forsake a man we discover him to be a fool, but nobody could find it out in his prosperity – *Jean de La Bruyère*

The gratification of wealth is not found in mere possession or in lavish expenditure, but in its wise application – *Miguel de Cervantes Saavedra*

Wealth is not his that has it, but his that enjoys it – *Benjamin Franklin*

Many a beggar at the cross-way, or grey-haired shepherd on the plain, hath more of the end of all wealth than hundreds who multiply the means – *Martin Farquhar Tupper*

If thou art rich, thou'rt poor; / For, like an ass whose back with ingots bows, / Thou bear'st thy heavy riches but a journey, / And death unloads thee – *Shakespeare*

In proportion as nations become more corrupt, more disgrace will attach to poverty and more respect to wealth – *Colton*

Riches are gotten with pain, kept with care, and lost with grief – *Sir Roger L'Estrange*

Wealth, after all, is a relative thing, since he that has little, and wants less, is richer than he that has much, and wants more – *Colton*

It is only when the rich are sick that they fully feel the impotence of wealth – *Colton*

It is far more easy to acquire a fortune like a knave than to expand it like a gentleman – *Colton*

Wealth consists not in having great possessions, but in having few wants – *Epicurus*

The most brilliant fortunes are often not worth the littleness required to gain them – *François de La Rochefoucauld*

A great fortune is a great servitude – *Seneca*

Wherever there is excessive wealth, there is also in its train excessive poverty, as where the sun is highest, the shade is deepest – *Walter Savage Landor*

Wealth hath never given happiness, but often hastened misery – *Tupper*

Excess of wealth is cause of covetousness – *Christopher Marlowe*

No one is poor with love to spend – *George Webster Douglas*

The acquisition of wealth is a work of great labour; its possession a source
   of continual fear; its loss, of excessive grief – *from the Latin*

Worldly wealth is the devil's bait.

In the age of acorns, a single barleycorn had been of more value to
   mankind than all the diamonds in the mines of India.

Prefer loss to wealth of dishonest gain; the former vexes you for a time;
   the latter will bring you lasting remorse.

A heavy purse in a fool's pocket is a heavy curse.

If you would take your possessions into the life to come, convert them
   into good deeds.

It is poor encouragement to toil through life to amass a fortune to ruin
   your children.

Less coin, less care; to know how to dispense with wealth is to possess it.

To acquire wealth is difficult, to preserve it more difficult, but to spend it
   wisely most difficult of all.

Much learning shows how little mortals know; much wealth, how little
   worldlings can enjoy.

A man who possesses wealth possesses power, but it is a power to do
   evil as well as good.

Without a rich heart wealth is an ugly beggar.

A philosopher may despise riches; but I'll bet his wife doesn't.

See also FORTUNE, GOLD, PROSPERITY, RICHES.

WELCOME

A table full of welcome makes scarce one dainty dish – *William
   Shakespeare*

Small cheer and great welcome makes a merry feast – *Shakespeare*

Welcome as happy tidings after fears – *Thomas Otway*

Welcome ever smiles, / And farewell goes out sighing – *Shakespeare*

Welcome as kindly showers to the long parched earth – *John Dryden*

Welcome the coming, speed the parting guest – *Alexander Pope*

WICKEDNESS

Wickedness may well be compared to a bottomless pit, into which it is
   easier to keep oneself from falling than, being fallen, to give oneself
   any stay from falling infinitely – *Sir Philip Sidney*

The happiness of the wicked passes away like a torrent – *Jean Racine*

To see and listen to the wicked is already the beginning of wickedness –
   Confucius

What rein can hold licentious wickedness, / When down the hill he holds
   his fierce career? – *William Shakespeare*

Wickedness may prosper for a while, but in the long run he that sets all knaves at work will pay them – *Sir Roger L'Estrange*

No wickedness proceeds on any grounds of reason – *Livy*

There is a method in man's wickedness; it grows up by degrees – *Francis Beaumont and John Fletcher*

The sure way to wickedness is always through wickedness – *Seneca*

There is wickedness in the intention of wickedness, even though it be not perpetrated in the act – *Cicero*

The disposition to do an evil deed is, of itself, a terrible punishment of the deed it does.

If the wicked flourish, and thou suffer, be not discouraged; they are fatted for destruction, thou art dieted for health.

See also VILLAINY.

WIFE

Sole partner, and sole part of all my joys, dearer thyself than all – *John Milton*

A wife's a man's best piece – *James Shirley*

A light wife doth make a heavy husband – *William Shakespeare*

Her pleasures are in the happiness of her family – *Jean Jacques Rousseau*

A wife is essential to great longevity; she is the receptacle of half a man's cares, and two-thirds of his ill-humour – *Charles Reade*

You are my true and honourable wife, / As dear to me as are the ruddy drops / That visit my sad heart – *Shakespeare*

Hanging and wiving goes by destiny – *Shakespeare*

She is mine own, / And I as rich in having such a jewel / As twenty seas, if all their sand were pearl, / The water nectar, and the rocks pure gold – *Shakespeare*

Of earthly goods, the best is a good wife; a bad, the bitterest curse of human life – *Simonides of Ceos*

I chose my wife, as she did her wedding-gown, for qualities that would wear well – *Oliver Goldsmith*

No man can live piously or die righteously without a wife – *Jean Paul Richter*

An ideal wife is any woman who has an ideal husband – *Booth Tarkington*

Her husband's eye, the truest mirror that an honest wife can see her beauty in.

If you would have a good wife marry one who has been a good daughter.

Unhappy is the man for whom his own wife has not made all other women sacred.

In the election of a wife, as in a project of war, to err but once is to be undone forever.

For a wife take the daughter of a good mother.

If you want to pull the wool over your wife's eyes, use a good yarn.

WILL

He wants wits who wants resolved will – *William Shakespeare*

At twenty years of age the will reigns; at thirty, the wit; and at forty, the judgement – *Gratian*

No action will be considered blameless, unless the will was so, for by the will the act was dictated – *Seneca*

The will of man is by his reason sway'd – *Shakespeare*

He who has a firm will moulds the world to himself – *Johann Wolfgang von Goethe*

The general of a large army may be defeated, but you cannot defeat the determined mind of a peasant – *Confucius*

It is the will that makes the action good or bad – *Robert Herrick*

Man is made great or little by his own will – *Johann Christoph Friedrich von Schiller*

People do not lack strength; they lack will – *Victor Hugo*

To deny the freedom of the will is to make morality impossible – *James Anthony Froude*

If we make God's will our law, then God's promise shall be our support and comfort – *Tryon Edwards*

To will what God wills is the only science that gives us rest – *Henry Wadsworth Longfellow*

Great souls have wills; feeble ones have only wishes – *Chinese proverb*

In the mortal world there is nothing impossible if we can bring a thorough will to do it. Man can do everything with himself, but he must not attempt to do too much with others.

Where there is a will there is a way.

In idle wishes fools supinely stay; / Be there a will and wisdom finds a way.

Do God's will as if it were thy will, and he will accomplish thy will as if it were his own.

WILLS

He that defers his charity until he is dead is, if a man weighs it rightly, rather liberal of another man's goods than his own – *Francis Bacon*

Those who give not till they die show that they would not then if they could keep it any longer – *Bishop Hall*

You give me nothing during your life, but you promise to provide for me at your death. If you are not a fool, you know what you make me wish for – *Martial*

Posthumous charities are the very essence of selfishness when bequeathed by those who, when alive, would part with nothing – *Charles Caleb Colton*

No one admires thrift more than an heir.

What you leave at your death let it be without controversy, else the lawyers will be your heirs.

You can't take your money with you when you go!

There are no pockets in a shroud.

WIND

Perhaps the wind wails so in winter for the summer's dead – *George Eliot*

God tempers the wind to the shorn lamb – *Laurence Sterne*

Ill blows the wind that profits nobody – *William Shakespeare*

The sobbing wind is fierce and strong; its cry is like a human wail – *Susan Coolidge*

Seas are the fields of combat for the winds – *John Dryden*

There's a strange music in the stirring wind.

As the wind blows you must set your sail.

WINE

A vine bears three grapes, the first of pleasure, the second of drunkenness, and the third of repentance – *Anacharsis*

Wine turns the good-natured man into an idiot – *Joseph Addison*

Wine and youth are fire upon fire – *Henry Fielding*

As fermenting in a vessel works up to the top whatever it has in the bottom, so wine, in those who have drunk beyond measure, vents the most inward secrets – *Michel Eyquem de Montaigne*

There is a devil in every berry of the grape – *Koran*

The first glass for myself; the second for my friends; the third for good humour; and the fourth for mine enemies – *William Temple*

Wine has drowned more than the sea – *Publius Syrus*

Polished brass is the mirror of the body and wine of the mind – *Aeschylus*

Wine is a noble, generous liquor, and we should be humbly thankful for it; but, as I remember, water was made before it – *John Eliot*

O God! that men should put an enemy in their mouths to steal away their brains; that we should, with joy, pleasance, revel, and applause, transform ourselves into beasts – *William Shakespeare*

The conscious water saw its God, and blushed – *Richard Crashaw*

A driver is safer when the road is dry; the road is safer when the driver is dry – *Earl Wilson*

Wine heightens indifference into love, love into jealousy and jealousy into madness.

Wine is a turn-coat; first, a friend; then, a deceiver; then, an enemy.
Old friends and old wine are best.

WISDOM

He must be a wise man himself who is capable of distinguishing one –
   Diogenes
Common sense in an uncommon degree is what the world calls wisdom
   – *Samuel Taylor Coleridge*
There is one person that is wiser than anybody and that is everybody –
   Charles Maurice de Talleyrand-Périgord
Very few men are wise by their own counsel, or learned by their own
   teaching; for he that was only taught by himself had a fool to his
   master – *Ben Jonson*
You read of but one wise man and all that he knew was – that he knew
   nothing – *William Congreve*
What is it to be wise? 'Tis but to know how little can be known – to see all
   others' faults and feel our own – *Alexander Pope*
Much wisdom often goes with fewest words – *Sophocles*
Wisdom is to the mind what health is to the body – *François de La
   Rochefoucauld*
No man can be wise on an empty stomach – *George Eliot*
Among mortals second thoughts are wisest – *Euripides*
The proverbial wisdom of the populace at gates, on roads and in
   markets, instructs him who studies man more fully than a thousand
   rules ostentatiously arranged – *Johann Kaspar Lavater*
Wisdom allows nothing to be good that will not be so forever; no man to
   be happy but he that needs no other happiness than what he has
   within himself; no man to be great or powerful that is not master of
   himself – *Seneca*
We ought to judge of men's merits not by their qualifications but by the
   use they make of them – *Pierre Charron*
The wisest man is generally he who thinks himself the least so – *Nicolas
   Boileau*
He that thinks himself the wisest is generally the greatest fool – *Charles
   Caleb Colton*
It is more easy to be wise for others than for ourselves – *La Rochefoucauld*
Perfect wisdom hath four parts, viz., wisdom, the principle of doing
   things aright; justice, the principle of doing things equally in public
   and private; fortitude, the principle of not flying danger, but meeting
   it; and temperance, the principle of subduing desires and living
   moderately – *Plato*
He who learns the rules of wisdom without conforming to them in his life
   is like a man who ploughs in his field but does not sow – *Sádi*

The first point of wisdom is to discern that which is false; the second to know that which is true – *Lactantius*

Wisdom is oft times nearer when we stoop than when we soar – *William Wordsworth*

The sublimity of wisdom is to do those things living which are to be desired when dying – *Jeremy Taylor*

A man's wisdom is his best friend; folly his worst enemy – *William Temple*

In seeking wisdom thou art wise; in imagining that thou hast attained it thou art a fool – *Rabbi Ben Azai*

Wise men know that the only way to help themselves is to help others – *Elbert Hubbard*

A wise man is never less alone than when he is alone – *Jonathan Swift*

Tell not all you know, nor do all you can – *Italian proverb*

A wise man's day is worth a fool's life – *Arabic proverb*

Wisdom is the pursuit of the best ends by the best means.

If you must hold yourself up to your children as an object lesson, let it be as a warning and not as an example.

If you are a master be sometimes blind; if a servant sometimes deaf.

Wisdom is ever a blessing; education is sometimes a curse.

What it is not possible to change must be borne in silence.

The wisest are those who can best adjust their disadvantages.

Oil and water – woman and a secret – are hostile properties.

A wise man never attempts impossibilities.

The art of being wise is the art of knowing what to overlook.

Quick speed is good, where wisdom leads the way.

No one is old enough to know better.

He is wise who knows the sources of knowledge – who knows who has written and where it is to be found.

It's a maxim of a wise man never to return by the same road he came.

Our chief wisdom consists in knowing our follies and faults, that we may correct them.

It is as great a point of wisdom to hide ignorance as to discover knowledge.

God gives men wisdom as he gives them gold; his treasure house is not the mint, but the mine.

It is too often seen that the wiser men are about the things of this world the less wise they are about the things of the next.

There are but two classes of the wise; the men who serve God because they have found him and the men who seek him because they have found him not.

Wisdom prepares for the worst, but folly leaves the worst for the day when it comes.

True wisdom is to know what is best worth knowing, and to do what is best worth doing.

The wisdom of one generation will be the folly of the next.
Even a fool, when he holdeth his peace, is counted wise.
Be wiser than other people if you can – but do not tell them so.
To some purpose is that man wise who gains his wisdom at another's expense.
The intellect of the wise is like glass; it admits light and reflects it.
Wise men learn by other men's mistakes; fools, by their own.

WISHES

Every wish is like a prayer with God – *Elizabeth Barrett Browning*
There is nothing more properly the language of the heart than a wish – *Robert South*
Happy the man who early learns the wide chasm that lies between his wishes and his powers! – *Johann Wolfgang von Goethe*
Men's thoughts are much according to their inclination – *Francis Bacon*
What we ardently wish we soon believe.
Why wish for more? Wishing of all employments is the worst.
Wishing – the constant hectic of the fool.
Wishes are, at least, the easy pleasures of the poor.
To a resolute mind, wishing to do is the first step toward doing.

WIT

Less judgement than wit is more sail than ballast – *William Penn*
Where judgement has wit to express it, there is the best orator – *William Penn*
To place wit above sense is to place superfluity above utility – *Marquise de Maintenon*
As it is the characteristic of great wits to say much in few words, so small wits seem to have the gift of speaking much and saying nothing – *François de La Rochefoucauld*
Wit is the salt of conversation, not the food – *William Hazlitt*
The impromptu reply is precisely the touchstone of the man of wit – *Molière*
He who has provoked the shaft of wit cannot complain that he smarts from it – *Samuel Johnson*
Wit is not levelled so much at the muscles as at the heart.
Let your wit rather serve you for a buckler to defend yourself, than the sword to wound others.
Be rather wise than witty.
Wit should be used as a shield for defence rather than as a sword to wound others.
Even wit is a burden when it talks too long.
See also HUMOUR.

WOMAN

The height of power in women rests in tranquillity – *Marquise de Maintenon*

The most effective water power in the world – women's tears – *Wilson Mizne*

When a woman begins to think, her first thought is dress. When Eve first ate the apple she reached for the fig leaf – *Heinrich Heine*

Women are wiser than men because they know less and understand more – *James Stephens*

Men at most differ as heaven and earth; but worst and best, as heaven and hell – *Alfred, Lord Tennyson*

To the disgrace of men it is seen, that there are women both more wise to judge what evil is expected, and more constant to bear it when it is happened – *Sir Philip Sidney*

The most dangerous acquaintance a married woman can make is the female confidante – *Mme Deluzy*

A handsome woman is a jewel; a good woman is a treasure – *Sádi*

There are three classes into which all old women are divided: first that dear old soul: second, that old woman; and third, that old witch – *Samuel Taylor Coleridge*

The greater part of what women write about women is mere sycophancy to man – *Mme de Staël*

A woman's heart, like the moon, is always changing, but there is always a man in it – *Punch*

All men who avoid female society have dull perceptions and are stupid, or else have gross tastes, and revolt against what is pure – *William Makepeace Thackeray*

No one knows like a woman how to say things which are at once gentle and deep – *Victor Hugo*

Women are ever in extremes; they are either better or worse than men – *Jean de La Bruyère*

One reason why women are forbidden to preach the gospel is that they would persuade without argument and reprove without giving offence – *John Newton*

They are the books, the arts, the academes, / That show, contain, and nourish all the world – *William Shakespeare*

I have often had occasion to remark the fortitude with which women sustain the most overwhelming reverses of fortune. Those disasters which break down the spirit of a man and prostrate him in the dust seem to call forth all the energies of the softer sex, and give such intrepidity and elevation to their character, that at times it approaches to sublimity – *Washington Irving*

'Tis beauty that doth oft make women proud; / . . . 'Tis virtue that doth

make them most admir'd; / . . . 'Tis that makes them seem divine –
Shakespeare

Women govern us; let us try to render them more perfect. The more they
are enlightened, so much the more we shall be. On the cultivation of
the minds of women depends the wisdom of man – *Richard Brinsley
Sheridan*

Men are women's playthings; woman is the devil's – *Hugo*

Women see through and through each other; and often we most admire
her whom they most scorn – *Charles Buxton*

The happiest women, like the happiest nations, have no history – *George
Eliot*

Most females will forgive a liberty, rather than a slight; and if any woman
were to hang a man for stealing her picture, although it were set in
gold, it would be a new case in law; but if he carried off the setting,
and left the portrait, I would not answer for his safety – *Charles Caleb
Colton*

Kindness in women, not their beauteous looks, / Shall win my love –
Shakespeare

She is not made to be the admiration of all, but the happiness of one –
Edmund Burke

Women wish to be loved without a why or a wherefore – not because
they are pretty or good, or well-bred, or graceful, or intelligent, but
because they are themselves – *Henri Frédéric Amiel*

A man without religion is to be pitied, but a Godless woman is a horror
above all things – *Miss Evans*

A woman's lot is made for her by the love she accepts – *George Eliot*

He is a fool who thinks by force or skill / To turn the current of a woman's
will – *Samuel Tuke*

Men have sight; women insight – *Hugo*

Women never truly command till they have given their promise to obey;
and they are never in more danger of being made slaves, than when
the men are at their feet – *George Farquhar*

To feel, to love, to suffer, to devote herself will always be the text of life of
a woman – *Honoré de Balzac*

Most men like in women what is most opposite their own characters –
Henry Fielding

There are a few things that never go out of style, and a feminine woman
is one of them – *Jobyna Ralston*

It is not education which makes women less domestic, but wealth –
Katharine Jeanne Gallagher

Just as a stream can rise no higher than its source, so no race can be
higher than its womanhood – *John Roach Straton*

Painted lips do not change the hearts beneath them – *Virginia C.
Gildersleeve*

A woman's advice is a poor thing, but he is a fool who does not take it –
Spanish proverb

The average woman can't keep a secret without getting a few friends to
help her.

All too often the clever girl who knows all the answers is never asked.

The forward girl casts many a backward glance.

Because a girl has dreamy eyes it does not follow that she is not wide
awake.

Some women are like angels because they are for ever harping.

A wise girl is judged by the company she keeps at a distance.

The reason women do not love one another is – men.

A woman conceals what she knows not.

A woman's face is her fortune and these fortunes often run into good
figures.

The finest compliment that can be paid to a woman of sense is to address
her as such.

Next to God we are indebted to women, first for life itself, and then for
making it worth having.

A good and true woman is said to resemble a fiddle – age but increases its
worth and sweetens its tone.

Nearly every folly committed by woman is born of the stupidity or evil
influence of man.

The deepest tendernes a woman can show to a man is to help him to do
his duty.

Women are the poetry of the world in the same sense as the stars are the
poetry of heaven – clear, light-giving, harmonious; they are the
terrestrial planets that rule the destinies of mankind.

The best woman has always somewhat of a man's strength; and the
noblest man of a woman's gentleness.

Woman is the Sunday of man; not his repose only, but his joy; the salt of
his life.

Women have more strength in their looks than we have in our laws; and
more power by their tears than we have by our arguments.

Woman – last at the cross, and earliest at the grave.

If we would know the political and moral condition of a state, we must
ask what rank women hold in it. Their influence embraces the whole
of life.

A woman's chief asset is a man's imagination.

God forgives, man forgets, but women remember for ever.

A philosopher may despise riches; but I'll bet his wife doesn't.

Sometimes the wolf is at the door at the daughter's invitation.

A woman too often reasons from her heart; hence two-thirds of her
mistakes and her troubles.

Pleasure is to a woman what the sun is to the flower; if moderately

enjoyed, it beautifies, it refreshes, and improves; if immoderately, it
  withers, deteriorates and destroys.
I have often thought that the nature of women was inferior to that of men
  in general, but superior in particular.
If thou wouldst please the ladies, thou must endeavour to make them
  pleased with themselves.
A spinster is a symptom of inflation – too many women chasing too few
  men.
What every girl should know is a rich young man.
Career girl: One who would rather bring home the bacon than fry it.
Womanhood is entitled to the best in manhood. Without it she cannot
  realize the best in herself.

WONDER

All wonder is the effect of novelty on ignorance – *Samuel Johnson*
It was through the feeling of wonder that men now and at first began to
  philosophize – *Aristotle*
The first wonder is the offspring of ignorance, the last is the parent of
  adoration – *Samuel Taylor Coleridge*
Wonder is involuntary praise.
Wonder is the source of all knowledge and discovery.
'Wonder' is the first cause of philosophy.

WORDS

Words are the counters of wise men, and the money of fools – *Thomas
  Hobbes*
Words should be employed as the means, not as the end; language is the
  instrument, conviction is the work – *Joshua Reynolds*
Words are the wings of actions – *Johann Kaspar Lavater*
I would rather speak the truth to ten men than blandishments and lying
  to a million – *Henry Ward Beecher*
Words are like leaves; and where they most abound, / Much fruit and
  sense beneath is rarely found – *Alexander Pope*
A good word is an easy obligation; but not to speak ill requires only our
  silence, which costs us nothing – *John Tillotson*
When words are scarce they are seldom spent in vain – *William
  Shakespeare*
He who seldom speaks, and with one calm well timed word can strike
  dumb the loquacious, is a genius or a hero – *Lavater*
Such as thy words are, such will thy affections be esteemed – *Socrates*
Learn the value of a man's words and expressions, and you know him –
  Lavater

A man cannot speak but he judges and reveals himself – *Ralph Waldo Emerson*

'Tis a kind of good deed to say well: / And yet words are no deeds – *Shakespeare*

Words are things; and a small drop of ink, falling like dew upon a thought, produces that which makes thousands, perhaps millions, think – *Lord Byron*

Words are but pictures of our thoughts – *John Dryden*

A word unspoken is a word in the scabbard; a word uttered is a sword in another's hand – *Francis Quarles*

Syllables govern the world – *Edward Coke*

Words are not essential to the existence of thought – only to its expression – *Dugald Stewart*

We should be as careful of our words as of our actions, and as far from speaking ill as from doing ill – *Cicero*

It is as easy to call back a stone thrown from the hand, as to call back the word that is spoken – *Menander*

The knowledge of words is the gate of scholarship.

What you keep by you you may change and mend; but words, once spoken, can never be recalled.

Seest thou a man that is hasty in his words? There is more hope of a fool than of him.

Words may be either servants or masters.

A good word maketh a glad heart.

Words, when written, crystallize history; their very structure gives permanence to the unchangeable past.

He that uses many words for explaining any subject, doth, like the cuttlefish, hide himself in his own ink.

WORK

We must labour for all that we have; nothing is worth possessing, or offering to others, which costs us nothing – *John Todd*

Never mind where you work; let your care be for the work itself – *Charles Haddon Spurgeon*

We enjoy ourselves only in our work – in our doing; and our best doing is our best enjoyment – *Friedrich Heinrich Jacobi*

All men, if they work not as in the great taskmaster's eye, will work wrong, work unhappily for themselves and you – *Thomas Carlyle*

Work does more than get us a living; it gets us our life – *Henry Ford*

The day's work must be done in a day – *Benito Mussolini*

As a cure for worrying, work is better than whisky – *Thomas Edison*

Never do owt for nowt, but if tha does owt for nowt, make sure tha does it for thy sen – *Yorkshire wisdom*

Men who have a half-a-dozen irons in the fire are not the men to go crazy.

Motion is all nature's law – action is man's salvation.

Work as though you would live forever; but live as though you would die today.

The world has not a man who is an idler in his own eyes.

Many a man wastes his present by dreaming of his future.

He has done much who leaves nothing over for tomorrow.

We always think every other man's job is easier than our own, and the better he does it, the easier it looks.

If you think nothing of the work you do you may find the opinion's shared.

Men tire themselves in pursuit of rest.

Absence of occupation is not rest.

The best way to kill time is to work it to death.

When easy does it, somebody usually has to do it again.

The man who has no push may get it.

Repose is work's greatest achievement.

The man who wants his dreams to come true must wake up.

Always begin somewhere. You can't build a reputation on what you intend to do.

Enthusiasm is the strongest motive force for production.

Pleasantness may be OK but nastiness gets results.

WORLD

The only fence against the world is a thorough knowledge of it – *John Locke*

You have too much respect upon the world: / They lose it that do buy it with much care – *Shakespeare*

The world is a comedy to those who think, a tragedy to those who feel – *Horace Walpole*

Contact with the world either breaks or hardens the heart – *Nicolas Sébastian Roch Chamfort*

He who imagines he can do without the world deceives himself much; but he who fancies the world cannot do without him is still more mistaken – *François de La Rochefoucauld*

The meek may inherit the earth – but not its mineral rights – *John Paul Getty*

What is meant by a 'knowledge of the world' is simply an acquaintance with the infirmities of men – *Charles Dickens*

The world is God's workshop for making men – *Henry Ward Beecher*

It is the way in which love is given, which constitutes worldliness – *Frederick William Robertson*

Knowledge of the world is dearly bought if at the price of moral purity.

Trust not the world, for it never payeth what it promiseth.

Hell is God's justice; heaven is his love; earth, his long-suffering.

We may despise the world, but we cannot do without it.

To understand the world is wiser than to condemn it.

WORSHIP

My words fly up, my thoughts remain below: / Words without thoughts never to heaven go – *Shakespeare*

A church-going people are apt to be a law-abiding people.

First worship God; he that forgets to pray / Bids not himself good-morrow or good-day.

WORTH

Worth begets in base minds, envy; in great souls, emulation – *Henry Fielding*

Worth makes the man, and want of it the fellow – *Alexander Pope*

Real worth requires no interpreter; its everyday deeds form its blazonry – *Nicolas Sébastian Roch Chamfort*

Many a man who now lacks shoe leather would wear golden spurs if knighthood were the reward of worth – *Douglas William Jerrold*

The difficulty is not so great to die for a friend, as to find a friend worth dying for.

WRITING

Setting down in writing is a lasting memory – *Henry Fielding*

Thoughts come maimed and plucked of plumage from the lips, which, from the pen, in the silence of your own leisure and study, would be born with far more beauty – *Lady Blessington*

A man with a clear head, a good heart, and an honest understanding, will always write well – *Robert Southey*

Show me a man's hand-writing, and I will tell you his character – *William Shenstone*

Writing is a cold and coarse interpreter of thought. How much of the imagination, how much of the intellect, evaporates and is lost while we seek to embody it in words!

To write well is at once to think well.

The writer does the most who gives his reader the most knowledge, and takes from him the least time.

WRONG

A man should never be ashamed to own he has been in the wrong, which is but saying in other words that he is wiser today than he was yesterday – *Alexander Pope*

To persist / In doing wrong extenuates not wrong, / But makes it much more heavy – *William Shakespeare*

There are few people who are more often in the wrong than those who cannot endure to be so – *François de La Rochefoucauld*

Wrong is but falsehood put in practice – *Walter Savage Landor*

It is better to suffer wrong than to do it, and happier to be sometimes cheated than not to trust – *Samuel Johnson*

A noble part of every true life is to learn to undo what has been wrongly done.

Be not familiar with the idea of wrong, for sin in fancy mothers many an ugly fact.

To revenge a wrong is easy, but religion teaches the contrary, and tells us it is better to neglect than to requite it.